Process and Method in Canadian Geography

Water

Process and Method
in Canadian Geography

Water

Selected Readings
edited by
J. G. Nelson
M. J. Chambers

Methuen

Toronto   London   Sydney   Wellington

Library of Congress Catalog Card Number 74-94433

SBN 458 90440 6 (Hardbound)

SBN 458 90450 3 (Paperback)

Design by Hiller Rinaldo

Printed and Bound in Canada

73   72   71   70   69   1   2   3   4   5   6

Preface

This volume is part of a series on Canadian geography. Companion works include *Geomorphology, Vegetation, Soils and Wildlife,* and *Weather and Climate.* Volumes on other topics are being planned.

Each volume comprises a collection of recent articles gathered, for the most part, from learned journals. The series is Canadian in the sense that the papers deal with Canadian topics or have been prepared by geographers working in Canada; it is geographic in the sense that they are concerned with the landscape, and the physical and cultural processes at work on it. For purposes of general definition the landscape can be thought of as *that zone at or near the surface of the earth that is perceived, used or affected by man.* This zone obviously includes surface phenomena such as vegetation, animals, and soils. The zone changes, however, with changes in knowledge and technology, so that more and more contemporary geographers are becoming concerned about human penetration into the oceans and into space. A process can be thought of as *a change that varies in space and time.* A process can be considered as cultural when it is *totally or primarily a result of the activities of man.* Examples are: urbanization with its cities and towns; agriculture with its fields and crops. A process can be considered as physical when it is *totally or primarily a result of forces independent of man.* Examples are ocean currents and hurricanes. As the articles in these volumes will show, however, the distinction between cultural and physical processes is, in many cases, increasingly difficult to draw. Floods are influenced by cultural activities, such as lumbering, as well as by physical processes, such as thunderstorms. Climate is affected by cities as well as by the general circulation of the atmosphere.

In recent years geographers have placed increasing emphasis on the study of processes. While this is partly a result of improved instrumentation, research methods, and technique, it also reflects a general trend in geography toward a more analytical approach. In this and companion volumes, stress has therefore been placed on articles illustrating research techniques and the study of processes. An attempt, however has also been made to add to the usefulness of the volumes by including studies that are concerned with many parts of Canada in order to provide knowledge and appreciation of the Canadian landscape.

In our initial thinking about the volumes, we recognised that it would be necessary and desirable to include relevant research undertaken by biologists, geologists, and members of other landscape-oriented disciplines. Geography, as with other disciplines, interrelates with many fields of study, and a considerable amount of cross-fertilization of thought and technique occurs. Now that a number of volumes have been formulated and organized, we find that some of them contain more work by practitioners in related disciplines than we had originally anticipated. Our concern, however, is to deal with those processes, techniques, problems, and topics that we believe to be of interest and importance to geographers in the wide sense. Moreover, the broader content of some of the volumes may make them extremely useful to members of related disciplines, as well as to those many scholars and students whose work and interest carry them into the so-called interdisciplinary areas where so many important contemporary problems lie.

Aside from their possible interest and value to some members of the public, the various volumes in this series should be useful at a variety of academic levels. Many of the articles in each volume will be of interest to the beginning student. They would also seem to be suitable for more advanced undergraduate courses, for example, the first courses exclusively on biogeography, geomorphology or climatology, or for broader courses in resources or conservation. The volumes could also be valuable in certain graduate courses as they describe important recent developments in research fields. They are a guide to the state of the art—or the science—in Canada. For those wishing to investigate a topic further, all the original bibliographies have been retained. These references are considered to be of greater value to the reader than other material that might be introduced, such as comments and reviews interjected between articles by the editors. Most of the maps, diagrams, and photographs have been retained in each article.

Contents

Contributors

Ballance, R. C.
Public Health Engineering Service, Department of Health, Toronto, Ontario.

Boan, J. A.
Department of Economics, University of Saskatchewan, Regina.

Brown, I. C.
Secretary, Canadian National Committee, International Hydrological Decade, Ottawa.

Burgess, L. C. N.
Canada Department of Energy, Mines and Resources, Ottawa.

Burton, I.
Department of Geography, University of Toronto.

Cass-Beggs, D.
Special Advisor, Science Secretariat, Privy Council Office, Ottawa.

Jeffrey, W. W.
Faculty of Forestry, University of British Columbia.

Kerr, D.
Department of Geography, University of Toronto.

Lloyd, T.
Department of Geography, McGill University, Montreal.

MacKay, D. K.
Canada Department of Energy, Mines and Resources, Ottawa.

McNaughton, A. G. L.
Late of the Royal Society of Canada.

Mayer, H. M.
Department of Geography, Kent State University, Kent, Ohio.

Menzies, J. R.
Late of the Department of National Health and Welfare, Ottawa.

Minghi, J. V.
Department of Geography, University of British Columbia.

Moss, F. E.
United States Senator for Utah.

Neatby, H.
Department of History, University of Saskatchewan, Saskatoon.

Philbrick, A. K.
Department of Geography, University of Western Ontario, London, Ontario.

Pleva, E. G.
Department of Geography, University of Western Ontario, London, Ontario.

Raby, S.
Department of Geography, University of Saskatchewan, Saskatoon.

Schramm, G.
Formerly Department of Economics, University of Manitoba, Winnipeg. Now Associate Professor of Resource Economics, University of Michigan.

Sewell, W. R. D.
Department of Geography, University of Victoria.

Thompson, M. W.
Engineering Advisor, International Joint Commission, Ottawa.

Introduction

In compiling this volume an attempt has been made to include articles instructive, not only in process and method, but also in the important substantive fields relating to water in Canada. On a broad subject matter basis, the articles in the volume can be divided into four parts. A series of papers on water supply, water use, and flooding constitute the first section. Four papers on pollution make up the second section. Water management and planning is the basic theme of the third block of contributions. Two papers on research complete the book. As a result of the complicated nature of water problems, authors have written articles that could sometimes be included in more than one of the divisions described above. Readers certainly will become aware of this and are, of course, in a position to compare articles or to use them in any order that suits their purposes or point of view.

In the first paper in the volume, Cass-Beggs discusses water supply in terms of precipitation, run-off and other aspects of the hydrologic cycle. Estimates are made of annual water consumption in the principal regions of Canada to 1990. Demand is then related to supply, and problem areas such as the Prairies are discussed. Brown is concerned about groundwater and the lack of knowledge of its origin, movement, distribution and quantity. He discusses basic geologic mapping, nuclear and sonic probes, chemical tracers and other techniques which can be used to find out more about groundwater. MacKay uses various statistical and graphical techniques to describe discharge and run-off. Variations in stream flow among river basins and drainage areas are considered, as are factors influencing these variations.

Floods are among the most destructive of the hydrologic processes. Burgess' paper aims to show how flood susceptibility can be determined by aid of aerial photographs. The widespread nature of the flood problem in Canada, our short memory of flood effects, and the lack of a Federal flood policy are all discussed in Ian Burton's article. Burton also refers to United States' evidence for increases in damage costs following the construction of levees and other technological devices to exclude floods. The devices encourage urban encroachment on the floodplain. Higher damages then follow the occurrence of a flood greater than that which the engineering devices were designed to exclude. Burton calls for wider use of other protective measures such as floodplain zoning and flood proofing.

The dam and the reservoir are frequently part of flood control projects. J. A. Boan claims that, aside from their value for this— irrigation and other purposes — reservoirs can be employed for recreation, although this use seems to have been insufficiently considered by planners in Canada. In this connection he comments on the need for acquisition and control of reservoir shorelines and the need to minimize the destructive effects of reservoirs on anadromous fisheries, bird and animal habitats, and natural land forms and vegetation. Many dams and reservoirs have been constructed for the production of water power. The desirability of continuing to do so is often questioned in the light of other alternatives such as thermal and nuclear power and the environmental damage that follows dam construction. This point is commented upon by Gunter Schramm in his paper on the importance of low cost hydro-electric power to certain power intensive industries such as aluminum. He concludes that the traditionally accepted cost advantages of hydro power have been drastically reduced in recent years. But, in his final footnote, Schramm indicates that, because of the size of Canadian generating systems and for other reasons, the best course of action in Canada may still be to install more hydro units.

The importance of water for transport is recognized in papers by Neatby and Kerr. Mayer briefly discusses some interactions between transport improvements, water, shoreline, industry, and recreation, and Minghi deals at length with a problem in the use of water for fisheries.

Neatby's approach is historical and, like Kerr, her river is the St. Lawrence. She tells something of the use of the river for transport ranging from local movement of wood to a far-flung international traffic in fur. Physical limitations, such as the short ice-free season, clearly have been problems since the days of earliest settlement. The obstacles to large modern craft moving upriver into the Great Lakes were considerably reduced by the completion of the St. Lawrence Seaway in 1959. Kerr's paper is a brief summary of the effects of the Seaway on the movement of various commodities and on the economic geography of the Great Lakes region as these effects were evident in 1963, only a few years after the completion of the project. One year later Harold Mayer expressed his concern about the effects of the Seaway on the metropolitan shorelines of the Great Lakes. He noted that, by improving transport, the Seaway had stimulated demand for more industrial and port development. At the same time, pressures were increasing for the use of the shoreline for recreation and for the conservation of scenery and "other amenities". For Mayer the resulting conflict represented a major challenge to city, metropolitan, regional, national, and international planning for the Great Lakes area.

Julian Minghi's study of the conflict of salmon fishing policies in the North Pacific is of general interest because it deals with fish, an organism of importance to users of both water and the biome, and the oceans, a realm of increasing concern to students of water problems. Minghi also raises a number of points of more specific interest: for example, the difficulties posed by scale (continents as well as oceans are involved as will be seen later in the N.A.W.A.P.A. papers); the relatively rapid rate at which seemingly innumerable fish or other organisms can decrease over large areas; the problem of finding a reason or reasons for reduction, whether cultural (related to use) or physical, and of instituting control measures; and the danger of founding use legislation and agreements on a small amount of scientific evidence, "rather than determining if a certain type of legislation would be effective scientifically, and if so, establishing measures accordingly."

Much waste has flowed under the bridge since the publication of J. R. Menzies' paper, *Water Pollution in Canada by Drainage Basins.* The paper was one of many prepared as background material for Canada's momentous Resources for Tomorrow Conference held in Montreal in 1961. Some seven years later Canada is still confronted by a growing number of pollution problems. In 1966 a special conference on pollution was held in Montreal. Detailed descriptions of pollution in various parts of Canada were provided on that occasion, among them R. C. Ballance's work on the St. John River. Like many rivers of Canada, the St. John is used for numerous purposes, including the transport of pulpwood and sawlogs, swimming, boating, sport fishing, commercial fishing, power generation and, particularly, waste disposal. Few treatment facilities exist along the river—none for the treatment of industrial waste. According to Ballance, the major industrial polluters, a pulp and paper plant and a food processor, produce more pollution than would a population of two million people. A regional development plan is underway for the river and attempts are being made to provide for increased power production, recreation, and for the conservation of fish, scenery and other so-called intangibles. The resolution of a variety of conflicts is involved in such multiple use planning, the most important being the threat that pollution ultimately poses to all other users of the river.

A large-scale example of the process of pollution can be found in the Great Lakes-St. Lawrence system. In his paper M. W. Thompson discusses problems posed, not only by pollution, but also by lake level fluctuations, making special reference to the role of the International Joint Commission in the amelioration or resolution of such problems. On October 7, 1964, the governments of Canada and the United States requested this Commission to investigate and report on the lake level and pollution problems of Lake Erie, Lake Ontario and the international section of the St. Lawrence River. Since that time the Commission and various co-operating bodies and groups have undertaken a number of research programmes focusing largely on physical or technical matters such as the chemistry, physics, and biology of the lakes, the assimilation of pollutants, and the effects of fertilizers, pesticides, and herbicides on aquatic life. Although agreeing that such research—and education—are necessary, E. G. Pleva stresses the political and administrative difficulties and says the most urgent need is to find means whereby unitary control programmes may be developed by the many distinct political units involved, including the governments of Canada and the United States, the nine states of Minnesota, Wisconsin, Illinois, Indiana, Michigan, Ohio, Pennsylvania New York and Vermont, and the two provinces of Ontario and Quebec.

The articles in the third section of this volume are devoted to various aspects of water management and planning. The first two papers, by Sewell and Lloyd, are broad in scope and touch on many important matters ranging from data, personnel and research needs, to a description of the geography of water supply in Canada. One of Sewell's more pressing concerns is the jurisdictional problem posed by the imperfect sharing of responsibility for water between the provincial and Federal governments. Essentially the province presides over water when thought of as a resource, while the Federal government retains exclusive jurisdiction over the use of water for navigation or fisheries. The Federal government also has responsibility for interprovincial and international relations including those concerning water. Trevor Lloyd is particularly interested in the establishment of a national water policy which, among other things, would involve provision for more research on, and long-term planning for, the future water requirements of Canada as a whole, without regard to provincial or local boundaries.

Following Lloyd's paper is a series of articles more or less specifically devoted to a given technique or aspect of water management and planning. Burton addresses himself in general to the matter of investment choices in public resource development and specifically to the use of the technique of cost-benefit analysis in making these choices. He would move away from the justification of water or other resource developments in terms of vaguely specified human values to a testing based in part on careful use of cost-benefit analysis. He would also use other criteria including budget constraints and the difficult-to-measure, so-called intangible benefits associated with such things as wildlife and scenery. Allen Philbrick sees water problems as being related to certain traditional views, particularly the idea that water needs must be met either directly or indirectly from precipitation through the hydrologic cycle. He speculates about water policy and planning changes which might follow technical advances. Specifically, he suggests the possibility of a break-through in the search for cheaper ways of producing fresh water through desalinisation of seawater. Philbrick sees this break-through as paving the way for the abandonment of the hydrologic cycle and the watershed as the basis of water management. A new operational unit is possible, the nodal water region. Philbrick briefly considers an example, the Great Lakes Nodal Water Region, which would largely be based on the diversion of desalinised water from James Bay. Stewart Raby's article is a critical evaluation of the Prairie Provinces Water Board, an advisory body set up in 1948 with the major function of recommending the use and allocation of water flowing through the three provinces of Alberta, Saskatchewan and Manitoba. Raby does not consider this Board, which represents one method of co-ordinating water management and planning, to have been successful, largely because of the difficulties arising from the Federal government's decision to build the South Saskatchewan dam. In contrast, E. G. Pleva describes the successes achieved by the Ontario Multiple Purpose Land and Water Districts, "a device for carrying out a coherent set of programmes that draw upon the experience and skills of several departments of the provincial government." A District also can get financial assistance from the provincial and Federal governments, notably through the Conservation Authorities Act of Ontario and the Canada Water Conservation Assistance Act.

The last block of articles in the third section of this volume deal with N.A.W.A.P.A. or the North American Water and Power Alliance, a grand and controversial example of water diversion as a method of solving apparent water shortages. Sewell discusses N.A.W.A.P.A. from the standpoint of a geographer, describing the basic elements of the scheme, which essentially involves diversion of water from northern Canada and Alaska, south, through western Canada into the Great Lakes, parts of the Great Plains, the Great Basin, the American southwest and Mexico. The papers by Sewell, Moss, and McNaughton make it clear that a number of contentious issues are associated with N.A.W.A.P.A. Among these are the traditionally wasteful North American methods of water use and their effect on water demand, the generally low cost of water in North America and its effect on demand, the continued heavy subsidisation of water developments in semi-arid and arid areas, a national as opposed to a continental policy on water use, and the destructive effects of the N.A.W.A.P.A. dams, reservoirs and canals on land use and ecology in many parts of North America. Obviously these and related points cannot be discussed in any detail here, but they can be studied in the three N.A.W.A.P.A. articles, which are included to give an idea of the scale, complexity, and differences in viewpoint, that are characteristic of North American water problems today.

The last two papers are specifically devoted to research. Jeffrey's paper on water yield improvement research in Canada reflects the physical and technical interests shared by foresters, physical geographers, biologists, meteorologists and engineers. The article by Sewell focuses on the contribution that can be made to water management through social and scientific research by geographers, sociologists, economists and members of other related fields. A number of major research topics are suggested, for example, the role of social guides in water development, or investigations leading to an improved framework of laws, policies, and administrative arrangements. In discussing these research possibilities Sewell refers directly or indirectly to a variety of opportunities for the geographer, such as studies of floods and human response to them, or of the ways in which people perceive water management alternatives and how this perception has influenced the solutions reached by them.

J. G. NELSON
M. J. CHAMBERS

Calgary,
June, 1969.

1

Water as a Basic Resource

D. Cass-Beggs

Water Supply
The problem of water supply in Canada is the control and redistribution of runoff according to the needs and location of her increasing population. The supply factor in the supply and demand relationship is the available runoff.

Precipitation
In an attempt to assess Canada's water resources, a study of precipitation and runoff was undertaken. Canada was divided into reasonably uniform natural regions, each one of which was subdivided into settled and unsettled areas: geographically, the southern and northern part of the territory. Settled portions were delineated on the basis of maps showing density of population, and the boundaries were further adjusted to follow the principal watersheds. Areas of the selected regions are listed in Table I.

While the settled zone of each region has been selected for more detailed discussion of water supply and use, the population density in these regions varies widely. For example, Ontario and Quebec, the most populous provinces with nearly two-thirds of the national population, together contain slightly over one-third of the settled area. About the same settled area lies in the more thinly settled Prairie Provinces, which have only one-fourth as much population. See Table II.

The area in each settled and unsettled zone was measured and the volume of precipitation was found by using a map with isohyetal

Background Paper, *Resources for Tomorrow Conference, 1961,* Vol. 1, pp. 173-89. Reprinted in edited form by permission of the Queen's Printer, Ottawa.

TABLE I. SETTLED AND UNSETTLED AREAS IN PRINCIPAL REGIONS OF CANADA[a]

1	2	3	4	5	6	7
	THOUSANDS OF SQUARE MILES[c]			PER CENT OF ALL CANADA		
Region	Settled Area	Unsettled Area	Total Area	Settled Area	Unsetted Area	Total Area
Maritimes[b]	106	88	194	3.5	2.9	6.3
Quebec	216	310	526	7.1	10.1	17.2
Ontario	149	211	359	4.8	6.9	11.7
Prairie Provinces	333	367	701	10.9	12.0	22.9
British Columbia	241	91	332	7.9	3.0	10.8
Yukon	./.	205	205[d]	./.	6.7	6.7
Northwest Territories	./.	744	744	./.	24.4	24.4
Canada	1,045	2,016	3,061[e]	34.1	65.9	100.0

[a] Defined by major watersheds.
[b] Newfoundland included.
[c] Calculated by planimeter.
[d] Included are the Districts of MacKenzie and Keewatin of the Northwest Territories.
[e] Compares with 3,018,000 square miles as recorded by D.B.S. (All Canada —less Franklin District).

TABLE II. POPULATION OF CANADA IN PRINCIPAL REGIONS, 1956

1	2	3	4	5	6	7
	THOUSANDS OF PERSONS			PER CENT OF ALL CANADA		
Region	Settled Area	Unsettled Area	Total Area	Settled Area	Unsetted Area	Total Area
Maritimes	1,764	./.	1,764	11.0	./.	11.0
Quebec	4,629	./.	4,629	28.8	./.	28.8
Ontario	5,405	./.	5,405	33.6	./.	33.6
Prairie Provinces	2,854	./.	2,854	17.7	./.	17.7
British Columbia	1,398	./.	1,398	8.7	./.	8.7
North and North-west Territories	./.	31	31	./.	.2	.2
Canada	16,050	31	16,081	99.8	.2	100.0

lines of one-inch precipitation difference.[1] The areas between the isohyetal lines were calculated by planimeter, and a mean value of precipitation was applied.

The calculated total volume of annual precipitation for settled and unsettled zones within each region is shown in Table III. The concentration of precipitation in settled areas is of interest. The settled area (34 per cent of the total area) receives 48.7 per cent

[1] Map supplied by Department of Mines and Technical Surveys, with isohyetal lines representing long-term averages.

TABLE III. ESTIMATE OF PRECIPITATION FOR SETTLED AND UNSETTLED AREAS OF CANADA

1	2	3	4	5	6	7
	DEPTH IN INCHES			RATIO TO CANADA AVERAGE		
Region	Settled Area	Unsettled Area	Total Area	Settled Area	Unsetted Area	Total Area
Maritimes	41.2	30.8	36.5	2.04	1.52	1.81
Quebec	37.6	23.8	29.4	1.86	1.18	1.46
Ontario	30.3	25.0	27.2	1.50	1.24	1.35
Prairie Provinces	16.6	15.5	16.0	.82	.77	.79
British Columbia	31.3	19.7	28.1	1.55	.99	1.39
Yukon	./.	13.2	13.2	./.	.65	.65
Northwest Territories	./.	9.6	9.6	./.	.48	.48
Canada	28.7	15.7	20.2	1.42	.78	1.00

of the total annual precipitation. But regional inequalities in distribution of the total precipitation are very noticeable. The settled portion of the Prairie Provinces, containing 32 per cent of the settled area of Canada, and 11 per cent of the total territory, receives only 19 per cent of the precipitation falling on settled areas, and nine per cent of all precipitation.

While the average annual precipitation for all Canada is about 20 inches (Table III), that for the settled areas is nearly 29 inches as against some 16 inches for the unsettled areas. While this no doubt reflects a normal settlement pattern for temperate zone territory, it foreshadows problems of increasing population and wider settlement. Of the presently settled areas, only the Prairie Provinces have precipitation below 30 inches, with a bare 17 inches. This figure is only a little below the Canadian average, but it is only half of the figures for the more humid regions.

The Northwest Territories with less than 10 inches, the Yukon with about 13, and the unsettled portions of the Prairie Provinces with 15.5 inches, are below the average for the unsettled areas, and well below the average for all settled areas of 28.7 inches. A general indication of the distribution of precipitation for Canada is given in Figure 5 which shows isohyets at 10-inch intervals.

Runoff in Settled Areas

There are not sufficient gauging stations in unsettled areas to permit any estimate of runoff in such zones. However, it is possible to compile estimates of runoff in settled areas from the long-term average flows recorded for the rivers draining the regions previously delineated and for which precipitation figures were compiled.

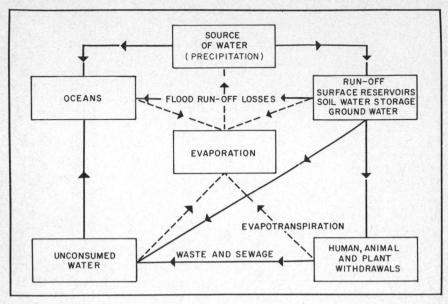

Figure 1. Hydrologic Cycle Modified by Water Use.

Runoff in total volume, in inches and as a percentage of precipitation for the settled areas, is presented in Table IV. The seasonal variation illustrated by monthly runoff in inches and as a fraction of the average month, is shown for the five regions in Table V.

The estimated runoff in the settled regions of Canada appears to be about 48 per cent of total precipitation. The remaining part of the rainfall can be considered to have disappeared into the atmosphere through evaporation and transpiration and through other very minor consumptive uses of water. A portion of the rainfall is, of course, delayed temporarily in surface and ground reservoirs,

TABLE IV. ESTIMATE OF ANNUAL RUNOFF FOR SETTLED AREAS OF CANADA
BY PRINCIPAL REGIONS (LONG TERM AVERAGE)

1	2	3	4	5	6
		Runoff			
Region	*Precipitation (Millions of Acre-Feet)*	*Millions of Acre-Feet*	*Per cent of Precipitation*	*Depth in Inches*	*Ratio to Canada Average*
Maritimes	234	145	62.0	25.6	1.95
Quebec	433	167	38.6	14.5	1.10
Ontario	240	89	37.1	11.2	.85
Prairie Provinces	295	51	17.3	2.8	.21
British Columbia	402	314	78.1	24.4	1.85
Total Settled Area	1,604	766	47.7	13.2	1.00

Table V. Seasonal Pattern of Runoff for Settled Areas of Canada by Principal Regions
(Long Term Average)

1	2	3	4	5	6	7	8	9	10	11	12	13	14
Region	Jan.	Feb.	Mar.	Apr.	May	June	July	Aug.	Sept.	Oct.	Nov.	Dec.	Average Month
(A) *Depth in Inches*													
Maritimes	1.14	.83	1.33	4.59	6.44	2.29	1.43	1.03	1.02	1.60	2.29	1.57	2.13
Quebec	.71	.61	.80	1.94	2.84	1.97	1.10	.84	.78	.93	1.05	.80	1.20
Ontario	.82	.79	.86	1.07	1.35	1.05	.92	.88	.83	.87	.89	.86	.93
Prairie Provinces	.16	.12	.12	.12	.27	.39	.38	.32	.29	.26	.22	.18	.24
British Columbia	.69	.61	.57	1.21	3.51	5.36	4.24	2.62	1.76	1.50	1.20	.89	2.01
Canada	.56	.48	.56	1.28	2.22	2.05	1.53	1.06	.84	.87	.88	.68	1.08
(B) *Ratio to Average Month*													
Maritimes	.53	.39	.62	2.15	3.02	1.08	.67	.49	.48	.75	1.07	.74	1.00
Quebec	.59	.51	.67	1.62	2.37	1.65	.92	.70	.65	.78	.87	.67	1.00
Ontario	.88	.85	.92	1.14	1.45	1.12	.99	.95	.89	.93	.96	.92	1.00
Prairie Provinces	.68	.50	.51	.51	1.15	1.65	1.62	1.35	1.24	1.10	.91	.78	1.00
British Columbia	.34	.30	.28	.60	1.74	2.66	2.11	1.30	.87	.75	.60	.44	1.00
Canada	.52	.44	.52	1.18	2.05	1.89	1.41	.98	.78	.80	.81	.63	1.00

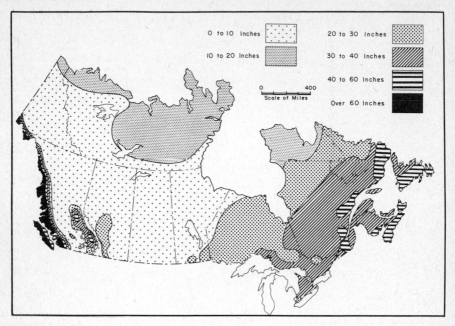

Figure 2. Precipitation in Canada.

where it affects the seasonal distribution, augmenting runoff during periods of lower flow, but in the long run is included in the measured runoff.

The regional variations in the percentage of precipitation that becomes runoff are startling. In the settled areas of British Columbia, the geology and slope of the terrain, the high annual rainfall and lower evaporation and transpiration, and the occurrence of seasonal floods from rainstorms and rapid snow-melt combine to bring the annual measured runoff to 78 per cent of precipitation (Table IV). This constitutes 41 per cent of the total estimated runoff in all Canadian settled areas. Much the same conditions prevail in the Maritimes, where runoff is 62 per cent of precipitation and nearly 19 per cent of the Canadian total.

Runoffs in Ontario and Quebec at 37 per cent and 39 per cent of precipitation account for some 12 per cent and 22 per cent of the Canadian total (for settled areas), respectively, or about one-third of the total when combined. The Prairie Provinces start with the smallest precipitation, and of this the smallest fraction appears as runoff. In the settled portion, only 2.8 inches of runoff occurs out of 16.6 inches of precipitation. While this area is more than 30 per cent of the settled area of Canada, the volume of runoff is only 6.7 per cent of the corresponding total. These relationships are

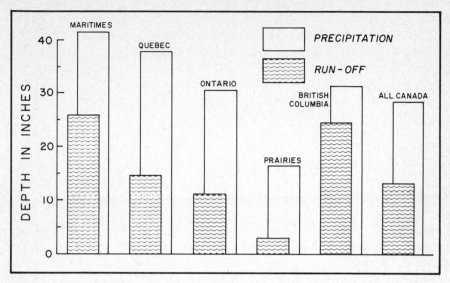

Figure 3. Precipitation and Run-Off in Settled Regions of Canada. (Long-Term Average)

illustrated graphically in Figure 3. Seasonal variation in runoff is illustrated in the graphs of Figure 4.

The scarcity of water for agriculture in the Prairie Provinces is somewhat alleviated by the concentration of rainfall in the growing season of May to August. The Prairies also experience 48 per cent of their total annual runoff in these four months. The over-all

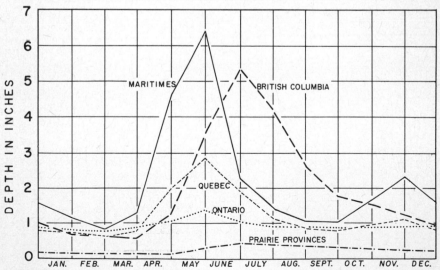

Figure 4. Seasonal Pattern of Run-Off for Settled Regions of Canada. (Long-Term Average).

rate of runoff, however, is reasonably steady throughout the year, the peak month of June experiencing only some 50 per cent more than the average monthly volume, and the lowest flow being about half of the average.

In British Columbia, by contrast, the peak month flow is nearly 2.7 times the average monthly flow, and in both June and July the runoff is double that of the average month. The lowest flow, 28 per cent of average, occurs in March. Thus, it can be surmised that a considerable part of the runoff is lost in flood flows.

Similarly, the runoff in the Maritimes, in April and May is over twice the average runoff, and in February, it drops to a low of 31 per cent of average.

Since runoff is the gross supply of water it is reasonable to examine the runoff per capita for each settled area. Figure 5 shows the variation in runoff per capita, expressed as a fraction of the Canadian average, in comparison with the runoff in inches. On a per capita basis the Prairie region and Ontario are approximately equal, with little more than a third of the Canadian average, while British Columbia has four or five times the average.

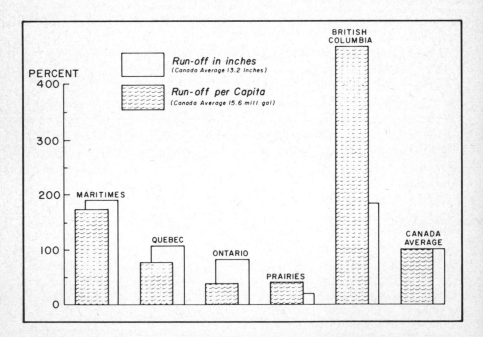

Figure 5. Run-Off Per Capita for Settled Areas of Canada as percent of Canadian Average.

Demand For Water

A demand for water arises out of almost every phase of human activity. Some demands do not involve removing the water from its natural location. These include such activities as fishing and the conservation of fish and wildlife; swimming and recreational activities; navigation on rivers and lakes; and the disposal of waste. These are the *nonwithdrawal* uses. Under most conditions, hydro developments are in this category.

Withdrawal uses of water, which involve continual removal of water from its natural location, include public water supplies, rural domestic and stock watering use, irrigation, industrial use and also hydro power, insofar as it involves diversion of water to a different watershed or directly to the ocean.

Of water withdrawn for various uses, only about 25 per cent of the total is actually consumed or lost to current supply. Various activities consume the water they withdraw in different proportions; public supply and rural household uses consume 10 per cent each; stock watering consumes nearly all the water withdrawn; irrigation consumes 60 per cent of delivered water; self-supplied industries about 2 per cent; and hydro power none.

This 25 per cent of water that is consumed does not include evaporation losses or water such as sewage lost through discharge into the ocean. Also, if the quality is impaired, re-useability of waste withdrawals depends on local facilities for purification. The water, however, is physically present and is re-useable. Ordinary sewage after suitable treatment can be and is re-used as drinking water, when necessary. Used water returning to the supply may occur far down-stream from the original diversion or even in another watershed. Thus the contribution that is relevant at any particular withdrawal point would be the return flows from withdrawals upstream. These are hard to assess and might be considered unreliable.

In computing the Canadian demand for water, only the gross withdrawal uses have been considered, without allowance for the proportion returned to the supply. Net withdrawals could not be assessed, but the appropriate factors might be examined under critical circumstances. Thus demand or consumption has been equated to withdrawal use. However, hydro power use has been excluded from the withdrawal use and demand, and considered separately.

Estimate of Present Use of Water

To make the best use of available data, the year 1956 was selected as the base year for the computation of the total regional demand for water. The compilation of these data required the use of various source materials, incidental evidence, and statistical procedures. The methodology followed is available as an appendix. Briefly, the following components were obtained:

(1) residential and commercial consumption in urban areas;

(2) industrial consumption both urban and rural; and

(3) rural non-industrial consumption.

Total urban consumption was obtainable for selected centres from a 1949-56 Canadian water use survey[2] supplemented by specific enquiries made for this study. However, these included the industrial establishments within urban areas. To separate these consumptions, recourse was had to a survey published by the American Waterworks Association Journal[3], the data of which could be adapted to the Canadian situation. Thus, residential and commercial consumption in urban areas was calculated by subtraction.

No statistics were available of Canadian water consumption in industry. Consequently, American data listed in the United States Census of Manufacturers[4] were adapted to fit Canadian Dominion Bureau of Statistics classifications. The American data also had to be adapted as to size of establishments to fit the Canadian pattern. Using the number of employees per establishment as a criterion for size, the relationship between water intake and number of employees for each industrial group was obtained. Since Canadian data[5] furnish regional breakdowns by industrial group of the average number of employees per establishment, the total industrial consumption per region for each industrial group was obtained.

Rural consumption was divided into household use, animal use and irrigation use. For rural household use, American[6] consumption figures were used without modification, since average conditions are reasonably similar. Canadian census figures provide the animal population by regions from which the animal consumption was derived.

Irrigation use was difficult to obtain both as to volume of water used per acre and total acreage irrigated. Adequate past records

2 J. F. J. Thomas, "Industrial Water Resources of Canada", Department of Mines and Technical Surveys.

3 American Waterworks Association, "A Survey of Operating Data for Waterworks in 1955" (May, 1957). H. F. Siedel and E. R. Bauman, "A Statistical Analysis of Waterworks Data" (December, 1957).

4 "Census of Manufacturers" (1954).

5 Dominion Bureau of Statistics, "General Review of Manufacturing Industries of Canada" (1956).

6 "Estimated Use of Water in the United States", *Geological Survey Circular No. 398* (1955), p. 6.

TABLE VI. ESTIMATE OF ANNUAL WATER CONSUMPTION FOR PRINCIPAL
REGIONS OF CANADA, 1956-1990
(*Thousands of Acre-Feet*)

1	2	3	4	5	6	7	8	9
Region	1956	1960	1965	1970	1975	1980	1985	1990
Maritimes	558	674	843	1,052	1,321	1,669	2,082	2,619
Residential and Commercial	129	147	174	205	243	287	338	399
Industrial	416	513	654	831	1,061	1,364	1,725	2,200
Farm and Irrigation	13	14	15	16	17	18	19	20
Quebec	2,615	3,386	4,477	5,836	7,493	9,533	12,027	15,070
Residential and Commercial	295	353	431	529	641	777	943	1,150
Industrial	2,270	2,979	3,987	5,241	6,780	8,676	10,996	13,817
Farm and Irrigation	50	54	59	66	72	80	88	103
Ontario	4,009	5,148	6,827	8,912	11,516	14,732	18,749	23,775
Residential and Commercial	465	560	698	868	1,079	1,337	1,667	2,069
Industrial	3,450	4,188	5,947	7,778	10,085	12,974	16,592	21,142
Farm and Irrigation	94	100	182	266	352	421	490	564
Prairie Provinces	1,586	2,159	2,761	3,474	4,336	5,366	6,589	8,058
Residential and Commercial	123	144	174	212	258	311	377	458
Industrial	518	736	1,085	1,537	2,129	2,873	3,804	4,957
Farm and Irrigation	945	1,279	1,502	1,725	1,949	2,182	2,408	2,643
British Columbia	1,417	1,728	2,173	2,747	3,478	4,412	5,599	7,122
Residential and Commercial	139	170	216	274	347	438	554	704
Industrial	690	947	1,324	1,817	2,453	3,273	4,321	5,670
Farm and Irrigation	588	611	633	656	678	701	724	748
Canada	10,185	13,095	17,081	22,021	28,144	35,712	45,046	56,644
Residential and Commercial	1,151	1,374	1,693	2,088	2,568	3,150	3,879	4,780
Industrial	7,344	9,663	12,997	17,204	22,508	29,160	37,438	47,786
Farm and Irrigation	1,690	2,058	2,391	2,729	3,068	3,402	3,729	4,078

were available only for Alberta. Insofar as irrigated area could be
determined for 1956, a total volume was estimated.

The results of these calculations for the year 1956 appear in the
first column of Table VI. The consumption is given for each settled
region as previously defined, and for Canada as a whole, in total
and broken down between residential and commercial; industrial;
and farm (including irrigation) uses. A diagramatic representation
of these principal uses is given in Figure 6. The areas of the circles
represent the relative total use of water in the regions, while the
sectors of the circles show the relative magnitude of the uses.

Projection of Water Consumption, 1960 to 1990

Referring to American sources, it was assumed that consumption
per capita in urban, residential, and commercial categories will

increase at an approximate rate of two per cent a year. Projections of population for each region on the basis of recent trends, adjusted to be consistent with the Gordon Commission forecast, were used in conjunction with per capita consumptions to obtain the total residential and commercial consumption up to 1990.

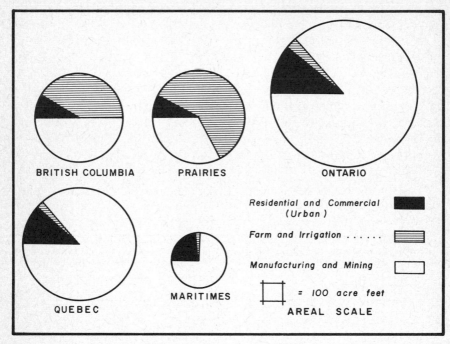

Figure 6. Principal Uses of Water in Canada, 1956.

The projection of industrial water use to 1990 was a very complex problem. The basic assumption made was that the water used in manufacturing would bear a fixed ratio to the value added in manufacturing. Statistics (1949 to 1956) made it possible to determine the value added in all manufacturing, per capita, for each region together with the rate of growth of this factor. The rates, of course, varied with the magnitude of the factor, being highest for the least industrialized areas and lowest for the most industrialized. Combining the appropriate levels and growth rates provided a projection of added value per capita for the next 30 years. Using the 1956 figures, the water use per dollar of added value was deduced for that year and applied to the projection. Incorporating population estimates gave the total water use in manufacturing.

There are obvious limitations in the procedure, but it is unlikely to have over-stated the water demand. For example, the use of a fixed consumption per dollar of added value pre-supposes essentially the same industrial technique throughout. Advancing techniques might be expected to involve more water per unit of production. On the other hand, the increasing scale of operations might lead to some economies.

Projections of rural consumption were made separately for rural household, animal and irrigation uses. The rural household use was projected on a population basis with the per capita use of ten gallons per day assumed constant. This may involve an under-estimate, but the total is not very significant.

Animal use was based on an estimate of animal population which in turn was assumed to have a fixed relationship to human population, since animals will presumably remain the source of milk, meat and other commodities upon which the human population depends. It has been assumed that there will be no major change in import and export ratios.

Irrigation use was projected as far as possible in accordance with known policies and trends in the regions where irrigation is most relevant. The figures developed indicated some 2.7 million acres irrigated in total by 1990, or about three times the present area. The figure may be reasonably satisfactory.

The estimated demand for water in these categories, for each region, for 1956 and at five-year intervals from 1960 to 1990 is shown in Table VI. The growth of the Canadian demand for water for residential and commercial uses, for industrial use and for farm (including irrigation) use up to 1990 is shown graphically in Figure 7. Industrial use is by far the most significant component and shows too, the highest growth rate. By 1990, Canada may expect to require five times the present industrial water supply.

These figures refer to the gross industrial withdrawal use. If pollution is avoided, the net requirement for industry may be significantly less.

Supply and Demand

When the apparent supply of water in the form of runoff is set against the demand, even as projected 30 years ahead, the demand seems an almost trivial proportion of the supply and no possible problem could exist. However, there is an enormous difference between the theoretically available supply in the form of runoff and that which is in fact available to meet the demand. In the first place, unless we assume a vast system of regulating reservoirs, which indeed may be available in due course, it is necessary to take the minimum flow as being all that in practice is available to meet the demand, which is essentially constant over the year. Some storage exists and it may not be unreasonable to take the minimum average monthly flow as being the normally available supply. This greatly reduces the supply in most regions, as reference to Figure 8 demonstrates. Relatively, the supply for the Prairie Region increases, since there the runoff is more uniform. In British Columbia, in particular, large summer peaks are obviously lost without storage developments.

Expressing the demand as a fraction of this reduced supply, of twelve months of minimum flow, the position is not nearly as favourable. Ontario will use 31 per cent of its supply in 1990; British

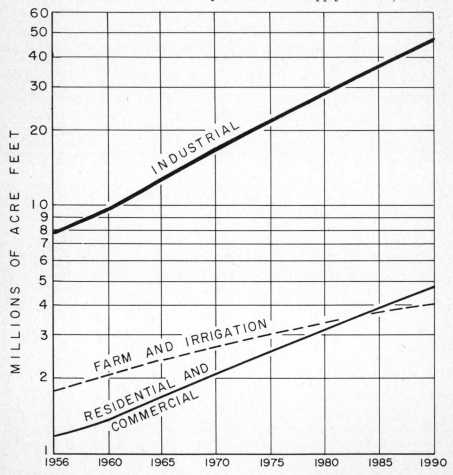

Figure 7. Projection of Principal Uses for Water in Canada, 1956-1990.

Columbia only 7½ per cent; while the Prairie Region will use 33 per cent. These relationships are illustrated in Figure 8.

These levels already indicate that storage, conserving the peak flows may well become essential. The runoff figures used for computation of the gross supply included whatever storage was available and in use above the points at which the river flow measurements were taken. However, these were taken generally at the mouth of rivers flowing into the Great Lakes, and the regulating effect of these major reservoirs was not included.

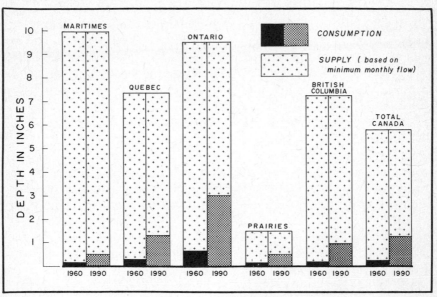

Figure 8. Water Supply and Demand in Canada, 1960 and 1990.

Effect of Non-withdrawal Uses

Obviously it is impossible to use the whole of the flow in months of minimum flow to meet the withdrawal uses. Even though, in Canada, navigation is not involved in the winter months when these minima occur, there remains the need for an adequate flow to dispose of or dilute waste water and sewage. Moreover, hydroelectric requirements are also critical in the winter months.

Sewage and industrial wastes represent an important part of the return flows from the withdrawal uses and have been excluded from the calculations by taking the gross withdrawal uses as the demand. Insofar as sewage and industrial wastes can be treated and rendered potable, they can be returned to the supply and the withdrawal requirement can be reduced accordingly. This is not in itself very significant. The more important aspect of waste treatment is that if it is returned to a river or lake in a raw state, while a natural purification process will occur, very large volumes of water will be required to dilute it, to transport it and to enable the purification to proceed. Unless an adequate minimum flow is maintained, the whole flow may become unsuitable for domestic use.

It is difficult to assess the minimum flow that is needed for this purpose; the amount will vary from place to place. The situation may be illustrated from the experience of the North Saskatchewan River. It represents an excellent source of water for the city of Edmonton, Alberta, where it arrives essentially pure from the mountains 200 miles to the west. But the effluent from the city, even with some degree of control, renders it virtually unusable at certain seasons 500 miles downstream at Prince Albert, Saskatchewan. Without treatment or without the provision of more water as a dilutant, the total minimum flow is unavailable as a supply for withdrawal uses.

In most populous areas, it is already true that the minimum flows of the local rivers are inadequate or nearly inadequate to handle the waste disposal problem and they would certainly be inadequate for the situation in 1990. Control of pollution thus emerges as one of the major uses of available runoff water, and waste treatment becomes possibly the most important method of increasing the effective water supply.

If it be assumed, but only by way of illustration, since no generalized figures exist, that 50 per cent of the minimum monthly flow in any river must be allowed to flow to the sea for waste disposal, the available supply is halved and demands become a formidable proportion of the remaining supply.

Navigation uses of water in Canada have been rather casually dismissed as not applying in the winter months. Yet extensions and improvements to waterways, while they will impound more water, will not in general involve decreased flows. At the time a new reservoir is filled, there is of course a depletion of the flow for a season or two. Navigation improvements would rather tend to improve water supply, unless attempts were made to secure increased depths by increasing the flow rather than by constructing canals, dams, locks or deepened channels. Water is used for moving logs downstream on many rivers, but serious conflicts are not likely to arise in this class of use.

Hydroelectric Power

The extraction of energy from flowing water is possible whereever a change of level or head can be developed. The amount of energy developed is proportional to the product of the volume of water that can be passed through the turbines and the head available. The rate at which energy can be extracted, or the power available at a given site is proportional to the flow.

Hydro installations have been of two general types. *Run of the River* developments take the water essentially as it comes and generate what energy it can provide at such times as it is available. Because of the cost of providing equipment that would operate only occasionally and on an uncontrollable schedule they discard the flood flows and are geared only to the dependable average flows. Such plants cannot generally meet the energy demands of a system since the fluctuating requirements would not match up with the variable supply.

If seasonal variations in flows are to be made to match up with daily and seasonal fluctuations in electrical load, very large storage developments become the second general type. Sometimes large natural reservoirs can be utilized. For example, Lake Winnipeg and Lake Erie are capable of providing almost perfect control for the flows in the Nelson River and at Niagara Falls, respectively, but control works are required. The South Saskatchewan River Project, by creating a reservoir some 130 miles long and giving about eight million acre-feet of storage, will be capable of smoothing out seasonal variations in flow over say three years and at the same time releasing the average flow available in almost any pattern required to meet the demands for electric power.

Hydro developments with large storage facilities can be developed for peaking purposes and can be used over short periods each day, in the winter months, when energy demands are particularly high, to supplement energy drawn on a constant basis from base load stations using coal or, in due course, nuclear energy. Indeed, the peaking function of hydro plants is becoming recognized as their most important contribution.

All hydro plants using storage will have some beneficial effect on gross water supply by conserving flood waters and increasing minimum flows. Any diversion of water above or around a hydro plant will represent a direct loss of energy, but not necessarily a reduction in its power capability (for peak loads), if storage is available, since water could be used at the same rate over a shorter period.

Power developments on the headwaters of rivers or on rivers, at points outside the settled areas, are beneficial or irrelevant to the water supply problem. Examples of these may be the Columbia,

Peace and Hamilton rivers. It would appear that most of the remaining undeveloped hydroelectric capacity of Canada lies in areas or is of a type that cannot impair the water supply at least for a population that can be expected over the period of several generations.

However, plants located close to or downstream from major centres of population can be seriously affected by water diversions and a serious conflict of interest could arise. Diversion of water from Lake Erie or Lake Huron for use in southern Ontario, with the return flows possibly going to Lake Ontario, would reduce the energy developed at Niagara Falls. Similarly water diverted from Lake Ontario and all points in the Great Lakes watershed would reduce the energy available at the St. Lawrence power plants. In these cases, however, the diversions may for many years be very small compared with the flows available for power.

The situation is much more critical at the South Saskatchewan River Project, where future diversions may well reduce the amount of energy available to less than half its initial value. In this case the installation of a plant at all, at this primarily irrigation project, had to be justified in other terms than its energy production. The plant is regarded as a source of power over the peak hours of the winter months for the central part of Saskatchewan, supplementing the base load energy from lignite coal. The ultimate installation may well exceed half a million kilowatts, although all the energy available might be generated with less than one-tenth of the installation. When storage exists or can be economically developed, an increased hydro installation represents by far the least expensive method of meeting daily and seasonal peaks on an electrical power system.

This position perhaps offers the solution to the apparent conflict of interest between hydro and other water uses, at least in the highly populated areas. The development of nuclear energy as a source of electric power will make the total energy capacity of hydro developments of less and less importance; but the economics associated with the problem of meeting peak electrical loads will make the power capability of hydro plants, where storage is available, more and more significant and will lead to their expansion in spite of a diminishing amount of energy to be secured.

Thus we are likely to see the re-development of old schemes to provide more storage, aimed at increased peak capacity rather than more energy production. New hydro schemes will emphasize storage and peak capacity and will be economically justified even with decreasing flows. Finally, pumped storage projects which in their operation do not deplete the water flow at all, but simply move water from one reservoir to another to store water at night for generation in the daytime or on a larger scale in the summer for winter generation, are likely to develop increasingly as river flows are relatively less available and other sources of base-load energy are developed.

Some existing and potential hydro developments divert water from relatively useless watersheds into much more useful areas, provide power and at the same time increase the available water supply. An example of this is the diversion from the Hudson Bay watershed to the Great Lakes in northwestern Ontario.

While increasing water use for domestic industrial and irrigation purposes will decrease the energy that might otherwise have been generated, the emphasis on storage type of developments will conserve flood flows and increase the total effective supply, possibly compensating over a long period for increasing water uses. Even though in the long run water uses may decrease the hydro energy available, the installations will still be economically justified for peaking purposes and the energy deficiency will be provided from nuclear sources.

Location of Supply in Relation to Demand

Estimates and comparisons of supply and demand made so far have used the total supply for each of the selected regions in relation to the population of the region. On this basis the average availability appears to be not too unreasonable. However, it does not take account of the distribution of runoff in relation to the location of population.

Most cities or large urban populations are naturally established on lake shores or close to major rivers. In these cases they have access not only to the runoff from their immediate district but to the unused runoff from areas hundreds of miles upstream. For example, cities on the Great Lakes and the St. Lawrence have access to water entering Lake Superior a thousand miles away. As population increases in the more remote areas, this surplus water will be reduced and cities will become more dependent on the runoff from territory in their vicinity.

Obviously, most of the cities have developed in locations having adequate water supplies, and they can secure supplies, subject to considerations of pollution, with relatively little cost for pumping, treatment, and local storage reservoirs.

Some cities, however, are not so well situated. Regina, the capital city of Saskatchewan has no adequate local supplies. Its require-

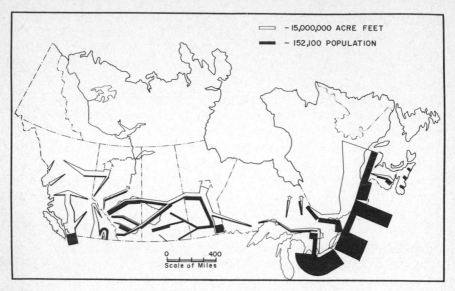

Figure 9. Location of Main Run-Off and Associated Population for Canada.

ments can, of course, be met from the South Saskatchewan River (as witness the situation of Saskatoon) but only at a continually expanding cost for pipelines or canals. Present supplies for Regina and Moose Jaw are drawn from a reservoir midway between Regina and the South Saskatchewan River which can be replenished by gravity from the completed South Saskatchewan Project.

While no other large cities appear to be as unfavorably placed as Regina, the position of the small cities and towns is frequently serious. The smaller centres have developed as the trading centres of farming districts and their locations are frequently not favorable for water supplies. They face the cost of obtaining supplies by pipeline over considerable distances. It is necessary to envisage water distributing grids over most of the rural areas of Canada to supply the smaller cities and towns. The cost of these facilities will be enormous. A survey of the problem in Saskatchewan indicated an expenditure of about $100 million to bring adequate water supplies to an urban population in small communities of about 150,000. Such an investment of some $700 per capita is far more than the urban communities could undertake. Moreover, these pipelines would not serve the farming population without greatly increased costs. Farms must therefore continue to depend primarily on ground water or locally impounded runoff.

Even if distributing grids were developed and maximum use was made of the natural movement of water in rivers to bring the runoff to the centres of population, important sources of runoff water, within technically populated regions, will remain unused unless water is moved in large volumes to the more populated areas. This situation is illustrated in Figure 9. The major rivers included in the computation of runoff are shown as bands, the width of which at any point represents the runoff approximately to scale. The population in the areas tributary to the river and which might be served at reasonable cost by local diversion is shown to scale by the width of the band on the lower edge of the river. The enormous disparity in distribution is obvious. Clearly the waters of many major rivers already included in the estimated supply for 1990 will have to be moved hundreds of miles to find the populations they will be required to support; or the population will have to move to the rivers.

The rivers flowing into the Pacific on the British Columbia Coast; the Peace and the Athabaska; the Saskatchewan in part, and many of the rivers flowing into the St. Lawrence east of Quebec City are examples of water resources that can only be counted on as part of our national supply under the above conditions. The cost of the necessary works will be extremely high, even if full advantage is taken of existing geographical features such as the Qu'Appelle Valley in Saskatchewan, through which water could be diverted from the South Saskatchewan Reservoir to serve communities accessible to the Valley over a 500 mile route to Winnipeg.

Hydroelectric developments may help in this area of major water movements. Simple diversions from one watershed to another occasionally exist. But if hydro developments were to form a complete chain of reservoirs with installations capable of functioning for pumped storage use, it is only necessary to visualize the pumping operation exceeding the generating operation to have reversed the flow of the river and moved water upstream to a point where a gravity diversion might take it to the location desired. Nuclear energy might well provide the excess energy required and the basic peaking function could still be performed by the hydro installations and largely pay for their cost.

There remain some minor factors which could improve the supply-demand position. The reduction of evaporation loss by means of surface films of evaporation inhibitors, such as cetyl alcohol, might be developed for use on a relatively large scale. When applied to the water surfaces of artifically created reservoirs, it would not interfere with the natural equilibrium of the hydrologic cycle and would make more water available for use. The seeding of clouds to concentrate precipitation in the most useful areas, although the subject of doubtful success to date, may have possibilities for the future. Similarly, the extraction of potable water from sea water may prove economically feasible on a significant scale in some water-short areas, although it is difficult to see its application in Canada.

A scrutiny of our uses of water would no doubt be rewarding. Much of our industrial use of water is for cooling purposes. Ultimately, almost all the energy dissipation required occurs through evaporation. Perhaps much more use should be made of air cooling. It is encouraging to note the completion of the first major thermal power station in Great Britain cooled entirely by air.

It may be concluded that while in total Canada's available water resources are adequate to meet her needs for the foreseeable future, this will be achieved in practice only by thorough planning of all aspects of water use together with positive and necessarily expensive measures for overcoming the problems of seasonal flow, location and pollution.

The planning phase must be based on far more adequate data as to water supply and use than exist today. For instance, we have an almost complete lack of ground water information; not only as to its extent today, but as to its trends, its relation to precipitation, the rate a which depletion will be naturally replenished and the feasibility of artificially increasing the water stored in this greatest of reservoirs. On the other hand, we have amazingly little data on water use. Future demands of industry will be the greatest water need, but we have no specific information as to Canadian industrial water uses comparable with the statistics now compiled on labour fuel required by industry.

Of the conservation measures required, perhaps elimination of pollution is the most urgent! This involves rigid control of untreatable industrial effluents and full treatment of sewage. But at the same time measures to regulate the runoff, such as reforestation of denuded watersheds, small control dams in the small streams, and major reservoirs on the larger rivers, are of enormous significance in certain areas. With these measures too, go the wise use of the water that is available for agriculture by proper agricultural techniques supplemented where feasible by irrigation and drainage.

The movement of water on a relatively small scale by transmission grids to supply smaller centres from the reasonably accessible sources is urgently required. In many cases, possibly at a later stage, such grids would also involve the movement of water on a much larger scale from remote resources to supplement those that are locally depleted.

The more expensive projects, geared to an increasing population and spread out over many years, perhaps many generations, can presumably easily be provided as required, but the less spectacular remedial measures and particularly the serious co-ordinated planning of water supply and use cannot long be delayed.

While long term climatic changes may have been contributing factors, it is salutary to note that the North African deserts once produced much of the wheat for the Roman Empire and that the Garden of Eden presumably lay in the desert of Mesopotamia.

2

Groundwater— An Undeveloped Resource

I. C. Brown

To those who rely on wells for water supply it may seem ridiculous to say that groundwater is an undeveloped resource; but, how much do you know about the amount of water you can pump, how long you can keep pumping at a given rate, how did it get there, where did it come from, why is it soft or hard? Without the answers to these questions and others the vast groundwater reserves of Canada cannot be used to their fullest extent, and at present the answers are available only for a limited number of wells and well fields.

Canada is blessed with more lakes and rivers than any equal area in the world and with all this fresh water available on surface it may seem unnecessary to develop a largely hidden water resource even though this resource is larger and more evenly distributed than the surface one. Rough estimates suggest that there is some thirty times as much water in the ground as in lakes and rivers. However, the cost of a well and the cost of a pipeline per foot are roughly the same, so it becomes a matter of economics. It is often cheaper to pump water from a few hundred feet below surface than to pipe it a mile or more on surface. As an extra bonus, groundwater is more consistent in temperature and quality and less likely to be polluted and consequently requires less expensive treatment than surface water. Obviously a resource that can give us a better and cheaper product is worth knowing about.

Reprinted in edited form from *Canadian Geographical Journal*, Vol. LXIX, no. 6 (1964), pp. 212-21.

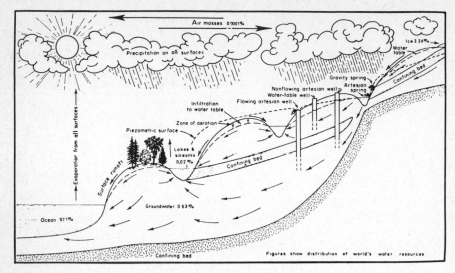

Figure 1. The never ending hydrologic cycle. Evaporation raises water from all water and land surfaces to be moved by winds in the atmosphere and precipitated on all surfaces where some runs off to the oceans, some evaporates and the rest seeps into the ground to percolate through it and eventually discharge back to surface or into the sea. The approximate amount of water present at all times in each part of the cycle is shown. (Adapted from diagrams prepared by the U.S.G.S.)

All the water on earth is travelling through a never ending cycle, the hydrologic cycle, and groundwater is only a part of this cycle. (Figure 1.) Ever since the earth's atmosphere became cool enough for water to condense, rain has been falling on the earth's surface. The first rain fell on barren rock and later on rock plus deposits of gravel, sand and silt which it had helped to form. These conditions continued for many thousands of millions of years. Some of the rain ran off, some evaporated, and some soaked into the openings in the rocks and surface deposits to become groundwater. With the advent of plant life, some three hundred and fifty to four hundred million years ago, came the development of soil and this complicated the cycle in that more of the rain was now held by the soil and evaporated slowly, or was extracted and transpired by plants, but the rest still sank deeper and became part of the groundwater.

Rainfall over the earth varies from practically nothing to more than a hundred inches per year, and we know that even the driest deserts today were once regions in which much rain fell. In Canada the average rainfall is now about 20 inches per year and, if we assume conservatively that only one half inch per year sinks into the ground as groundwater, then in a mere one million years this would add up to almost eight miles of water. Obviously all this water cannot just sink into the ground and disappear; it has to keep moving through it, while at the same time keeping the materials of the earth pretty well saturated.

Water that soaks into the earth fills cracks and holes in rock and the pore spaces between fragments in gravel, sand and clay. The upper surface of this saturated zone is termed the water-table. Some water evaporates from this surface and eventually finds its way back to the atmosphere. The configuration of this water-table is, broadly speaking, a subdued replica of the earth's surface.

Above the water-table, water moves largely downward due to the pull of gravity, but below, it becomes a part of groundwater and is subject to gravity, the pressure in surrounding water, and molecular forces. The molecular forces bind some of the groundwater to the surface of the materials and thus place it in dead storage. The rest, being lazy, follows the path of least resistance—up, down, or sideways—to the place where its potential energy is lowest, ultimately the sea.

Channel ways through the ground are extremely complex and numerous and extend to great depths. Consequently water generally travels through them very slowly, in great quantities and sometimes for great distances, but eventually it has to find some place to run out or the earth would be waterlogged. Groundwater completes its part of the cycle when it is discharged by seeps or springs to the surface or into streams, rivers, lakes or the oceans. This discharging groundwater keeps rivers flowing during long periods when there is no rain, thus rivers are drains both for surface run-off and for groundwater. Over long periods of time this cycle is always in balance and groundwater is a continuously flowing system or a renewable and, as we shall see later, a re-usable resource.

Considering the area of Canada it is obvious that there is a very large quantity of water stored in the ground, but only part of this is available for withdrawal. In saturated clay very little water can move even under high pressure. In coarse sand and gravel, on the other hand, water can move more easily. There are of course all gradations from unfractured solid rock or a very compact clay to open solution channels and coarse gravels. Any material from which enough water can be withdrawn for a given requirement at a reasonable cost is called an aquifer. Thus the term aquifer is relative only and an aquifer capable of supplying just enough water for scattered individual homes might not be considered an aquifer by someone looking for a large industrial supply.

The study of groundwater depends on a detailed, three dimensional knowledge of its geologic distribution system plus the knowledge of how it reacts to these geological materials both physically and chemically. To study all these factors requires scientists and engineers trained in a wide variety of disciplines and there are only a limited number of such specialists available in Canada. Most of them are in the Provincial and Federal Government groundwater agencies. Groundwater is considered a mineral and consequently responsibility for its administration and control rests with the provinces. Most provinces have well established groundwater agencies who carry out these responsibilities and actively assist in the development of groundwater resources. There is much to be learned before we can properly use groundwater and while much data have been gathered in the past, interpretation of these data and basic research into the where and why of groundwater is only in its infancy. But it is a very healthy and energetic infant.

Many other government and private organizations and consultants are also doing research and gathering data that have a direct bearing on the subject. Such organizations are those dealing with geology, mining, oil and gas, agriculture, forestry, health, waterpower, water supply and engineering. It would take too long to describe all the wide variety of research projects being worked on, so that the remainder of this paper will describe what the study of groundwater involves and how these studies will enable us to fully and intelligently use and control this vast resource.

The primary concern of the hydrogeologist, the groundwater specialist, is to find out where the groundwater flows from the time it enters the ground until it leaves. We know that groundwater drainage basins coincide with the surface drainage basins at shallow depths. We also know that at greater depths the effects of geologic formations become more important and groundwater flow systems are no longer defined by surface drainage basins. By intensive study of a number of typical drainage basins, theories and methods are developed that can be used not only to predict conditions in similar basins for which only a limited amount of information is available, but can also be applied to the more difficult and expensive studies of deeper flow systems.

Basin studies now being undertaken in Canada vary greatly in size. One of the smallest is the 3½- to 4-square-mile Marmot Creek basin in the front ranges of the Rockies in Alberta. This is primarily a forestry research project, but trees depend on water and the hydrogeology is being studied by the Research Council of Alberta.

At the other end of the scale is the research being conducted by the Geological Survey of Canada in the huge Assiniboine drainage basin, more than 41,000 square miles in area. This is a ten-year project with the objective not only of studying the groundwater in a large drainage basin under semi-arid prairie conditions but also of developing methods and techniques suitable to these conditions. This study, started in 1962, has already provided methods that are being applied to smaller basin studies across Canada.

The first requirement in any basin study is as complete a knowledge as possible of the geology even at great depth. By compiling all existing information from all possible sources such as, geologic maps, soils maps, aerial photography, water well inventories, oil and mining company drilling records and geophysical data, an incomplete framework is first built up. Much of this information has been gathered by highly trained specialists and is reliable. Some, such as well inventories, depends to a large extent on well owners' memories of what materials were encountered perhaps 30 years before and must be very carefully assessed before it is used.

Many direct and indirect methods are then used to fill in the details of the framework. The most direct method is to study the materials in the field and map the unmapped areas. This completes part of the framework but must be supplemented by mapping and studying the formations below the ground. It would be ideal to have a large number of mine shafts and actually go underground and see the formations but this can only be done where there is a mine. The next best method is to drill holes and get all possible information from them. The most accurate record is obtained from a continuous large diameter core but this is very costly, so other methods are often used that give less perfect information but at lower cost. These vary from small diameter continuous cores to samples of the cuttings being washed out of the drill-hole.

Because groundwater always contains dissolved materials and reacts with the surrounding geologic materials it has various electrical properties and these can be measured by probes lowered down test holes. These are designed to measure the natural electrical properties or to introduce artificial currents and measure their effects. Nuclear probes, which measure the effects of certain types of radiation, and sonic probes which measure the effect of ultrasonic vibrations, are also used. Many of these methods have been adapted from the oil industry and give much information about the type of formation, its porosity and water content and composition and will give more when we learn all their capabilities. They are most useful in indicating changes from one formation to another and formations, identified from core samples in one hole, can be traced long distances by simply drilling and electrologging—which is much cheaper than core sampling.

While drill-holes give good reference sections at a point, it is much too costly to drill at close enough intervals to give a complete picture of the geology except for detailed studies of small areas. Atomic Energy of Canada Limited has had to do very detailed studies of groundwater movement in waste disposal areas at Chalk River, Ontario, and has drilled holes a few feet or tens of feet apart. Saskatchewan Research Council, on the other hand, drills test holes many miles apart in support of their reconnaissance mapping program.

Various indirect methods are used to fill in between the areas where drilling information is available and to provide guidance as to the best places to drill. If the type or age of formation is known, geologists can often predict what is likely to be found, even many miles from any outcrop. Also, a host of geophysical methods are available for measuring various physical properties of the rocks beneath our feet, including airborne means. However, little can be said of these latter as some are still under military security and others have not yet been tested in the field. If successful they could revolutionize our methods of study.

Seismic techniques, long used in the oil industry, are being adapted for use at shallower depths. These depend on the speed of travel of sound energy through the ground, the refraction method, or its reflection from denser layers. The source of energy in groundwater seismic work can be a blow on the ground by a hammer or heavy weight, which makes it much easier to use in settled areas than the dynamite explosion used for exploration to greater depths. This technique was used by the Geological Survey of Canada during a hydrogeological study in the Vaudreuil area, Quebec, to outline in detail an old buried valley of the Ottawa River that was known to contain thick deposits of permeable sand and gravel, and to be an excellent artesian aquifer. It was also found possible to indicate quite closely changes in the type of bedrock underlying these deposits.

By introducing an electric current into the ground the resistance of materials at various depths can be calculated. This method has been used on the Prairies in tracing buried valleys in which the material filling the buried valley was so similar to that of the sides of the valley that seismic techniques could not be used. It was also used successfully near Winkler, Manitoba, where a sand and gravel aquifer had been located near the town and had been traced for some miles to the north by a drilling program. An experimental resistivity survey of the area was able to not only outline the aquifer accurately beneath its clay cover, but indicate the type of material that would be found in various parts of it, though it could not tell whether there was water in these materials or not. Subsequent test pumping proved large amounts of water available.

Gravity methods that can detect masses of lighter or heavier materials have been used to trace buried valleys. The deposits filling the valleys are not as well consolidated as the surrounding bedrock and consequently have a lower gravity.

Having built a fairly adequate picture of the geology in three dimensions the next problem is to find where the water is flowing within it. In a very general way we know from the surface of the water-table that flow is from high areas to low areas and maps are constructed using this surface to indicate the general direction of groundwater flow. Such maps are first approximations only as they do not indicate how the water flows below the water-table nor how it is affected by the materials through which it flows.

A more accurate picture can be obtained by measuring variations in pressure even though we are dealing with diffuse flow through a porous medium that is not uniform. After determining the pressure at numerous points within the system we can construct sections showing lines of equal pressure. The water flow must be at right angles across these lines.

On the Prairies where we have a large amount of data on wells, and wells are constructed to considerable depths, it has been possible to use pressure data to construct sections showing the flow pattern across many miles of the country. These show that in general the water flows downward through the less permeable materials near surface into more permeable sandy materials at depth and then flows laterally toward lower areas where it flows upward and discharges at surface. Such studies are very general in character as there is no way of telling whether these wells are actually giving the pressure at the bottom end of the well or have developed leaks at other points.

More accurate results may be obtained from piezometer (pressure-measuring) points, which are nests of three or four small diameter wells very carefully sealed so that they indicate the pressure at the well point only, and at three or four different depths. The results show that groundwater flow may be much deeper than ex-

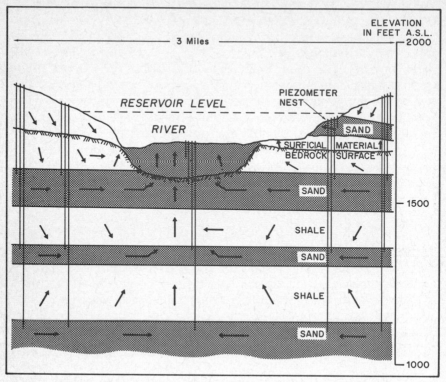

Figure 2. Section showing piezometer installation across the South Saskatchewan River near Riverhurst used to study the effect on ground-water of flooding the reservoir. The arrows show where the greatest amount of flow occurs. Pressure in some of the sands is sufficient to raise water into the piezometers almost to the future reservoir level. In areas of upward flow the water level or pressure in deeper piezometers is higher than that in shallower ones.

pected. One section of such nests across the South Saskatchewan River, with the deepest point at 860 feet, indicates water coming from even greater depths to discharge into the river (Figure 2).

Various other approaches have been tried to see if it is possible to predict the probable depths of flow systems so that piezometers can be installed at the best points rather than by trial and error. Electrical models can be built to simulate natural conditions on a small scale. More complex physical and electrical models capable of giving more accurate and even quantitative results, if sufficient data are available, have been constructed in other countries and will soon be in use in Canada. Such models will be of great use when our knowledge reaches the stage that we can use them to make predictions of changes in flow systems due to either natural or man-made causes.

The chemistry of water also can be used to tell us a lot about where it is flowing. For example, water flowing through limestones and dolomite will be high in carbonate and that flowing through rocks containing gypsum will be high in sulphate, while that flowing through clean sand and gravel or crystalline rocks will be very low in dissolved contents. Work in other countries has shown that in long groundwater flow systems there is a continuous change in certain chemical characteristics of the groundwater regardless of the materials through which it flows. Water at surface starts out being characteristically a bicarbonate water and proceeds through a series of changes until it finally ends up as a chloride water much like sea water. Studies of the chemistry of the groundwater in the Red River Valley, south of Winnipeg, showed that the bedrock artesian aquifer underlying the area receives its water from the Sandilands Forest Reserve area many miles to the east and further that within this aquifer the zones of greatest flow can also be outlined.

Tracer materials can be injected into groundwater but various chemicals and dyes which have been used for this purpose tend to react with the materials through which they are travelling, and groundwater flow systems are so complex that tracers soon become so diffused that they cannot be identified. Atomic Energy of Canada have made use of radioactive isotopes in their waste disposal areas to do extremely detailed studies of groundwater flow and by means of these tracers have shown that even different layers in a sand-filled basin can have different directional properties and water in one layer just a few feet above another may be flowing in an entirely different direction.

Perhaps the best tracer is tritium, the radioactive isotope of hydrogen that is present in all water. Since the advent of atomic bombs there have been periods when the rainfall was particularly high in tritium. By combining knowledge of these periods with knowledge of the rate of decay of tritium it is possible to determine the age of the water up to approximately 30 years. By knowing the age at various points the direction of flow can be deduced. Similar age determinations can be done using radioactive carbon that is naturally present in water but this method is not being used in Canada as yet.

Study of groundwater flow systems leads us to both ends of the system and it is important to know where, when and how water is recharged from the atmosphere to the ground. In general, recharge takes place on a large scale during the fall rains after plant growth has died down or ceased, and in the spring during break-up. During the rest of the year, much of the precipitation that falls is taken up by plants and returned to the atmosphere without ever reaching the groundwater table. This information is obtained from observation wells. These wells are measured weekly or monthly to determine the longer term changes, or have continuous recorders installed to record fluctuations in the water-table of as little as one hundredth of a foot and operate unattended for long periods. In Canada only about 250 observation wells are being maintained by the various groundwater agencies. This compares with some 7,000 permanent observation wells in the United States. The Canadian network is being expanded so that over the years we will not only have some accurate knowledge of what the natural fluctuations in the water-table are, but also what changes are due to man's withdrawal of groundwater in heavily pumped areas.

At one time, it was generally considered that sloughs and swamps which have no external drainage must be places from which water soaked into the ground and recharged the groundwater. Studies using piezometers have shown that the opposite is usually true. Groundwater is recharged on the high ground between these depressions, flows quite deeply into the ground and back up into the depression. This has radically changed the ideas bearing on the area of ground available for recharge.

In some areas the groundwater flow system may be capable of handling more water than is available from natural recharge and in others water may be being drawn out faster than it can be recharged naturally. Research is now being conducted in Alberta, Saskatchewan, and Ontario into the possibilities of artificial recharge. This can be done by allowing water to sink in from the surface or by injecting it by wells directly into an aquifer. Much has been done in studying these problems in other countries but few of these have Canada's winter problems to contend with. Some of the answers may come from the oil companies who inject water into the oil-bearing formations to drive oil out. In withdrawing large quantities of groundwater for cooling purposes, disposal of the water may be a problem and in some areas this is returned to the ground far enough away to be naturally cooled and reused. It is even possible now to take the treated effluent from sewage disposal plants and return it to the groundwater system for re-use, though this is not done in Canada at present except through septic tanks.

Seeps and springs have long been known as discharge areas for groundwater but pressure studies have shown that there is also much diffuse discharge into rivers along their bottoms and sides.

In fact, it is more usual for rivers to be drains for groundwater than for them to feed groundwater. This may help account for mysterious gains and losses in flow along stretches of certain rivers. Many arid areas of sodic soils are unsuitable for agriculture and it has been considered that these could be improved by adding fresh water to leach out the excess salts. However, in many of these areas, the groundwater movement is upward and the visible salts are the result of evaporation of groundwater very slowly seeping up to the surface. Adding water on surface would only result in water-logged land as there would be no place for it to go.

Plant life is also used to study circulation systems. If the flow system is comparatively short as in a small slough, there has been little chance for chemical change, the water being discharged is fresh, and plants grow that will not tolerate any amount of salt, such as willow. Conversely if the flow system is long, and the water being discharged is high in dissolved salts, then plant growth is salt tolerant. Thus, by mapping areas of salt tolerant plants it is possible to outline areas of diffuse discharge. Deep wells drilled in such areas of upward flow are almost invariably artesian. Unfortunately they are also salty.

Many plants can survive considerable periods without any moisture, but others, known as phreatophytes, feed on groundwater and have to have their roots wet all the time. Such phreatophytic plants indicate that groundwater is flowing close enough to surface to be reached by their root systems. Such plants can transpire large amounts of groundwater to the atmosphere and studies are now underway to determine just how much this is. Possibly by selective removal or planting we will some day prevent large water losses along streams or canals, or reclaim unusable land.

The practical uses of the study of flow systems require knowledge of how much gets in, how much is travelling through any part of the system, how much is coming out, and its composition. The answers to these questions are still largely in the future as we have to understand much more about where water travels before we can say how much. Water is a moving medium that varies greatly in quantity and quality from day to day, month to month, and year to year. Thus a relatively long period of a decade or more is required to study the fluctuations.

The United Nations Educational, Scientific and Cultural Organization, the World Meteorological Organization, and the International Association of Scientific Hydrology, and other international organizations have realized this and have endorsed an International

Hydrologic Decade. UNESCO convened in May, 1963, a proprietary meeting of experts to prepare a tentative program for an International Hydrologic Decade to begin in 1965. In April of 1964, a second meeting was convened to discuss programs of the countries that have agreed to participate.

Canada has agreed to participate in this program and at the time of writing government organizations at all levels, universities and private organizations are preparing programs of research. All that remains to be decided is the extent of these programs. It has been estimated that more than three billion dollars will be spent in Canada on water resource development programs in the next decade. Much of this development will take place in remote areas where hydrologic data are meagre and studies have not even been begun. Such expenditures should be based on sound knowledge and it is to be hoped that Canada's research program will be sufficient to provide this knowledge so that groundwater will no longer be an undeveloped resource.

3

Characteristics of River Discharge and Runoff in Canada

D. K. Mackay

Introduction

A great amount of streamflow data has been collected for many of Canada's river basins by the Water Resources Branch of the Department of Northern Affairs and National Resources, but the geographical aspects of runoff in Canada have received little study. A knowledge of the areal differences in runoff, its seasonal components, and its recorded variability over the years is basic to the intelligent use and conservation of our water resources. This paper is a continuation of the work involved in the preparation of the map of Canadian drainage basins compiled for the Atlas of Canada by the Geographical Branch.

Although Canada's supply of fresh water is very large, the technological demands of a modern society and an expanding population can cause regional shortages which demand national attention. This is particularly true if solutions to the problem of shortages involve water diversion. There are a number of ways of satisfying water shortages other than by diversion of streams from basins of relative nonuse to those of overuse. These could include pollution control and multiple use, curbs on industrial expansion in specific areas, development and expansion of reservoir systems, and

Reprinted from *Geographical Bulletin*, Vol. 8, no. 3 (1966), pp. 219-27. By permission of the Queen's Printer, Ottawa.

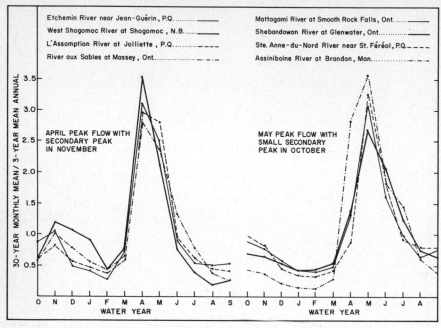

Figure 1. Hydrographs of river discharge (dimensionless).

desalinization. In any event, there is a definite need for basic information about Canada's water resources. Some of the general characteristics of runoff and of the regional differences that exist with respect to these characteristics are discussed in this paper.

Runoff

Runoff is the residual of precipitation which flows into a surface stream. In other words, it is that portion of precipitation which reaches a natural channel after loss by evaporation and transpiration, and after soil moisture deficiencies have been satisfied. To reach the channel, the water moves both over the surface and through the ground and its movement is influenced and regulated by such factors as landforms, soils and vegetation, as well as by the activities of man.

Runoff is variable in space and over time. Spatially, it is variable not only from river basin to river basin, but as indicated by differences in area-yield ratios at gauging locations along a stream channel, it varies within a basin as well. Fluctuations between the source and mouth of a stream reflect basin differences in precipitation, evapotranspiration, soil porosity and stratigraphy. Discharge data recorded at a stream gauging station are therefore integrated values, only representative of the area above the gauging site. This is a problem when it is desirable to develop an understanding of runoff conditions within a basin or over a larger area containing a number of basins. Inevitably, a considerable amount of information is lost through the processes of generalization.

There is an advantage in averaging runoff observations over convenient periods of time such as, for example, one month. The masking of small fluctuations in such a time series tends to throw into relief fundamental patterns in the variation of the series which are repeated to a certain degree from year to year. It also establishes a yearly curve which probably does not differ to any marked extent from curves at other locations along the channel because there must necessarily be a strong measure of serial correlation among observations taken at various points along the same river. These basic curves, taken over a period of years, can be used to classify rivers and separate them into regional categories.

Classification of Rivers

Rivers may be classified by comparing monthly flow hydrographs for similarities and differences. For purposes of comparison it is best to derive a dimensionless hydrograph by determining the percentage of the annual flow occurring in any given month or, using a similar transformation, by dividing the river's mean monthly flow by its mean annual flow (Browzin, 1962). In this way, differences in the rates of river discharge are resolved, and the hydrographs may be compared by overlaying one on another (Figures 1, 2 and 3).

The significant features in the form of the curve are the peaks and troughs, i.e., the months of high and low flow respectively. In the course of the water year, which runs from October through the following September, runoff may peak more than once, depending mainly on the precipitation regime. Another important factor is the stability of the curve over any given period of time. The flow in a given month will vary from year to year, in some months more than in others. The variability may be so great in fact, that in some instances mean monthly runoff values may be misleading. The confidence which can be placed in an annual runoff curve must be related not only to the length of the runoff record but also to its variability.

In this study, monthly discharge means, standard deviations, and coefficients of variation based on the 30-year period, 1921 to 1950, were determined for 101 rivers in Canada, exclusive of those in the Arctic islands. The variation in maximum and minimum runoff is discussed with reference to five major basin complexes.

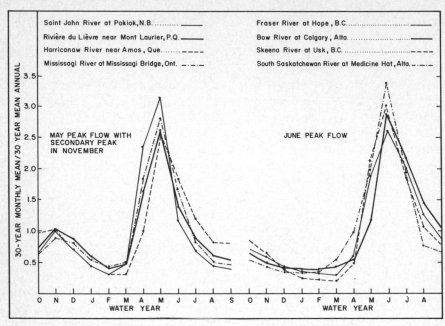

Figure 2. Hydrographs of river discharge (dimensionless).

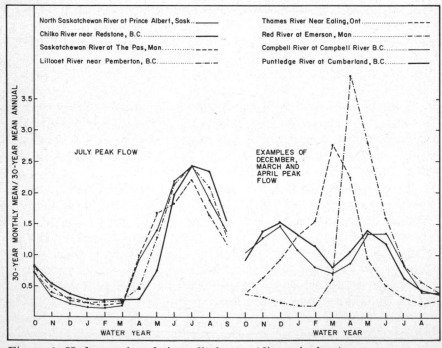

Figure 3. Hydrographs of river discharge (dimensionless).

Where long-term observations were not available, shorter records were used; the Arctic basin, for example, is discussed solely on the basis of available short-term records, and reference to the Gulf of Mexico drainage is made on the basis of one 30-year record plus a few shorter ones. Much more information is available for the other three basins: seventeen 30-year records were processed for the Pacific basin, thirty for the Hudson Bay basin, and fifty-three for the Atlantic basin. Records of shorter duration were used to supplement the long-term data.

Pacific drainage

Two flow curves are typical of the Pacific basin which covers an area of approximately 400,730 square miles. One curve shows a winter maximum, the other a late spring-summer maximum (Figure 4). A December maximum is general for the Vancouver Island streams such as Campbell River (Figure 3), probably for those of the Queen Charlotte Islands, and for some streams draining parts of the Coast Mountains and the area of Vancouver's north shore. December is a month of high precipitation, much of which falls in the form of rain in the mild winter climate of the lowland coastal belt. Snow that falls on the mountain slopes and the lower levels can also make a considerable contribution to December runoff because the freezing level fluctuates with incursions of warm air. Minimum runoff in this area occurs in August, the end of a period of relative drought and the month in which temperatures begin to drop, thus effectively reducing snow and glacier melt at higher elevations.

Over the rest of the Pacific watershed, which encompasses a considerable part of British Columbia and the Yukon Territory, the highest runoff usually occurs in June or in cases such as the Bridge, Lillooet, and Chilcotin basins, in July. On the basis of the very limited data available, exceptions can be found among the small streams draining the west front of the Coast Mountains, but those that penetrate to the interior of the mainland have June maxima. One outstanding exception is the upper Yukon River which, as a result of a combination of high precipitation and intense glacier melt reaches its maximum discharge in late July or early August—mean monthly maximum at Whitehorse occurs in August. The same condition may also hold for the river's western tributaries, the White and Nordenskiold rivers, but as Robinson (1945) has observed, "Snow-fed streams, such as Teslin, Pelly and, to a lesser extent, the Stewart, heading into the southeast and east, come quickly into flood at break-up in late May, and, by late July and

August are dependent entirely on rainfall and may become quite shallow."

Minimum runoff in the interior mainland part of the Pacific basin occurs in February or March, months of low temperatures and low precipitation.

Gulf of Mexico drainage

This covers the relatively small area of about 10,000 square miles in southern Alberta and Saskatchewan which is drained by the Milk River and its tributaries. The Milk River rises in the Rocky Mountains of Montana, flows north into Alberta and then turns back into the United States near the Alberta-Saskatchewan provincial border. Its peak monthly flow coincides with the precipitation peak in June.

The Saskatchewan portion of this basin is drained by such tributaries of the Milk River as Lodge and Battle creeks, and the Frenchman and Poplar rivers. These tributaries rise in an area which suffers from a moisture deficiency and their flow is at a maximum in May and a minimum in January. In a water-deficient area such as this, stream flow may often peak before the ground thaws completely, i.e., before the infiltration capacity seriously limits the surface runoff, and this early maximum may occur in spite of increasing precipitation in later months. The January minimum is related to the combination of low temperatures, low precipitation, and a negligible ground water flow.

Arctic drainage

Although the Arctic drainage system covers an area of 1,380,895 square miles, there is only a limited amount of streamflow data available and estimates of months of maximum and minimum flow are based on very limited direct evidence. The Mackenzie and its western tributaries usually have a peak flow in June following a May break-up. (Figure 4). One anomaly is the Athabasca River, the most southerly tributary of the Mackenzie, whose mean monthly flow over the years of record reaches its maximum in July. Discharge data, however, reveal that the yearly peak flow occurred as often in June as in July, only the long-term mean monthly flow being greater in July. The reason for a July maximum rate of flow in the Athabasca basin is the increase in precipitation over that of the previous month. This is in contrast to basins south of the Athabasca where June precipitation is generally higher than that of July. Precipitation data for the Peace River basin to the north show little difference in the amount of rainfall occurring in these two months.

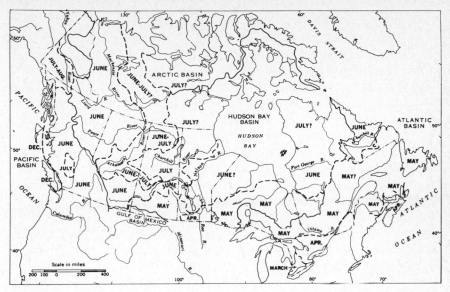

Figure 4. Months of maximum runoff.

To the north and east of the Mackenzie River meteorologic and hydrologic data are lacking and this poses a problem in determining the months of maximum and minimum runoff. The scattered accounts of flood conditions and the dates of river break-up—break-up being a reasonably good indicator of the period of maximum runoff —suggest later periods of peak flow than are characteristic of the Mackenzie River and its western tributaries. The lower Coppermine River, for example, breaks up approximately two weeks later than the Mackenzie at Aklavik and it may therefore be assumed that the period of maximum runoff would be similarly retarded. March is the month of expected minimum flow for Arctic drainage with the exception of the Athabasca River basin where runoff is lowest in February. The March increase in the Athabasca flow may be due to radiational melting of snow and ice in the region of its southernmost headwaters.

Hudson Bay drainage

This is a vast area of over 1,400,000 square miles in which there are considerable differences in the periods of maximum and minimum runoff. Peak flow can occur April through July, and minimum flow January through March or occasionally, even into April.

Of all the streams in the Hudson Bay drainage basin, only the Red River has a maximum monthly flow in April (Figures 3 and 4). This river rises in the United States and flows north into Manitoba as far as Lake Winnipeg, 100 miles north of the border. It is probable, however, that maximum runoff in the Canadian portion of the Red River basin occurs in May, the same month as in the Assiniboine basin to the west. As in the case of rivers which flow north in northern latitudes, snow melt begins in the headwaters area, and this in combination with the vagaries of river break-up can result in floods at downstream locations. If the Red River and its principal tributary the Assiniboine River reach their maxima at nearly the same time, the result can be a flood of major proportions such as occurred in 1950.

A July peak flow is typical of the Saskatchewan and Churchill rivers (Figure 4) and is probably characteristic for all rivers on the western side of Hudson Bay north of the Churchill basin. This, however, has been inferred from examination of the fragmentary evidence of runoff conditions available for rivers in the Mackenzie River area far to the west.

In some parts of the Hudson Bay basin a small secondary maximum occurs, usually in October and November. This is particularly evident in the discharge records of streams in the Moose River basin (e.g., Mattagami River, Figure 1), and to a lesser extent in other rivers draining into James Bay.

Minimum flow occurs earliest in the headwaters of the South Saskatchewan basin. A January minimum is normal on the main stream at Medicine Hat (Figure 5) and at various points on its

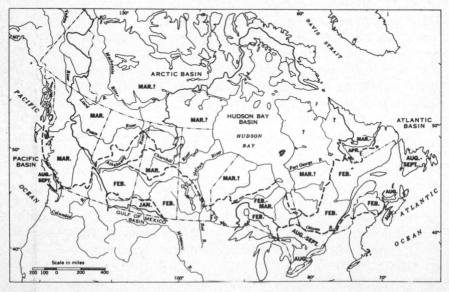

Figure 5. Months of minimum runoff.

tributary, the Oldman River, and appears to be a result of the January minimum both of precipitation and of temperature in the headwaters area. The remainder of the Prairie drainage network has minimum runoff in February. Hudson Bay rivers which drain portions of the Canadian Shield generally reach their minimum in March, somewhat later than the Prairie rivers.

Atlantic drainage

This area of approximately 580,097 square miles shows considerable variation, with peak runoff occurring as early as March in the Thames basin of southwestern Ontario (Figure 3), as late as June in the Churchill (formerly the Hamilton) basin of Labrador (Figure 4) and possibly even later farther north in Labrador. Throughout most of the area a small secondary peak occurs in November, although in Nova Scotia the secondary maximum occurs in December, and in Prince Edward Island during January. The periods of low flow normally occur in February and in August-September. If the primary minimum is in the fall, the secondary minimum will occur in the spring, and vice versa.

Typical Runoff Regimes

Figures 4 and 5 illustrate that similar periods of maximum and minimum flow are common to rivers that drain large contiguous areas although the limits of these areas do not necessarily always coincide for both phenomena. Over large areas hydrographic curves are very similar in shape (Figures 1, 2 and 3) with the period of maximum flow being the dominant feature. The month of minimum flow falls at the lowest point in a nearly horizontal part of the curve and, with relatively short records, is subject to change if extreme runoff conditions occur in any given year. If monthly runoff values are grouped into seasonal components, some information will be lost although broad characteristic differences are discernible among many basin complexes.

The approximate percentage of runoff occurring in specific drainage areas during winter (December, January, February), spring (March, April, May), summer (June, July, August) and fall (September, October, November) are shown in Table I. Although the selection of areas and rivers appears arbitrary, the list is a reflection of two conditions: the availability of data and the grouping together of basins displaying similar seasonal runoff components.

Table I illustrates the dominance of spring runoff in Canada east of the Lakehead and of summer runoff in western Canada, with

TABLE I. SEASONAL RUNOFF

Drainage area	Approximate percentage of runoff occurring in:			
	Winter	Spring	Summer	Fall
Pacific basin				
Vancouver Island/Vancouver north shore mountains	**33**	26	*18*	23
Pacific watershed				
(except Pacific basin)	8	20	**53**	19
Pacific-Hudson Bay basin				
Pacific watershed/Saskatchewan River system (omitting Pacific basin)	7	23	**52**	18
Hudson Bay basin				
Red/Assiniboine basin	5	**56**	30	9
English/Winnipeg basin	*15*	28	**35**	22
Moose/Harricanaw drainage system	*10*	**43**	27	20
Atlantic basin				
Ontario/St. Lawrence North Shore drainage	19	**43**	21	*17*
St. Lawrence south shore/New Brunswick drainage	16	**50**	19	*15*
Nova Scotia	30	**40**	*11*	19

the two notable exceptions of the Vancouver Island/Lower Mainland region and the Red/Assiniboine basin. The former is the only area of Canada in which winter runoff is the primary seasonal component; the latter resembles eastern Canada in that it has a spring runoff maximum but lacks the eastern Canada tendency toward a secondary peak in November or December.

The average range in discharge

The range between mean minimum and mean maximum monthly discharge is an important variable as it bears on such problems as the maintenance of a constant water supply and by implication, the provision of storage facilities, on the development of hydro-electric power stations, on land use and on other related aspects of land management and conservation. If the range is calculated as a percentage of a river's mean discharge, the resulting value is dimensionless, and it can be compared directly with those for other rivers across the country. Table II lists values of river complexes that are combined on the basis of similarities in range within specific drainage areas. Areas are subjective and the resulting values are only designed to show the differences that exist across the country.

It should be noted that the use of mean values effectively masks the range in discharge that can occur over very short periods particularly in streams that exhibit flash characteristics. If, for example, the rate of discharge just prior to a storm is taken as a base value, and this value is then compared with the peak discharge

TABLE II. TYPICAL RANGE BETWEEN MAXIMUM AND MINIMUM MEAN MONTHLY DISCHARGE (IN EQUIVALENTS OF MEAN ANNUAL DISCHARGE)

Drainage area	Average range
Vancouver Island rivers	1.1
British Columbia mainland rivers	2.6
Red/Assiniboine rivers	3.4
North Saskatchewan/Saskatchewan system	2.4
South Saskatchewan headwater rivers (Oldman, Belly, St. Mary)	3.4
Atlantic drainage in Ontario	2.4
Moose River basin	3.5
Matane River/St. Lawrence south shore drainage	4.2
Nova Scotia rivers	1.8
New Brunswick rivers	3.0

value resulting from the storm, the range can greatly exceed those shown in Table II. The same is true of the range between the instantaneous minimum and instantaneous maximum rates of discharge that occurs in a stream over a typical water year.

Variability of Monthly Runoff

The coefficient of variation is a parameter which can be used to measure runoff variability. It is computed by dividing the standard deviation of a sample by its mean and multiplying the result by 100; in other words, the standard deviation is taken as a percentage of the mean. In this study, 101 thirty-year records of river discharge were examined and the coefficients were computed for each on a monthly basis. Figure 6 illustrates some of the differences.

On both the east and west coasts, high runoff periods generally show less variability than low runoff periods. The same situation appears to hold for rivers draining the interior of British Columbia. This relationship changes in the Prairie drainage systems. For example, runoff for the North and South Saskatchewan rivers in the Nelson basin is least variable during the winter minimum and the summer maximum but highly variable during break-up and freeze-up. Runoff from the Red and Assiniboine rivers, also in the Nelson basin, is most variable during May, the month following break-up, and during the summer period of high flow. In northern and western Ontario the winter period of minimum flow is least variable, although in southwestern Ontario the Thames and Saugeen rivers are least variable during the spring period of maximum flow.

Summary

Figures 4 and 5 illustrate the significant regional variation of the months of maximum and minimum river flow in Canada as well as a latitudinal effect in the southern regions which cuts across all

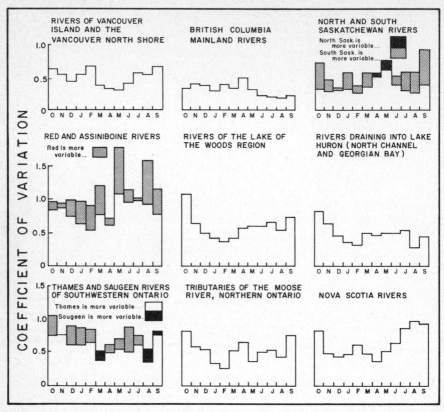

Figure 6. Approximate variability of monthly runoff for selected drainage.

basins. If runoff values are grouped on a seasonal basis (Table I), spring runoff is seen to be dominant in eastern Canada and summer runoff in western Canada. Figures 1, 2 and 3, showing the basic types of hydrographs typical of various parts of Canada, indicate that rivers separated by great distances may still have similar annual regimes. Figure 6 shows the nature of the variation in monthly runoff values that occur in different parts of the country. The least variation in year-to-year flow occurs in British Columbia, and the greatest is shown by the Red and Assiniboine rivers in Manitoba and by the Thames and Saugeen rivers in southwestern Ontario.

The results show that very real regional differences exist with respect to runoff characteristics and that these characteristics require careful study in the interests of the use and conservation of Canada's water resources.

References

Browzin, Boris S., "On classification of rivers in the Great Lakes-St. Lawrence basin", Institute of Science and Technology, Great Lakes Resources Division, pub. no. 9 (University of Michigan, 1962) pp. 86-92.

Department of Northern Affairs and Natural Resources, Water Resources Branch, "Water supply papers for climatic years 1921-63".

Robinson, J. L., "Water transportation in the Canadian Northwest", *Canadian Geographical Journal*, Vol. XXXI, no. 5 (1945), pp. 236-256.

4

Airphoto Interpretation as an Aid in Flood Susceptibility Determination

L. C. N. Burgess

". . . along most rivers there seems to be a general relationship between frequency of flooding and certain alluvial features of the valley bottoms. . . . The relation of terrain to floods as an aspect of human geography has hardly been studied, at least not nearly so extensively as river hydraulics and hydrology."[6]

Introduction and Background

The recent flooding in northern Italy has perhaps received wider publicity than any flood in recent history, because of the damaged art treasures at Florence, and the great strain that has been placed upon the Italian economy by the magnitude of the general flood losses. However, few floods receive anything like this amount of publicity. Generally, the news media seem to report damaging floods more in terms of the number of persons drowned and families driven from their homes than in terms of the dollar value of damages incurred. It is also true that many floods do not merit worldwide or even national news coverage, even though today's sophisticated news media are fully capable of providing it. Even in the personal experience of residents of our many flood plains,

Text of a paper presented to the *International Conference on Water for Peace*, Washington, D.C., May 1967. Published by the Canada Department of Energy, Mines and Resources. Reprinted by permission of the Queen's Printer, Ottawa.

flooding may be a relatively rare occurrence, for these disasters are unevenly distributed over time and directly affect only a small fraction of the total population. Furthermore, man has a propensity for forgetting the unpleasant. These factors would seem to be the main reasons for the insufficient awareness on the part of the public of the enormous damage caused by floods.

The gravity and chronic nature of flood problems may in large measure be appreciated, when one considers that in the United States, the country for which most complete figures are available, $4,000,000,000 was spent on flood control measures from 1936 to 1957. However, in spite of this expenditure, average annual flood damages continued on an upward trend which began about the turn of the century.[12] This increasing average annual damage is accounted for in large part by continued encroachment of development upon the flood plains.[6] Flood-plain development will, however, continue to take place regardless of whether absolute flood damages increase or decrease because this land form still has many obvious advantages for agriculture, transportation and urban development. There are several noteworthy examples of continuing flood-plain encroachment in Canada, one of which is the Lower Fraser River Valley. Here in 1948, one of the most extensive and certainly the most costly flood in the river's recent history occurred. Despite this disastrous flood, during the subsequent 1951-1961 census period, the population growth rate on the flood plain was double that of the valley as a whole, while the rate for the metropolitan Vancouver portion of the flood plain was almost four times as fast as for the rural area.[11]

Proponents of flood-plain zoning acknowledge the inevitability of further encroachment on flood plains and the impossibility of providing complete flood protection by structural measures. Indiscriminate flood-plain development is wasteful because unnecessary flood damage occurs sooner or later. Complete prevention of flood-plain use is equally wasteful since the flood plain's distinct advantages for development are needlessly forfeited. The need for compromise between these extreme positions has been recognized by advocates of flood-plain zoning. Even zoning is but one of many alternative adjustments to floods, among which must be found the optimum compromise. Ideally, zoning should occupy the pivotal position in this group of flood adjustments in order to minimize costs and maximize benefits.

There are three main reasons why flood-plain zoning has not been accepted more widely and rapidly in the three decades since it was first introduced: (1) unwarranted faith in the ability of engineering structures to control floods, (2) aversion to restrictive laws, and (3) lack of a composite picture of the flood-plain environment upon which to base zoning regulations, particularly lack of flood susceptibility information. The purpose of this paper is to discuss a new method, namely airphoto analysis and interpretation, which can aid in eliminating this third obstacle.

But before going on to discuss the role of airphoto analysis and interpretation, it is desirable at this stage to digress briefly in order to show why comprehensive pictures of flood-plain conditions are not available. When zoning was first introduced, flood-plain information was only available as rather isolated facts such as stream gauge data that were difficult to interpret for planning purposes. It was not until the 1950's that in Canada and the United States a more composite picture of flood-plain conditions during flooding, was incorporated in reports that could be used by planners, thereby partially fulfilling a long standing need. These reports dating from the 1950's fall into three general categories: (1) comprehensive watershed planning reports, (2) flood control planning reports, and (3) flood hazard mapping reports. Although three different purposes lie behind the preparation of these reports as indicated by the titles, from the point of view of their usefulness to the prospective flood-plain zoner, they are remarkably similar in content.

Hydrologic data, historical records and field interviews provide the main basis for the flood-plain investigations which constitute all or a portion of these reports. Supplemental information on the major floods cited in these reports is sometimes obtained from specially flown flood or post-flood photography. However, unfavourable weather conditions or delay in arranging contracts, often prevents acquisition of this photography. Flood photography is unexcelled in depicting the outline of flood water at a particular point in time and is valuable in helping interpret pre-flood photography. Such flood photography, when obtainable, is also of great value to the hydrologist for the purpose of checking stage-discharge and stage-inundation relationships, but is less valuable to the regional or city planner because much of the flood plain is obscured by water during and after these relatively rare events.

Although such conventional flood-plain studies provide information on extent, frequency and depth of flooding, they neglect to include important aspects of the flooding phenomenon, aspects which are necessary for more rational flood-plain use or regulation. The reports commonly include maps showing the area inundated by one or two major historical floods, as well as the area expected to be covered by the "design" or maximum probable flood. Stream profiles indicate the water depth at various stations for both historical and probable floods. Dramatic newspaper photos, either ground level or aerial obliques, serve to emphasize the hazards of flood-plain occupancy even more than eyewitness accounts of specific floods. In sum, whereas hydrologists and flood control planners have, in presenting these flood-plain studies, considerably improved our knowledge and understanding of the frequency distribution of flooding of various depths and extent, little has been done to place these vital studies in an all-embracing framework. These more conventional studies have tended to emphasize flooding per se, but have neglected to specify the characteristic features of floods and flood plains which are crucially important for would-be users of flood plains. This apparent lack of emphasis on interpretation of data for the use of planners, stems, I should imagine, partly from public pressure for flood damage prevention and also public apathy, heretofore, toward rational land use planning.

The foregoing pin-points the need for a more integrative approach to the study of flooding. A young but extremely promising discipline which can be and is being used to integrate the work of both hydrologist and planner is Air Photo Analysis and Interpretation which attempts among other things to comprehend the problem in its entirety.

In the industrialized countries, for instance, interpretation of aerial photographs taken under *non-flood* conditions can supplement flood-plain studies and watershed planning with information that is useful to the hydrologist and invaluable to the planner. The hydrologist concerned with minimizing damage from watershed runoff must pay heed to more than stage-discharge and stage-inundation relationships. For example, constrictions in the stream channel and the location of natural floodways each warrant his attention, and are given his consideration, but are not usually discussed in reports in such a manner that their full implications become apparent to those engaged in flood-plain regulation, use or development. On the other hand, there is apparently little awareness on the part of hydrologists, of the presence or importance of such terrain features as slack-water areas, in which flood water will be ponded for extended periods of time, nor of scoured areas, in which the highest overflow current velocities may be expected. Such information may be of limited use to the hydrologist, but it is essential for evaluation of the potentials and hazards of flood-plain occupancy—a vital element in rational flood-plain planning and development.

In the developing countries airphoto interpretation can be effectively used as a substitute for the more sophisticated and costly flood-plain studies alluded to above. Meaningful and detailed hydrologic studies require engineering expertise and a backlog of long-term hydrologic data. As will be described below, airphotos capture the effects of long-term stream flow and flooding. Furthermore, the information gained from the photos, will have potential for broader application than the more specialized but unobtainable hydrologic information.

What Is Airphoto Interpretation?

Airphoto interpretation consists of three increasingly sophisticated levels of procuring information from aerial photographs. Photo reading, the simplest level, is the identification of physical and cultural features and the determination of their spatial relationships. Stereo viewing is helpful but not essential for this data-gathering procedure. Photo analysis, the intermediate level, includes the procedures of photo reading but goes further to allow analysis of the arrangements and physical characteristics of photo features. This analysis provides a basis for the classification of residential areas, soils, land use, and so forth. Stereo viewing is usually essential for this approach. The most advanced level, photo interpretation, goes on from a background of photo reading and analysis to "explain the meaning of information obtained from airphoto study in terms of some particular objective."[9] It may also be thought of as the technique of obtaining information of an inferential nature not directly visible on the photograph. Stereo viewing is essential to this approach, which depends for success upon the relevance of the interpreter's experience and training to his particular objective.

Airphoto interpretation is an effective method of obtaining unique flood susceptibility information. We will address ourselves to the perceptive interpretation of aerial photography, which has already been acquired at considerable expense for other purposes in nearly all countries. Though up-to-date information is lacking, one-half the land area of the world had been photographed at least once by 1959[4] Most of the more developed countries have been covered by photography completely one or more times. So much new photography is obtained each year that it is now probably safe to say that even in the least advanced countries, practically any area of interest to a water resource administrator or specialist has photographic coverage. Since much of the world's aerial photography has been obtained by military agencies and aerial survey firms located in Canada, the United States, Great Britain and France, much of the information on overseas coverage is available through sources located in these countries, and not always in the country photographed. A national, seeking information in his own country on photo coverage, should direct his inquiries to those government departments which are concerned with Defence, Resources, and Development. Finally, in regard to the acquisition of aerial photography, it is worthwhile making a comment on the costs likely to be involved. The cost of 1:20,000 scale contact prints can range from a few cents to a few dollars per square mile of stereo-coverage. On the other hand, new photography will cost from a few dollars to a few tens of dollars per square mile. The economic advantage of utilizing available photography need scarcely be emphasized.

Airphoto Evidence of Major Floods

The large volumes of water involved in major floods and the resultant high velocity currents, ensure that these rarer floods leave conspicuous evidence of their impact. Property damage of one sort or another is usually the first to catch the eye of the ground observer, and because of the clarity of this evidence it is usually the first to be eliminated, primarily through repair and cleaning-up operations.[1] But even if vertical photos are taken immediately after a flood they are unlikely to record the full extent of the damage unless they are supported by aerial obliques.[4] Major floods may also leave new or accentuated flood evidence in the form of modifications of the natural landscape. These modifications may be as dramatic and significant as a newly cut channel section, though, even in the case of a major flood, are more likely to be confined to more subtle alterations of existing features such as sand splays or scour marks. Although on the ground this "natural" evidence of severe flooding is usually less obvious than property damage, from the air it stands out distinctly. Light greyish or brownish sand splays which may be nearly concealed from view in a weedy vacant lot appear as dazzling white on postflood photography. Deepened scour marks will stand apart from portions of abandoned channels, a distinction less easily made on the ground. The existing features which may be high-lighted following severe flooding, are in most cases features that result from the effect of more frequent but less extensive overflows.

Airphoto Evidence of Minor Floods

Minor and more frequent floods differ from major floods more in degree than kind, at least as far as direct evidence upon the flood plain is concerned. These more frequently occurring floods cover a smaller portion of the flood plain, and the frequency-inundation relationship, which is so familiar to hydrologists, provides the basis for separating frequently and infrequently flooded areas. Minor floods do not erode, deposit or damage as extensively or severely as major floods. However, the relatively short time interval between minor floods means that this direct evidence may remain almost unmodified through natural processes or man's activities during the interflood periods. The frequent intensification of this flood evidence in susceptible areas helps to distinguish them, because the evidence on less frequently flooded areas may be more subdued through modification over a longer interflood time period.

Frequently flooded areas are also characterized by the closer adjustments of man's activities to flood-plain conditions. Indirect evidence of this type, subtle though some of it may be, is just as useful as that direct evidence which is left behind after a particular flood. Compensating for the sublety of the indicators is the degree of sensitivity expressed by adjustment of life to flood susceptibility. Flood-plain farmers, probably because they live "close to the land" often demonstrate a keen awareness of flood-plain conditions and a discrete response to them that their urban counterparts almost completely lack. By way of contrast, in urban centres where physical structures tend to obstruct a comprehensive view of the physical geography of the area, and where residents are forever on the move, it is small wonder that some residents can live within a stone's throw of a channel and be unaware of its significance. There seem to be more maladjustments to the flood plain in the urban than in the rural environment. Whereas in the rural situation maladjustment to flood-plain conditions often reflects misguided gambling with nature, in the urban situation maladjustment more often reflects decisions made in ignorance. It is important to recognize flood-plain maladjustments during airphoto interpretation which otherwise could result in erroneous flood susceptibility evaluation. Ways of avoiding this error are discussed subsequently.

The type and distribution of vegetation is a sensitive indicator of soil and moisture conditions which in turn reflect flood susceptibility. The relationship of vegetation distribution and crop condition to flood-plain conditions seems closest in the generally more flood-prone areas, because here soil conditions change most rapidly. Just as existing flood-induced physical features on the most susceptible portions of flood plains are accentuated by the more extensive major floods, so the adjustment of vegetation in these areas is likewise sharpened.

It is necessary to emphasize here that since major floods occur infrequently, and since any aerial photo records the cumulative impact of all preceding floods, most photographs whether taken before or after a major flood, will no doubt reflect approximately the same evidence with perhaps varying degrees of clarity. Thus, it would appear uneconomical to acquire "post-major flood" photography unless all existing photography fails to provide certain requisite information, because the disproportionate high cost of these photos is unlikely to be offset by the additional information.

Flood Susceptibility Determination

Direct and indirect evidence of flooding takes many forms, only a few of which have been mentioned in the preceding section. In providing an unbiased cumulative record incorporating all this evidence, the airphoto facilitates its compilation and analysis for the determination of relative susceptibility of an area to flooding. The value of this flood susceptibility information is superior in some respects to that which is or could be accumulated by ground methods alone, because it derives from a critical four dimensional examination of the total flood-plain environment. The photo background from which the information is gleaned, is at one and the same time a three dimensional panoramic and detailed view of the flood plain, while time, the important fourth dimension is captured in the stream's geomorphic history and man's adaptations, as already noted.

In Canada, which was one of the first countries to obtain substantial airphoto coverage for peaceful purposes, sequential photography covers a span of more than four decades. The repetitive aspect of this coverage adds a time dimension of a different nature. Old photography which has captured the scene at intervals over the past few decades, has added value such as, permitting study of natural flood-plain features long since obliterated by urbanization, or facilitating land use change studies.

A complicating factor encountered in attempting to determine relative frequency of flooding is the wide variation in absolute flood frequency on different streams. Although recognized authorities have stated that a 1.5 year frequency of "bank full" stage seems a good average, little affected by physiographic setting or stream size, our perusal of many watershed planning reports indicates that in a substantial number of watersheds being treated for flood control, the streams flood up to 10 or 15 times per year.[8] This apparent contradiction is accounted for in large part by their definition of "bank full". Since it is defined as the difference in elevation between the stream channel profile and the flood-plain profile, both being average lines drawn through a number of points, it follows that many points along the bank will be topped by flood water before the "average bank full" stage is reached. Many factors account for this very wide variation in absolute flood frequency, but this frequency should be recognized and taken into account in the determination of the relative susceptibility to flooding of different portions of flood plains.

For this and other reasons that are covered subsequently, no attempt is made to present a formal key for flood susceptibility classification. Rather, those indicators, visible or inferable from airphotos, which bear a positive or negative relationship to flood susceptibility, or which are otherwise useful in estimating susceptibility are grouped in Table I under six indicator classes: (1) Meteorologic, (2) Physiographic, (3) Geomorphic, (4) Topographic, (5) Pedologic and, (6) Socio-Economic. Some indicators have undoubtedly been omitted from this table, but it is believed the most relevant are included. The value of the indicators is not only for determining relative susceptibility of an area to flooding, but for determining other flood characteristics such as potential hazard from erosion, sedimentation and extremes in flood-water velocity as well as relative duration, depth and areal extent of inundation. In fact in many instances it is easier to ascertain characteristics of flooding or the susceptibility to certain types of flood hazards, than it is to determine relative flood frequency.

The characteristics of flooding are determined in the main by meteorologic and physiographic factors, thus, the meteorologic and physiographic classes are composed mainly of causative flood factors. On the other hand the geomorphic, topographic, pedologic and socio-economic indicators in large part *result* from flood characteristics and hence are derivative in nature. These six classes of indicators should also serve to guide the utilization of any available meteorologic, geologic, soil or economic reports for susceptibility determination. Information in such reports may serve to strengthen conclusions drawn from the airphotos.

In the following treatment, selected indicators will be discussed to illustrate their value for flood character determination and to show their interdependence. Some consideration is given to the rela-

TABLE I. FLOOD SUSCEPTIBILITY INDICATORS

CLASS I—METEOROLOGIC
Climate
  Seasonality
  Temperature
  Precipitation
    Distribution
    Intensity
Storm Type
Storm Direction
Orographic Effect

CLASS II—PHYSIOGRAPHIC
Bedrock Composition
Bedrock Structure
Upland Physiography
Watershed Shape
Valley Orientation
Flood-Plain Shape
Proportion of Watershed in Flood
  Plain
Stream Drainage Pattern and
  Density
Discharge to
  Next Order Stream
  Much Larger Stream
  Lake
  Tidewater
Underfit Streams

CLASS III—GEOMORPHIC
Flood-Plain Type
  Meander Plain
  Cover Plain
  Bar Plain
Alluvial Fans
Terraces
Levees
  Active
  Abandoned
Point Bars and Swales
River Bars
Deltas
Channel Configuration
Channels
  Abandoned
  Oxbows
  Filled
Backswamp Areas
Marshes
Former Lake Beds
Dunes
Landslides
Springs and Seeps
Depth to Water Table
Swamping
Valley Trenching

CLASS IV—TOPOGRAPHIC
Relative Elevation
Slope
Slope Changes
Slope Complexity
Micro-relief

CLASS V PEDOLOGIC
Structure
Texture
Organic
Salinity
Depth
Vertical Uniformity
Permeability
Drainage
Erosion
  Type
  Extent
  Severity
Deposition
  Type
  Distribution
  Freshness

CLASS VI—SOCIO-ECONOMIC
Land Use (Rural and Urban)
  Character
  Intensity
  Changes over Time
  Boundaries
  Alternatives
  Limitations
Building
  Type
  Location
  Condition
Transportation
  Type
  Location
  Condition
Flood Alleviation Measures
Channel Constrictions
Repair Work
Farm Characteristics
  Size
  Type
  Location
  Management Practices
  Crop Condition
Vegetation Removal
  Logging
  Land Clearing
Revegetation

tive significance and dependability of the different lines of evidence, both in terms of inherent reliability and in terms of variability that results from characteristics of the photography.

Meteorologic Indicators

Much of the meteorologic information of the type listed in the table will come from reports or be common knowledge, but this information has unequalled relevance to flooding and must be considered for accurate photo interpretation, whether it is derived from the photo or a report. For obvious reasons these indicators lend themselves to evaluation through airphoto interpretation less than those of any other class. However, when one considers the scarcity of meteorologic information which exists in many areas, even in the industrialized countries, the value of airphotos in obtaining and utilizing meteorologic information can be better appreciated. Commonly rainfall data are only available for a municipality in the lower reaches of a watershed. The distribution of rainfall in the watershed due to storm direction and the orographic effect can be determined on airphotos, at least in relative terms, from consideration of the topography and vegetation distribution. These and other considerations can lead to the determination of the relative amounts of runoff from different tributaries. This alone allows prediction of higher flood stages on the mainstem reaches below these tributaries. Small scale photography which provides the more all-inclusive view might be helpful for such meteorologic studies.

Seasonality in rainfall distribution that indicates when floods may be expected, takes on added significance when airphoto interpretation reveals the seasonal development of sand bars or spits at river outlets, which may restrict flow with the return of the rainy season. Winter temperatures which are extreme enough to allow ice to form on rivers are common in many countries in the high latitudes. The very long northward flowing rivers common to Canada and the Soviet Union are particularly prone to this complicating flood factor. The extent of inundation which is forecast on the basis of standard hydrologic procedures becomes an unreliable guide, under those conditions where ice jams form. On streams where ice jamming is a common event, careful airphoto study may reveal diagnostic clues. Alternatively, it may be possible to draw inferences about ice jam frequency and probable location from apparently unrelated evidence. A classical example of such airphoto interpretation "detective" work was in the case where "the grooves in lake bed sediments made by (wind blown) pan ice were related to shallow water of the (post-Ice Age) lakes, and thus to more salty soils."[2]

The frozen condition of flood plains during spring runoff floods accounts for the anomalous indistinctness of scour marks on flood plains characterized by this seasonality of flooding. Deposition from such spring floods is not so greatly diminished because the channel acts as a source of sediment.

Physiographic Indicators

The gross physiographic characteristics of a watershed are indicative of the nature and frequency of flooding. The bedrock structure of an area has a profound influence upon the shape of watersheds, while the bedrock composition closely controls the drainage density and pattern. Nearly circular watersheds for example may develop in structural basins. Other factors being equal, frequent flooding is indicated for watersheds which tend to be circular and characterized by mountainous uplands and a dense drainage network. Some watersheds of this nature which are known to flood frequently over very broad flood plains show surprisingly little in the way of flood-plain scour and sediment damage. In these cases, however, it is in accord with flood-water ponding which results from constriction of the flood plain down stream or results from backwater effects where streams empty to tidewater. This observation also illustrates the point that there is a close relationship between the larger features of the watershed and the smaller features of the flood plain. Flooding of this nature also may occur in limestone terrain, because limestone solution which has resulted in the development of a discontinuous surface drainage system, has not yet advanced far enough to carry storm runoff into the underground without prolonged surface ponding.

In any area where a stream empties into another, there may be the problem of the common flood plain, however, it may be quite evident from the pattern of flood deposition on photographs which stream dominates the flood problem. Also the diminution of certain kinds of flood evidence in the lowest reach of a stream may indicate frequent flooding and backwater from the one into which it empties. For the purpose of assigning damage costs and benefits it is important that the problem of common flooding be accurately resolved.

In this brief discussion, the physiography of a watershed has been shown to be relevant to flood susceptibility, erosion and sediment damage, flood-water velocity, and duration and extent of flooding. As in the case of meteorologic indicators, the photo characteristic of most significance is probably scale, since small scale photography facilitates appraisal of gross watershed characteristics.

Geomorphic Indicators

The numerous land forms and landscape features cited as geomorphic indicators are more easily grouped to designate expected flood characteristics than relative flood frequency. The reason lies in the fact that flood-plain features are quite well understood in terms of processes involved, texture, depositing water velocities and duration of inundation.[8] But little has been written on the relation of these flood-plain features to frequency of flooding. Geologists claim that meander plains built primarily through lateral channel migration and resultant point bar deposits, flood less frequently than cover plains which are blanketed by vertical accretion deposits. However, they have not gone much beyond this highly questionable gross generalization.

The comparative elevation of different flood-plain or terrace levels clearly shows relative potential for flooding, but it is their subtle surface features which tell whether or not they are still subject to flooding. Terraces exhibit the same surface features as lower portions of the flood plains. Some of these features of course may be relicts from the time when a terrace was a more active floodplain bottom, but others are present day features whose distinctness reflects the frequency of flooding. Especially on higher terraces, these clues may be so subtle as to be indistinguishable except from the air. Tonal and vegetational changes may be the most obvious expression of levee and slack-water deposits on a terrace.

Alluvial fans present flood problems that are peculiar to them alone, because of their relatively steep gradient and the transitory and branching nature of their multiple channels. Flood-water velocities, sediment load and texture are reflected in the channel configuration, cross-section shape and character of scour marks, which are most easily assessed on airphotos. Sequential photography records channel location changes which help predict new channel courses and areas of increasing flood hazard.

Along the larger streams, natural levees may provide almost the only land suitable for intensive development. Abandoned levees are less susceptible to overtopping than active ones, as indicated by the less distinct scour marks running down their back slopes. The soils on abandoned levees will be more mature and of higher productivity than texturally comparable soils on active levees, making them more attractive for agriculture. Much soil information of this nature can be obtained by airphoto interpretation. On abandoned levees, flood proofing specifications for buildings could be adjusted to take account of the diminished hazard from high velocity currents and intense scour and sedimentation which characterize flooding on active levees. The activity of a channel and consequently the degree of abandonment of a levee, can perhaps be better determined from examination of these features in the context of the whole flood plain on airphotos than any other way. Slackwater areas behind active levees may be more susceptible to flooding than the levees themselves, because water may move down the flood plain behind the levee before it is topped. Areas where the bank full stage is first reached are readily located by the large scour marks which identify them. If the soil at the time of photography is either too dry or too wet, or the flood plain is heavily vegetated, then less use can be made of soil tone changes in the recognition of scour marks, and more reliance must be placed upon vegetative and topographic clues to overbank flow. The configuration of the main channel will also indicate where overflow can be expected when other clues are weak.

A particularly easy guide to flood susceptibility is the presence of stabilized or vegetated sand dunes on river terraces. The persistence of these land forms in a stabilized condition is precluded by flooding, therefore their presence indicates non-susceptible areas. But certain other factors relevant to land development are then apparent. Special treatment of dune sand is required for road subgrades and severe wind erosion may follow soil disturbance resulting from other development. In the case of dune plains traversed by relatively small streams, the dunes may modify channel configuration and contribute substantially to flood hazard by decreasing its capacity.

Heavy rainfall on saturated ground which forebodes maximum flood hazard, also sets the stage for landslides in areas where soils are susceptible to this phenomenon. Particularly in areas of residual soils this hazard not only coincides in time and space with the flood hazard, but increases it, especially by contributing vast amounts of sediment and vegetative debris to flood waters. This was the case in the December, 1964 floods in the U.S. Pacific Northwest.[1] The value of airphotos for locating these hazard areas is well established.[7]

To optimize results from the interpretation of geomorphic indicators, photography should be large scale, and taken when the soil is quite moist and either before or after the growing season. In tropical areas photography that follows the harvesting of such rank growing crops as sugar cane may be most timely.

Topographic Indicators

The relevance of topographic considerations to flooding is so obvious that at first one may wonder why it merits mention here. But even if large scale topographic maps were available for all regions, which is far from the actual case, the use of airphotos would still be justified. Micro-relief, (changes in elevation of less than the contour interval) is one of the most important of the topographic considerations, because it is a definitive indicator of certain erosional and depositional conditions and soil types.[2] In some areas mounded soils which have a relief measured only in decimeters are found adjacent to, but not on, flood plains of small streams. The boundary of these soil types, so conspicuous on photos, accurately defines the extent of all but the most infrequent floods. No topographic map is made which does not lose some detail of relief between the contour lines that is relevant to flood susceptibility determination. When the scale of the photography is too small and/or the relief is too subtle for this relief perception, it may be accurately inferred from study of soil drainage patterns, photo tone changes and vegetation characteristics. Such detail is significant where soil drainage measures are to be carried out or where a river develops a flood plain on particularly flat terrain such as a coastal plain. On a somewhat larger scale, complex slopes along stream channels testify to local but intense scour and deposition.

Although all physiographic indicators except bedrock structure and composition may be derived from a topographic map, many of the geomorphic indicators, even larger ones, are lost between the contours. Study of all pertinent flood indicators can never be done from a topographic map, whereas the airphoto comes close to being the idea base. The largest scale photography possible facilitates study of micro-relief and when available, coverage avoiding the growing season should be used.

Pedologic Indicators

The indicators in this class have a high degree of dependence upon the indicators already discussed because the influence of climate, topography, and parent material upon soil formation is so great. As a result it becomes more difficult to discuss indicators as isolated entities. Indeed they are not! Like other clues to flood characteristics, they are closely interrelated. Especially when considered in conjunction with geomorphic indicators they can be very definitive.

The fine grained organic rich sediments characteristic of oxbow lakes, filled channels and backswamp areas, testify to quiet water deposition. Long inundation periods can be expected here. Scour marks too may exhibit a veneer of sediment with this texture, since they also are topographic depressions in which a small volume of water will be ponded. However, the foundation conditions underlying these features which exhibit rather similar surface textures, are almost certain to be significantly different. Urban development and levee construction are both critically dependent upon subsurface conditions which may be inferred from airphotos as engineers have been doing, preparatory to intensive investigations, for about 20 years.

In arid areas, the white distinguishing badge of alkali on airphotos helps define subtle depressions and the movement of groundwater.

Soil permeability and drainage possibilities are closely related. It may be entirely feasible to lower the water table on a sandy flood plain but impractical or at least less successful in many clay soils. These soils can be distinguished on photography even of forested areas in undeveloped regions.

Erosion in the usual sense of the word is absent from flood plains. The low gradients of most flood plains and the changes wrought upon them by flooding prevent development of anything but scour marks from water leaving, or returning to, the channel. It is important on photos to distinguish between scour marks caused by flood water returning over a terrace edge and normal terrace face erosion.

The type, distribution and freshness of flood sediment is one of the best indicators of flood susceptibility. Sequential photography may reveal marked differences in the appearance of areas subject to deposition which reflects timing of the photography relative to flooding. A deposit of fresh sand only a centimeter thick will appear just as white on post-flood photography as do thick sand drifts. Care must be taken not to over-estimate sediment damage because of the conspicuous appearance of fresh sediment. Photography which does not coincide with an immediate post-flood period is more reliable in this respect than that which does coincide. Distinction is more easily made between major and minor sand accumulations on the basis of tonal differences and other modifications when at least one growing season has elapsed between the time of deposition and photography.

Socio-Economic Indicators

If the pedologic indicators exhibited a degree of dependence upon other indicators, the socio-economic do even more so. In this class are presented man's adaptations to and his conflicts with the flood-plain environment. The background of other observations which we have built up allows very accurate and meaningful interpretation of these indicators in terms of flood characteristics. Generations of flood-plain residents have in some measure succeeded in synthesizing the information we have been discussing, albeit most of this has been done by rural residents. When they have struggled with the flood plain instead of adapting to it, their reasons can often be determined by airphoto interpretation.

Burton has dealt at length with the adaptations of farmers to flood plains, including the paradox involving flood hazard awareness and non-adaption.[3] A knowledge of local agriculture and economic conditions is certainly essential to get the most from socio-economic indicators in rural areas. Indeed for this work an airphoto interpreter must have an insight into the sociological conditions in the area. The farmer's decision-making process is influenced to a large extent by his motivation, which cannot be seen and not always inferred from airphotos. In fact we cannot always infer that he is motivated to maximize his monetary income as witnessed by the sub-marginal farmers in every country in the world, some of whom consciously forego financially advantageous urban employment alternatives. Nonetheless a high proportion of the (flood-plain) environment factor-land use relationships that were studied can readily be examined on air photographs, and their significance weighed in the light of other indicators. As Burton noted, the land use intensity-flood frequency relationship is rather weak, but in his study he explained the exceptions encountered, as for example the lack of non-flood-plain land to farm intensively, may force a farmer to crop even highly flood susceptible areas. One need not interview a farmer to ascertain such limitations to his land, a photograph will do as well. There is therefore, little danger of interpreting intensive use as indicative of a low frequency of flooding, especially in the light of other airphoto evidence to the contrary. On many flood plains there is a clear decrease in land use intensity with increasing flood frequency despite the exception just noted. Flood alleviation measures taken by local residents are accurate indicators of a high frequency of flooding, though these activities must be considered in the light of local economic and other conditions. Stream channel straightening, ditching and building of artificial levees by farmers indicate the location and extent of flood problems.

Land use boundaries on some flood plains coincide closely with lines separating areas of rather marked differences in flood hazard as determined from other evidence, thereby indicating a keen flood hazard awareness on the part of the farmer. This awareness of flood hazard by farmers is particularly evident in the case of farm house location and slightly less so for other buildings, though exceptions occur. In urban areas, the type, location and condition of buildings may or may not have a close relationship to flood frequency. Rundown dwellings are often noted on very susceptible areas, but extreme exceptions occur in the case of some recent housing developments where expensive homes are located on "choice" streamside lots. In the latter situation it may be necessary to examine photos pre-dating the development to determine flood susceptibility. In some situations the flood hazard is then so obvious as to suggest that ignorance of the hazard which can honestly be attributed to the purchasers, cannot be attributed to the developer. It must be admitted in defence of some developers however, that what is glaringly evident on photographs may be relatively inconspicuous on the ground.

Intensely increased runoff and sediment damage can be anticipated from areas subject to injurious logging practices or land development. New housing developments in rolling countryside contribute vast amounts of sediment during the construction stage and greatly increased runoff thereafter, as many a suburban dweller has learned to his sorrow. Study of socio-economic indicators is perhaps best facilitated by examination of photos spanning as long a time period as possible.

Summary

In the foregoing analysis I have endeavoured to show, among other things, the importance of certain specific flood susceptibility indicators, and indicator classes, but did not attempt to place priorities on them. This is not as easy as one would no doubt tend to imagine, because priorities tend to differ considerably with respect to desired objectives. If for instance one is concerned with a macro view, then one would probably be inclined in the initial stages of the inquiry to focus primarily on the meteorologic and physiographic indicators. On the other hand, if one's purpose is to examine in detail a relatively small area, then one, while not ignoring the previously named indicator classes, would be prone to place the greatest emphasis on the topographic and socio-economic indicators. However, this priority rating does not pretend to have universal applicability especially when it is recalled that flood susceptibility indicators have varying significance and import in various cultural, climatic and geographic regions of the world. For this reason it must be emphasized that meaningful analysis and interpretation must be based on the most appropriate combination of indicators that are dictated by the problem.

In sum, this paper has attempted to illustrate various ways in which airphoto analysis and interpretation can be profitably applied to flood-plain studies and by implication to watershed studies. I have shown at some length that airphoto interpretation is all-embracing in the sense that in its presentation of a comprehensive view of say a flood plain, it must perforce draw heavily on factors which fall within the purview of most disciplines in the natural and social sciences. One of the implications of this fact is that adequate studies of flood plains and watersheds are interdisciplinary activities, and airphoto analysis provides an integrative role based on a fairly comprehensive view of the region as a whole.

References

[1] Anonymous, "Deluge and Havoc in the Northwest", *Life*, Vol. 58, no. 1 (1965), pp. 20-28.
[2] Belcher, Donald J., "Microforms and Features", *Photogrammetric Engineering*, Vol. 30, no. 6 (1959), pp. 773-778.
[3] Burton, Ian, *Types of Agricultural Occupance of Flood Plains in the United States* (Chicago, Department of Geography, University of Chicago, 1962).
[4] Colwell, Robert N. (ed.), *Manual of Photographic Interpretation* (Washington, American Society of Photogrammetry, 1960).
[5] Howe, Robert L., "The Application of Aerial Photographic Interpretation to the Investigation of Hydrologic Problems", *Photogrammetric Engineering*, Vol. 26, no. 1 (1960), pp. 85-95.
[6] Hoyt, William G. and W. B. Langbein, *Floods* (Princeton, Princeton University Press, 1955).
[7] Liang, Ta and Donald J. Belcher, "Airphoto Interpretation", *Landslides and Engineering Practice, Highway Research Board Special Report 29* (1958), pp. 69-92.
[8] Leopold, L. B., M. G. Wolman, and J. P. Miller, *Fluvial Processes in Geomorphology* (San Francisco, Freeman and Co., 1964).
[9] Mollard, J. D., "Photo Analysis and Interpretation in Engineering-Geology Investigations: A Review", *Reviews in Engineering Geology*, Vol. 2 (1962), pp. 105-127.
[10] Nakano, T. M. Ohya, and T. Kanukubo, "Landform Classification for Flood Prevention Using Aerial Photographs", *Transactions of the Symposium on Photo Interpretation, International Archives of Photogrammetry*, Vol. 14 (1962), pp. 447-452.
[11] Sewell, W. R. Derrick, *Water Management and Floods in the Fraser River Basin* (Chicago, Department of Geography, University of Chicago, 1965).
[12] White, Gilbert F. et al, *Changes in Urban Occupance of Flood Plains in the United States* (Chicago, Department of Geography, University of Chicago, 1958).

5

Flood-Damage Reduction in Canada

I. Burton

Foreword
This report is based on an office and library review of all readily available materials. Considerable information has also been obtained by correspondence with provincial government agencies. Interviews have been conducted in Ottawa, Quebec City, Toronto, and Winnipeg. Field work has been undertaken in Toronto and Belleville, Ontario. Nevertheless, due to limitations of time and money available it has not been possible to make a complete canvass of all information relevant to the flood problem. It has not been possible to consult information in the files of some provincial agencies. It is thought, however, that the gaps and omissions in the information presented in this report are not enough to impair seriously the value of the conclusions reached.

Dimensions of the Problem
  Almost every year the media of mass communication report in sensational fashion the damage and loss of life caused by floods somewhere in Canada. On most occasions the floods are of short duration and the area of damage is small. The headlines are soon devoted to other more pressing matters and public interest and awareness rapidly recede with the flood waters.
  Although in many communities floods remain a constant threat to life and property, the threat is not always recognized and is

Reprinted in edited form from *Geographical Bulletin*, Vol. 7 (1965), pp. 161-85. By permission of the Queen's Printer, Ottawa.

sometimes ignored. Occasionally a major flood strikes some part of the nation—as in Toronto in 1954, the Red River valley in 1950, and the lower Fraser valley in 1948. Then everyone is made aware of the power of this natural hazard and its great capacity for destruction. In the Toronto flood of 1954, 81 people were drowned (Metro. Toronto and Region Conserv. Authy., 1959). In the Red River (Winnipeg) flood of 1950, damage was very heavy,[1] and if a similar flood were to occur prior to the completion of the Red River floodway damage would be higher, owing to further development of the land liable to flooding. In the Fraser River flood of 1948 some 16,000 people had to be evacuated from their homes and damage has been estimated at $20 million (Fraser River Board, 1958). This figure is probably substantially lower than the actual amount of damage since it does not include damage to railway property or such indirect damages as loss of income.

Disasters such as these, involving major cities like Toronto, Winnipeg and Vancouver, lead to action, and attempts are made to prevent the occurrence of similar events in the future. At such times also, major shifts may take place in government policy. New committees and commissions are established and old ones are galvanized into fresh activity. It is an apt comment that action almost invariably follows disaster. Flood hazards are recognized in many places, but the threat often seems remote until it is too late. A common approach to flood damage has been corrective rather than preventive.

The continued occurrence of destructive floods, both large and small, provides a measure of the nation's adjustment to this environmental hazard. In spite of highly advanced engineering and communications technology, floods continue to plague us, and there are no signs of a progressive reduction of flood damages. Intelligent and informed appraisals of the problem range from the view that individual managers of flood-plain property make adjustments consistent with their own best interests and that hence human use of flood plains tends toward an economic optimum; to the notion that flood protection provided at public expense serves only to subsidize and support uses of land that are already unduly expensive.

There is no panacea. It is not possible either to prohibit Canadian citizens from developing all flood plains, or to surrender those that do take such risks to the consequences of their actions. Engineering works such as dams, dykes, and channel improvements, reduce or control flood flows in part, but do not prevent, and may even encourage, the creation of new damage potential, without providing all the security that is sometimes attributed to them. It is only rare that dams can be built large enough to contain the largest possible floods, and such construction, even where technically feasible, is often of doubtful economic value.

The dilemma is real. For fear of flood damages of unknown extent that may come in the future, advocates of abandoning flood plains outright, or of prohibiting further development would deprive the nation of a valuable natural asset that can be used to produce income now. Human adjustment to floods is a problem calling for the exercise of a broad horizon of understanding and a high level of management skill. More of both are required, but this need not be allowed to prevent the full use of such knowledge and skill as is available.

Loss of life, the distress caused by property damage, and the suffering that results from the dislocation of the economic life of communities, are well known concomitants of a major flood. Much less well appreciated is the problem of numerous smaller floods, as for example the Timmins, Ontario, flood of 1961 (McMullen, 1962). In single cases, the loss of life, the property damage and the disruption of business are all insignificant on a national scale. Such floods are more often associated with inconvenience rather than disaster. Yet they occur often enough to constitute a significant problem for the nation if taken together. They are significant if only because they represent one way in which loss and inconvenience are consistently borne by a section of the population often least able to withstand them. Flood losses give rise to recurrent demands for public action to control floods and reduce damages. Insistent demands cannot usually be ignored indefinitely and action eventually results.

For governments to chart an equitable course among these paths is not easy. There is no acceptable and simple view of the flood problem. While it is true that insurance companies consider floods "acts of God" that cannot be covered by most existing policies partly because they are certain to happen in areas where flood insurance is sought, it is also true that flood damages are very largely a consequence of the acts of man. More than 70 years ago the geologist W. J. McGee (1891) noted that:

> "the flood remains a barely mitigated evil, a hardly appreciated obstacle to progress. Indeed as population has increased, men have not only failed to achieve means for suppressing or for escaping this evil, but have, with singular short-sightedness rushed into its chosen paths."

McGee refers to man's apparent affinity for flood-plain land. Although the elements of nature are not now regarded as inherently good or evil, and although floods are not now a significant obstacle to process, nevertheless his observation of man's attitude to the flood hazard is a fair comment on present-day human actions, even more so than in his own day.

Floods occur in a capricious, highly irregular, or random fashion. Dealing with the damaging and violent aspects of such a phenomenon is a problem of adjusting human occupancy to the flood-plain environment in such a way as to utilize its natural advantages most effectively, while at the same time doing whatever is feasible and practicable to minimize the detrimental impact of floods. Failure to do this will only serve to increase damage and suffering. It is then that acts of God are in danger of becoming human acts of criminal negligence.

In their own public decision-making, and in setting guide lines for the private decision-making of numerous individuals and corporate groups, governments tend to mitigate the apparent evil of flood damages. Yet in determining what policy to adopt no simple formula for economic optimizing is available. It is becoming increasingly fashionable to attempt to estimate the benefits and costs of flood-control schemes.[2] Predicting the outcome of present decisions, however, requires not only the sharp tools of economic analysis. It requires an adequate appreciation of the decision-making process, especially in the private sector, for no government policy is likely to be successful in the absence of understandings concerning the way in which flood-plain managers make their decisions and the principal factors that enter into those decisions (White, 1964).

The National Flood Policy

It is scarcely appropriate to speak of a Canadian policy in flood-damage reduction, for with very few exceptions there are no Canadian or national flood problems in the legal sense. Under the terms of the Canadian constitution as set out in the British North America Act, as amended, and as subsequently interpreted in court rulings, the regulation of natural resource development is a provincial and not a federal responsibility. This has discouraged the federal government from taking the interest in flood problems that has now come to be expected from the United States government. The federal government can take action on all rivers deemed navigable, and on interprovincial rivers but in general has refrained from doing so. Its reluctance to becoming involved in flood problems is evidenced on the occasion of major flood disasters beyond the capacity of a provincial government to handle. For example, during the 1950 Red River flood the then Prime Minister was asked in

Winnipeg if the government had formally recognized the flood as a national emergency. As reported in the *Winnipeg Free Press*, May 22, 1950, he replied,

"I do not like the words 'national emergency'. When something happens to Canadians, then all Canadians are interested. Already there is ample proof of the widespread effect upon Canadians that this flood has had."

This statement in part reflects the constitutional position described above. It also reflects the state of uncertainty exhibited by successive Canadian governments as to the appropriate role to play in the alleviation of flood problems.[3]

Eventually, of course, the federal government has become intimately involved in the Winnipeg flood problem and is bearing a substantial portion of the cost of building a large diversion channel to carry the flood waters around the eastern side of the city. This floodway is now under construction.

In the absence of a major disaster, however, flood problems remain almost entirely in provincial hands. In consequence, the attention paid to the problem varies greatly from place to place, for not only is the severity of the problem different, as is to be expected, but also the ability of the provinces to help themselves in this regard is not equal. The provincial view of flood problems differs widely—from considerable concern in some provinces to outright discounting in others, or as one official puts it: "There are no recognized flood problems in this province."

The United States Experience

Valuable insights into Canadian flood problems and policies can be gained by an examination of the American experience.

Until the present century the problem of floods in the United States was regarded primarily as a local or at most a state concern. More recently the federal government has been deeply involved. The shift in responsibility from the local to the federal level began with federal government involvement in major flood-problem areas such as the lower Mississippi, well documented by Robert W. Harrison in his *Alluvial Empire* (Pioneer Press, Little Rock, Ark., 1961). The Flood Control Act of 1936 acknowledged federal responsibility for flood control on navigable waters, and encompassed urban flood problems, while the Watershed Protection and Flood Prevention Act of 1954 broadened federal responsibility still further into the realm of floods on small watersheds in agricultural areas.

A major element in the flood-control program has been heavy reliance on engineering works such as dams, levees and floodwalls, while other possible adjustments such as land-use regulation, flood proofing, encroachment statutes, building codes and the like (White, 1945) have been little used. The engineering works constructed have been sound, and have prevented considerable damage that would otherwise have occurred. In spite of an average annual expenditure of between $300 million and $400 million on flood-control works, however, the rising toll of flood losses has not been arrested. A major reason for this is continuing human invasion of flood-plain land (White *et al.*, 1958). A recent Corps of Engineers report indicates that at the present rate of spending, flood protection will "just about keep up with the increase in flood damage that may be anticipated by 1980 as a result of the flood plain development over the next two decades" (U.S. Senate, 1960, p. 29). Under 1938 conditions, the average annual economic loss to the United States from floods was about $700 million. In 1980 it will be about $760 million, if by that time a total investment of $11.5 (1959 dollars) billion has been made in flood-control projects. The position has been aptly summarized by White and Cook (1963, p. 345) who point out that, "if future flood-control efforts are confined to the construction of engineering works, while the Nation's citizens continue to develop its flood-plains without regard for the effect on flood losses, expenditures of Federal funds will have to exceed $300 million annually, on the average, to keep flood losses from increasing. In other words, the cost to the nation of permitting uncontrolled development of flood-plain lands averages more than $300 million annually."

A rapidly expanding literature[4] on alternative adjustments has been accompanied by a growing realization of the need for a broader approach to flood problems. Still more knowledge is required, but at least the direction of movement is clear.

Application to Canada

One simple, broad implication for Canada of this experience is clear. At a time of rapid urban growth, future flood problems may be created by unthinking invasion of hazardous areas. The large expenditures on flood control that have become necessary in the United States can still be avoided in Canada if steps are taken to ensure that development of flood-plain land, particularly in urban communities, is guided in such a way as to make maximum use of the land while at the same time exposing life and property to a minimum of risk. With carefully planned development based on sound hydrological studies this can be achieved. Undoubtedly it is being achieved in some places. But in general, urban expansion continues on the flood plains without careful study of the possible consequences. The growth of flood-damage potential in Winnipeg has already been cited. Similar developments have been reported at Kamloops in British Columbia (Fraser River Board, 1958), and can be seen in many other cities.

The British Experience

Unlike developments in the United States, flood problems in Britain are regarded primarily as a local or regional concern, not the business of the central government. Flood-control schemes are financed by regionally supported River Boards, and decisions to undertake engineering works made by the local authorities entail responsibilities for a substantial proportion of the cost. The central government participates in the financing of schemes in roughly inverse proportion to the ability of a given River Board to meet the full cost. In consequence central government assistance for flood-control work is frequently smaller in urbanized river basins such as the River Trent area, than in rural and agricultural basins such as the River Great Ouse area.

Town and country planning is also more highly developed and effective in Britain than in the United States, and local planning regulations frequently, though not always, prohibit or restrict further flood-plain development. The avoidance of flood-hazard areas has also been facilitated by a rural settlement pattern in which nucleated villages are often located on terraces above the level of the present flood plain. Modern expansion of these villages has been guided away from flood plains by careful planning (Burton, 1961b). In consequence heavy expenditures on flood control have been avoided in Britain, although the country is densely populated and heavily urbanized. Flood losses occur, but there is insufficient evidence to indicate whether they are increasing or decreasing.

In Britain, as in Canada, there are no figures of flood losses recorded on a consistent basis. In both countries, it is difficult to isolate from the expenditures of all the levels of government involved, the amount of money spent on flood-control works.

The success of the British policy, however, has been dependent, in part, on central government initiative. The closest approach to the British River Boards in Canada are the Ontario Conservation Authorities. Both are organized on a river-basin basis, their activities being controlled largely by constituent local governments that provide money in the form of a tax for most of the normal expenditures of the Boards and the Authorities. In Britain it was found necessary to make the establishment of such Boards obligatory. In Ontario this has not been considered necessary, and parts of the province still remain outside the jurisdiction of any Conservation Authority (Pleva, 1961).

Application to Canada

A major implication for Canada is that heavy expenditures on flood control are not a necessary corollary of densely populated and urbanized areas. It also seems that the involvement of a national government can be avoided except in the case of the largest and most disastrous floods. When the problem is handled primarily at a local or regional level, however, it may become more difficult to integrate flood-control work with other elements of water-resource development. There is also less likelihood of collecting and recording data on trends in flood control, flood losses and flood-plain management on a national scale, thus inhibiting a nation-wide attack on flood losses.

A flood policy for Canada need not follow closely either those of Britain or the United States. It may, however, seek to profit from their experience, and then to show the way toward a more rational and effective approach. It would involve the collection of damage data on a national, standard pattern, and the analysis of this data to indicate the direction of rational solutions. The effort would require at least three steps: (1) the precise definition on maps or air photographs of areas subject to flooding, and an analysis of the hydrological characteristics of the flooding including expected depths and frequencies; (2) the collection of flood damage estimates for all floods immediately after their occurrence; and (3) a continuous monitoring of changes in flood damage potential by mapping and/or sampling land use in the areas defined under point (1) above. When more data becomes available, and when a better knowledge of flood problems than is now possible is a reality, it may, of course, prove that present arrangements are generally effective in mitigating flood losses. There is considerable circumstantial evidence that this is not likely to be the case. It is the main purpose of the remainder of this paper to establish beyond a reasonable doubt the need for a new look at Canadian flood problems.

Types of Flood

Defining a flood is as difficult as mapping a flood plain. Common definitions include the notions of bank-full stage and damage stage.

Bank-full stage is that elevation of a river or stream at which it begins to overflow its banks. Damage stage is that elevation at which damage begins.

At least four types of flood may be recognized according to the physical factors involved. These are:

(1) Snow-melt floods
(2) Ice-jam and ice break-up floods
(3) Convectional storm floods
(4) Cyclonic storm floods

This typology is useful because it is possible to associate certain characteristics with each, although it is an oversimplification because there are many other contributory factors, and rarely can a flood be ascribed to a single cause.

Snow-melt floods occur in the early spring when a winter's accumulation of precipitation may be liberated and flow off a watershed within a short period. Such floods are most likely to occur after an unusually heavy season of snowfall, and in areas where snowfall is normally heavy. They are also associated with a rapid thaw process as when the temperature rises rapidly after a long cold period and stays high for several days. The hydrograph associated with snow-melt floods often demonstrates a flat curve, and the flood-to-peak interval may last several days or even weeks. The Red River flood of 1950 is an example of a snow-melt flood. There was heavy snowfall in the winter and an above-normal accumulation at break-up. Important contributory factors were that the thaw or break-up came later than usual, the soil moisture content was high due to a wet autumn, the ground was frozen and above-normal rainfall also occurred during break-up. Ice-jams were an additional cause of flooding on a few tributaries.

At Winnipeg the river reached flood stage (746 feet) on about April 23, flood peak was in mid-May (approximately May 18) and the river did not return to below flood stage until the end of the first week in June. The flood-to-peak interval was about 25 days and a further 20 days were required for the river to drop back to flood stage (U.S. Geol. Surv., 1956).

Ice-jams and ice break-up floods also occur in the early spring, and are a type of flood common to most of Canada. Ice-jam floods may occur at any time during break-up and are not necessarily more likely to happen when the stage of the river is high. Such floods are more frequent when there is an abundant quantity of ice jammed together to form a temporary dam. Ice-jams notoriously occur at constriction points such as a sharp bend, a gorge or a bridge-crossing or any other physical obstacle. They may also occur where the gradient of a channel changes from steep to gentle, or at the point where a stream discharges into a lake. Other contributing factors are the thickness of the ice and the direction of the river. For example, problems may arise on north-flowing rivers such as the Red, Moose, Chateauguay and Chaudiere, where the downstream sections remain last frozen while the upstream southern sections are in freshet. Once a jam develops the water often rises behind it very rapidly so that the hydrograph of an ice-jam flood is often much more peaked than that of a snow-melt flood.

An example of the ice-jam flood is the Belleville, Ontario flood of 1936. Belleville is situated at the mouth of the Moira River on Lake Ontario. Frequently the ice on the river goes out while the Bay of Quinte is still frozen. The ice carried by the river may then jam up against the ice on the lake, causing water to back up and flood the city.

In 1936 this type of flooding resulted in water five feet deep on Front Street. An area of 75 acres in the city was flooded, 200 people were homeless and damage was estimated at between $100,000 and $250,000. The flood was eventually brought to an end when the ice-jam was successfully dynamited. The flood lasted from March 12 to March 19, but both the rise of flood waters on the 12th and the fall on the 19th were rapid (Ont. Dept. Planning and Dev., 1950).

Convectional storm floods are associated with violent local storms caused by convectional flows of air. Such storms occur most frequently in summer in southern Canada and are often accompanied by thunder and lightning. They tend to be of short duration and to produce floods only in small watersheds and in urban areas when storm drains are sometimes inadequate to take large flows. The frequency of thunderstorm days has been examined by Kendall and Petrie (1962). Rainfall probabilities in the Prairie provinces have been studied by McKay (1964).

The hydrograph for floods associated with convectional storms demonstrates a sharply peaked curve. Flood waters rise very quickly and subside equally as rapidly. The convectional storm typically lasts not more than a few hours and is usually responsible for flash floods. Basement and cellar flooding occurs every summer in many cities as a result of convection storm flooding. Frequently also highway underpasses beneath railway tracks are filled with water for short periods.

Cyclonic storm floods are of variable length and magnitude depending in a large part upon the nature of the storm. The rainfall associated with cyclonic storms is usually more widespread, less intense, but of longer duration than that associated with convectional storms. In consequence the rise of flood waters is slower, but larger drainage areas are more easily affected.

Although the distinction between these two kinds of storms is a useful one, floods are frequently caused when frontal activity is particularly violent and is associated with convectional currents as in the Timmins, Ontario flood of 1961. Considerable latent instability existed in the area on the day of the storm and was triggered by the passage of a weak centre of low pressure. A rainfall of eight inches fell in less than twelve hours in a very limited area around the city. This was sufficient, however, to cause the Town Creek to flood (McMullen, 1962).

The most severe cyclonic storm flood to occur in Canada this century was caused by a hurricane in 1954. Hurricanes are frequent along the east coast of the United States in late summer and early fall. Their normal course takes them from Caribbean area where they originate, in a parabolic arc parallel to the east coast, and they eventually sweep out into the North Atlantic Ocean off New England. Infrequently they go directly north into southern Quebec or the Maritimes. A hurricane that moves further inland, however, is unusual. Such an event occurred in October 1954, when Hurricane Hazel turned across New York State and into Ontario passing over the Metropolitan Toronto area. The catastrophic effects of this storm are well known. It is an example of the violent kind of cyclonic storm, and although 32 hurricane-spawned storms are known to have occurred in Ontario since 1878 (Metro. Toronto and Region Conserv. Authy., 1959), few were as severe as Hurricane Hazel.

Human Response to Floods

Most of southern Canada was settled at a time when technology was much less advanced than at present. Rivers were widely used for both transportation and power. It was therefore both natural and logical that many settlements should be located on or near rivers. The earliest settlements were located on the large rivers because these were the only available means of access to the lakes and the sea and to the market for products in the Old World. Settlement on flood plains was further encouraged where the alluvial soils of the valley bottoms was more fertile than those of the uplands. The streams themselves were also used as sources of power to turn the wheels of many grist mills.

When settlements grew larger, the streams became important sources of water in some instances, and were also a convenient means of disposing of wastes. Railway as a new form of transport served to emphasize the value of the valley floors, for they could often be most cheaply constructed by following the low gradients of the valleys. Industrial development, often associated with railway transport, took place in towns and cities and it was found that construction of large factories was easier on the level land of flood plains than on hill slopes. Low-lying land was also favoured as being cheaper to supply with water because less pumping was required.

All these advantages of river and flood-plain sites have helped to shape a distribution of settlements strongly associated with flood-hazard areas. Flood damages are the price paid for utilizing the natural advantages of the flood plain, but the comparative advantages are not so great as they once were. Smaller streams are no longer used for power or navigation, and where hydro-electric power is developed with modern technology it can easily be transported out of the flood-hazard area. Large-scale earth-moving machinery has also made it possible to create level building sites on sloping land. Under present conditions there is much less need to locate cities in the path of floods. Once a settlement has been established, however, the chances of removing it to another site are slim. The heavy investment in streets, water and gas supply, drainage, electricity and other services are not readily abandoned. Nor are the owners of property anxious to transfer to another site at their own expense. In consequence efforts are often made to protect the settlement from floods, and when protection is provided there is added reason for expanding and developing the site. Despite the fact that modern highways are less demanding of easy gradients than were the railways, nevertheless they too tend to follow the river valleys, if only because they connect cities located in flood plains.

Four Case Studies

The following four cities together illustrate something of the range and variety of flood problems, and the kinds of adjustment that are being made.

Belleville, Ontario, illustrates the failure of a community to secure flood protection and the lack of other alternatives for it to turn to as a means of reducing future flood damages. Calgary, Alberta, is a city where expansion has been taking place in the flood plain in the face of a recognized flood hazard. Red Deer, Alberta, is a smaller community seeking sites for industrial expansion and turning to the flood plain for this purpose, while trying to guide development into the least hazardous sections. Toronto, Ontario, is the site of a major flood disaster that has spurred the establishment of a multi-purpose recreation and flood-control scheme.

Belleville, Ontario—This community has suffered from periodic ice-jam floods on the Moira River, and has recently been engaged in an attempt to gain financial assistance for the construction of a flood-protection (ice-control) dam. A brief was prepared for the Moira River Conservation Authority and submitted to the provincial and federal governments in 1958. The brief comprised a benefit-cost analysis of the proposed flood-control dam as requested by the federal government, and a request for $165,000 from each of the governments. This relatively small sum of $330,000 is 75 per cent of the total cost of the scheme. The city would be required to pay $107,800 towards the cost or 98 per cent of the balance. The remaining 2 per cent would come from other communities in the Moira watershed.

This was the latest of a series of attempts to obtain support for a flood-protection scheme for Belleville. The earlier attempts are described in a summary presented to the city of Belleville by the Conservation Authority and dated February 13, 1961. Two attempts had been made following the maximum flood on record in 1936. The failure of these attempts by Belleville alone led to the formation of the Moira River Conservation Authority, in the hope that a more powerful and united front would prove successful. Other communities in the valley joined in the establishment of the Authority, and a third proposal presented in 1948 to the federal government was rejected on the grounds that the stream was not navigable and did not therefore qualify for federal assistance. Negotiations with both senior governments were continued sporadically without any significant progress for the next ten years. Meanwhile some work was carried out by the Authority in obtaining designs and cost estimates for the proposed dam.

The latest approach was made in 1958. The damages that would occur in the event of a repetition of the 1936 flood were measured by sending a questionnaire to 233 establishments in the flood plain. Only 79 replies were received, on which estimates for the whole study were based. As it was also estimated that construction of the ice-control dam would permit $1,095,000 of these damages to be prevented, this amount is listed as a benefit from the scheme. The proposal was rejected by the federal government, not only on the basis of the analysis which found a positive benefit-cost ratio, but because it was not considered to qualify as a major project under the Canada Water Conservation Assistance Act. Local officials in Belleville obtained the impression that it was rejected because projects of less than $2,500,000 were too small for federal government participation (personal communication). Federal officials claim that no lower limit for project cost was ever specified and that each project was considered as its application was received (personal communication).

The Authority then decided that there was little point in making further representations to the federal authorities and that the matter should be referred to Belleville for action. The city decided to consult the persons involved, and sent a letter of enquiry with a questionnaire to be completed by all residents and businessmen in the flood-prone area. The response was most discouraging. Of some 800 questionnaires distributed, only 215 were returned and of these only 60 indicated support for the city to go ahead with the scheme. Accordingly, the city drew the conclusion that the people were not sufficiently interested in receiving flood protection and abandoned the project. Interviews conducted in the area in September 1962* revealed that many residents have little or no awareness of the flood hazard. Some did not recall the last severe flood in 1936, and among those who did, most felt that such a flood would not occur again. These residents ascribed their optimism to the very existence of the Conservation Authority and to the greater degree of preparation by the city. This latter reason is in part valid. A flood-warning system has been set up for the city in conjunction with the Moira River Conservation Authority, and Civil Defence Authorities. Preparations have also been made to meet the flood emergency should it arise, and instructions for city personnel were printed in the City Engineer's Annual Report in 1961. Nevertheless, the optimism of residents and businessmen in the flood-hazard area is not justified by the facts. A flood equal to, or greater than, the 1936 flood could occur at any time in late winter or early spring when ice is being carried downstream and conditions are right for an ice-jam to develop. The 1959 Moira River Authority brief puts the return period of the 1936 flood at

*By the author with assistance from C. W. Bridge, M.A. Church, M. Foty, H. Gordon, G. J. V. Kokich, C. Lewis, D. Rigby and J. Westman.

20 years. If this is a correct estimate, floods of much greater magnitude can be expected over a longer period.

The flood-warning system and the emergency measures proposed by the City Engineer would help to reduce damages when another flood comes, although considerable damage could still occur. The choice facing governments at all levels has largely been one of building the dam or doing nothing at all. While the dam was under consideration, nothing else was done, but since the final abandonment of the scheme, plans for warnings and emergency action have been formulated. However, in theory there are many other possible adjustments that could be made in Belleville. Private citizens could be informed about the nature and degree of the hazard. Many of them are now unaware of it. Technical advice could also be made available on how best to remove valuable property from the flood-hazard area, and how to make buildings themselves flood-proof. Facilities for sandbagging and other emergency measures could be kept constantly available. Some managers have made preparations to meet an emergency, among the more elaborate of which are those made by the manager of the Eaton's store on Front Street. Many others do nothing.

In addition to the planning that private citizens can initiate, there are more ambitious public alternatives. The city of Belleville has turned its back on the river. Travelling down Front Street by car the casual visitor does not suspect the existence of the river immediately behind the buildings and shops that front onto the west side. Yet the river with its rushing water and rocky bed is one of the most attractive features of the town. Front Street is also congested, and there is a lack of public open space. There are no gardens and no places for the weary shopper to sit in the shade of trees. Nor are there adequate parking facilities for the cars that jam the main shopping area and business section.

An ambitious plan would be to attempt the phased withdrawal of all property in the central business section that lies between Front Street and the river. This would open up the city and give a broad view from Front Street across the river. Space would be created for gardens and for additional parking facilies. Small recreation facilities such as a miniature golf course might also be provided. In addition to these benefits which might revitalize the centre of Belleville, considerable reduction in future flood losses would be achieved. The plan could be carried out over a number of years, and arrangements might also be made to provide flood-plain properties with a subsidized flood-insurance program while they remain in the hazard zone. Funds for the scheme might be justified both on the grounds of flood-damage reduction and the need for urban renewal. Such an ambitious alternative is not now available to Belleville because no existing legislation provides for financing of such multi-purpose schemes. The possibility has its merits, however, and on closer examination may prove to be economically feasible. An effort to broaden the range of choice where flood protection cannot be provided would give cities like Belleville an incentive to seek alternative methods of solving the flood problem.

Calgary, Alberta—Calgary is located on a flood-plain at the junction of the Bow and Elbow rivers. It was founded as a North-West Mounted Police fort in 1875, and the site selected for the post was a flat terrace just above the junction of the two rivers (Putnam, 1952). In 1883 the C.P.R. transcontinental railway reached Calgary along the flood plain of the Bow River, and the town became the major maintenance centre for the railway company in the western section of the prairie provinces (Bussard, 1935). The town grew up around the fort and railway station in the land above the confluence, and this area is now occupied by the downtown section of the city. Calgary has grown out from the centre in all directions, extending along the river valleys and also out onto the surrounding uplands. Growth has been particularly rapid since 1948, and in the period 1951-1956 the city's population increased by 42.5 per cent from approximately 140,000 to 200,000. Expansion has been conditioned by the feasibility of water and sewer line extensions, and has tended to concentrate in the flood plains, especially that of the Bow River to the southwest and southeast of the city (Smith, 1962), although the Planning Board is now making efforts to keep further development out of the flood plain.

Several major floods have occurred since the site was first settled. One in 1897 is said to have been the largest known but information on it is very slight (Hendry, 1915, pp. 30-31). A number of other damaging floods have occurred and on them the information is more complete. A summary of gauge heights and discharges for four of them is given in Table I.

TABLE I. SPRING FLOODS AT CALGARY

Date of flood	Gauge height (feet)	Discharge (cu.ft./sec.)
June, 1897	17.52	99,000*
July, 1902	16.7	90,000*
June, 1915	—	41,600
June, 1932	12.5	53,600

* Estimated.

It is known that these floods were caused by sustained rainfall and in the case of three by melting snow. A repetition of either the 1897 or 1902 floods would be catastrophic, causing millions of dollars worth of damage in the Calgary area. A small measure of alleviation is afforded by storage reservoirs on upper tributaries which may be expected to reduce a flood of the magnitude of the 1902 flow in the order of 20 per cent. Land fill in various parts of the flood plain would reduce flooding in these places but cause higher stages elsewhere. Little information is available on rainfall in the watershed at the time of these floods, except that the 1932 flood is known to have been caused by rain concentrated mainly in the foothills and east of the second range of the Rocky Mountains (i.e., below Banff).

The highest flow on record for the Elbow River, 26,000 cfs, also occurred in 1932. A limited measure of control is provided by the Glenmore Dam (built mainly for water-supply purposes) but a repetition of the 1932 flow would cause considerable damage in the residential area from the dam to the Bow River confluence. By fortunate chance the Glenmore Dam had just been completed in 1932 and the reservoir was being filled at the time of the flood (A. H. Nicholson, City Engineer, Calgary, personal communication).

In more recent times comparatively minor flooding has been caused by ice-jams during severely cold periods. Inundations by back-up water behind ice-jams have been controlled by the construction of dykes along both banks of the river in affected areas. The dykes are only located, however, in the central portion of the city upstream from the Pearce Estate. No protection is provided by dykes for the predominantly industrial section in the Inglewood area. The elevations of four recent winter floods are given in Table II.

TABLE II. SOME WINTER FLOODS AT LANGEVIN BRIDGE, CALGARY

Date of flood	Gauge height (feet)
January 14, 1948	12.1
December 16, 1949	10.9
December 1, 1950	15.3
December 19, 1951	13.4

The dykes would probably contain safely a flow of 50,000 cfs but any future flood of 70,000 cfs or more would undoubtedly result in severe property damage from Bowness to the south city limit (T. D. Stanley, personal communication). A recurrence of the estimated 99,000 cfs discharge of 1897 would not necessarily follow exactly the same pattern of flooding. Dyking and land fill would result in some areas then flooded remaining dry. This would have the effect of raising stages elsewhere so that areas unaffected in 1897 could well be flooded by a future discharge of like magnitude.

There is also the possibility of floods greater than that of 1897. The probability of such a flood occurring in any one given year is low. At some time in the future, however, such a flood is certain to occur.

The absence of severe summer flooding in the Calgary area for many years, and the recurrence of less severe winter flooding caused by ice jamming has led to much greater attention being given to the latter—the lesser danger of the two. Winter floods, as indicated in Table II, are of a lower order of magnitude than late spring floods.

More than a decade ago an Alberta Royal Commission was established to examine the cause of flooding in the Bow Valley. The Commission devoted its report primarily to a consideration of winter flooding. A careful analysis was made of the available evidence, and the Commission was able to conclude that "while the complete solution to the problem has not yet been found, worthwhile advance in knowledge and experience has been gained" (Alberta, 1953).

One recommendation of the Royal Commission was that the Bearspaw power development should be constructed as soon as possible since it offered the most important single solution to ice jamming and flooding in the Calgary-Bowness area. This has now been constructed but has not solved the winter ice-packing problem. By reduction of the length of open ice making the river upstream of the area subject to ice packing it has reduced the incidence, but not the severity, of the problem. Dykes have been constructed by the provincial government since 1952 to a stage equivalent to gauge height 17 feet at Langevin Bridge. These dykes are now the main and most effective means of preventing surface flooding in the affected part of the city.

Other recommendations of the Royal Commission called for the establishment of a Control Board to deal in an advisory capacity with the question of flood control, seepage and remedial measures; the elevation of the Bowness steel bridge to a suitable height to prevent its loss or damage by ice jamming; the extension of dykes in Calgary and cribbing or dyking in places in the Bowness area; consideration to be given to increasing the height of the present dykes to take care of high spring or summer floods; further investigation into the seepage problem and draining down of water level in storage dams when severe snow-melt floods are expected, under the direction of the proposed Bow River Control Board.

One other recommendation of the Royal Commission is of particular importance. It was recommended that legislation be passed to,

"(a) prevent settlement or building on areas which in the opinion of authority are subject to serious danger from flooding;

(b) to cause to have buildings removed from critical areas where reasonable protection cannot be provided."

This recommendation stems from the Royal Commission's finding that, "The whole question of allowing buildings to be built in critical flood areas is alarming, not only on the Bow River but elsewhere in Canada and the United States." A comparison of two air photographs taken in 1926 and 1949 respectively shows that, "in 1926 there were less than a dozen buildings situated near the banks of the Bow River in the Bowness area, while in 1949 almost the whole area has been built up. Some of these buildings have been built on areas where incipient ice jamming or spring or summer floods occur which can cause serious damage. This is especially true of Bow Crescent and a portion of Bowness."

Calgary provides evidence from an official source that urban development of flood plains has been taking place rapidly in the face of known flood hazard, but without careful study as to the likely, or possible, consequences of such development. Here is a case where flood problems of the future are in the course of creation. Some steps are now being taken to arrest further growth of the problem. The Alberta Water Resource Act Amendment of 1960 gives the Minister the necessary authority to prevent development of flood-plain lands. These powers are being used and permission has been refused for the building of a hospital and two subdivisions. A problem still remains, however, and is likely to continue at least until there is another major flood. Then demands will be placed on government authorities to provide some flood protection. Whether such protection is or will become economically justifiable is not known. To the extent that present attempts to limit further development are successful and to the extent that some damage potential is created will depend upon the amount of benefits to be derived from further flood protection. Surely the important point is that developments have been taking place under conditions of ignorance as to their possible consequences. A more rational approach would be to attempt to weigh the comparative value of the development, against the risks being taken.

Red Deer, Alberta—The city of Red Deer is located on the flood plain of the Red Deer River, close to the point where it is crossed by the main railway line from Calgary to Edmonton. The main part of the city lies below the bluff of a former meander scar on the southeast bank of the river. There is a small community on the northwest side of the crossing, and in recent years the city has expanded both along the flood plain and on to the top of the bluff.

The valley is subject to ice-jam floods during the winter months, and snow-melt floods in spring and early summer especially when a rapid thaw is associated with heavy and persistent rainfall.

The highest stage recorded due to ice-jams was in 1943. The highest summer flood stage was in 1915. Details of these and other floods are given in Table III.

The flooding has occurred mostly in flood-plain reaches above and below the city, and in areas peripheral to it. The 1913 flood was dangerous but did not prove disastrous. The water rose 14 feet and was reported by the *Red Deer Advocate* (April 11, 1913) to be at its highest since the flood of 1901 when a new bridge was washed out. Ice from Waskasoo Creek (a small tributary that occupies, in part, the former course of the Red Deer in its abandoned meander southeast of the centre of the city) jammed at the Gaetz Avenue bridge, and the next bridge upstream.

TABLE III. SELECTED FLOOD STAGES AND DISCHARGES AT RED DEER

	Ice-jams			Summer floods	
Date	Peak stage (feet on the gauge)	Daily discharge (cu. ft./sec.)	Date	Peak stage (feet on the gauge)	Daily discharge (cu. ft./sec.)
April 8, 1913	17.86	4,000	June 28, 1915	19.05	56,000 (68,250 peak)
April 7, 1925	17.46	10,600	June 2, 1923	14.51	34,800
April 4, 1943	21.95	9,690	June 4, 1929	14.23	34,200
April 7, 1955	18.40	12,000	June 24, 1952	14.82	37,900
April 8, 1958	15.36	3,110	August 26, 1954	16.70	42,620

Ice-jams in Waskasoo Creek almost caused water to flood into Holt Avenue (52nd Avenue), and jams at the bridge on Gaetz Avenue caused water to flow over the concrete wall along Gaetz Avenue in one place. At a subsequent meeting of the Council, Town Commissioner Stephenson advised the Council that a recent *Calgary Herald* report of April 9, 1913, concerning ice-jam flooding and flooding along creeks was sensational exaggeration which if not stopped might cause cancellation of all insurance policies in the city.

The flood in June, 1915 was described by the *Red Deer Advocate* as the highest flood in 30 years. The Clearwater bridge two miles east of the city was washed away and other minor property damage resulted.

Perhaps the worst flood on record is that of April, 1943, which was described by the *Red Deer Advocate* as doing thousands of dollars worth of damage. The Red Deer River rose more than 15 feet in less than one hour about 4 a.m. The ice-jam broke at 6 p.m. and the water fell eight feet in one hour. People living on the west side of the river had hardly time to get out of their houses before the water rushed in. Some heavy losses were reported. One farmer lost 90 head of cattle, 17 hogs, a team of horses and 40 sheep. His loss was estimated at $12,000 to $15,000. A number of houses were flooded to depths of 18 inches.

Five deaths were attributed to the ice-jam flood of March 26, 1947 in Red Deer. This flood made the people of Red Deer more aware of the hazards, so that a firm of consulting engineers was engaged to advise what flood-plain land could reasonably be used for industrial development. They reported in 1960 to the city of Red Deer that there were two separate land areas on the flood plain usable for industrial development, and that each could be enlarged considerably by land filling and berm construction (Hadin, Davis and Brown, 1960). The report does not describe in detail the calculations upon which these recommendations were based, but the suggested fill and berm construction is considered protection for the areas recommended for development from floods of a 200-year frequency. Such a flood has not occurred in the period since the establishment of the city. The summer flood of 1915 has an estimated frequency of once in 50 years, or more correctly, one chance in 50 that it will occur in a given year. Estimates of the frequency of the same flood by others (Hadin, Davis and Brown, 1960), range from 1 in 40 to 1 in 135. The recommendations made, are therefore on a design flood of elevation 24 feet on the gauge (compared with 21.95 feet for the highest recorded stage in 1943) or an elevation of 2,806 feet above sea level, which has an estimated frequency of 1 in 200. Extrapolations of the frequency of high discharges are notoriously uncertain, however, and clearly a flood of much higher proportions than those previously experienced is possible. Virtually the whole of the city of Red Deer lies below 2,820 feet, so that the possibility of a super-flood occupying the whole of the valley floor and flooding all property, some to a considerable depth, cannot be ruled out.

It is not clear, therefore, whether further development of the flood plain by industrial users is desirable. The recommendations made by the consultants meet with the terms of reference given to them by the city of Red Deer. It is assumed that the risk of less than 1 in 200 is low enough to be worth taking. While it is impossible to measure this degree of risk with great precision, it should be possible to assess the benefits of developing flood-plain land instead of using higher land not subject to floods. There is no acute shortage of suitable nonflood-plain land around the city of Red Deer.

The city of Red Deer presents a problem distinct from that of Calgary. Here the city government has determined upon expansion in the flood plain as a matter of policy and has been quite precise about the level of risk to be taken. A basis for evaluating the policy will be lacking, however, until the value is known of the benefits that accrue from use of flood plain rather than upland. This value may never be known.

Toronto, Ontario—The flood-control project for Metropolitan Toronto currently under construction provides an example of a way in which flood-damage reduction may be combined with other goals into a multi-purpose project. It also illustrates only cursory consideration of alternative methods of damage reduction.

As at Belleville, a benefit-cost study was made. In the Toronto case, it was successful and the project was approved by the provincial and federal governments (Metro. Toronto and Region Conserv. Authy., 1950). Contrary to the theoretical objective of benefit-cost analysis—the evaluation of alternatives*—the technique was used to justify a previously designed project (Burton, 1965).

The background to the present Toronto plan also illustrates one of the prevailing national flood policy. In the absence of a required systematic study of potential flood problems, little is done until a disaster has occurred. Even where floods are known to have taken place in the past, there is a tendency to assume that they will not come again. In 1950 the Don Valley Conservation Authority in Toronto published the following statement:

On the whole the floods of the Don now do only a small amount of damage compared to those before 1880 and there seems little likelihood that the amount will increase. Flooding is not a very serious problem on the Don and does not call for costly measures of control (Ont. Dept. Planning and Dev., 1950, p. 19).

Four years later the catastrophic flood associated with the passage of Hurricane Hazel caused considerable property damage in the

---

* *See* Sewell *et al.*, 1962; Inter-Agency River Basin Committee, 1950 and Hufschmidt *et al.*, 1961.

Toronto area (including an estimated $3.5 million in the Don Valley alone) and resulted in the loss of 81 lives. Five years later in 1959 a *Plan for Flood Control and Water Conservation* for the Metropolitan Toronto area was presented to the federal government. The plan set out in part that:

It is the purpose of this plan to point out the urgent need for flood control and water conservation measures, to outline a program of proposed measures and to analyze the engineering, economic and social aspects of the proposed program. The Metropolitan Toronto and Region Conservation Authority respectfully requests financial assistance from the Government of the Dominion of Canada and the Province of Ontario in respect of an integrated flood control and water conservation Program for Metropolitan Toronto and Region (Metro. Toronto and Region Conserv. Authy., 1959).

It is widely acknowledged that Hurricane Hazel (1954) changed views of flood problems in Toronto and southern Ontario. By this time (1959) the Don Valley Authority had merged with several other authorities into the Metropolitan Toronto and Region Conservation Authority to present a united front on the flood problem.

The 1959 request was for contributions of $12,795,488 each from federal and provincial governments. However, this request was not entirely or even largely for flood-control measures. As indicated in Table IV only 22 per cent of the benefits were for flood damage reduction and over 40 per cent were derived for public recreation.

TABLE IV. TANGIBLE BENEFITS OF THE METROPOLITAN TORONTO PLAN

Type of benefit	Value of benefit	Per cent
Flood-damage reduction	$12,447,000	22.4
Recreational use of reservoirs	$21,203,000	37.6
Indirect benefits	$ 9,335,000	16.5
Others (including water supply, fishing outside reservoirs, pollution abatement, and recreational use of acquired flood-plain lands)	$13,240,600	23.5
Total	$56,225,600	100

On close examination it appears likely that the Hurricane Hazel flood had the effect of generating activity and concern that will eventually lead to the provision of excellent public recreation facilities for Toronto. Government approval and funds have been forthcoming and a series of dams is to be built around the periphery of the Metropolitan area, and the lakes developed for public recreation. Construction is already under way.

The opportunity to develop public recreation may have helped to direct attention away from a consideration of alternative adjustments to floods. Some of these alternatives seem, on the grounds of circumstantial evidence, to offer substantial prospect of considerable reduction in flood losses without the large-scale costs of dam construction. The total area of developed flood-plain land is small, due to the ravine-like nature of the major valleys. Main lines of communication pass over the ravines on viaducts, and residential development in general stops short at the top of the valley walls. In a few places where the valleys open out to enclose wider expanses of flood plain, especially in their lower courses, there are both industrial and residential properties. These are the exception rather than the rule. Even in those places where the flood plain is crowded with development, the total area subject to flooding is relatively small.

It might be objected that if flood-damage potential is so small, it would not have been possible to justify the dams in a benefit-cost analysis. In fact this is the case. There are insufficient flood-control benefits, and it is only by adding a considerable sum of recreation and other benefits that the Toronto scheme has been justified.

What might an alternative plan have included? Since the total amount of flood-plain property is small in relation to the size and wealth of the city, a scheme involving removal of buildings from the hazard area in a program of phased withdrawal should be possible. This could be accompanied by flood-proofing measures, and an improved flood-forecasting system for those properties that remain temporarily in the flood plain. Many of the present buildings in the flood-hazard area are old and in any case would be due for reconstruction in the next decade or so. A government sponsored insurance scheme might also be offered to those remaining on condition that they agree to evacuate by a certain date. The plan does include provision for flood forecasting and some flood-plain land acquisition, but these were not regarded as elements in a comprehensive approach to flood-damage reduction.

The architects of the Toronto plan may legitimately claim that such alternatives were not open to them. The necessary legislation, the necessary administrative and financial arrangements are all lacking, and in any case the alternatives suggested would not help in providing badly needed public recreation facilities. The point here is not that the Toronto plan is a bad one. It is not. The issue is simply that it may not be the best alternative, and that the pre-project planning studies did not consider other schemes. Had other choices been open to them, the resultant plan might have been very different and the cost to the nation much less.

The Choice of Adjustments

There is a wide range of theoretical possibilities for flood-damage reduction. Many of these were described by White (1945), and since then the choice has been elaborated by many students of flood problems (Tennessee Valley Authy., 1963). A convenient chart in use by the Tennessee Valley Authority presents a framework of many of the alternatives, and is reproduced in Figure 1.

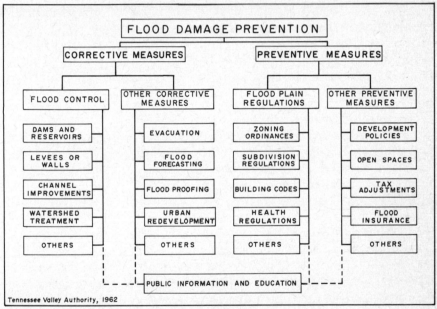

Figure 1. Alternative adjustments to flood.

As shown in the Belleville and Toronto cases, not all of these alternatives may be open to selection by the decision makers involved, even if they are aware of the theoretical choice. An examination of flood problems across Canada shows that where action has been taken it usually consists of some type of flood control.

Methods in common use

There are extensive dykes on the lower Fraser River in British Columbia (MacDonald, 1957). A flood-diversion channel is under construction to divert Red River flows around the city of Winnipeg (Dept. Res. and Dev., 1953). Several flood-control dams have been built in southern Ontario, such as the Fanshawe Dam on the North

Branch of the Thames above London (Ont. Dept. Planning and Dev., 1952), and others are proposed such as the dams around Metropolitan Toronto (Metro. Toronto and Region Conserv. Authy., 1959).

In addition to these structures, watershed treatment has often been advocated as a means of reducing flood flows. While deforestation of watersheds may increase run-off rates and add to flood crests, it should not be assumed that reforestation and other watershed treatment will eliminate floods. These methods are playing a role in reducing flood hazards on some watersheds in southern Ontario, and in other parts of the country.

Frequently these and other methods of flood control are blocked by the very limitations inherent in the type of remedial action recommended. For example there is a real danger when recommendations are based primarily on benefit-cost analysis that the community will be given no more than one choice of action—either to carry out the recommendation or do nothing at all; no alternatives are offered.

The neglected choices

Flood proofing—Flood proofing as one such choice has been examined by Sheaffer (1960). This is a form of flood-damage reduction that requires individual buildings to be made water-tight by minor structural changes. Lower windows can be bricked up, steel bulkheads can be made to fit over door spaces and valves can be installed on drains and sewer outlets. For example in Winnipeg and Regina many buildings have sewer caps which can prevent back-up into basements. Shaeffer discussed such adjustments in some detail, and after a careful study concluded that flood proofing is a valuable alternative method of flood-damage reduction and suggested six kinds of situations in which flood proofing of buildings may be especially desirable. These are: (1) where low-stage, low-velocity, moderate flooding of short duration is experienced; (2) where the more traditional kinds of flood protection such as dams and dykes are not feasible; (3) where individuals desire to solve their flood problems without collective action or where collective action is not possible; (4) where cultural groups shun government aid and subsidy but wish to mitigate their flood losses; (5) where activities which demand riverine locations in order to function, need some degree of protection; and (6) where a resource manager desires a higher degree of protection than that provided by a flood-control project.

Flood proofing is a flexible adjustment to flood hazard and can be used either by itself or in conjunction with flood-control projects, flood-plain regulations, or flood-damage insurance as in the Golden Triangle area of Pittsburgh (Sheaffer, 1960). It can also be undertaken privately or at government expense or under a cost-sharing arrangement.

Urban redevelopment—Many cities with flood problems have large sections of their central business districts on the flood plain. These urban cores and the surrounding zone of mixed housing and industry are commonly the oldest part of the city, and many of them are now or soon will be in need of renewal.

Accordingly a program aimed at eliminating flood damage in addition to removing damageable property leads directly to urban redevelopment. Such cities as Galt (Bell, 1963), and Belleville, Ontario, where the main street parallels the banks of a river and where the backs of main street properties stand directly on the bank of the river, are examples of a situation common in many smaller cities. Urban redevelopment in such situations could fulfill a triple function by (1) removing damageable property from the path of floods, (2) creating more public open space along the waterfront and thus adding to the attractiveness of the business centre, and (3) providing more parking space and thus helping to revitalize the central business district.

Flood-plain regulations—Under this broad heading a number of social guides are possible that will channel development in the most desirable places and avoid undue creation of new flood-damage potential. Such guides include encroachment statutes, building codes, zoning ordinances and the like. It is not necessary to view this as negative legislation, the only purpose of which is to prohibit development. On the contrary, it can be used to ensure that flood plains are utilized to their maximum advantage, while reducing, in so far as is possible, the risks taken by private citizens.

Flood insurance—The private insurance business has not ventured into the field of flood-damage insurance (Am. Ins. Assoc., 1956). There are good reasons for this. Most property is not subject to flood and would, therefore, have no need for flood insurance; but property located on flood plains will be flooded sooner or later and the group of people involved would have to share the burden of a flood-damage insurance program. Basic data needed for determination of fair and equitable premiums for areas of varying flood risks are not yet available. Hence flood insurance is prohibitively expensive and for most practical purposes is not available. There remains the possibility of government-sponsored flood inurance. This would produce problems of accelerating movement into flood plains, unless premiums were realistically related to risks.

Flood forecasting—Flood forecasting is being widely used and modern communications make this method of flood-damage reduction potentially one of the most effective. How effective it is at the present time is difficult to assess. A fruitful study could be made of the amount of damages prevented by flood forecasting in relation to the cost of providing the forecasts. It seems likely that such a study would show very large benefits from flood forecasting in relation to costs.

Although flood forecasting is capable of further refinement and development it is not a neglected alternative in the sense of the other methods discussed above. One qualification is needed here. Flood forecasting by itself is less effective than when combined with public efforts to increase flood hazard awareness. If citizens located on the flood plain are made aware of the danger then they will be better prepared to take emergency steps to reduce damage. Such steps may include evacuation of people and valuable property from the hazard area, elevation of property beyond the reach of flood waters, emergency sandbagging and the like. Where flood hazard awareness is low, plans for dealing with an emergency may be relaxed or poorly developed and even the receipt of a timely flood warning may not allow effective measures to be taken. For example, sand and sandbags may not be readily available and transport for the removal of goods may not be quickly obtained.

A second point about flood forecasting is that great care needs to be exercised to make warnings accurate. A series of unfulfilled warnings can rapidly diminish the effectiveness of future warnings.

Extending the Range of Choice

The present study has presented evidence to show that if a wider range of choice can be offered with inducements to decision-makers in question of flood-plain land use and the reduction of flood damages, there is reasonable prospect that the periodic distress and suffering brought about by floods can be reduced substantially. In particular more vigorous steps are needed to prevent further undue growth of damage potential; to remove buildings from areas of high hazard; and to encourage flood proofing of those buildings that must remain in the path of floods. If these methods do not result in a substantial reduction in flood damages, at the very least they may be expected to restrain further growth. On the other hand if the range of choice to decision-makers is not extended, there is every prospect that flood damages will increase and that additional burdens will be thrown on governments in the form of the need to provide relief and rehabilitation for an increasing number of flood victims, and also to provide increasingly large-scale engineering works for flood control.

In order that the range of choice may be extended and that adequate guides to the choice can be made available, several innovations are required as well as extensions to present practice. There is need for more work on the hydrological aspects of floods. Studies of regional flood frequency and extent would be a useful starting point.

There is also need to recognize flood proofing of buildings as a legitimate method of reducing flood damages. If governments are prepared to spend large sums of money on engineering works for flood control, why not spend some small sums to assist flood-plain managers to flood-proof their buildings? A cost-sharing scheme would ensure that the money is well spent and is only used by those sufficiently concerned to make a contribution to their own protection. Another possible application of flood proofing is in those areas where the flood hazard is of a low order of frequency and the advantages of using the land for development are seen to outweigh the risks of infrequent flood damage. Here requirements for flood proofing could be added to the building code so as to ensure that, in the event of a flood, damages would be minimized.

Urban renewal and redevelopment legislation does not provide for use of funds to achieve other desirable and worthwhile objectives in addition to its main purpose. Where urban renewal projects are in prospect, steps could be taken to ensure that new uses of land conform to the national interest by minimizing the risk of future flood losses. There are also areas where the flood hazard itself could be the catalyst in starting an urban renewal scheme. This is particularly the case where engineering methods of flood control are found to be unfeasible.

A comprehensive program of flood-loss reduction would also include an increased emphasis on the flood-plain zoning work that is now taking effect in some cities. Local planning agencies are in need of assistance in drawing up suitable flood-plain regulations. For this purpose and for urban renewal schemes, it would be useful to have hydrometeorological studies of flood frequency, extent, depth and duration, in all the areas of the country where major flood damage potential exists. Such studies would aim at providing planners with a basis for rational choice of boundaries of hazard zones. For example, it may be possible to recognize parts of a flood plain as having distinctly different degrees of flood hazard. Regulations could be shaped accordingly to permit the maximum level of development consistent with the aim of minimizing flood damages.

Not all places with flood problems have established planning authorities to take action on flood-plain zoning, and even where planning authorities do exist there is frequently no readily available method of communicating information on flood hazard to private citizens. Often decisions to develop flood-plain land are taken by citizens who remain ignorant of the risks they are taking and to which they may be exposing others. There is need, therefore, for a flood-plain information program, both for the benefit of planners and for private citizens. In such a program flood-plain areas could be designated and shown on topographic maps, together with hydrological information on the nature and degree of hazard. Such a program could be made into a logical extension of the mapping work of an existing agency at an appropriate level of government.

It would be most helpful if the agency preparing information on flood hazards could also be made responsible for collecting flood-damage data. This leads to the suggestion that a central collection and depository office be established to gather together in one place information on flood hazard, flood damages, and changes in flood-damage potential. Such an office could probably be established in an existing agency of government at relatively little extra expense. It could certainly expect to pay for itself in flood losses prevented by the wise policies of adjustments to floods which it would encourage.

It would be unwise to rush headlong into the establishment of a government-sponsored flood insurance program. Some possible advantages of such a scheme, however, suggest that it may be worthy of special investigation by a government committee of enquiry. After careful thought it may be possible to devise a scheme in which flood insurance would play a useful role along with other methods of adjustment to floods.

In planning a flood policy for the next few years, there are advantages to be gained from a broader and more flexible approach than has yet been used. In particular flood-plain zoning, urban renewal for flood-damage reduction, and flood proofing merit more serious attention. These alternatives have been relatively neglected. Continued rapid population growth, and continued urban expansion can mean a much higher bill for flood losses and flood control works under existing policies and arrangements for flood-damage reduction.

References

Alberta, "Report of the Royal Commission to investigate the cause of flooding in the Bow River Valley, 1952", mimeo (1953).
American Insurance Association, "Studies of floods and flood damage, 1952-55", (New York, American Insurance Society, 1956).

Ausable River Conservation Authority, "Flood control and water conservation brief, Parkhill Creek watershed" (1959).

Bell, W. H.., "Galt and Guelph, a study in urban flood problems", unpublished B.A. thesis (Department of Geography, University of Toronto, 1963).

Burton, Ian, "Invasion and escape on the Little Calumet", Gilbert F. White (ed.), "Papers on flood problems" (Department of Geography, University of Chicago, 1961), Res. Paper 70, pp. 84-92.

Burton, Ian, "Some aspects of flood loss reduction in England and Wales", ibid., pp. 203-221.

Burton, Ian, "Review of flood-plain studies", Plan Canada, Vol. 3, no. 2 (1962), pp. 103-105.

Burton, Ian, "Investment choices in public resource development", A. Rotstein (ed.), The Prospect of Change: Proposals for Canada's Future (McGraw-Hill Co. of Canada, 1965).

Burton, Ian and Robert W. Kates, "The perception of hazards in resource management", Natural Resources Journal, Vol. 3, no. 3 (1964), pp. 412-441.

Burton, Ian and Robert W. Kates, "The flood plain and the sea shore: a comparative analysis of hazard zone occupance", Geographical Review, Vol. 54, no. 3 (1964), pp. 366-385.

Bussard, L. U., "The early history of Calgary", unpublished M.A. thesis (Edmonton, University of Alberta, 1935).

Department of Resources and Development, "Report on investigations into measures for the reduction of the flood hazard in the greater Winnipeg area, with appendices", A. H. Eng. and Water Resources Branch (1953).

Fraser River Board, B.C., "Preliminary report on flood control and hydroelectric power in the Fraser River basin" (1958).

Goddard, James E., "The cooperative program in the Tennessee Valley", Gilbert F. White (ed.), "Papers on flood problems" (Department of Geography, University of Chicago, 1961), Res. Paper 70.

Hadin, Davis & Brown (Alberta) Ltd. and H. G. Acres and Co., Niagara Falls, Ont., "Red Deer flood stages and industrial land development", a report to the city of Red Deer (1960).

Harrison, Robert W., Alluvial Empire (Little Rock, Pioneer Press, 1961).

Hendry, M. C., "Report on Bow River power and storage investigations", Department of Interior, Water Power Branch, Water Res. Paper 2 (1915).

Hufschmidt, M. M. et al, "Standards and criteria for formulating and evaluating federal water resources development", Report to Bureau of the Budget, Washington (1961).

Inter-agency River Basin Committee, "Proposed practices for economic analysis of river basin projects", Washington (1950).

Kates, Robert W., "Hazard and choice perception in flood-plain management" (Department of Geography, University of Chicago, 1962), Res. Paper 78.

Kendall, G. R. and A. G. Petrie, "The frequency of thunderstorm days in Canada", Met. Br., Department of Transport, Circular 3746 (1962).

MacDonald, J. L. "History of dykes and drainage in B.C.", Trans. 10th B.C. Natural Resources Conference (1957), pp. 75-86.

Manitoba, "Report of Royal Commission on South Saskatchewan River project" (1952).

Manitoba, "Report of Royal Commission on flood-cost benefit", (1958).

McGee, W. J., "The flood plains of rivers", Forum (April, 1891), pp. 221-234.

McKay, G. A., "Statistical estimates of probable maximum rainfall in the prairie provinces", Department of Agriculture, Prairie Farm Rehabilitation Administration (1964).

McMullen, D. N., "Timmins flood, Aug. 31-Sept. 1, 1961; a design storm for Ontario", Met. Br. Department of Transport, Circular 3746 (1962).

Metro. Toronto and Region Conservation Authority, "Plan for flood control and water conservation" (1959).

Moira River Conservation Authority, "Flood control and conservation measures brief, Moira watershed" (1959).

Murphy, F. C., "Regulating flood-plain development" (Department of Geography, University of Chicago, 1958), Res. Paper 56.

Ontario Department of Planning and Development, Conservation Branch, "Don Valley conservation report" (1950).

Ontario Department of Planning and Development, Conservation Branch, "Moira Valley conservation report" (1950).

Ontario Department of Planning and Development, Conservation Branch, "Upper Thames Valley conservation report" (1952).

Pleva, E. G., "Multiple purpose land and water districts in Ontario", H. Jowett (ed.), *Comparisons in Resource Management* (Baltimore, Resources for the Future, Inc., Johns Hopkins Press, 1961).

Putnam, D. F. (ed.), *Canadian Regions, a Geography of Canada* (Toronto, Dent and Sons, 1952).

Roder, W., "Attitudes and knowledge on the Topeka flood plain", Gilbert F. White (ed.), "Papers on flood problems" (Department of Geography, University of Chicago, 1961), Res. Paper 70, pp. 62-83.

Sewell, W. R. D. et al., "Guide to benefit-cost analysis", Northern Affairs and Natural Resources, Ottawa (1962).

Sheaffer, J. R., "Flood proofing: an element in a flood-damage reduction program" (Department of Geography, University of Chicago, 1960), Res. Paper 65.

Smith, P. J., "Calgary, a study in urban pattern", *Economic Geography*, Vol. 38, no. 4 (1962).

Sutton, Walter G., "Planning for optimum economic use of flood plains", paper presented to Environmental Engineering Conference, American Society of Civil Engineers, mimeo (1963).

Tennessee Valley Authority, "Flood damage prevention; an indexed bibliography" (1963).

United States Geological Survey, "Floods of 1950 in the Red River of the North and Winnipeg River basins", Water Supply Paper 1137-B (1956).

United States Senate, "Floods and flood control", Select Committee on National Water Resources, Committee Print 15 (1960).

Upper Thames River Conservation Authority, "Supplement A to brief on flood control measures for the Upper Thames watershed; benefit-cost analysis" (1957).

Upper Thames River Conservation Authority, "Flood control brief" (1958).

Upper Thames River Conservation Authority, "Supplement B to brief on flood control measures for the Upper Thames watershed; benefit-cost analysis" (1959).

White, Gilbert F., "Human adjustments to floods" (Department of Geography, University of Chicago, 1945), Res. Paper 29.

White, Gilbert F., "The choice of use in resource management", *Natural Resources Journal*, Vol. 1, no. 1 (March, 1961).

White, Gilbert F., "Choice of adjustment to floods" (Department of Geography, University of Chicago, 1964), Res. Paper 93.

White, Gilbert F. and Howard L. Cook, "Making wise use of flood plains", *Natural Resources: Energy, Water and River Basin Development*, Vol. 1 (1963), UN Conference on Application of Science and Technology for Benefit of Less Developed Areas.

White, Gilbert F. et al., "Changes in urban occupancy of flood plains in the United States" (Department of Geography, University of Chicago, 1958), Res. Paper 57.

6

The Significance of Reservoirs in Recreation

J. A. Boan

Visits at reservoirs by people seeking outdoor recreation indicate that man-made lakes have a significant value apart from their importance for such primary purposes as power, irrigation and flood control. Their usefulness in expanding the recreational resource base may be more dramatic in arid regions but they nevertheless have an equally important role to play in humid areas. The South Saskatchewan river reservoir will provide facilities for hunting, fishing, swimming, boating, picnicking, camping, and cottages in an area now almost devoid of such facilities. In humid areas reservoirs add to the natural recreational resource base which, over time, may become lost to cottage and industrial developments and destroyed through excessive use.

Considering the many recreational values resulting from the building of a reservoir, it is difficult to understand why these values have so often received insufficient consideration. This may be because recreational values are intangible.

Perhaps reservoir planners have overlooked the growing importance of recreation in an increasingly affluent society. Lack of coordination between the many different agencies concerned with the planning of a multi-purpose project may be another cause. It is

Background Paper, *Resources for Tomorrow Conference, 1961*, Vol. 2 (1961), pp. 1003-08. Reprinted by permission of the Queen's Printer, Ottawa.

imperative that all planning work be so co-ordinated as to avoid irreversible mistakes in the planning of structures, acquisition of land, and preparation of shore lines, that would add greatly to the ultimate cost of recreational developments and perhaps make it impossible to reap maximum benefits from these developments.

Two principles emerge. First, recreation should be on a par with other basic purposes in the planning, construction, operation and maintenance of reservoirs. Second, the provision of reservoir recreational facilities should be integrated with regional and national programs for recreation development.

1. *The Recreational Value of Reservoirs*

If the *demand* for water for recreational purposes continues to rise to the end of this century at the same rate as in the last fifteen years, reservoirs will gather increasing importance as an additional recreational resource. They will be needed to help overcome limitations of water supply in arid areas. They will also be needed to enlarge the supply in more humid areas where natural recreational resources for public use have been lost to housing, cottage and industrial developments and where population density is so great that excessive use is destroying existing recreational resources.

A reservoir may possibly exert its greatest impact in arid areas deficient in water-based recreational resources. Indeed, the building of reservoirs, in these areas, may help to *equalize* aquatic recreational opportunities throughout Canada.

The South Saskatchewan River Project affords an example of a multiple-purpose development with unique opportunities for immense recreational benefits. It will provide a reservoir with a shore line almost 500 miles in length along which there will be facilities for hunting, fishing, swimming, boating, picnicking, camping, cottages, etc. It would also permit the stabilization of the lakes, in the Qu'Appelle Valley which now support the core of the recreational development in southern Saskatchewan.

The reservoir can be expected to sustain the fish which are indigenous to the South Saskatchewan river, especially pike, pickerel, and gold-eye and deep cold water pools may permit the introduction of new species such as trout. Improved water conditions in the lakes of the Qu'Appelle chain could improve angling conditions in these areas. In the reservoir area migratory waterfowl should greatly increase. In the irrigation areas, the pheasant population should find conditions favorable to its propagation, as was the case in the irrigation districts of Alberta and the Dakotas. The tourist trade may also benefit from the project. The project will improve the attractiveness of an area almost devoid of trees, lakes and streams and good park sites. In brief, the reservoir will offer to the people living in the area many pleasures and satisfactions derived from outdoor recreation such as physical and health, esthetic and educational values.[1]

At least two-thirds of the people of Saskatchewan will be within a two-hour auto journey of a large body of water created or improved by this project. For the first time many people will have an opportunity to enjoy outdoor recreation on a grand scale. A recreation consultant has estimated that visits at this reservoir, for all kinds of recreation, will increase from about 269,000 in 1965 to about 467,000 in the year 2000.[2] With sightseeing about the only attraction, the construction site of the South Saskatchewan River Dam had over 82,000 visitors in 1960.

American experience illustrates the popularity of reservoir sites as recreational attractions. As one example, the following figures show the number of visits to reservoirs built by the United States Corps of Engineers in the southwestern States and the extent to which actual visits exceeded estimated attendance.[3]

Reservoir	1946 estimate of future annual visitor-days	1956 annual visitor-days
Dennison (Lake Texoma)	600,000	7,471,600
Canton Dam, Oklahoma	45,000	561,900
Great Salt Plains, Oklahoma	32,000	436,200
Hulah, Oklahoma	18,000	471,700

It is claimed that "the Lake Mead National Recreation Area, encompassing Hoover and Davis Dams and their reservoirs, is second only to the Blue Ridge Parkway in tourist attraction."[4] In its 25 years of existence more than 38 million visitors have come to this recreation area, 3,390,574 of them in 1959.[5]

In fairly humid areas, reservoirs are also needed to expand the natural recreational resources. The popularity of the Ontario-St. Lawrence Development Commission's facilities between Morrisburg

[1] *Report of the Royal Commission on the South Saskatchewan River Project* (Ottawa, Queen's Printer, 1952), p. 253.
[2] W. M. Baker, *The Recreation Prospects of The South Saskatchewan*. Part II—*The Plan of Development*. Chapter 1, "The Intensity of Use of Reservoirs for Recreation", p. 19, The South Saskatchewan River Development Commission (June, 1960), mimeo.
[3] *Army-Interior Reservoir Land Acquisition Policy*, Union Calendar No. 465, House Report No. 1185, 85th Congress; 1st Session, United States Government Printing Office (1957), p. 25.
[4] *The New York Times* (August 14, 1960), p. 80.
[5] *Loc. cit.*

and Cornwall is a case in point. These facilities are man-made structures that have to cope with the draw-down problem common to many reservoirs. Nevertheless, the number of visits there rose to 925,000 in 1960, which represents an increase of 20 per cent over 1959. The engineering features of the seaway undoubtedly drew many people to the area. However 9,000 overnight camping groups were accommodated in the park areas which is an indication of the recreational values of the area.[6] In the same year, visits at the Fanshawe Dam of the Thames Valley Conservation Authority just outside London, Ontario, totalled about 160,000.

As time goes by the need for more recreational resources in areas of high population density will become increasingly pronounced. Reservoirs offer a possibility of enlarging the recreational resource base of an area and they may also offset the destructive effects of excessive pressure or congestion on natural beaches and parklands. "It is one of the paradoxes of recreation that as increasing numbers of people grow to appreciate nature and seek enjoyment in the outdoors, they tend to destroy the values they came to find. Recreational uses of land are essentially extensive uses. For many people, the ideal man-land ratio in outdoor recreation is represented by the wilderness areas. Yet, an increasing intensity of recreational land uses is unavoidable if recreational opportunities are to be made available to a growing population of users."[7]

If the rate of increases in visits is any criterion, then there is no doubt as to the increasing popularity of reservoirs for recreation. Rates of increases in visits from the end of the last world war to 1958, at reservoirs and other recreational areas in the United States, were as follows:[8]

Recreational Site	Average Annual Percentage Increase
Corps of Engineers Reservoirs	28
T.V.A. Reservoirs	15
National Wildlife Refuges	12
National Forests	10
State Parks	10
National Park System	8
Municipal and Country Parks	4

[6] Data from correspondence with G. W. Arthurs, Public Relations Officer, The Ontario-St. Lawrence Development Commission, Morrisburg, Ontario (October 26, 1960).
[7] C. W. Loomer, "Recreational Uses of Rural Lands and Waters", *Journal of Farm Economics*, Vol. 40, no. 5 (December, 1958), p. 1333.
[8] M. Clawson, *Statistics on Outdoor Recreation* (Washington, Resources for the Future, Inc., April, 1958), p. 7.

It has been estimated that the *demand* in the United States for resource based recreation areas of an intermediate type which provide for all-day outings, for boating, fishing. swimming, etc., would increase 16 times in the next 40 years.[9] Since natural areas which can provide the necessary water resources for this type of development are limited, reservoirs will play an increasingly important role.

Because of differences in climate, customs and economic factors, the potential *demand* may increase somewhat less rapidly in Canada than in the United States; but because of the great similarities in the ways people spend their leisure in the two countries, the potential increase in Canada is likely to be of proportional magnitude. The popularity of reservoirs in the United States, the upward trend in water-based recreational activities in Ontario and elsewhere, and prospects for the next 40 years, all suggest that the significance of reservoirs in recreational programs has become so pronounced that it cannot be ignored.[10]

[9] M. Clawson, "The Crisis in Outdoor Recreation", *American Forests*, Vol. 65, nos. 3 and 4 (March and April, 1959).

[10] Experience in the United States indicates that recognition of public recreational values associated with reservoirs must still be fought for. On October 12, 1953, a new joint policy for land acquisition on reservoir projects was announced by the Departments of the Army and of the Interior. The effect of this policy, if it had been carried out without amendment, would have been to inhibit public recreational development on future reservoir shore lines, and to threaten the public development that had taken place on past projects. Before the announcement of the new policy and in fact even before the Flood Control Act of 1944, it had been recognized that "the recreation and conservation values inherent in the development of . . . reservoirs should, where practicable, be made fully available for public use". (Committee on Government Operations, *Army-Interior Reservoir Land Acquisition Policy*, Union Calendar No. 465, House Report No. 1185, 85th Congress, 1st Session, 1957, p. 23.)

According to the testimony given at Public Hearings held by the Public Works and Resources Subcommittee over a period extending from June 4 to July 2, 1957, recreational development based on the policy of the 1944 Flood Control Act would have been very difficult to carry out under the new policy. At the Hearings, 48 recreation, wildlife and conservation associations went on record as being opposed to the new policy. Two organizations approved of it; these were the Chamber of Commerce of the United States and the National Lumber Manufacturers Association. (See *ibid.*, p. 51). As a result, the land acquisition policy was clarified in 1959 to state categorically that "federal water storage reservoirs are important elements in the nation's outdoor recreation and fish and wildlife resources". (Department of the Interior Information Service, August 18, 1959). And further, "Recreation and fish and wildlife opportunities, both present and potential, shall be considered throughout the planning, construction, operation and maintenance of reservoir projects . . ." Thus, by indicating qualitatively the value that the public attaches to reservoirs for recreational purposes, policy with respect to reservoirs was oriented more positively than before, toward recreation.

2. *Some Problems in the Development of Reservoirs for Recreation*
(a) *The Need for Recognition of Recreational Values of Reservoirs*

Recreational values must be given due consideration in the initial planning of a reservoir project and at each phase of the ensuing development and operational program. Recent park and recreational planning work for the St. Lawrence Seaway and the South Saskatchewan river reservoir point to a growing acceptance of this viewpoint. Still all too frequently recreation is given little or no consideration in the planning of reservoir developments.

The day may yet come when reservoirs are built primarily for recreational purposes. Today, they are built chiefly for other purposes and recreational use is no more than an incidental purpose. If people better understood the importance of recreation in general and of water-based recreation in particular it would be considered as one of the multipurposes for development and not as an incidental benefit. Canada might profit from what has been done in the United States and initiate a continuing study of recreation. This study should follow the same general pattern as the work done by the National Outdoor Recreation Resources Review Commission in the United States,[11] but with broad enough powers to include all forms of outdoor recreation.

Two principles emerge from the premises that a) reservoirs may greatly enlarge the recreational resource base, both in arid and humid regions; b) it is desirable to minimize the destructive effects of a too intensive use of existing recreational areas; c) the cost of developing recreational facilities may be held to a minimum by planning, land acquisition and improvement before flooding. The first principle is that, at the planning stage, recreation should be placed on a par with other basic purposes of a reservoir and that this parity should be preserved through the subsequent stages of construction, operation and maintenance. When this approach is followed the agencies responsible for recreational developments have an opportunity to study the project and make recommendations about land acquisition, engineering requirements and management. The result: a better job at lower cost. The second major principle is that recreational developments should be considered in the general context of recreational programmes within a region.

Recreational values to be gained from reservoir construction are so obvious that it is difficult to understand why recreational uses have so often failed to receive due consideration.

---

[11] This Commission was set up in the fall of 1958 by Congress, and its report is expected in 1961. See Marion Clawson, "The Crisis in Outdoor Recreation", *op. cit.*, pp. 5 and 20 in the "Resources for the Future" reprint.

The significance of reservoirs in recreation may very well be overlooked because of a psychological bias rating natural lakes as *good* and fit for recreation, and artificial lakes as too elaborate and lacking in natural or primitive wonder. It is difficult to understand this bias when the popularity of reservoirs is so obvious, particularly when large developments frequently offer to the eye the breathtaking display of some of the finest engineering achievements.

Perhaps the tendency of reservoir planners to treat recreation lightly stems from their failure to recognize its importance in an increasingly *affluent* society.[12] This might be considered as a form of "cultural lag", understandable in view of the many pressing and persistent problems which public figures must contend with. However, it is surely not too much to ask that reservoirs built for other purposes be also developed for recreation. This would go at least some distance toward meeting the prospective potential *demand*.

In a market economy where measurable benefits and costs are the key to decisions, the use of resources for recreational purposes may tend to be overlooked because so many of the benefits of recreation are intangible. True enough, in recent years, an attempt has been made to place an economic value on recreational resources. However we have not yet been able to devise satisfactory methods for the economic evaluation of recreational resources.[13] We may have to develop techniques, other than market techniques, for the measurement of utility.[14] In the meantime we can do no better than rely on rather unrefined methods of measuring recreational benefits.[15]

---

12 Harry G. Johnson, "The Political Economy of Opulence", *The Canadian Journal of Economics and Political Science*, Vol. 26, no. 4 (November, 1960), pp. 552-564.

13 Andrew H. Trice and Samuel E. Wood, "Measurement of Recreation Benefits", *Land Economics*, Vol. 39, no. 3 (August, 1958) pp. 195-207. Also, "Measurement of Recreation Benefits: A Reply", *Land Economics*, Vol. 34, no. 4 (November, 1958), pp. 356-370.

14 For an excellent review of the work being done on utility measurement see, K. J. Arrow, "Utilities, Attitudes, Choices: A Review Note", *Econometrica*, Vol. 26, no. 1 (January, 1958), pp. 1-23.

15 Evaluation procedures in the United States have been summarized as follows: "Generally, the Corps of Engineers measures tangible recreation benefits by estimating the net income from recreational facilities, such as hotels, camps, and concessions. The Bureau of Reclamation obtains estimates from the National Park Service. The Department of Agriculture does not measure any tangible recreational benefits." See Subcommittee to Study Public Works, *Economic Evaluation of Federal Water Resource Development Projects*, House Committee Print No. 24, 82nd Congress, Second Session, Washington, United States Government Printing Office (1952), pp. 13-14.

An analysis which relies on a description of the type of recreation to be provided, the number of people to be served, the distances involved, and the various types of alternatives may not produce a numerical value but, nevertheless, it may have a great deal of significance. Moreover, planners could be enlightened by regional or local groups interested in recreational development if the groups could justify the need for a reservoir and were prepared to assume responsibility for certain aspects of a recreational development project.

(b) *The Need for Acquisition and Control of Reservoir Shore Lines*

Sufficient land should be acquired around the margins of a reservoir to make recreational development possible. All too often the *take-line* is determined almost entirely by engineering considerations such as erosion hazard or inundation during periods of excessive high water. Savings in land acquisition costs may be insignificant in comparison with the total expenditure for the project but, proportionately, the gains may be quite large. Many reservoir construction agencies are reluctant to become involved in problems of administration arising from the holding of land, even though their concern with such problems may be of short duration. Frequently these agencies do not wish to become tangled up with shore line development projects—recreational projects in particular —in which they have little interest. Their chief concern is with construction and engineering work and they tend to regard recreation as an added burden. There is a basic indecision as to who should be the prime beneficiary of greatly increased land values on the margins of the reservoirs. Should the newly created values accrue to the general public who have created the reservoir or should they be left to private owners to exploit at will and possibly in a manner detrimental to the intended purposes of the reservoir?

Whatever the basic causes of the present approach to shore line control it seems imperative that prospective uses for the reservoir, particularly for recreation, must be given full consideration in the land purchase programme. The determination of the *take-line* solely on engineering considerations is obviously too restrictive since it gives little or no recognition to other uses to which the reservoir can be put.

Sometimes a sharp conflict develops between public and private recreational developments on a reservoir. A major difficulty stems from the building of private cottages along the shore line. The subdivision of land for cottage sites may be permitted, but always in accordance with the judgment of the developing agency, and ownership of the shore line should be withheld from private individuals and agencies. The shore line area must be under the control of the impounding agency to ensure that the reservoir can be adequately policed and that the major purposes for which it was constructed are not frustrated.

(c) *The Need to Minimize Destructive Aspects of Reservoirs*

Destruction commonly occurs when rivers inhabited by anadromous fish, such as salmon, are harnessed for hydroelectric power development. The dam impedes the movement of the fish to their spawning grounds upstream and thus leads to a decrease in the fish population. This has an adverse effect on both recreational and commercial fisheries.[16]

Dams, however, have little adverse effect on non-anadromous fish such as white fish, pike, pickerel, and gold-eye. These fish populations usually increase rapidly during the first 10-12 years after the reservoir has been filled, and thereafter decrease and stabilize at about the previously existing level. The rise in the fish population in the first 10 or 12 years may be explained by a bountiful food supply; the cause of the subsequent decline is not well understood but is likely a function of the oxygen supply.

Bird habitats may be disturbed but the enlargement of the water surface leads to an increase in migratory waterfowl, an increase which may more than compensate for the loss of certain local species.

Animal habitats are likely to be destroyed. In some instances, the destruction of such habitat may entail the loss of educational values as well as the loss of the animals themselves. For example, an easily accessible beaver colony may have given young and older children an opportunity to appreciate the beauty and the industry of the animal kindom.

The most grievous losses in recreational value often result from the destruction of the landscape. Unsightly borrow pits, radical alterations in the natural contour of the area, and failure to clear the trees and shrubs from shore line areas that will be inundated are of particular significance in this respect.

Shore line clearance problems arise because, even in arid areas, the flooded river valley is usually wooded. Because of cost and other short-term considerations, the clearing of sites has often been neglected. However, these costs cannot always be avoided and

---

16 See M. E. Marts and W. R. D. Sewell, "The Conflict Between Fish and Power Resources in the Pacific Northwest", *Annals of the Association of American Geographers*, Vol. 50, no. 1 (March, 1960), pp. 42-50.

if clearing is postponed until after flooding they may be three or more times what they would have been before the flooding.

The trees which are killed by flooding eventually show up at the dam and then have to be removed. This is not a serious problem when the reservoir is used primarily for power. However when it is part of a multi-purpose project which includes irrigation, timber may damage the outlets to irrigation canals. When the reservoir is used for recreational purposes the shore line must be cleared of all obstructions that offer a threat to life, limb, and property (boats).

We know of three chief methods of clearing the shore line. The first one is the most popular, but not at all effective: do nothing. The second entails clearing and cleaning up before flooding, and the third clearing before flooding but postponement of the cleaning up which is done through a floatation process after the reservoir is filled. The second method is recommended for its contribution to esthetic values but the third is thought to be somewhat cheaper. In the Saskatchewan River project, young trees uprooted from the area to be flooded might well be transplanted to areas designated for park development, to hasten the day when trees will supply shade to the park visitors.

(d) *Timing and Co-ordination*

Maximum recreation benefits will be secured and destructive aspects adequately controlled only with proper timing and administrative co-ordination. Unless these two conditions are realized, recreational values may be seriously impaired and administrative agencies will likely face a series of crisis situations.

Recreational uses must be fully considered at all stages of reservoir planning, from the preliminary evaluation of the scheme to the final decisions on land acquisition and reservoir construction and operation.

Recreation is an explosive force, with tremendous social and economic implications, for both urban and rural people. Sound planning, that is planning that considers all aspects of a multiple-purpose project and relations between them, will minimize conflicts among uses and prevent the disruption of operational programs.[17]

Parks and recreation departments and agencies must be represented in the planning and administrative machinery set up for reservoir development. Frequently the governmental departments

---

[17] ". . . landowners, particularly resort owners around the reservoir, often exert pressures seeking to prevent necessary raising or lowering in the level of the conservation pool." See *Army-Interior Reservoir Land Acquisition Policy, op. cit.*, p. 21.

and agencies operating in this field are primarily interested in the engineering, agricultural, and power aspects of development, and hence recreation does not get the attention which it deserves.

There is often a recognition of the importance of the need to involve recreational agencies in the co-ordinated planning and administrative apparatus but the recreational agencies frequently are not in a position to undertake their part of the planning responsibilities because of budget or staff limitations. In the light of the sporadic nature of the need for competent staff to undertake this specialized type of recreational planning, consideration might be given to the establishment of a *reservoir* of talent to be made available on a consultant basis to provincial and municipal agencies.

7

The Effect of Low-Cost Hydro Power on Industrial Location

G. Schramm

Introduction

The purpose of the paper is to investigate the influence that low-cost hydro power sources may have on the location of new industrial plants. This is a question of considerable interest to us because Canada is one of the few industrialized western nations that still has substantial sources of undeveloped hydro power available. It is of even greater interest to a number of underdeveloped countries that are rich in hydro resources but unable to utilize them unless substantial industrial energy loads are developed at the same time.

Past experience shows that availability of low-cost hydro can significantly affect the locational decisions of power-intensive industries. The question which we will ask and answer here is whether the underlying cost-price relationships of these locational decisions are still valid for the present and the foreseeable future. In order to do so we have to define the meaning of "low-cost" power. This is obviously a relative concept; "low-cost" hydro power must be defined in terms relative to the costs of producing power by alterna-

Edited text of a paper read to the Second Annual Meeting, Canadian Economics Association, Calgary, 1968. Published in edited form in *Canadian Journal of Economics*, Vol. II (May, 1969), pp. 210-24, and reproduced here by permission of the Canadian Economics Association and University of Toronto Press.

tive means.[1] One of the central issues, therefore, is the question whether the historical cost advantage of favourable hydro sites still holds at present and, if it does not (for which there is overwhelming evidence), to which extent it has been reduced.

Section I will briefly discuss the historical evidence. Section II will indicate the various regions in Canada and elsewhere where the existence of undeveloped hydro resources could hold out the promise of similar industrial developments. Section III will investigate the effects of power costs on the overall costs of production of various products and commodities. Section IV will discuss recent technological changes that have taken place in the production of electric energy by means other than hydraulic turbines and will compare the relative price changes between hydro and thermal power that have resulted from these changes.

I.
HISTORICAL TRENDS

The historical evidence of the attraction of low-cost hydro power to power-intensive industries is certainly impressive. In the United States the developments of the Tennessee Valley Authority in the South-East and the Bonneville Power Adminisration in the North-West have led to large-scale settlements of such industries in areas which, with the exception of low-cost energy, generally offered neither suitable local raw material sources nor near-by markets. Similar developments took place elsewhere.

United States

In the Tennessee Valley aluminum smelters use more than five billion kilowatt-hours of energy per year, or nearly one-third of the industrial use of power in that region.[2] Ferro-alloy industries consume well over one billion kilowatt-hours of TVA power annually. Electrochemical plants producing elemental phosphorus, phosphoric acid, phosphates and other fertilizers, chlorine and

---

[1] Traditionally, the term "low-cost" power was applied to projects that produced at-site energy in the one to three mills/kwh range. Provisionally we will accept this range as meaning "low-cost" power until we investigate its merits in section IV of this paper.

[2] The 1965 year-end capacity of the three primary aluminum smelters in the area (Aluminum Co. of America's plant at Alcoa, Tenn., Reynold Metal Company's plant at Listerhill, Ala. and Consolidated Aluminum Company's plant at Johnsonville, Tenn.) amounted to 381,500 short tons, or about 14% of total U.S. capacity. Data from: Ivan Bloch and Samuel Moment, *The Aluminum Industry of the Pacific Northwest* (Portland, Oregon, Bonneville Power Administration, 1967), Table 28.

caustic soda, calcium carbide and acetylene, electrolytic manganese and titanium consume about five billion kilowatt-hours per year. As a U.S. Senate document points out: "Most of the raw materials for the electro-process industries that are based on TVA power are brought into the area and most of the products are shipped out."[3] In addition, the U.S. Atomic Energy Commission processing plants in the area use as much energy as the total of all other TVA customers combined.[4]

In the marketing area of the Bonneville Power Administration the 1965 primary aluminum capacity of the various smelters supplied with electric energy from BPA amounted to 803,000 short tons, or approximately thirty-three per cent of total U.S. smelter capacity.[5] 1964 elemental phosphorous plant capacity in the Pacific Northwest amounted to 145,000 short tons, or approximately twenty-six per cent of the U.S. total.[6] 1961 ferro-alloy production in the area was 121,667 short tons, or about 6.5 per cent of total U.S. production.[7] The silicon carbide capacity of the Carborundum Company's plant at Vancouver, Washington represented over fifty per cent of the 1962 rated U.S. capacity of 144,900 short tons.[8] Similar impressive statistics can be cited for other products requiring large quantities of electric energy for their production processes.

Norway

Similar developments took place in other countries, notably in Norway and Canada. Norway is rich in hydro resources but lacks almost any other source of industrial raw materials. Despite the lack of raw materials and domestic markets in 1960 forty-four per cent of the country's thirty-one billion kilowatt-hours of electric energy production were consumed by electro-process industries.[9] Most of

---

3 All data and quotation from: U.S. Senate, Committee on Public Works, *The Market for Rampart Power*, Yukon River, Alaska, 87th Congress, Second Session, Washington, D.C., 1962, pp. 26 and 27.
4 *Ibid.*, p. 28.
5 Ivan Bloch and Samuel Moment, *op. cit.*, Table 2.
6 Norman S. Petersen, *The Phosphate Rock Industry of the Pacific Northwest* (Portland, Oregon, Bonneville Power Administration, 1964), Table 19.
7 Gury A. Kingston and Robert A. Miller, *Alloy Metals Outlook in the Pacific Northwest States* (Portland, Oregon, Bonneville Power Administration, 1966), Table 4.
8 Norman S. Petersen and W. N. Hale, *Trends and Outlook for Manufacture of Abrasives in the Pacific Northwest* (Portland, Oregon, Bonneville Power Administration, 1965), p. 9.
9 All Norwegian data with the exception of aluminum production based on U.S. Department of the Interior, *Rampart Project, Alaska, Field Report*, Juneau (1965), pp. 505 ff. Aluminum data from Ivan Bloch and Samuel Moment, *op. cit.*, Table 5.

the raw materials for these industries were imported while most of their outputs were exported. By processing alumina imported from distant sources Norway produced 220,000 tons of primary aluminum in 1962, which made it the world's fourth largest producer. The country ranks second only to West Germany in the production of silicon carbide abrasives which are manufactured from imported carbon and native silica. Calcium carbide and calcium cynamide are important export products derived from domestic limestone and imported coal and coke. Except for scrap iron and quartz, the raw materials used in Noway's ferro-alloy industries are imported, while their export make Norway a leading supplier in Europe. Other important industries based on raw material imports, cheap hydro power and export markets are copper, nickel and zinc refining and pig iron and steel production in electro-furnace processes. Furthermore, magnesium refining (from sea-water) and dolomite and rockwool production are important electro-process industries that depend almost entirely on export markets.

Canada

Even more impressive is the Canadian record. Canada's 1962 magnesium production of 8,200 tons made it the world's fourth largest producer after the United States, the USSR and Norway.[10] The 1962 silicon carbide and fused aluminum oxide capacity of Canadian plants accounted for over 65 per cent and about 90 per cent of the total combined U.S.-Canadian production capacities respectively; almost the entire output of the Canadian plants was exported to the United States.[11] In addition Canada is an important producer of phosphate fertilizers,[12] ferro-alloys, electrolytic zinc[13] and other electro-metals and chemicals. Much of the output of these industries is exported.

But by far the most important electro-process industry that came into being as a result of the availability of low-cost hydro

[10] Frank B. Fulkerson and Jerry J. Gray, *The Magnesium Industry and Its Relation to the Pacific Northwest* (Portland, Oregon, Bonneville Power Administration, 1965), Table 7.
[11] These two materials are the basic compounds for the manufacture of artificial abrasives. Data from: N. S. Petersen and W. N. Hale, *op. cit.*, pp. 7 and 8.
[12] The major producers are the Consolidated Mining and Smelting plants at Trail and Kimberley, B.C. which utilize phosphate rocks imported from U.S. mines in Idaho and Montana and hydro power from company-owned powerplants. In turn Cominco sells much of its phosphate fertilizers in midwestern U.S. markets. Data from: Norman S. Petersen, *op. cit.*, p. 18.
[13] The Consolidated Mining and Smelting Company's electrolytic zinc smelter at Trail ranks with Anaconda's plant at Great Falls, Mon. as the largest in the world.

power is Canada's aluminum industry. Canada ranks second in the world as a producer of primary aluminum. All of the basic raw material, bauxite or alumina, must be imported, while most of the output is exported. Table I shows plant locations and capacities. All of them obtain their electric energy from company-owned hydro plants. All of them are located at tide water, allowing easy access for raw material supplies on the one hand and metal shipments to distant markets on the other. In 1965, 707,512 short tons, or about 84 per cent of the total production of 840,348 tons were exported.[14] This is in sharp contrast to the U.S. industry which produces mainly for the domestic market.[15] The almost exclusive raison d'etre for Canada's aluminum industry, therefore, is low-cost hydro power in close vicinity to tidewater locations.

TABLE I. SOURCE OF ELECTRIC POWER FOR CANADIAN PRIMARY ALUMINUM PLANTS AS OF DECEMBER 31, 1964*

Name of Company	Location	Capacity Short Tons	Source of Power and Ownership
Aluminum Co. of Canada	Arvida, P.Q.	373,000	Hydro-Alcan
	Isle Maligne, P.Q.	115,000	Hydro-Alcan
	Shawinigan, P.Q.	70,000	Hydro-Alcan/ Quebec
	Kitimat, B.C.	212,000	Hydro-Alcan
Chryslum Ltd. (leased from Alcan)	Beauharnois, P.Q.	38,000	Hydro-Alcan
Canadian British Aluminum Co.	Baie Comeau, P.Q.	99,000	Hydro-CBA (Manicouagan Power Co.)

What we must conclude from these past developments in Canada, in the United States and elsewhere is that the availability of favourable hydro-sites has strongly influenced the locational decision of major electro-process industries. These industries have moved to areas far from sources of raw materials and far from markets. But today most of the accessible low-cost power sites in the United States and in other industrial western nations have already been utilized. On the North American Continent there are only a few areas left, mainly in northern Canada and in Alaska, where undeveloped sites

---

* Ivan Black and Samuel Moment, *op. cit.*, Table 44.
[14] Dominion Bureau of Statistics, *Canada Yearbook 1967* (Ottawa), p. 565.
[15] In 1965, for example, total U.S. primary metal production amounted to 2,754,500 short tons of which only 286,850 tons (in ingot and mill-shapes) were exported, while net imports of primary metal amounted to 527,500 tons. Data from: Aluminum Association, *Aluminum Statistical Review 1966* (New York, July, 1967).

still exist. Much of the unexploited hydro potential of the world lies in underdeveloped countries, in South America, in Asia, and in Africa. Does that mean that in the future power-intensive industries will migrate to these areas? To answer this question we have to investigate the effects of power cost on total production costs on the one hand, and the costs of power production by means other than hydro power on the other. However, before we can turn to this issue let us quickly pinpoint the areas where potential hydro resources still await development.

II.
UNDEVELOPED HYDRO RESOURCES

United States Mainland

According to the 1964 National Power Survey a potential total of some 28,212 megawatts of installed hydro-electric generator capacity could still be developed in the United States. This compares to a 1964 existing capacity of 50,309 megawatts.[16] About forty per cent of the projected capacity is located in the Pacific Northwest. While these figures might sound impressive it should be noted that, according to the same source, the total existing and projected U.S. hydro capacity would account for only fifteen per cent of the country's total generating capacity needs for 1980. Furthermore, as a result of rapid increases in construction costs, an expected substantial upward revision in applicable interest rates for federally financed projects[17] and the decreased costs for energy from thermal power-plants much of the projected capacity may never materialize. Even under the more favourable 1964 conditions many of the proposed sites were marginal in economic terms; few, if any, could have been classified as low-cost sources of power.

Alaska

Alaska is one of the few remaining regions on this Continent that still contain large, undeveloped hydro power resources. The

---

[16] Federal Power Commission, *National Power Survey 1964 Part I* (Washington, October, 1964), pp. 99 and 113.

[17] Interest rates applied to federal water resources projects ranged from a low of 2.5% in 1952 to a high of $3\frac{1}{8}$% in 1967. However, in his January, 1968 budget proposal President Johnson directed the federal water resources agencies to develop "a more appropriate rate" — "that will be related to the average estimated current cost to the Treasury of long-term borrowing". This will probably mean that applicable interest rates will increase to about $4\frac{1}{2}$%. For a typical hydro project with a fifty year repayment period this would mean a cost increase of between 25 and 30% which would render many of the proposed federal hydro projects uneconomical.

total estimated potential has been estimated at 17,400 megawatts.[18] Remoteness of location and lack of internal Alaskan power markets have so far prevented the development of any of the larger projects. Only recently the U.S. Department of Interior turned down the well-publicized Rampart Dam proposal as uneconomical.[19] There may be some hope that the Yukon-Taiya project could come into being provided the highly uncertain construction cost estimates can be confirmed and U.S.-Canadian co-operation secured.[20]

Canada

Canada as a whole has still substantial undeveloped hydro power resources available. Table II lists estimated undeveloped and installed generator capacities by province. It is unlikely that all of the existing potential will ever be developed since some of the rivers lack adequate sites for generating stations or storage facilities, whereas at others the construction of hydro dams would interfere with valuable fisheries or recreational resources.

In the Maritimes most of the potential sites would yield only moderate to high-priced energy. The one notable exception is the Churchill Falls Project in Labrador on which construction has recently started. Located some 750 miles north-east of Montreal the projected installed generator capacity of 4,500 megawatts and its firm energy output of 34 billion kilowatt-hours annually will make it the largest single hydro project on the Continent. Site conditions are exceptionally favourable; it is estimated that average energy costs will be in the two mills per kilowatt-hour range.[21]

---

18 The mill-rates for all projects are based on 1964 construction costs, a federal financing rate of 3%, a repayment period of fifty years and the assumption of rapid industrial load growth in Alaska or a transmission intertie to southern power markets. All data except for Yukon-Taiya from: Gunter Schramm, *The Role of Low-Cost Power in Economic Development. A Case Study: Alaska,* unpublished doctoral dissertation, The University of Michigan, Ann Arbor, 1967, Tables 8 and 9. Yukon-Taiya data from: Gunter Schramm, *Annals of Regional Science,* Vol. II (1968) (forthcoming).
19 U.S. Department of the Interior, *Alaska Natural Resources and the Rampart Project* (Washington, June 15, 1967).
20 The Yukon-Taiya project would consist of a diversion of the flow of Upper Yukon tributaries through the coastal mountains to the valley floor below. The most favourable powerplant site would be located in Alaska while streamflow and storage sites would be almost entirely in Canada.
21 These cost estimates have never been officially confirmed. It is known, however, that the negotiated sales price to Quebec Hydro is very low although subject to various escalator and contingency clauses. One source has estimated that the sales price of energy delivered at the Quebec-Labrador border is about 2.45 mills/kwh. See W. R. Derrick Sewell, "The Churchill Falls Project", *Water Power,* London, England, Vol. 19, no. 3 (March, 1967), p. 101.

TABLE II. WATER RESOURCES, BY PROVINCE, AS AT JANUARY 1, 1966*

Province or Territory	Undeveloped Water Power Available continuous power at 88% efficiency and Arithmetic Mean Flow**	Developed Water Power Installed Generating Capacity
	megawatt	megawatt
Newfoundland	4,871	400
Prince Edward Island	2	—
Nova Scotia	165	143
New Brunswick	497	262
Quebec	32,500	10,339
Ontario	1,663	6,064
Manitoba	5,853	1,074
Saskatchewan	1,559	320
Alberta	4,866	445
British Columbia	24,665	2,616
Yukon Territory	5,689	28
Northwest Territories	3,322	35
CANADA	83,652	21,792

* Dominion Bureau of Statistics, *Canada Yearbook* 1967, p. 638.
** Installed generator capacity may exceed estimated continuous power at mean flow if storage is provided and generators operate at less than 100 per cent load factors.

Quebec has still large reserves of undeveloped hydro resources available. However, the more favourable sites have already been developed and additional installations can only be made at increasing costs. This is one of the reasons why the provincially owned Quebec Hydro has decided to defer further major construction projects for the time being. Instead it has contracted to purchase almost the entire output of Churchill Falls in order to satisfy increasing power demands in the coming decade.

Most of Ontario's available hydro potential has already been developed. In the three Prairie provinces the most favourable development appears to be the Nelson-Churchill project in northern Manitoba. Consisting of a number of plants along the Nelson River and along the planned Churchill River diversion route the ultimate capacity of the various sites has been estimated at about 6,000 megawatts at an eighty per cent load factor.[22] At site energy costs are

22 D. M. Stephens, "The Nelson River Power Development and Its Relation to Long-Term Water Resources Management in the Saskatchewan-Nelson Basin", paper delivered to the *80th Annual General and Professional Meeting of the Engineering Institute of Canada*, Winnipeg (May 25, 1966), mimeo, p. 4.

estimated to be about two mills per kilowatt-hour, whereas transmission costs to the vicinity of Winnipeg are claimed to be between 1.2 to 1.3 mills/kwh.[23]

British Columbia contains some of the largest and most favourable undeveloped hydro sites on the Continent. Conservative estimates place the existing potential at 24,665 megawatts, but some provincial authorities have stated that they may well be in excess of 100,000 megawatts.[24] At the present time the first stage of the Peace River power project is nearing completion. The ultimate capacity of the Peace is estimated at 3,700 megawatts. Energy from the project will be delivered to Vancouver at slightly more than four mills per kilowatt-hour. Also completed or under construction are three storage dams at the Canadian section of the Columbia River system. This development will ultimately support the installation of some 4,400 megawatts of generating capacity at Mica Creek and several downstream plants. Early estimates claimed that average at site energy costs of all Columbia installations would be two mills per kilowatt-hour or less.[25] The rapid increase in construction costs experienced on the projects, however, make these forecasts somewhat doubtful. By far the largest known hydro potential in the provinces is represented by the Fraser River and its tributaries. There are a number of exceptionally favourable dam sites at the lower reach of the Fraser. However, the existence of a valuable salmon fishery has so far precluded any plans for development. In the North-West the potential of the Nechako River has been partially harnessed by diverting it through the coastal mountains to supply the Alcan-owned Kemano power-plant. The presently installed capacity at Kemano is 707 megawatts. Drilling of another diversion tunnel would permit installation of another 550 megawatts. This, in turn, would permit the expansion of the Kitimat aluminum smelter to its ultimate design capacity of 550,000 tons of aluminum ingots per year.[26]

---

[23] Administrative Committee, Nelson River Board, *Report to the Programming Board*, Winnipeg (February 6, 1964), Table 4.

[24] Ray Williston, British Columbia Minister of Water Resources as reported in the *Financial Post*, Toronto (June 3, 1967), p. 5.

[25] B.C. Hydro and Power Authority Information Services, *Columbia River Development*, Vancouver (May 3, 1965), p. 14.

[26] While official figures apparently have never been published, one source suggests that the power costs to the smelter might be as low as 1.7 mills/kwh for the one-tunnel operation. The incremental costs for bringing the power project to its ultimate capacity are estimated at 2.1 to 2.6 mills. From: Ivan Bloch and Ass., *Background Papers for the Resources and Development Corporation, Market for Rampart Power, Yukon River, Alaska*, New York (1962).

Hydro Resources Outside of the United States and Canada

Most of the existing hydro capacity in the industrialized free-world nations outside of the North American Continent have already been utilized. But there exist exceedingly large, untapped potentials in many of the underdeveloped nations of the world. Table III lists estimated capacities in a number of regions or countries that are particularly well-endowed.

By far the largest potentials are located in tropical Africa. The Congo River alone has an estimated power potential at Q95 of more than 100,000 megawatts, which is greater than the combined capacity of all United States (including Alaska) and Canadian rivers combined. Engineering studies have estimated that large blocks of this power could be developed at costs of less than one mill per kilowatt-hour.[27]

TABLE III. ESTIMATED GROSS THEORETICAL POTENTIAL AT Q95* AND INSTALLED HYDRO-ELECTRIC CAPACITY IN VARIOUS REGIONS OF THE WORLD**

Area or Country	Estimated Gross Theoretical Potential Megawatt	Installed Capacity Megawatt
Central America	12,100	2,090
South America	50,750	6,865
Africa	176,677	3,185
India and Pakistan	37,560	2,796
Burma, Vietnam & Thailand	11,250	38
Indonesia	20,875	210
New Zealand	3,750	1,550
Papua	1,100	3

* Q95 refers to the power equivalent of flow available 95% of the time (i.e., flow availability without any storage).

** Data from Sterling Brubaker, *Trends in the World Aluminum Industry,* Johns Hopkins Press, Baltimore, 1967, Table 21.

However, owing to the political unrest in most of these areas and the very large capital requirements for hydro power and subsequent industrial developments few of these potential projects have been developed or are likely to be developed in the near future. The recurring hope of many of these hydro-rich countries that power-intensive electro-process industries would move to these sites has not materialized so far. Up to the present only three medium-sized export oriented aluminum smelters have been built in under-

[27] For an excellent and detailed discussion of the power potentials of the various countries of the world see Ivan Bloch and Samuel Moment, *op. cit.,* Chapter VI, pp. 139-175.

developed countries of the world.[28] As we will see below, not many are likely to follow for quite some time to come.

III
ELECTRICITY AS A FACTOR INPUT TO INDUSTRIAL PRODUCTION

Importance to Industry in General

Modern industry would be unthinkable without electricity. It feeds communication systems, electronic equipment, lighting fixtures and heating facilities; it is the major source of inplant motive power for production machinery; without it there could be no electro-process industry. Yet, while its use is all-pervasive, in most activities its share of overall production costs is surprisingly small. Table IV lists a number of major industries and their expenditures on fuel and electricity as a percentage of sales revenue for manufactured goods. As can be seen from column 3 in eleven of the twenty industries listed this percentage is less than one. For five others it is less than two and for only four industrial groups, papers and allied products, primary metal, non-metallic minerals and chemical and chemical products does it range from two to slightly over six percent.[29] Industry in general, of course, will not be insensitive to energy costs since substantial changes in the latter could have significant effects on profits. A comparison of pre-tax profits after depreciation and costs of fuel and electricity (columns 2 and 3) clearly shows that this holds even for industries with modest energy requirements. However, while there are significant variations in industry by industry percentage shares of energy costs between provinces it is safe to conclude that for most manufacturing activities these regional differences will have little effect on locational decisions. Factors such as costs and availability of raw materials and labor and transportation costs to markets will be more important determinants of plant locations.

---

28 These three smelters are a 57,000 ton annual capacity French owned smelter in Cameroun, the 165,000 ton Kaiser-Reynold Volta River smelter in Ghana and the 66,000 ton Alcoa smelter in Surinam. In addition, there are a number of aluminum plants in Mexico, Venezuela, Brazil, South Africa, Taiwan and India. However, the latter are mostly small-scale, high-cost producers that supply mainly domestic markets. For more details see *ibid.*, Chapter III.

29 The various percentages shown will not accurately indicate the importance of electricity as an input factor. Fuel requirements, for some industries or production processes, will be more important than electricity. Furthermore, the regional composition of industries that make up the broad industrial classifications will vary. Since electric energy requirements for individual processes vary by very large amounts the regional distribution of specific activities will have an important influence on the percentages shown for individual provinces.

TABLE IV. COSTS OF FUEL AND ELECTRICITY AS A PERCENTAGE OF THE VALUE OF SHIPMENTS OF GOODS OF OWN MANUFACTURE, BY PROVINCE, 1964*

Industry	Pre-tax Net Profits as a Percentage of Sales** Canada	Cost of Fuel and Electricity as Percentage of Value of Output											
		Canada	Nfld.	P.E.I.	N.S.	N.B.	Que.	Ont.	Man.	Sask.	Alta.	B.C.	Yukon & N.W.T.
Foods & Beverage	5.20	1.34	2.42	1.88	1.90	1.67	1.28	1.37	1.28	1.35	.94	1.29	5.38
Tobacco Products	—	.37	—	—	—	—	.34	.41	—	—	—	—	—
Rubber	5.71	1.48	—	—	—	—	.56	1.49	.59	—	—	3.16	—
Leather	—	.76	—	—	—	—	—	.93	.77	—	—	.98	—
Textile	2.16	1.48	—	—	—	—	1.45	1.52	—	.55	1.61	1.21	—
Knitting	—	.76	—	—	—	—	.68	.86	—	—	—	—	—
Clothing	—	.33	—	—	1.90	—	.32	.35	.34	.43	.24	.47	—
Wood	4.28	1.98	4.28	—	2.62	2.58	1.94	1.77	2.24	2.97	3.13	1.89	3.84
Furniture & Fixtures	—	.97	—	2.80	1.48	—	1.04	.92	.92	1.24	.98	.86	—
Paper & Allied Ind.	4.97	5.50	7.89	—	5.82	7.99	6.06	4.42	3.85	4.45	3.60	4.89	—
Printing, Publishing & A.I.	8.20	.72	2.09	—	1.16	1.29	.63	.69	.84	1.27	.86	.79	—
Primary Metal	5.75	4.17	—	—	—	3.15	4.67	3.86	10.75	—	2.12	3.04	—
Metal Fabricating	5.07	1.14	—	—	2.71	1.46	1.04	1.18	1.08	.92	.89	1.08	—
Machinery	7.02	.83	—	—	2.76	—	.71	.77	.73	1.09	1.43	.87	—
Transportation Equipment	3.71	.69	1.42	1.02	1.43	—	.92	.63	1.52	—	.99	.72	—
Electrical Products	2.95	.81	—	—	—	1.76	.84	.80	.86	—	.70	.78	—
Non-metallic Mineral	4.35	6.06	6.96	4.89	8.14	9.76	6.33	6.00	7.08	6.01	4.06	6.36	—
Petroleum & Coal Prod.	5.18	.88	—	—	—	—	.72	.77	.90	1.14	1.55	1.13	—
Chemical & Chem. Prod.	7.59	3.54	—	.65	1.86	5.47	2.93	3.69	.94	3.47	4.94	4.39	—
Miscellaneous Mfg.	5.85	.96	—	—	3.52	1.31	—	.91	1.08	1.18	1.32	1.44	—

* Calculated from *D.B.S. Canada Yearbook 1967*, tables 8, 9, pp. 681-95.

** Calculated from D.B.S., Business Finance Division, *Corporate Profits, 4th Quarter, 1967*, Cat. No. 61-003. Data refer to 1964 totals.

TABLE V. ELECTRIC ENERGY REQUIREMENTS PER TON OF OUTPUT
AND VALUE OF OUTPUT BY PRODUCT

Product	Electric Energy Required Per Ton of Output	Value of Output Per Ton
Titanium Sponge[c]	30,000	2,740.00[b]
Ferronickel 55%[f]	24,000	827.75[b]
Magnesium Electrolytic Process	19,000	745.00[a]
Aluminum[e]	15,000	490.00[a]
Elemental Phosphorus[i]	13,000	356.00[a]
Silicon Metal[f]	13,000	310.00[a]
Magnesium Silicothermic Process[d]	12,000	745.00[a]
Ferro-Silicon 75%[f]	10,000	310.00[a]
Ferro-Silicon 50%[f]	6,000	280.00[a]
Electrolytic Zinc[g]	3,600	333.20[b]
Silico-manganese[f]	3,600	188.00[b]
Ferro-manganese[f]	3,000	170.00[b]
Chlorine & Caustic Soda[h]	1,500	60.55[b]
Chemical Pulp[j]	1,000	114.80[b]

[a] delivered price.

[b] price f.o.b. plant.

[c] Frank B. Fulkerson & Jerry J. Gray, *The Titanium Industries and Their Relation to the Pacific Northwest*, Bonneville Power Administration, Portland, Oregon, 1964, 1962 prices.

[d] Frank B. Fulkerson & Jerry J. Gray, *The Magnesium Industry and Its Relation to the Pacific Northwest*, Bonneville Power Administration, Portland, Oregon, 1965, 1963 prices.

[e] Sterling Brubaker, op. cit. and The Aluminum Association, op. cit. 1965/66 prices.

[f] Gury A. Kingston & Robert A. Miller, *Alloy Metals Outlook in the Pacific Northwest*, Bonneville Power Administration, Portland, Oregon, 1966, 1963 prices.

[g] Richard W. Knostman & Gary A. Kingston, *Copper, Lead and Zinc Industries in the Pacific Northwest*, Bonneville Power Administration, Portland, Oregon, 1966, 1962 prices.

[h] Chlorine & Caustic Soda are joint products of the same electrolytic process. For each 2,000 lbs. of chlorine 2,285 lbs. of caustic soda are produced. Chlorine sells for $61.00 and caustic soda for $60.00 per ton, delivered.

[i] Norman S. Petersen. The f.o.b. sales price has been estimated here on the basis of production costs provided by Petersen, on the assumption of an 85% capacity utilization, a 15% pre-tax rate of return on capital investment and a 13% allowance to cover depreciation, delivery costs and miscellaneous expenditures, 1963 prices.

[j] DBS, *Canada Yearbook* 1967, p. 520 and U.S. Dep. of the Interior, *Rampart Project, Field Report*, p. 663.

Power-Intensive Industries

Let us turn, therefore, to the numerically small, but in terms of overall output important group of industries in which electricity as an input appears to play a much larger role than in others.[30] Most of these "power-intensive" industries utilize electricity for the purpose of smelting, refining or electrolytical processes. Only one of the four significant groups of Table IV, pulp and paper, does not fall into these use-classifications. While electric power requirements for machinery such as debarkers, chippers and others are large, the main reason for the significance of pulp and paper are the heavy non-electric fuel requirements in that industry.[31] Furthermore, the grouping "pulp and paper" is much more homogeneous than the other three industrial classifications which include many specific manufacturing activities that use relatively little electricity. A blast furnace steel smelting operation, for example, will utilize only relatively small amounts of electric energy compared to other inputs, while an all-electric ferro-nickel furnace will have large power requirements indeed. What we have to do, then, is to isolate those particular industrial processes in which electricity plays a major role.

A number of these processes or industries have been listed in Table V which shows electric energy requirements per ton of output and the value of output per ton.[32] Titanium sponge, a metal used for high-tensile, heat resistant sheeting in supersonic aircraft and similar applications leads the list with 30,000 kilowatt-hours per ton. It is followed with 24,000 kilowatt-hours by ferro-nickel, one of the group of ferro-alloys that are used in the production of specialty steels. Electrolytic production of magnesium requires 19,000, aluminum 15,000, elemental phosphorus 13,000 and 75 per cent ferro-silicon 10,000 kilowatt-hours. Compared to these materials the 1,500 kilowatt-hours for chlorine and caustic soda and the 1,000 kilowatt-hours for chemical pulp look almost insignificant. This impression can be misleading, however. What is important is not so much the energy input per unit of output but the relation-

---

[30] These four industries, papers and allied products, primary metal, non-metallic minerals and chemicals and chemical products accounted for about 25.8% of the value of Canada's 1964 industrial production.

[31] Unfortunately, no separate statistical data for electricity are available for Canada.

[32] This list is not exhaustive, but contains only a number of the more prominent production processes for which data were available. Some of the more interesting recent additions to this group are, for example, heavy water production and the manufacture of plutonium and enriched uranium fuels.

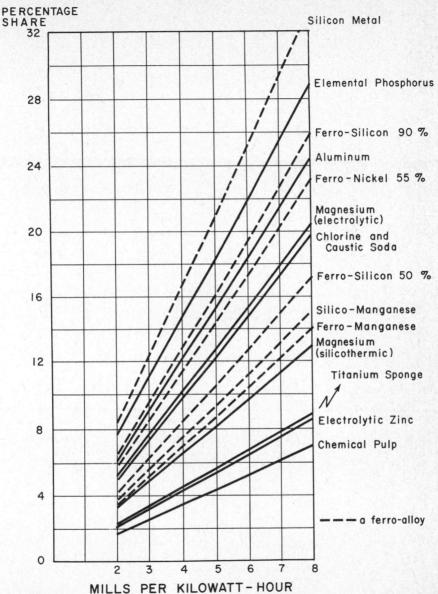

Figure 1.

ship of the costs of energy to the costs of other inputs (or the value of the finished product).

These input-output cost relationships have been shown in Figure 1 which, for the products listed in Table V, shows the percentage

TABLE VI. 1961 AND PROJECTED 1985 PRODUCTION OF VARIOUS ELECTRO-PROCESS METALS AND MINERALS[a]

Product	Area	Major Uses	1961 Production short tons	1985 Estimated Production short tons	1985 Estimated Value of Output in base year prices h $'000	Average Growth Rate per cent
Aluminum	Free World Total	bldg. products, transportation, electrical, consumer durables	4,698,000[c]	high 24,552,500 low 16,394,000	12,030,725 8,033,060	7[d] 6[d]
Magnesium	Free World Total	aluminum alloys, military aircraft	80,000	n.a.	n.a.	
	U.S.A.		45,533	350,000	260,750	8¾
Titanium Sponge	Free World	supersonic aircraft, missiles, submarines	9,800	100,000	2,740,000	10¼
Ferro-Alloys	U.S.A.	steel ingots, steel and iron casting	1,860,000	2,722,000		1¾[e]
Chlorine	U.S.A.	chemical industry, pulp & paper, water & sewage plants	4,600,000	11,500,000	701,500	4½[f]
Caustic Soda	U.S.A.	chemical industry, pulp & paper	4,900,000	12,250,000	735,000	4½[f]
Special High Grade Slab Zinc[g]	U.S.A.	die casting, galvanizing, brass	319,777	840,300	279,820	4¼
Elemental Phosphorus	U.S.A.	fertilizers, detergents, metal cleaning	432,000	1,288,000	458,564	4¾

a Where not mentioned otherwise production and projections are from sources listed in Table V.
b Area to which 1961 and 1985 production data refers to.
c The Aluminum Assn., op. cit.
d Sterling Brubaker, op. cit., p. 73; the 7% growth rate is Brubaker's own estimate; the 6% rate is from an earlier United Nations study.
e Based on the projected U.S. growth rate for primary steel production.
f Growth rate estimated from projected regional growth rate in the Pacific Northwest.
g About 74% of special high grade slab zinc was produced by the electrolytic method.
h Base years as stated in Table V.

share of electric energy costs on the value of output for a range from two to eight mills per kilowatt-hour.[33] The interpretation of the graph is simple; the more sensitive the production process to power costs the steeper the graph. A word of caution is necessary: the relationships shown are highly simplified. For some products alternative production processes with different electric energy inputs are available; for magnesium, for example, two such processes have been shown. Furthermore, even for given manufacturing methods power requirements are not immutable. Within certain limits, substitutions for electricity (more labor or more capital or more raw material inputs) are always feasible. Finally, technological improvements that result in reduced energy requirements are common. In the production of aluminum, for example, average power requirements per ton of metal have been reduced from over 20,000 kilowatt-hours in World War II plants to some 15,000 kilowatt-hours in the most modern plants today. This process is likely to continue.

Let us briefly discuss the importance of energy costs as a factor influencing plant locations for the various products shown. To put their importance into perspective Table VI has been added which shows major use categories, 1961 and projected 1985 production figures, output values and the estimated average annual growth rates for this 24 year period.

---

33 This range covers the likely variation in electric energy costs that would have faced power-intensive industries in the post-World War II period. However, average industrial costs (for all industries) are usually higher. For customers of the Ontario Power Commission, for example, average industrial rates charged in 1966 were slightly less than 10 mills per kwh (Toronto 9.1, Waterloo 9.6, Peterborough 7.6 mills) although for some isolated communities they were as high as 40.0 mills (Westport). Rates are a function of total demand and annual load factors of individual customers. Data from: The Hydro-Electric Power Commission of Ontario, *59th Annual Report for the Year 1966*, Toronto (May, 1967), Statement D, pp. 237-257.

Chemical Pulp

As we can see from the graphical presentation in Figure 1. chemical pulp is the least power sensitive product in the group. At eight mills electricity accounts for 6.96 per cent of sales prices f.o.b. mill. While this is not insignificant it is likely that transportation costs of pulpwood to a plant will be a much more important determinant of the location of a pulpmill.

Titanium Sponge

Surprisingly, the most power-intensive material, titanium, proves to be one of the least sensitive to variations in power costs. Even at eight mills energy costs account for only 10.9 per cent of the value of the metal. Interestingly enough, however, two of the major inputs of titanium production, magnesium and chlorine[34] also require large inputs of electric energy; therefore it is likely that a new titanium producer would attempt to locate close to sources of supplies of these two inputs since their transportation costs, particularly those for chlorine, are high. A location with favourable power costs that has attracted magnesium and chlorine production may, as a result, be a particularly favourable location for a titanium producer as well.

Ferro-Alloys

The material most sensitive to energy costs is silicon metal. However, plants that produce this alloy usually produce a number of other ferro-alloys as well. As a result total average energy requirements per unit of combined output and, hence, sensitivity to energy costs will be considerably lower. Furthermore, most of the ferro-alloys are by-products of various metal smelting and chemical manufacturing operations. Quantities produced in individual plants are small. For these reasons electric energy costs will have only a relatively minor effect on plant locations. This is born out by a survey of U.S. plants which shows that most ferro-alloy plants are located in the eastern United States where power costs (at least in the past) were moderately high.

Zinc

Zinc occupies a special position because there are two distinct smelting processes in use, the electrolytic and the distillation process. The 3,600 kilowatt-hours per ton shown in Table V apply only

[34] The major input requirements for the production of 1 ton of titanium sponge are: Rutile or titanium slag (the basic raw material) 2½ tons, magnesium 1 ton, chlorine 3 tons and insert gas 1,800 cubic feet. Data from: Frank B. Fulkerson and Jerry J. Gray, *The Titanium Industries, op. cit.,* p. 14.

to the former; for the latter power requirements are small. Of the eighty primary zinc smelters in the world outside of Russia thirty-two recover the metal by electrolysis. While there are some technical advantages to electro-smelting[35] it is unlikely that the process would be used in areas where power costs are high. Availability and location of large mines and orebodies will be the determining factors for smelter locations.

Chlorine and Caustic Soda

In terms of quantities produced the joint products of chlorine and caustic soda are far more important than any other electro-process metal or mineral. They are quite sensitive to variations in electric energy costs. At eight mills per kilowatt-hour energy costs would amount to almost twenty per cent of the delivered price. In addition, however, the weight/price ratio of both materials is much higher than that for any other electro-process material. As a result they are much more sensitive to freight charges (both materials must be shipped in special corrosion resistant tank cars). For example, chlorine shipping costs between Portland and Eugene, Oregon are $8.00 per ton whereas between Portland and Los Angeles they amount to $20.20 while the delivered price of $61.00 per ton is the same at both locations.[36] By comparison energy costs would amount to $4.50 at three mills or $12.00 at eight mills per kilowatt-hour. Even if the costs of electricity at a particular location are extremely low in comparison to other areas, therefore, freight charges will restrict chlorine and caustic soda producers to limited regional markets.

Phosphorus

The same conclusions do not hold for elemental phosphorus despite the fact that shipping costs per ton over similar distances are usually higher than for chlorine or caustic soda. The reason is, of course, the much higher value of phosphorus which has been estimated here at $356.00 per ton. What is important, however, is a favourable plant location with respect to phosphate rock deposits since 10.5 tons of the latter are needed to produce one ton of elemental phosphorous.[37] Such a location may be either a plant at tidewater which could take advantage of low ocean freight

---

[35] Electrolysis lends itself more readily to the production of special high grade zinc (zinc with a purity of 99.99% and better); this grade has seen the most rapid growth in demand since 1954.

[36] Donald J. Morey, *op. cit.*, p. 50.

[37] Other important inputs are 1.5 tons of coke and 1.4 tons of silica. Data from: Norman S. Petersen, *op. cit.*, p. 34.

rates from major rock supply sources such as Florida, North Africa or the Middle East or, on the North American Continent, a location within reasonable rail shipping distance from the major deposits in Florida, Tennessee or the Western U.S. states. Representative rail shipping charges are, for example, $9.19 per long ton from Soda Springs, Idaho to Kimberley, B.C. or $19.44 from Florida to Bismarck, North Dakota.[38] Freight charges, therefore, could vary from virtually zero (for a plant adjacent to a phosphate rock deposit) to as much as $200.00. By comparison, energy costs per ton of phosphorus could range from a low of $26.00 at two mills to $104.00 at eight mills. As a result, a favourable location with respect to a source of raw material will have a more important effect on plant location than variations in energy costs despite the fact that phosphorus is more sensitive to changes in the latter than almost any other product.

Magnesium

Magnesium, which in terms of projected demand growth ranks second only to titanium has usually been produced by either of two distinct processes. Both are power-intensive, but the so-called silicothermic process less so than the electrolytic method. In the silicothermic process dolomite serves as the basic raw material. Since 14.41 tons of the latter are needed to produce one ton of magnesium plants must locate close to the mineral source since freight charges would be prohibitive otherwise. The energy demand of 12,218 kilowatt-hours even for this process is still substantial. However, of this some 11,000 kilowatt-hours are needed in the production of ferro-silicon which serves as an intermediary in the production process. In areas where energy costs are high ferro-silicon could be brought in from elsewhere. One of the major disadvantages of the process is its high labor content; seventy man-hours per ton of magnesium are needed as against thirty hours for the electrolytic process.[39] Mainly for this reason magnesium production by the silicothermic process has been discontinued in the United States after the end of World War II; today it is used only in countries such as Great Britain where power costs are high. The electrolytic process uses seawater as the basic raw material source. Warmwater locations with their higher mineral concentration are somewhat more suitable than colder, northern waters. Another major

---

[38] *Ibid.*, Table 13.
[39] Frank B. Fulkerson and Jerry J. Gray, *The Magnesium Industry, op. cit.*, Tables 3 and 4.

input is salt; some eight tons are required per ton of magnesium.[40] Energy requirements, at 19,000 kilowatt-hours, are very high. Major locational determinants, therefore, are a good source of undiluted, clean seawater, cheap electric energy and access to a large low-cost source of salt.

Aluminum

This leaves aluminum which in almost every respect—in terms of quantities produced, value of output and sensitivity to power costs—is the most important electro-process product known. At a price of eight mills per kilowatt-hour the costs of electricity would amount to almost 25 per cent of the delivered price of the metal. The basic raw material, bauxite or alumina, must be brought in from distant tropical or southern hemisphere countries. No wonder, then, that in the past low energy costs and access to tidewater locations were generally the two most important determinants of smelter locations.[41]

Conclusion

What we can conclude from the foregoing discussion is that for practically all electro-process products the cost of electric energy is an important determinant of plant locations. Nevertheless, for many of them transportation costs, either for raw materials or for finished products, are even more significant. While such producers will try to locate in areas where both energy and transportation costs can be minimized, in many cases they will accept moderate to high power rates in order to escape the penalty of prohibitive freight charges. Any attempt to determine most likely plant locations for specific processes will have to be based on more than just a comparison of power costs. In most cases a whole series of factors will mutually determine the best potential location for a plant.

---

40 In addition, the process requires some 3.2 tons of lime (which could be produced from limestone, dolomite or oystershells), 3 tons of chlorine, 3.4 tons of hydrochloric acid and 172 mega-cubic feet of natural gas. Fixed capital costs of $1,200 per annual ton of capacity are lower than the estimated $1,515 for a silico thermic plant. *Ibid.*

41 However, under certain circumstances shipping costs of metal to markets may be higher than shipping costs of bauxite or alumina to a plant. For this reason some aluminum smelters have been built close to major metal consuming markets despite the fact that energy costs in these areas were higher than elsewhere.

IV

Conventional Thermal and Atomic Power Plants

In our introduction we have stated that in the past "low-cost" power meant energy in the range of one to three mills per kilowatt-hour. This is still true today. Until very recently only hydro developments (and then only from particularly favourable sites) could supply energy in that range while alternative means of producing energy were much more costly. This, however, is no longer true today.

In this section we will review the reason why this is so. We will assess the changes that have taken place in conventional thermal and atomic power generating technology and trace their effects on the relative attractiveness of hydro versus thermal power generation. In addition, we will try to evaluate the trends that could affect this relationship in the future.

The Basic Technology of Producing Electricity

Electricity can be produced by a variety of means. However, in order to produce it in the huge quantities required by modern industry only one basic process is economically feasible. This is by driving heavy, rotating electric generators. What is needed, then, is a source of mechanical motive power. The first commercial generator set installed on this Continent was a waterwheel-driven plant by the Rochester Electric Light Company, founded in 1880. In 1882 Edison made history by installing the first steam-driven electric generating plant in New York. Ever since that time falling water or the driving force of high-pressure steam have been the major sources of mechanical energy that turned the generators which fed the ever growing demands for electric power.[42]

Hydropower has three advantages. First of all, the energy content of falling water is essentially costless, replenished as it is by the never-ending hydrological cycle. Secondly, the mechanical efficiency of hydraulic turbines is very high. Modern turbines utilize something like 88-92 per cent of the gravitational energy content of the water. Thirdly, the energy content of the water can be stored in reservoirs, to be utilized only when needed. But hydropower has also disadvantages. Its supply is limited and plants have to locate where favourable sites exist.

---

[42] Other alternatives are direct-fuel-driven diesel generators or gas turbine sets. However, for both fuel requirements and, hence, operating costs are high so that their utilization is limited to isolated areas or for peaking power purposes.

Steam-driven power plants are more flexible; they can be built almost anywhere provided fuel can be brought to the site and provided a minimum amount of boiler and cooling water can be made available. But in order to produce steam a source of fossil or atomic fuel is needed. Neither of them is costless. Furthermore, the thermal efficiency of steamplants is much lower than the mechanical efficiency of hydraulic turbines. In 1900 thermal efficiencies were as low as five per cent. By 1940 they had reached thirty per cent[43] but this was still low by hydraulic turbine standards. A further disadvantage of thermal power generation is that neither steam nor electricity can be stored in a meaningful way; what is not used while it is being produced is wasted. Thermal plants cannot be turned on and off at a moments notice; when demand fluctuates much of the energy content of the fuel heating the boilers is lost.

Recent Technological Developments

(a) Conventional Thermal Power Generation.

By the late 1940's a steamplant that produced high load factor energy at six to seven mills per kilowatt-hour was considered to be highly efficient. In terms of aluminum production, for example, this meant that a smelter would have had to pay some $114 to $123 per ton of metal, or more than forty per cent of then prevailing delivered metal prices.[44] No wonder that the industry was looking hard for hydro sites that held out the promise of low-cost power.

Since that time, however, important changes have taken place in the field of thermal power generation. Two general trends developed. One was a rapid increase in unit size to reduce capital and operating costs of steam electric power plants. The other was a substantial increase in boiler temperatures and operating pressures to attain greater thermal efficiencies. These factors were highly interrelated. In 1946 the largest boiler on order had a capacity of one million pounds of steam per hour. In 1964 the largest boiler on order, a twin-furnace type, had a generating capacity of over 6.5 million pounds. The largest turbine set ordered in 1946 had a capacity of about 150,000 kilowatt, but by 1962 a one million kilowatt set was under construction.[45] Further factors reducing overall

---

43 Federal Power Commission, *op. cit.*, p. 62.
44 Assuming then prevailing average energy requirements of 19,000 kwh's per ton of aluminum. Average aluminum prices between 1943 and 1947 were US$280.00 per ton. They increased to $294 in 1948, $320 in 1949 and $325 in 1950, the year in which Alcan decided to proceed with the development of the Kitimat smelter in northern British Columbia. Price data from: The Aluminum Association, *op cit.*, p. 47.
45 Federal Power Commission, *op. cit.*, pp. 64-67.

generating costs were the introduction of more efficient coal mining methods and the advent of high-speed, low-cost coal haulage systems. Between 1952 and 1962 average productivity at all types of bituminous coal mines increased from 7.47 to 14.72 tons per manday. At the same time average mine costs decreased from $4.90 to $4.48 per ton.[46]

How substantial the impact of these technological changes were on the costs of thermal power generation can be seen from Table VII.[47] Estimated average energy costs for the three projects listed range from a low of 2.90 mills per kilowatt-hour to a high of 4.16 mills for a private utility plant that would have been built close to a major load center. Compared to the early 1950's these changes represent a reduction in generating costs of some fifty to sixty per cent, a reduction that took place despite the substantial increase in overall price levels that occurred in the same period.

(b) Atomic Power.

While improvements in fossil-fuel power plant technology have had a deep impact on the cost structure of power generation, recent developments in the atomic power field have been ever more dramatic. Many of the fossil-fuel improvements benefit atomic plants because atomic plants are essentially thermal power stations which utilize a different type of fuel. Until the early 1960's most nuclear plants in operation or under construction were relatively small and consequently inefficient because of the high investment-cost/output ratio. As a matter of fact, most of these plants could still be classified as experimental, and almost all of them received, implicitly or explicitly, some form of governmental support.

All this changed, rather drastically, in early 1964 when the Jersey Central Power and Light Company announced an order for a 620,000 kilowatt nuclear powerplant, stating that:

. . . the station is expected to produce electric power at a total cost of less than 4 mills per kilowatt-hour which is appreci-

---

[46] *Ibid.*, Part II, p. 321. The fact that average mine costs did not decrease proportionally to labor productivity increases is mainly the result of two factors: increased use of capital per unit of output on the one hand and labor cost increase (through higher wages) on the other.

[47] It should be noted that none of these three plants were to be built because they were not competitive with nuclear alternatives. However, the cost ranges shown are representative for large, coal-fired plants that are being built today. Canadian cost ranges are similar. For example, Ontario Hydro's 2 million kws (4 turbine-generators of 500,000 kws each) Lambton Generating Station has estimated capital costs of Can. $108.90 per installed kw; this compares favourably with the U.S. $114.00 estimated for the Oyster Creek coal-fired plant. Ontario data from: The Hydro-Electric Power Commission of Ontario, *op. cit.*, p. 61.

TABLE VII. ESTIMATED MILL RATES PER KILOWATT-HOUR, COAL-FIRED STEAM ELECTRIC PLANTS

Project	Year of Estimate	Capacity kw	Pay-out Period Years	Fuel Costs Cents per btu $x\ 10^6$	Rate of Return or Interest	Load Factor %	Costs mills/kwh
Bolsa Island[1]	1965	617,000	30	35.4	3.5	90	4.05
Oyster Creek[2]	1964	620,000	30	26.0	6.3775	60[4]	4.165[5]
Cumberland City[3]	1966	2,206,000	35	18.9	4.5	85	2.90

1 United States Atomic Energy Commission, *Engineering and Economic Feasibility Study for a Combination Nuclear Power-Desalting Plant, Summary,* TID-22330 Vol. III, Reactor Technology, Clearinghouse for Federal Scientific and Technical Information, National Bureau of Standards, U.S. Department of Commerce, Springfield, Virg., Jan., 1966, Table 5-1, Comparison of Fossil- and Nuclear-Fueled Plants. The data refer to a power-only alternative, plant location Southern California.

2 Jersey Central Power & Light Company, *Report on Economic Analysis for Oyster Creek Nuclear Electric Generating Station,* Table 1, p. 21 Feb. 17, 1964. The data refer to the coal-fired alternative at Oyster Creek.

3 Tennessee Valley Authority, Office of Power, *Comparison of Coal-Fired and Nuclear Power Plants for the TVA System,* Chattanooga, Tennessee, June, 1966.

4 Weighted average load factor over life expectancy of plant.

5 Average rate throughout life expectancy of plant.

ably below the expected total cost of power from any other type of station that Jersey could install at this location.[48]

What brought about this sudden change? A nuclear expert, Gale Young, Assistant Director of the Oak Ridge National Laboratory, summed it up in a nutshell:

> The significance of Oyster Creek lies in one thing—*capital cost*. For many years nuclear electric capital costs have been substantially higher than for fossil electric plants, until it had almost come to be accepted as a matter of course that this was fact and would remain fact. The dispelling of this fog has been the great contribution of Oyster Creek. Actually the gain comes from standardization, quantity production, scaling up, simplification, and compaction.[49]

Since then the nuclear power industry has never looked back. On July 1st, 1964, the total installed U.S. nuclear capacity had been 1.074 million kilowatts; in the spring of 1968, not even four years later, ninety plants with a total capacity of 60.8 million kilowatts were either under construction or in operation.[50] This is considerably more than the total existing hydro capacity in the United States and the trend towards more and more nuclear plants is accelerating.

Table VIII lists data for a few representative installations. Their expected generating costs which depend on size, location and type of financing range between 2.37 and 4.04 mills per kilowatt-hour. Considering the fact that nuclear power plants can be built close to major load centers because transportation costs for atomic fuel are negligible this is attractively priced power indeed.[51]

Future Prospects

But what about the future? Will the multiplying demands for uranium fuels not quickly exhaust the rather limited known sources of supply? Will present inflationary cost trends in North America's

[48] Jersey Central Power and Light Company, *op. cit.*, p. 1.
[49] Gale Young, "The Fueling of Nuclear Power Complexes", *Nuclear News* (November, 1964).
[50] Another 10 million kws are expected to be ordered in 1968. When the 1964 National Power Survey was published it projected that 40 million kws of nuclear capacity would be installed in the U.S. by 1980 (N.P.S. Part I, p. 89), while today's projections for 1980 call for a nuclear capacity of some 180 million kws. Data from: *Electrical World* (May 6, 1968), p. 95.
[51] This does not mean that the locating of nuclear plants presents no problems. Safety regulations require considerable distances from inhabited areas; furthermore, large quantities of cooling water are required; these are not easily found because of the danger of thermal pollution to many of North America's already overtaxed and polluted rivers and lakes. Taken together these conditions create considerable difficulties in finding suitable sites for atomic powerplants.

TABLE VIII. PRESENT AND FUTURE NUCLEAR POWERPLANT COST DATA

	Oyster Creek[1]	Diablo[2]	Browns Ferry[3]	1990 Projection[4]
Capacity MW	620	1,060	2,129	2,000+
Capital Costs Dollars/kw	110	n.a.	116	50-100
Load Factor	88-56	90	85	80-90
Energy Costs Mills/kwh	3.42-3.97	4.04	2.37	1.05-2.04

1 Jersey Central Power & Light Company, *Report on Economic Analysis for Oyster Creek Nuclear Electric Generating Station*, Table 1, p. 21. The analysis is based on a declining load factor over the thirty years' life expectancy of the plant.

2 *Electrical World*, February 27, 1967. The plant will be built by Pacific Gas and Electric Company at a site 190 miles south of San Francisco.

3 Tennessee Valley Authority, Office of Power, *Comparison of Coal-Fired and Nuclear Power Plants for the TVA System*, Chattanooga, Tennessee, June, 1966, p. 4.

4 Gale Young, *Oak Ridge Institute on Nuclear Science and World Politics*, "Aspects of Nuclear System Economics", April 12-30, mimeo, p. 37.

manufacturing and construction sectors not take their toll in the building of nuclear power stations, just as they have taken their toll in the construction of hydroplants in recent years?

Both trends are visible at present. Order books of U.S. nuclear plant manufacturers are bulging. Deliveries quoted today are in excess of five years. Considering the various cost escalator clauses built into recent contracts, prices have risen by twenty to thirty per cent compared to only two years ago. Prices for atomic fuels are rising too. Long dormant in the range of $5.50 to $6.50 per pound of natural uranium they are expected to reach eight to ten dollars by the mid 1970's.[52] These price changes affect nuclear energy costs. For example, TVA's recently ordered identical third nuclear unit for the Brown's Ferry Plant will have average generating costs of 2.75 mills compared to the 2.37 mills of the original two units.[53]

These trends towards higher costs will be offset in part by economies to scale. The first Oyster Creek unit had a capacity of 620,000 kilowatts. Today there are sixteen units on order with capacities in excess of one million kilowatts each.[54]

But more fundamental changes are on the horizon. Most of the U.S. nuclear plants under construction now are of the pressurized boiling water type. These types of plants utilize only about two per cent of the total energy content of the enriched uranium fuel. Fuel costs, as a result, are high, amounting to some 1.4 to 1.6 mills per kilowatt-hour.[55] Within a few years graphite, helium-cooled reactors are expected to be on the market. These will allow the utilization of much higher temperatures, resulting in better fuel economies. Forecasts call for total fuel costs in the 0.7 to 0.8 mills per kilowatt-hour range. Farther into the future (most forecasts call for 1980 to 1990) are the so-called "breeder" reactors which have the fascinating characteristic that they produce more fuel than they consume.[56] Sodium cooled breeders are expected to have fuel

---

[52] George White, "Adequate Uranium Foreseen to Fuel Nuclear Power Growth", *Electrical World* (May 6, 1968), p. 84.

[53] *Power* (October, 1967), p. S8.

[54] *Electrical World* (May 6, 1968), p. 96.

[55] These and the following fuel cost data from: *Ibid.*, "Physicist Hans Bethe Views Nuclear Power", pp. 93-94.

[56] It is not possible here to outline the basic principles of various types of nuclear powerplants. For two brief, highly readable accounts see: (1) *Ibid.*, (2) Gale Young, "The Fueling of Nuclear Power Complexes", *Nuclear News* (November, 1964), p. 23 ff. A more detailed, technical account can be found in Gale Young, "Aspects of Nuclear Systems Economics", paper presented at the *Oak Ridge Institute on Nuclear Science and World Politics* (April 12-30, 1965).

costs of 0.5 to 0.7 mills, whereas helium-cooled breeder reactors are expected to have fuel costs of as little as 0.2 mills per kilowatt-hour.[57] Fast "breeder" reactors are more complex than present-generation reactors. Their capital costs, therefore, are likely to be higher. Nevertheless, the nuclear power industry is rather confident that overall generating costs will fall substantially. As can be seen from the last column of Table VIII, this range is expected to be in the one to two mill range, a range which in the past was obtainable only from exceptionally favourable hydropower sites. These are heady prospects; but they are prospects that will also deeply affect the future of presently undeveloped hydropower sites.

Summing Up: Hydro Versus Thermal Power

What we must conclude from the preceding discussion is that the historical cost advantage of hydropower vis a vis other generating methods has been rather drastically reduced. Today there are still a number of very large potential Canadian hydropower sites in existence that could provide at-site energy in the two mill per kilowatt-hour range. This is less than the 3-4½ mills for modern coal-fired stations. It is also less, although by a narrower margin, than the 2.4 to 4.5 mills for modern nuclear plants. But these potential hydro sites are far removed from centers of industry and population. Many of them (and some of them that are being developed now) will have higher delivered energy costs at load centers than the large thermal and nuclear stations now under construction.[58] Fifteen, twenty years ago power-intensive industries found it advantageous to move their plants to sites where cheap hydropower was still available. Today, with generating cost differentials reduced so drastically, these advantages have all but disappeared.

---

[57] The coming of breeder reactors will also solve the threat of any possible uranium shortage. While today's known resources will barely last until the late 1970's, more deposits will undoubtedly be discovered. Bethe estimates that total ultimate world reserves may be in the range of ten million tons; assuming a total world nuclear capacity of 1 billion kws this reserve would last for 125 years; with graphite-helium-cooler reactors it would last for 800 years, whereas with breeder reactors it would be sufficient for 5,000 years. In addition, somewhere in the distant future we are likely to master the technology of fusion reactors. These would utilize deuterium from seawater. There is enough deuterium in existence to power 100 billion kws of fusion-plant capacity for 1 billion years. From: *Electrical World*, "Physicist Hans Bethe Views Nuclear Power", *op. cit.*, p. 94.

[58] At this point the often-heard question may be raised "why even bother with developing more hydro-sites in Canada? Why don't we build nuclear stations instead?". The answer is that, first of all, hydropower stations can be better regulated to suit fluctuating power demands. Furthermore, if their construction costs are estimated correctly (i.e. if likely cost inflation

during construction has been taken into account) once they are built they are less sensitive to price increases because the share of operating and maintenance costs rarely amounts to more than 15 to 20 per cent of total costs. The main reason is, however, that most Canadian generating systems are simply too small. As an editorial in *Power* (July, 1967, p. 93) pointed out: "It has been proven that, to be economical, a nuclear reactor must have a capacity of at least 500 MW." By comparison, the total installed March, 1966 generator capacity of the integrated Manitoba Hydro-Winnipeg Hydro system was 1,183 MW. As a rule of thumb the reserve capacity of a system at any time ought to be about 15%. This means that no single generator unit should be larger than 15% of total system capacity (because of the danger of outages). In the case of the Manitoba system this means a maximum unit size of 118 MW, a far cry from the 500 MW minimum-size nuclear reactor. Today only Ontario Hydro and Quebec Hydro could install economic minimum-size nuclear plants although both of them would have to think twice before accepting the risk of installing such mammoth units as the 1,124 MW TVA nuclear generator sets. For these reasons for most Canadian utilities the best course of action may still be to install more hydro units, even if their generating costs are appreciably higher than those of our southern neighbours.

8

That Great Street: The St. Lawrence

H. Neatby

The St. Lawrence has a magnificent history as the living centre of a great commercial empire, the continental road of the fur trader, the explorer, and the missionary. There is also a quieter story to be found in its more intimate relations with those who lived along its banks and who gradually learned how to get the most profit and pleasure from this splendid but reluctant and occasionally treacherous servant. The achievement of these individuals, often taken for granted, underlies the triumphs of the commercial empire.

Many writers expatiated on the economic, the social, the strategic, and the political significance of this river, quite literally the gateway to an entire continent. From it the French created their magnificent sketch of an empire in North America, an empire extending from Newfoundland to the Rockies, and from Hudson Bay to the Gulf of Mexico. In the exploitation of that great North American staple, fur, the St. Lawrence finally emerged victorious in the long struggle with two other famous waterways, Hudson Bay and the Hudson River. The dominion, or kingdom, or federation of Canada is only a part, although a large one, of the old fur-trading kingdom created largely from the St. Lawrence.

All this and much more is familiar ground. In recent decades it has been brilliantly and meticulously set forth by those who have done so much to reinterpret our history, notably H. A. Innes and

Reprinted from *Water Resources of Canada,* ed. C. E. Doleman, pp. 49-62. (University of Toronto Press, 1967). By permission.

D. G. Creighton. My purpose in this paper is only to add to this great and striking picture of one of the great rivers of the world a few homely details—one could even call them housekeeping details —that have come to my attention in an examination of some of the sources of the history of the Canadian community during the thirty years which followed the conquest of the country by the British in 1760.

Although the St. Lawrence first aroused the interest of explorers as a possible road to the western sea, it was soon attracting attention because of the wealth contained within its waters. Along the whole length from the gulf up through Lake St. Peter and to the great lakes beyond, it yielded a great variety and quantity of fish. This fish was used as a trade article. It was also used by the community living along the river banks as food for man and as fodder for cattle during the long winter. Great stacks of frozen fish were piled up and were used to supplement the sometimes scanty supply of hay. The St. Lawrence from early times attracted seal fishers, although this ancient sealing differed from the modern industry that has lately caused so much discussion. The early sealers were interested in the adult seals, which they caught by means of nets stretched across the passages between the rocky shores and the nearby rocky islands. These passages were frequented by the seal in their seasonal migration. The adult seals were wanted for their oil and for their skins; the skins were not luxury furs but were sold chiefly in the colony for the making of winter moccasins.

The wealth of the St. Lawrence fisheries was, however, in no way extraordinary. The importance of the river lay in its potentialities as a road, or as Chief Justice William Smith picturesquely called it, in relation to the community, "a great street." Primarily men saw it as a means of entry to the tremendous interior of the continent. Going up from Montreal, the highest point to which a ship of any size could penetrate, traders and missionaries from the mid-century set off for the certain privation and uncertain perils of the wilderness, intent like earlier travellers elsewhere, on gospel, gold, and glory. In the other direction, ships leaving Quebec on its massive rock opposite the Island of Orleans, at the point where the river widens into a gulf, found their way to the ocean routes which linked the colony and the missionary and fur-trading enterprise to the metropolis in Europe—to Paris before 1760, to London afterwards. As historians have pointed out, the whole economy of our country during its early history was geared to a metropolis. There were very sound economic reasons for Canadian loyalism.

The stretch of river from a few miles above Montreal to some distance below Quebec thus served a double purpose. First, it was the "great street' on which centred the economic life of the community, which by 1760 comprised perhaps 75,000 people. Secondly, it was the hinge on which turned the total operation of the fur trade, the complex relationships between the few hundreds of traders scattered over tens of thousands of miles of territory, and the few men in London who initially financed the trade, and ultimately disposed of the furs. Almost every merchant in Quebec, Montreal, and in the towns and villages between, was, directly or indirectly, involved in this double function. Immediately after the conquest and even before it was completed, traders from the colonies and the British Isles moved in. Along with Canadian associates and rivals they began the task of reorganizing, largely on free enterprise principles, and with London as the metropolis, economic operations hitherto carried on either through the French government or under very close government supervision.

The service of the river to the river community, while it may seem obvious and unexciting, presents in its details a vivid picture of the methods of satisfying the daily wants and needs of the people. From far down the river and the gulf, fish of all kinds—cod, green and dry, salmon, oysters, and eels—along with the seal skins and the seal oil to feed the lamps during the long winter evenings, went up-river to Quebec. From the country districts about Quebec there was collected the local homespun cloth, used for clothing by habitants generally and by the working classes. No doubt this cloth was made everywhere in the province, but evidence seems to show that a great deal went up-river for sale. This may be because the cloth was in demand for making bags for the shipping of grains and flour, produced in far greater quantity on the rich farming lands of the Richelieu River and the upper St. Lawrence than lower down.[1] From the district of Quebec also lime and stone for building

[1] Merchants at this time were constantly preoccupied with securing suitable containers for goods that moved up and down the river or overseas by ship. Those concerned with transportation today, when the making of packages and containers of all sorts has become not only a science but an art—if a rather debased art—would find it hard to imagine the time and effort spent by their eighteenth-century predecessors in securing suitable containers. Packages had to be of a convenient size and shape for handling and for getting on and off the ships without modern mechanical aids. They had also to be secure against the rough treatment that they might receive in loading and unloading, and also the inevitable rough treatment from winds and waves, especially damaging if they had not been skilfully stowed on board. It was also desirable that the packages should be at least partially waterproof. Much use was made of casks or barrels of all sizes from the small

purposes went up-river. These last commodities may have gone in smaller boats rather than in ships. From Montreal down-river went wheat, oats, peas, flour, and biscuit. Flour and biscuit were not exported much in the early part of this period, but they were used to supply the fishing stations of the lower river and the gulf. Montreal also sent apples and pears (especially the much prized pears from the orchards of the Seminary), nuts, pumpkins, wooden staves for the construction of casks and barrels, and timber for building purposes; and from Montreal and the upper districts came the bearskins, which seem to have been generally used throughout the province as winter blankets.

In the midst of this stretch of river the little town of Three Rivers supplied melons and tobacco, for which commodities it seems to have been famous throughout the province. Three Rivers also had a minor ship-building industry. Ships and canoes were constructed and repaired there. Everywhere on the river, no doubt, there were innumerable local exchanges which have left little trace behind them in the papers of the period. There is, however, much evidence of the brisk trade in fire-wood that was conducted by water in the neighbourhood of the cities and especially of Quebec. Many of the city houses were built with large lofty rooms and spacious windows in the fashion of the day. Exposed as they were to the bitter rigours of the northern winter, they were kept comfortable by open fire-places in every room and iron stoves in every passage. Coal not being used at all, these all had to be fed by wood. The consumption must have been enormous.

Another but related business on this mid-stretch of the river was the distribution of the commodities that came in from overseas for local consumption. It is easy for one absorbed with the needs of the fur trade to forget that even this relatively small community did demand a considerable store of luxuries and comforts from abroad. It is true that the habitant was largely self-supplying in food and in clothing. However, it seems quite clear that the habitants of Quebec, unlike the European peasants, did not manufacture their holiday clothing at home. The women of Quebec of all classes in society dressed as fashionably as their means would permit. Probably not many women of the countryside were able

---

keg to the hugest of casks; they had the great advantage that they could be rolled and otherwise manoeuvred with relative ease and with a minimum of damage. Drygoods generally came out from Europe in trunks, probably relatively small trunks with handles. Shoes, however, were often shipped in casks, at least within the province. Wheat and other grains and flour went in casks or bags.

to afford the twenty-five yards of white silk brocade such as one merchant purchased for his wife's new dress. Perhaps few of them even managed to purchase the fashionable white silk stockings. Yet, as a small town like Terrebonne was said to rival and even surpass Quebec and Montreal in its fashionable life, costly clothing was certainly not confined to the cities, and everywhere there would be some demand also for the striped, checked, and flowered cottons, which were used both for dresses and for household hangings. Merchants took great pains to explain to their English correspondents the taste of Canadian women in these matters. The many little stores which were now appearing throughout the province would have to be supplied with these articles, and also with such things as vinegar, wine, olive oil, imported cheese, spices, sugar, molasses and, to judge from certain lists which have survived, a large and various store of drugs. The local storekeepers often acted as grain buyers in the country, extending credit on the pledge of the coming crop. Occasionally they may also have been the local innkeepers, although it seems likely that the local cabaret was a separate and rather less respectable undertaking.

Far more complicated, however, than the demands of the local trade, was the total organization of the fur trade, which also took place along the stretch of river between Quebec and Montreal. Much of the planning and labour, and much of the risk involved in transferring the pelt of the beaver from its original owner in some far western stream to the ultimate owner — perhaps Gainsborough's lovely Georgiana, Duchess of Devonshire, who, it will be recalled, enhanced her charms with a beaver hat of impressive proportions —much of this labour and risk rested on the shoulders of a handful of merchants at Quebec and Montreal. When Montreal became a common resort for ocean-going ships, the undertaking was greatly simplified. But at least for two or three decades after the conquest the great import-export centre for goods was Quebec, the chief source of canoes and tobacco essential to the trade was Three Rivers, and Montreal was the assembling place for the goods, the canoes, and the crews ready to go up-country, as well as the receiving centre for the returning crews and their cargoes. The operations at Montreal were, in the early days, complicated by the fact that all passes for canoes going up-country had to be secured from the secretary of the province down at Quebec. On these passes it was necessary to state the name of the owner of the canoe, all the items of its cargo, the names of all members of the crew, and their place of origin. Later the securing of the passes was much simplified by a provision which permitted the commander-in-chief at Montreal to issue them to the traders.

The result of these combined operations meant that there was an enormous amount of coming and going and of correspondence between Quebec, Montreal, and, to a lesser extent, Three Rivers. Travelling in winter was by sleigh and could be quick, easy, and pleasant. William Smith wrote to his wife in the fall of 1786 that he was going to buy himself a closed sleigh in which he could lie down comfortably at full length and perhaps even sleep on his journey. Trains of sleighs could be used for necessary winter freighting, especially in late winter and early spring, when goods were sent by sleigh from Quebec to Montreal to be ready for the departure of the canoes. Even in the summer, travellers and letters went by the road as being more speedy than the river. But toward the end of this period river vessels did attempt a regular passenger service. In one of the local newspapers of the 80s there is a vivid description of a passage from Montreal down to Quebec. It appears to have been one long picnic, with plenty of conversation and plenty of liquid as well as other refreshment.

From the beginning, however, nearly all the freight in summer went by river, an easier route than the indifferent dirt roads and the numerous ferries which had to be negotiated on the north shore between Quebec and Montreal. The river traffic in summer must have been impressive for the size of the community. Up and down the river would pass canoes and small boats, heavy whaling boats, little sloops and schooners with crews of only three men, and others much larger, up to the ship drawing 16 feet of water, the largest ship that could penetrate as far as Montreal. In addition to these conventional craft there were rafts of all kinds, particularly the peculiar rafts fashioned by the men who cut staves up the Richelieu and floated them in long trains down to Quebec in spring.

But the St. Lawrence, now famous the world over for its magnificent stretches of water, its lovely islands, its shore alternating peaceful pastoral scenery with wild and wooded rocky stretches, was not to be used with impunity by the ignorant or the reckless. The whole rhythm of life in the colony had to be adapted not only to the nature of water transport, but to the whims of a particular river which could be extremely whimsical.

It had been known for many years that the St. Lawrence was an exceedingly difficult river to navigate. Not only did the ebb and flow of the tide make it all too easy for ships to become grounded unless conducted by skilled and knowledgeable pilots; the river-bed was also in some places broken by rocky shelves and ridges which at low tide came dangerously close to the surface. American and British invaders under the French régime had paid their tribute to the river by the pains they took to secure Canadians to pilot them up the gulf even as far as Quebec. Captain Cook, later the explorer of the Pacific, was employed in charting the river soon after the conquest. The Canadians themselves were under no illusion about its dangers. The Jesuits lay claim to having established the first university in Canada, because they instituted classes in hydrography for those preparing to act as pilots on the St. Lawrence. Throughout the period following the conquest, in response to petitions from merchants and others, successive ordinances were passed regulating the training, the apprenticeship, certification, and conditions of work of the pilots on whose services the whole safety of commerce depended.

In addition to this fundamental and special problem was the general problem with which all Canadians are familiar. The St. Lawrence does not provide an open winter port. All the commercial operations of the country had to be geared to the very short season from some time in May until early November. The spring ships from London might reach Quebec late in April, but they were much more likely not to arrive until the first, second, or even the third week of May.

The concern of the merchants in Quebec and Montreal was to get their goods and to distribute them to retailers throughout the country as quickly as possible. The Quebec merchants were in an advantageous position. They could clear their goods immediately, giving the customs officer a note for the amount of the duty if they had no ready money. In those early days, there being no customs buildings, the officer was only too glad to get rid of his responsibility. The Montreal merchants always tried to get the London suppliers to put their goods on ships bound for Montreal. Often this was impossible. Also, many Londoners were probably as vague about the relative positions of Quebec and Montreal as some Canadians still are about those of Australia and New Zealand. The Montreal merchant who had to receive his goods in Quebec could confide them to Quebec commission merchants, who would send them up-river for a commission of one half of one per cent, in addition, of course, to the freight charges. Montreal merchants resented this additional expense, and it seems likely that many merchants of Montreal and Quebec performed these and similar services for each other without charge. It was taken for granted that goods would be forwarded as promptly as possible. Occasionally, however, a commission merchant in Quebec, instead of sending on goods by the first boat, would keep them waiting in order to be able to send them on his own private vessel later when business should slacken.

It might also happen for a special reason that no ships were available. Ordinarily river ships would wait at Quebec in the spring for the arrival of the ocean fleet. They would then load on goods for Montreal and intermediate points and, on the return journey, would bring down wheat from the winter threshing along the Richelieu and upper St. Lawrence. This was the ideal plan. Unfortunately, it required ideal weather conditions: an early break-up in the gulf and steady winds from the north-east to bring the ocean-going ships up to Quebec. Then, especially if the northeast winds continued to favour them, the little ships could make their way up-river before the ebb of the spring floods made navigation of the Richelieu impracticable for them. When the ocean ships were long delayed, local ship-owners and captains had to make a series of agonizing reappraisals, which sometimes resulted in the schooners going up-river without a cargo in order to reach the Richelieu in time. Captains who lingered too long at Quebec might miss both the arrival of the London ships and the Richelieu flood-time. If merchants occasionally became short-tempered during the busy season, and they did, they had ample excuse.

The goods that came out in the spring then were forwarded more or less promptly from Quebec to Montreal. They would arrive too late for the great event of the spring, the dispatch of the fur-trading canoes up-country. Canoes which were to return from the upper country in the fall had to start as soon as the ice broke in the spring. Preparations for this were made in the late winter. If necessary, trains of sleighs would take goods from Quebec up to Montreal to be ready for the dispatch of the canoes as soon as the ice broke. The Quebec merchant, François Baby, was accustomed to go himself to Montreal at this time to send off his fleet of canoes to his brother and partner, Duperron Baby, in Detroit. The canoes set off in May, often to face during the journey the hideous discomfort of bitter cold rain or very light snow. They struggled up-river and along the lakes, the men sheltering at night as best they could under their canoes. Nothing could match the horror and scorn of the hardy captain of militia when he had to report that men impressed for the *corvée* (in this case the transport of goods along the lakes) were demanding tents to sleep in.

All goods for these spring canoes would have come out in the previous year by the fall ships. Seamstresses worked in the winter at making the lengths of cotton and linen into shirts, petticoats, and so on, suitable for the Indian trade. The spring ships from overseas supplied the needs of the community, and also stock for the canoes which left later in the summer. These would winter up-country, and return in the following spring.

Ships from overseas needed a return cargo if ocean rates were not to be impossibly high. There would always be available, no doubt, some furs from the winter take at the King's Posts down-river, and from the trade which came into Three Rivers. Ships could also get furs from the canoes that had wintered up-country and come down in the spring. Furs, however, took relatively little space. The returning ships would also take the staves which had been cut in the Champlain district and elsewhere during the winter, and had been brought down the river to wait for them at Quebec. Smaller ships might load up with flour and biscuit for the supply of the fishing islands and sealing stations in the gulf before return-ing to the colonies or Europe with a supply of fish.

A most important, and increasingly valuable, commodity on the journey back to Europe was wheat. As has been mentioned, one of the preoccupations for the owners of river schooners was to get their little ships up the St. Lawrence as early as possible in order to take advantage of the spring floods on the Richelieu. If the harvest had been plentiful the previous year and if the price in Europe was good, wheat was a welcome cargo to the various ships gathered at Quebec. A most profitable arrangement for the ship-owner and for the merchant was to fill the holds of the ships with wheat, and to pile the bundles of staves on the decks, thus making use of every possible space.

The busy exchange in the few months of spring and summer constantly provides illustrations of the embarrassment of merchants in the face of inadequate and uncertain means of transport on the river. The season was so short that ship-owners wanted to be certain of full employment during the summer. This meant that in the busiest periods there was never enough transport. A merchant in Montreal might well be faced with an acute shortage of some com-modity urgently demanded by his customers. He would write fran-tically to Quebec, telling his correspondent there to get it up to him in any way he could, though fully aware that want of shipping might make this impossible. Meanwhile he might be communicating with Three Rivers, on the chance of there being a surplus there which he could secure, or he would be going about the town of Montreal to see what he could get from his fellow merchants. Evidence of a considerable variety in prices even between Montreal and Three Rivers confirms the impression of a serious transport problem. Sometimes a merchant would have on his hands a large quantity of wheat which he must send down immediately if he would catch the ships before they left for Europe, and which in any case he would wish to get rid of for want of a suitable place to store it. Again he would encounter the problem of shipping. The owners of the river schooners had a sellers' market and knew how to make the most of it.

However, ship-owners, many of whom were merchants, had their own troubles. Having secured a schooner, their next task was to get a reliable crew, and this was often difficult. Too many competent captains were illiterate and therefore incapable of handling bills of lading. One merchant, for example, writes to another asking if he knows of any capable man who can read and write, and who would be willing to serve on his schooner and help the captain, who cannot read, with the paper work. Sometimes the captain and crew were unsatisfactory in other ways. Montreal merchants learned to count carefully the bundles of dried cod that came up to Montreal, because it was entirely possible that the crew might have been living at their expense on the journey from Quebec. It was more important still to make sure not only that the casks of wine were full, but that the contents were wine and not wine and water. An ingenious captain might draw off quantities of the wine for the refreshment of himself and possibly of his crew, compensating at least in weight by adding water.

The ship-owner also had to meet special hazards such as might occur in war. It is true that the vastly increased needs of transport in war-time might enable him to make large profits; but then his ship might be taken over by the government, with unfortunate results. One ship-owner complained that his boat had been conscripted and used to convey goods up to Montreal. On the way back it became grounded in Lake St. Peter. He was not able to get it free until the following spring, when he found it much damaged. The total compensation that he could obtain from the government was £45, the rental agreed on for the month that the ship was in service.

It is quite clear to any reader of mercantile correspondence that what was needed in order to make the best use of the short season and all shipping available was ample and secure storage space. Given such a provision the goods could always be ready and waiting for the ships and their crews, which could thus be maintained in constant employment. Failing storage facilities, one might find, for example, that a ship would arrive in the spring in the Richelieu River ready to take on a whole cargo of wheat, and would have to wait impatiently while the grain merchant hurried round to the homes of all the habitants, who were storing it in their granaries, trying to persuade them to leave their farm work in order to bring it as quickly as possible to the wharf. In fact the province was very poorly supplied with storehouses. It is true that the stone houses along St. Paul's Street often had ample, well-constructed, dry stone-lined vaults, which were used by merchants for storing the furs that came down from the upper country, and the woollen goods that might be waiting to go up. There were, however, far too few of these vaults, and from time to time furs and woollens were damaged by damp, moths, or rats.

Much bigger in every way was the problem of storing wheat. Not only were granaries needed at the regular pick-up points along the Richelieu and St. Lawrence rivers; larger ones were needed at Montreal, and most of all they were needed at Quebec, where the wheat was gathered to await shipment overseas. Gradually, as the wheat trade grew, the province did become equipped with suitable granaries, but this was a work of time. The whole wheat trade was built up empirically in the post-conquest era. Before 1760 there had been not much free enterprise, as the government was likely at any time to take the wheat at a fixed price from the habitants or other owners. Peace and security, the growth of population, and possibly the influence of Englishmen interested in farming who bought up some of the seigneuries, appear to have sent wheat production up rapidly. The difficulty was, however, that until a trade was regularly established with Europe (and this trade depended on the uncertain fluctuation of European prices), it was not worth while to invest in granaries. Yet without the granaries it was almost impossible to have a regular trade at all. What was needed, as in any new enterprise, was faith and capital. Fortunately the merchants, although they had little capital, had much faith, but their real trials, their risks, and their losses during the experimental beginnings are vividly recorded in their letters.

The merchants of Quebec during this period have been criticized as narrow-minded bigots, unfriendly to Canadians and anxious to domineer over them. These charges are partly true. It should be remembered, however, that Canadians worked with English in this trade and that all of them displayed a perseverance, a courage, and a tenacity which in themselves inspire respect, if they do not quite atone for the want of other virtues. The wheat trade was patiently and courageously built up by the Quebec merchants and the Montreal merchants association themselves with local shopkeepers, with individual buyers, with operators of the river schooners and of the ocean ships, and with the London correspondents who ultimately disposed of the shipments. Like the timber trade which followed it, the wheat trade was absolutely dependent on the river. Furs, if necessary, could have gone down from Montreal to Quebec overland in the winter. With wheat and wood this was impossible.

The most complicated problem encountered by the merchants in using the river I have left to the end. This was important in itself, and was also curiously interwoven with a mass of potentially conflicting interests: merchant and merchant, Canadian and English, official and private person, army and civilian. This problem is the obvious one of wharves. It is easy to speak of a river road while forgetting the great question of access and egress. In order to use the river the tiniest boat had to have a beach or a landing stage. The larger ships were proportionately more exacting in their requirements. Montreal merchants who dealt only with canoes, boats, and the smaller ships seem to have settled their problem without much trouble. They had enough room along their waterfront for the building of wharves. Quebec, with many more ships, and larger ones, all huddled in the relatively short space running from the foot of Cape Diamond to the mouth of the St. Charles River, gave much trouble before any satisfactory arrangements could be made.

Early in Governor Murray's régime, a natural conflict of interest between local and provincial trade appeared. Merchants and others at Quebec asked for concessions of the available space in order to build wharves, and a number were granted. Serious trouble broke out, however, when the Council was asked to consider disposing of the stretch of beach customarily reserved for the vendors of firewood, who were accustomed to put in their boats anywhere, stack up their piles of wood, and make sales on the spot to private purchasers. No fees were charged for this privilege. The merchants who wished to secure a grant of this beach, or part of it, apparently urged that space could be left for the wood lot, and that even if all land were taken, the service through a regular wharf would be more efficient. They may have had in mind that wholesalers could take over the fire-wood and pass it on at retail to purchasers. They argued, reasonably perhaps, that it was wrong to retain valuable land for one purpose only. The retort was obvious. Little boats carrying fire-wood which would suffer no material damage from wetting or rough handling needed no expensive facilities. Construction of wharves would be certain to send up the price.

The issue lay between the general body of consumers and the small group of merchants. It also lay, to a considerable extent, between English and Canadians. The promoters of wharves had to win in the end. Time was on their side. Meanwhile, it is interesting to note, even in this minor matter, the alignment of the conservative forces standing ostensibly for community interests, against English "improvers"—in this instance each being so much in the right that only a very imaginative and sympathetic compromise could have satisfied both. The information on the working out of this particular problem is fragmentary, but a wharf was erected on this place eventually.

A long and bitter controversy involving mercantile rivalry, the interests of government, and the privileges of the army developed over the one large and adequately constructed wharf which dated from the French régime. The King's Wharf at Quebec was situated up-river at the place where the beach begins to narrow to a point below Cape Diamond. It was an irregular quadrilateral, pierced from the river side by a long narrow slip for the construction and repair of ships. At the lower end of the wharf as the river flowed was the *cul de sac,* a kind of inlet sheltered from above by the wharf as it projected into the river. Here ships were stored in winter, and here, during the busy season, they crowded together, waiting to unload.

Unfortunately, this wharf, perhaps damaged during the siege, had fallen partially into ruin, and not for ten years after 1760 could arrangements be made for its adequate repair and maintenance. It was crown property, but for some years after the conquest the province yielded practically no crown revenue. Governors met necessary expenditures by drawing bills on the British treasury, with the encouraging assurance that if the British authorities found their expenses unnecessary, the amount of the bills would come out of their own pockets. There was no money for public works except for defence.

Thomas Ainslie, a merchant, and a friend of Governor Murray, who had appointed him collector of customs in 1763, made some use of the wharf and the buildings on it in his official duties. Realizing its potential value he offered to repair and lease it. His fellow-merchants immediately petitioned against the lease, offering to raise £2,000 for the repair of the wharf rather than see it in private hands. This was probably an empty gesture intended to prevent the customs collector (by his office unpopular, as the merchants were vigorously protesting the customs duties) from extending his commercial advantages.

However, it was clear that the wharf could be put into full service only through private enterprise. Lieutenant-Governor Carleton, who arrived in 1766, passed over Ainslie. Ainslie was Murray's friend, and Carleton, always suspicious of officials, often with justification, thought his personal fees too high. There was a sharp tussle between other firms tendering for the lease. Accusations of undue influence, and of spying into private papers with a view to undercutting bids, were rather freely bandied about. Eventually the lease went to the firm of Johnston and Purss, after much bargaining about the upkeep of the wharf, the fees that might be charged to ships tying up at the wharf or moored in the *cul de sac,* and on all goods landed. There were precise specifications on repair and upkeep, apart from the obvious repairs that had to be made immediately to the wharf itself. The wharf was to be surrounded on the landward side by a heavy stone wall pierced by two gates; the slip in the centre was to be maintained, and the whole frontage on the river and on the *cul de sac* was to be faced with heavy timbers. In addition the river bottom in front of the wharf and in the *cul de sac* was to be kept clear of stones.

In return for this, and for a rental of five shillings a year, the lessees could charge dues on all ships tying at the wharf or moored in the *cul de sac.* They could also charge specified rates (over which there was much haggling) on every tun, pipe, butt, barrel, cask, or quarter-cask containing brandy, rum, wine, or sugar, and on other goods and containers in proportion. "King's Ships," however, were to be free of charge. There was inevitably a brisk debate on "King's Ships," the lessees insisting that contractors carrying government stores were not to claim exemption as King's Ships.

And so at last, after ten years, on the eve of Carleton's departure for Britain in 1770, the lease was signed, and the wharf—the only adequate wharf in the city—was on the way to being rendered serviceable. The merchants complained that Quebec, of all cities in North America, was the worst provided with wharves—and yet in five years it was to become not only the main entry to the continental fur-trading country but an essential base of operations in the American Revolutionary war.

There is nothing in this story of the mid-stretch of the river to compare with the great epic of the inland fur trade. Yet the historian, charged in a sense to do justice to all, must pay tribute to the energy, the ingenuity, the endurance, and the ceaseless toil of innumerable men—from the wealthy, or at least ambitious, merchants through traders, shopkeepers, and agents, through captains, sailors, boatmen, and pilots, to the humblest habitant negotiating the rapids on his rickety raft to get his staves down to Quebec. By their efforts local industry and trade were stimulated and coordinated to serve the fur trade, and to cut down freight rates by ensuring that the great ships need not always return to Europe with empty holds. But for them, that "great street," the lovely but captious and treacherous St. Lawrence, could not have been forced to provide the essential link that joined the great inland fur country to its metropolis overseas.

Note on Sources

The information for this article has been gathered piecemeal from a variety of sources, going all the way from official or semi-official reports on economic matters to the most casual references in personal letters. The dispatches to and from the Colonial Office (C.O. 42), often carrying interesting enclosures, have been useful. The minutes of the Legislative and Executive Councils of the province, and the accompanying collections of papers filed in the Council office (S. series), contain important material. Most fruitful for colourful detail, however, are the collections of business and personal correspondence (Baby Letters, Jacobs Papers, Lindsay-Morrison Papers, etc.). All these collections are available in the Public Archives of Canada.

9

The St. Lawrence Seaway and Trade on the Great Lakes, 1958-63

D. Kerr

The opening of the St. Lawrence Seaway in 1959 marked another stage in the building of canals to circumvent rapids and falls on the St. Lawrence River upstream from Montreal, making it possible for moderately large ocean-going vessels and domestic bulk carriers to enter and leave the Great Lakes. The effects of this enlarged waterway on the economic geography of the Great Lakes region in general, and on the movements of cargo and changing status of ports in particular, invite attention. Substantial research on these topics, however, must be delayed until the statistical record is longer and more complete. None the less, a preliminary examination of the changing and emergency patterns of trade serves not only as a report on current trends, but also, and hopefully, as a stimulus to further research. An inquiry of this nature raises more questions than it answers, but such is the primary purpose of the paper.

General Statistical Review[1]

In the years just preceding the opening of the seaway, cargo shipped through the old canals averaged 11 million tons annually

Reprinted in edited form from *Canadian Geographer*, Vol. VIII, no. 4 (1964), pp. 188-96.

[1] For period 1959-63, based on St. Lawrence Seaway Authority, *Traffic Report of the St. Lawrence Seaway* (Ottawa, Queen's Printer, annually); for period before 1959, based on D.B.S., *Canal Traffic* (Ottawa, Queen's Printer, annually).

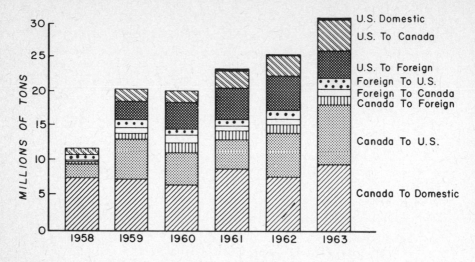

Figure 1. Cargo tonnage through St. Lawrence canals, 1950-1963.

(Figure 1), comprising mainly shipments between Canadian ports, in particular Montreal and Prescott (Figure 2). In 1959, the tonnage of cargo through the new canals increased sharply but rather more slowly thereafter reaching almost 31 millions tons in 1963. (As this article goes to press it appears that the 1964 trade has reached at least 38 million tons.) Direct overseas shipments, insignificant in 1958, rose very quickly to account for almost one-third of all ship-

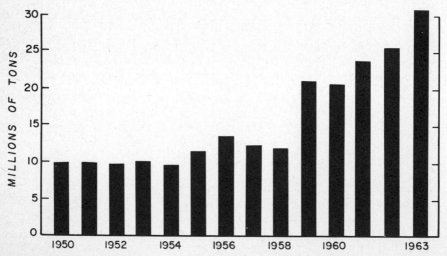

Figure 2. Total Shipments on the St. Lawrence Seaway by origin and destination, 1958-1963.

ments in the early 1960's. A relative decline set in, however, and by 1963 direct overseas shipments had dropped to 25 per cent of the total.

In terms of origins and destinations of shipments, almost 75 per cent of the traffic remains intracontinental, mainly within Canada or between Canada and the United States, although a substantial and increasing amount is American grain which moves by large lake bulk carriers through the seaway to be transferred to ocean vessels at Montreal, Trois Rivières, or Bai Comeau. In short, the historic function of the St. Lawrence canals in trans-shipping goods to and from the interior has by no means been eliminated. In fact, it may very well be strengthened in the future!

Although foreign shipments through the St. Lawrence canals have increased in the last few years, most still originate at Canadian ports. For example, in 1963, 9.7 million tons moved between Canadian ports, 8.6 million tons from Canadian ports to American ports, and 1.3 million tons from Canadian ports overseas, comprising in total 63 per cent of all seaway shipments.

From the period of earliest commercial traffic to the present an imbalance of shipments favouring downbound over upbound has characterized the flow pattern in the St. Lawrence canals. Although outgoing shipments still exceed those coming in, the discrepancy has been considerably narrowed since the opening of the seaway. In 1963, 17.4 million tons or 56 per cent moved downbound, 13.5 million tons or 44 per cent moved upbound. Agricultural commodities comprised 79 per cent of all downbound shipments—wheat 42 per cent, corn 15 per cent, and barley 6 per cent (Figure 3). Bitumi-

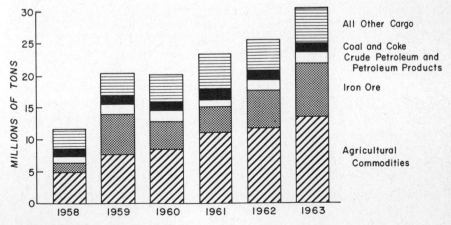

Figure 3. Major commodities shipped on the St. Lawrence Seaway, 1958-1963.

nous coal and coke account for 4 per cent of all downbound shipments, miscellaneous manufactured goods 3.6 per cent, and scrap
iron 2 per cent. Approximately 60 per cent of all cargo moving into
the Great Lakes is made up of iron ore shipped from Sept Iles and
Port Cartier to, in most cases, American ports on Lake Erie. Other
commodities are fuel oil, 10 per cent, and various manufactured
goods, mainly iron and steel products, 17 per cent.

The Grain Trade

Grain remains the most important commodity moving through
the St. Lawrence canals. In the past, it was almost entirely of Canadian origin shipped in canalers from the lower lakes or upper St.
Lawrence ports to lower St. Lawrence ports, mainly Montreal, for
final transfer to ocean vessels. Since the opening of the seaway the
volume of American grain moving through the canals has increased
enormously from approximately 150 thousand tons in 1958 to over
5 million tons in both 1962 and 1963, reflecting in terms of transport
costs the increase in accessibility of the American midwest to
Europe. It should be added that during this period American exports
of grain rose from 20 million tons to over 35 million tons, but the
movement through Atlantic ports declined from 5 million tons (25
per cent) to about 4.7 million tons (13 per cent).[2] Shipments through
Gulf ports in 1958 amounted to 10 million tons or 50 per cent of the
grain export but by 1962 had increased to 20 million tons or 57 per
cent of the total. In short, while Pacific and Atlantic ports showed
both relative and absolute declines in grain trade, Great Lakes and
Gulf ports showed a vigorous growth.

Perhaps the single most profound effect of the seaway on grain
has been the great upheaval in domestic freight rates. The eastern
railways cut their export rates in 1959 to fight the seaway. Many
western railways followed suit by reducing their rates into lake
ports to meet the eastern rail competition. Railways to the Gulf then
reduced their rates to fight both northern rates. This forced barge
operators on the Mississippi and its tributaries to cut their rates.
Truck operators have been struggling, through the midwest, to meet
these new rate changes.[3]

The American grain trade on the Great Lakes is handled almost
entirely by three ports, Duluth-Superior, Chicago, and Toledo, which

[2] For a detailed statistical record see "Changing Shipping Pattern on the
St. Lawrence Seaway", *U.S. Department of Agriculture, Marketing Research Report,* no. 621 (Washington, 1963), p. 113.
[3] R. C. Liebenow, "Grain Movements via the Seaway", *Proc. Inst. on the
St. Lawrence Seaway* (Great Lakes Commission, May 1964).

account for 94 per cent of the total. Undoubtedly this concentration will continue and perhaps even intensify as new bulk freighters carry more and more of the cargo. In 1960, 80 per cent of the American grain moved directly overseas on scheduled European freighters and in tramps, but in 1961 and 1962 the direct shipments had fallen to approximately two-thirds. By 1963, direct shipments of grain had dropped to less than 40 per cent of the total and trans-shipments at lower St. Lawrence ports had become dominant. A flow pattern has developed on the lower St. Lawrence River in which many of the large lake freighters, having unloaded a cargo of grain, return upbound with iron ore from Sept Iles or Port Cartier.

Iron Ore

In recent years shipments of iron ore have accounted for about one-quarter of all trade through the seaway. In fact, the concept of a modern seaway is based to a very large extent on iron ore from Quebec and Labrador moving upbound to balance the traditionally high downbound movement of grain. Concern over the depletion of high-grade iron ore in the Lake Superior region coupled with the possibility of developing large bodies of ore in Labrador to feed American steel mills made the argument to build the seaway very convincing to many members of the American Senate and Congress in the early 1950's. That shipments of ore through the new canals have failed to reach the volume anticipated has been very disappointing to supporters of the venture and is worthy of a brief investigation.[4]

Among the various factors, that of the continued vigour of iron mining in the Lake Superior region is the most important. Surprisingly, the flow of iron ore from ports on Lake Superior has diminished only slightly. In recent years between 50 and 60 million tons have been shipped from various ports mainly Duluth-Superior, Twin Harbours, Taconite, and Silver Bay (Figure 4). Although the tonnage is approximately two-thirds that of peak years during World War II, the iron content may, in fact, be just as high because an increasing amount moves in the form of concentrated iron pellets. In fact, most mid-western steel mills continue to rely very heavily on this traditional source, and in 1962 ore from the upper lakes supplied 62 per cent of all iron (direct shipment and concentrates) consumed in the United States. Even the mills at Hamilton, Ontario, continue to draw almost entirely on this source, mainly because of

---

4 Preliminary figures for 1964 indicate that iron ore shipments have risen to 10,000,000 tons.

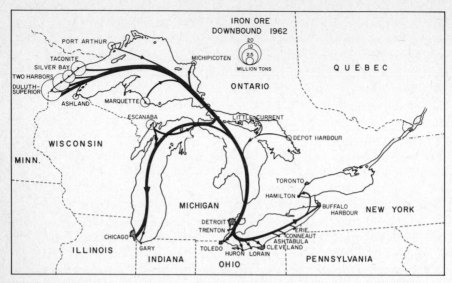

Figure 4. Ports at the western end of Lake Superior remain the most important in the shipment of iron ore (concentrate and direct shipments).

ownership patterns.[5] The Steel Company of Canada, for example, has invested in the taconite process in Minnesota. However, both of the large producers at Hamilton are participating with a number of other companies in the development of ore bodies at Wabush in Quebec so that when production begins in 1965 they will draw an increasing proportion of their supplies from the source and consequently via the seaway.

To be considered in any analysis of iron ore shipments through the seaway is the competition of the east coast or Atlantic route. Whether ore for American steel furnaces moves from the Quebec ports of Sept Iles and Port Cartier via the St. Lawrence or via the Atlantic depends on a number of factors of which transport costs and the ownership of iron ore are the two most important. On the basis of a ten-year average (1954-63), the division of shipments to the United States has been approximately equal: half via the St. Lawrence route and half to the Atlantic ports of Baltimore and Philadelphia. It is quite obvious that steel mills on the Atlantic seaboard, consuming at least in part Quebec-Labrador ore, would be supplied by the Atlantic route just as mid-western mills on the shores of the Great Lakes would be served by the St. Lawrence route. That most of the ore production in the Labrador trough has

5 Donald Kerr, "The Geography of the Canadian Iron and Steel Industry", *Economic Geography*, Vol. XXXV, no. 2 (April 1959), p. 155.

been financed by mid-western interests suggests a mid-western destination, and, indeed, a relatively large amount of ore unloaded at Baltimore and Philadelphia moves inland to the Ohio Valley. Here, beyond doubt, is found the focus of competition of the two routes—much farther inland than most adherents of the seaway anticipated.

Over the last decade shipping rates on the two routes have fluctuated rather widely in response to the size and availability of ships. For example, in the late 1950's and early 1960's ocean rates from Sept Iles to Baltimore oscillated between $0.75 and $1.60 per long ton (U.S. dollars), while water rates from Sept Iles to Cleveland average $2.75 per long ton, including the seaway toll of $0.45 per long ton. In the last two years the introduction of large bulk carriers on the St. Lawrence-Great Lakes route has improved the efficiency of handling ore with a corresponding lowering of rates to an average of $2.15 per long ton from Sept Iles to Cleveland (including the toll). Even so, rates on the Atlantic remain lower and help to explain the success of forwarding ore inland. It becomes apparent from Table I that the Pittsburgh region lies at a point where total transport costs via the seaway and the Atlantic route are approximately the same. If tolls are raised on the seaway and ocean rates are lowered, the Atlantic route becomes more attractive. Conversely, lower tolls and reduced seaway freight rates would favour the St. Lawrence route.

Although the directions of most shipments are determined by transport costs alone, some are influenced by patterns of ownership of iron ore, water carriers, and consuming mills. Companies such as the Republic Steel Corporation, having steel mills only in the midwest and part-ownership in the Iron Ore Company of Canada, will tend to favour the seaway route from Sept Iles. On the other, the Bethlehem Steel Corporation, also a participating investor in the Iron Ore Company of Canada, may load a shipment to be sent to its mill at Sparrows' Point, Maryland, one day, and to Buffalo via the seaway the next day. Furthermore, the U.S. Steel Corporation, owners of the Quebec-Cartier Mining Company, may ship ore from Port Cartier in its carriers via either the seaway or the Atlantic according to the availability of ships.

Direct Overseas Trade

It is noteworthy that the exchange of goods, bulk and general cargo, between overseas ports and those on the Great Lakes in ocean vessels reached a peak in 1962 and has been declining since. As

TABLE I. Selected Shipping Costs per Long Ton of Iron Ore from Sept-Iles, 1962*

(U.S. dollars)

| To | Via seaway and Lake Erie ports | | | | | Via east coast ports | | | |
	Rail charges from Cleveland	Unloading charges	Seaway tolls	Freight rate to Cleveland	Total	Rail charges from Philadelphia	Unloading charges	Ocean freight rate	Total
Johnstown, Pa.	3.02	0.50	0.45	1.70	5.67	3.50	0.50	1.50	5.50
Monessen-Donora, Pa.	2.86	0.50	0.45	1.70	5.51	3.62	0.50	1.50	5.62
Pittsburgh, Pa.	2.73	0.50	0.45	1.70	5.38	3.76	0.50	1.50	5.76
Youngstown, Ohio	2.08	0.50	0.45	1.70	4.73	4.03	0.50	1.50	6.03

*Compiled from a variety of sources and in particular the Mineral Resources Division, Department of Mines and Technical Surveys.

emphasized, bulk trade, especially grain, has been dropping, and consequently the focus should be put on direct overseas general cargo which in 1963 comprised about 3 million tons.

Before the opening of the seaway, several European shipping companies opened offices in major lake ports and developed trade with small ocean vessels able to navigate the old fourteen-foot canals.[6] The trade was of necessity modest, but formed the basis of a considerable expansion which occurred after 1959. Those ports able to engage in this trade were recognized quite early, and continue to dominate. Two ports, Toronto and Chicago, stand out, and, on the basis of 1963 figures, handle 22 per cent and 21 per cent of the total direct overseas general cargo trade respectively (Figure 5). Five other ports, namely Detroit, Hamilton, Cleveland, Milwaukee, and Toledo, account for most of the remaining trade. Direct overseas trade at Lake Superior ports remains less than 5 per cent of the total. Among the large ports, Chicago, Toledo and Detroit have the most favourable balance of imports and exports. Although Toronto's trade remains mainly that of imports, it is suggested that

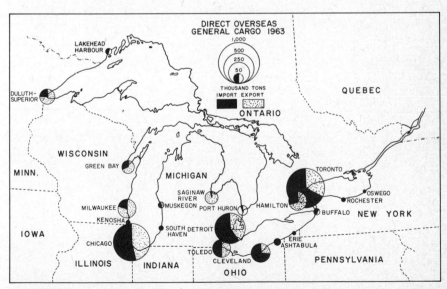

Figure 5. Only a few ports have a substantial share of the direct overseas general cargo trade.

6 See H. M. Mayer, "Great Lakes-Overseas: An Expanding Trade Route", *Economic Geography*, Vol. XXX, no. 2 (1954), pp. 117-43; and also D. P. Kerr and J. Spelt, "Overseas Trade at the Port of Toronto", *Canadian Geographer*, no. 8 (1956), pp. 70-79.

the western end of Lake Ontario may eventually prove to be attractive as a turning basin for some vessels, especially in view of Hamilton's dominant export trade.

Conclusion

In view of the preliminary aspect of the present paper, there are no real conclusions. Quite obviously, no transportation route can be studied in isolation, for the lowering of a rate here, or the widening of a canal there, may set off chain reactions which often return full cycle. Reference has been made to the effect of the Atlantic route on seaway shipments of ore, and, undoubtedly, further attention should be paid to other cargos and other routes of competition. Many questions regarding the exchange of cargo, such as that of grain for ore in large carriers at ports on the lower St. Lawrence, remain unanswered. The apparent need to establish a fairly rigid schedule of ore shipments for the whole navigation season may, upon further investigation, suggest the difficulty of attaining any theoretical equilibrium of cargo shipments on the basis of transport costs. Further attention must also be directed to the impact of the seaway on the functions of various ports, in particular, Montreal and the major Great Lakes ports.

10

Metropolitan Shorelines
of the Great Lakes

H. M. Mayer

After six years of operation, the enlarged St. Lawrence Seaway is still an immature water route, in the sense that many of the facilities which are required in order to realize its full potentials are yet not adequate. Among these are port terminals. Few of the Great Lakes ports in either country are developed to the point at which the maximum-sized vessels—particularly salt water ships—can be handled with full draft and with efficiency comparable to that of the traditional salt water ports. Pressures will continue for many years for additional development of port facilities, and for port-oriented industries on deep-water channels in the ports along the Great Lakes-St. Lawrence waterway route. Although smaller ports may, in some instance, develop specialized facilities for large-scale water movement of bulk industrial materials, most of the pressure for comprehensive port terminals and large concentrations of port-oriented industries will be in the larger metropolitan areas. Here, the demands for port and industrial development are coming into sharp conflict with the demands for other uses of the shorelines, especially for recreation, and for the conservation of the scenic and other amenities, which are receiving a new emphasis as the metropolitan populations produce ever-increasing pressures.

Reprinted from *Canadian Geographer*, Vol. VIII, no. 4 (1964), pp. 197-202.

Along the St. Lawrence and Great Lakes shores is the nodal region—the urban and industrial belt—of Canada and a significant portion of the core region of the United States. Bordering these waterways is a high proportion—in the case of Canada, the majority —of the population of both countries. Of the 212 standard metropolitan statistical areas recognized by the 1960 United States census, 17 have shorelines on the Great Lakes. Of 37 Canadian metropolitan and major urban areas, as of the 1961 Canadian census, 15 have shorelines on the Great Lakes or the St. Lawrence River and its tributaries. These include the two largest metropolises in Canada. Two pairs of metropolitan areas—Detroit-Windsor and Buffalo-Niagara Falls—are in effect international urban agglomerations with substantial daily commuting across the border, which in both instances lies in the waterway between the two countries.

This article is devoted to brief consideration of some of the problems of shoreline development within the metropolitan areas of the two countries along the Great Lakes, and incidentally the St. Lawrence River. These problems are numerous and varied. Some are of purely local concern; others are subject to determination by the states and provinces; still others involve the interest of one or the other of the two nations, while a few are of international concern. The problems of shoreline development which are most urgently in need of attention by the planners and by the governmental authorities, at whatever level, are summarized here.

Land is a scarce resource. With the population pressures produced by the expansion of metropolitan agglomerations, accelerated by increased comparative regional advantages induced by the St. Lawrence Seaway and projects associated with it, shoreline land uses are increasingly competitive. It is generally accepted in both nations that some degree of official intervention into the operation of the land market is necessary in order to secure patterns of shoreline use which are socially desirable, and which cannot be left entirely to the operation of the laws of supply and demand in the real estate market. So we have planning, and the implementation of planning by police powers, the exact limits of which vary from state to state, province to province, nation to nation. All units of government, however, are generally agreed upon the desirability of some control of shoreline development.

What are the major considerations which affect decisions relative to development of the shorelines? First, of course, are those considerations which relate to the physical character of the shoreline itself, and to the nature of the water and land areas adjacent to the shorelines. Of major significance among these is that of the levels of the lakes and river surfaces, which, in turn, are reflected in the depths available for shipping in the harbours and connecting channels, and in problems of beach stabilization and shoreline erosion.

It is, of course, well known that the lake levels are subject to fluctuation in short periods, seasonally, and in longer-term cycles of from three to five years on the one hand to twenty or more years on the other.[1] At the low stages of the cycle, as this year, the shipping and port interests complain bitterly that the lack of availability of full vessel drafts greatly reduces the efficiency, and thus increases the costs, of water transportation, and renders some ports, such as Lake Calumet Harbor in Chicago, marginal because of restricted vessel access. On the other hand, at the high stages of the cycle, protection of shorelines and beaches from erosion becomes a serious problem.

On the principal issues relative to the Great Lakes which is of international concern is the amount of water which is permitted to be diverted from Lake Michigan, in order to allow the dilution of the sewerage effluent from metropolitan Chicago as it flows across the drainage divide into the Illinois-Mississippi River system. This issue has been a recurring one almost since the completion of the drainage canal by the Sanitary District of Chicago in 1900. Since 1930 the diversion has been limited to 1,500 cubic feet per second in addition to an approximately equal amount for domestic pumpage. In order to prevent the pollution of the waters of Lake Michigan, from which Chicago and nearby suburbs derive their water supply, the wastes of the metropolitan area have been diverted away from the lake since 1900. For several decades, the major municipal wastes have been treated, although there is still much industrial waste and discharge from suburban communities which do not receive treatment, or for which, as in the case of household detergents, the treatment is inadequate. Under pressure from port, shipping, and power interests in both the United States and Canada, the amount of diversion, if any, which is to be permitted has again been subjected to judicial review. All of the testimony is in hand, and a decision may be expected from the courts within the next year or two. It is to be hoped that the decision will be made on the basis of hydrology, and not politics. Chicago,

---

[1] W. T. Laidly, "Regimen of the Great Lakes and Fluctuations of Lake Levels", *Great Lakes Basin* (Washington, American Association for the Advancement of Science, 1962), pp. 91-105.

straddling the drainage divide, has interests both pro and con. In spite of the adverse effects of diversion upon the shipping and port interests of Chicago, it appears to be very decidedly in the interests of the metropolitan area to do everything in its power to prevent any decrease in the amount of permitted diversion, and, if possible, to support efforts to increase the diversion.

As contrasted with the amplitude of the natural fluctuations in the levels of the Great Lakes, the effects of changes in the amount of water diverted from the lakes at Chicago are very minor. It has been demonstrated, in the course of the recent hearings, that the existing diversion decreases the level of Lake Michigan, and of Lake Huron which is hydrologically the same as Lake Michigan, by about two and one-half inches. By contrast, the amplitude of the longe-range cyclical fluctuation is as much as five to six feet. It is only at the extreme low end of the cycle, as this year, that the diversion effect of a few inches would significantly affect the availability of maximum vessel drafts in the harbours and the connecting channels.

The diversion issue at Chicago is significant for other Great Lakes cities in ways other than those related to shipping and port operation. Should the diversion be considerably reduced, the cost to the metropolitan area, and possibly also to other metropolitan areas on Lake Michigan, of additional treatment of its wastes, would far exceed the costs of the two or three inches loss of vessel draft which results from the present diversion in one or two years out of ten. Chicago has a magnificent shoreline park and beach development of over twenty miles, the utility of which would be greatly impaired should the lake waters be subjected to additional pollution that may result from reduced diversion through the drainage canals. The beaches would become useless for swimming and bathing and the entire shoreline less attractive, unless additional treatment works were to be provided, at a cost of many millions of dollars per year. Furthermore, expensive modifications to the system of collection and treatment of the municipal water supply of Chicago, and possibly of other cities, would be required. Many of the basic industries, which now secure water directly from the lake, would require additional water intake and treatment facilities. Thus one of the natural advantages of location on Lake Michigan would be impaired or lost.

A second aspect of the physical configuration of the shoreline areas, which significantly affects the character of development, is the scenic and ecological aspect. With the rapidly expanding populations of the metropolitan areas along and near the Great Lakes and the St. Lawrence River, the demand for recreational and open space is increasing at the same time that the supply is decreasing under pressure from the spreading urbanization. This is a problem in the Oshawa-Toronto-Hamilton area, the Niagara Peninsula, and other areas in Canada, as well as in the vicinities of most of the Great Lakes cities to the United States. In the northern lakes, too, scenic and recreational conservation is a problem, even though the areas are more remote from large-scale urban development. In such areas, public control of substantial stretches of shoreline and adjacent land is imperative. Closer to the metropolitan areas, the conflict between urbanization and industrialization on the one hand and conservation and recreation on the other is critical. The battle to preserve the remaining natural shoreline of Lake Michigan in northwestern Indiana, adjacent to the metropolitan complex of Chicago and Gary, has been documented extensively elsewhere, and need not be repeated here.[2] Analogous battles are shaping up near and within several other of the Great Lakes metropolitan areas.

In the United States, there has in recent years been a substantial shift in emphasis at the federal level in the planning of national parks, and in other recreational and conservational policies. Most of the existing national parks and monuments are located in areas of particularly interesting or significant scenery, primarily in the sparsely populated areas of the west, whereas there has been little federal development of recreational resources accessible easily to the vast metropolitan populations. The recent report of the Outdoor Recreational Resources Review Commission proposed a classification of outdoor recreation resources into six categories, including two—high-density recreation areas and general outdoor recreation areas—which are typically located within or close to major population concentrations.[3] The same commission recommended that the federal government embark upon a programme of acquiring, developing, and operating shorelines of national significance for recreation, scenic beauty, wildlife habitat, or biotic communities, and that it assist state and local governments where other financial needs cannot be met in areas of high recreational impact by providing financial assistance for the planning, acquisition, and develop-

2 For example, Harold M. Mayer, "Politics and Land Use: The Indiana Shoreline of Lake Michigan", *Ann. Assoc. Am. Geog.*, Vol. LIV, no. 4 (1964), pp. 508-523.
3 Outdoor Recreation Resources Review Commission, *Outdoor Recreation for America* (Washington, Government Printing Office, 1962), p. 7.

ment of shoreline recreation areas, providing technical assistance, and specifying programme standards for federal participation in shoreline development.[4] Two national lakeshores have been proposed. One embraces the Sleeping Bear Dunes area on the northern Lake Michigan shoreline, and the other the Indiana Dunes National Lakeshore now in a bill before the Congress. In addition, studies are under way in the Apostle Islands area of northern Wisconsin, in Lake Superior.

A recent change in the National Housing Act provides for federal assistance up to 20 per cent of the cost of acquisition by local governments of open space, or 30 per cent where there is a regional planning agency to co-ordinate the local planning into a metropolitan or regional open space plan. The possibilities of securing public use of lake and river shorelines in this way are now open to the metropolitan areas of the United States around the Great Lakes. Unfortunately, metropolitan government, along the lines pioneered in Toronto, is not characteristic of the United States; on the contrary, the typical pattern is fragmentation of the metropolitan geographic areas into numerous local governments, including both municipalities and special-purpose districts, each with its vested interest in an area or a particular function. In metropolitan Chicago there are over a thousand such local governmental units,[5] and in the New York region over 1,400.[6] In the 212 standard metropolitan statistical areas of the United States in 1960, there were 18,442 local governments,[7] or an average of 87 local governments per metropolitan area.

The fragmentation of metropolitan areas among states, counties, and municipalities is a troublesome aspect of the problem of shoreline development. On the one hand, there is relatively little co-operation among the local governmental units—in spite of the encouragement by the federal government—on behalf of the entire metropolitan and nearby population, in the securing of public ownership and recreational development of the shorelines and adjacent land areas. It is not unusual for suburban municipalities to place restrictions on the uses of beaches and other facilities by

4 Outdoor Recreation Resources Review Commission, *Shoreline Recreation Resources of the United States* (Washington, Government Printing Office, 1962), p. 7.
5 United States 87th Congress (1st sess., H.R.), *Governmental Structure, Organization and Planning in Metropolitan Areas* (Washington, 1961).
6 Robert C. Wood, *1400 Governments* (Cambridge, Harvard University Press, 1961).
7 *Municipal Yearbook 1963* (Chigaco, International City Managers' Association, 1963), p. 21.

non-residents of the community, while at the same time the suburbanites are at liberty to make unrestricted use of the facilities provided in the central areas of the major cities.

The central city-suburban dichotomy is only one aspect of the conflict of interests represented within the major metropolitan areas with respect to use and development of shorelines. Another is the common divergence of interest with respect to public versus private development along the shores. Many suburban communities, especially the smaller ones, have little or no portions of their shoreline accessible to the public, including even their own residents, because riparian ownership by the adjacent property-owners is usual. Very often the location along the shore—as northeast of Detroit, the North Shore north of Chicago, and in the suburbs east and west of Cleveland—encourages development of upper-income suburbs where public access to the shoreline is not desired by the residents, while, on the other hand, much of the shore in the adjacent central cities is utilized for industrial, port, railroad, and other non-recreational use.

Although it is generally recognized that central city and suburbs constitute, geographically and functionally, single units, and that comprehensive planning for the interests of all parts of the respective metropolitan areas is essential, there are few, if any, examples of planning for the development of the entire shoreline of the metropolitan entity. Perhaps the metropolitan municipality of Toronto furnishes the best example, but, then, we do not have metropolitan municipalities along the shores of the Great Lakes in the United States, and, indeed, few are the cities which have been successful in achieving a balance among the conflicting demands for their own shoreline.

The opening of the St. Lawrence Seaway has focused attention upon the need for improved port facilities, deeper and more accessible harbors, and additional shorefront lands for industrial development. But at the same time the expanding city and metropolitan populations require recreational facilities, including especially the use of the increasingly scarce shorelines. The task ahead consists of making, and more important, of effectuating, plans for appropriate allocation of the scarce shorelines among the competing and conflicting uses. If an excess of shoreline is in private riparian ownership for use by abutting residents, the total use for any purpose by the public is restricted. If the shoreline is developed for public recreational use, its availability for port and industrial use is restricted. If port and industrial use dominates, a major amenity value of the city and metropolitan area is alienated. What is a proper allocation?

Chicago, the largest city on the Great Lakes, has not solved this problem. It has twenty miles, almost without interruption, of lakshore devoted to park and recreational use, largely on fill created after the riparian owners turned over their rights to the Chicago Park District or its predecessors. The major port development was forced to locate six miles inland, up the difficult, narrow, shallow, winding Calumet River, because of unavailability of the lakefront. Expansion by fill lakeward from its present site by the largest steel mill in Chicago, even though such expansion is proposed for a portion of the lake unsuitable by location for any but industrial development, is opposed by most Chicago organizations, which have been, through the years, "sold" on the Burnham Plan tradition of lakefront recreational development exclusively. If such industrial expansion cannot take place, the city of Chicago is very likely to lose its largest single manufacturing plant, which can easily transfer to an expanded plant of the same company in nearby Gary.

On the other hand, portions of the lakefront park have been diverted to non-recreational uses, including an exhibition hall surrounded by a sea of parking lots and masses of trucks unloading or loading exhibit material, a chain of obsolete guided-missile bases —with weapons poised as if an invasion from Michigan were expected any moment— a lakefront airport, and two water treatment plants. Meanwhile, to reach the major port and many of the port-associated industries, ships must take several hours to negotiate the difficult Calumet River, with tugs fore and aft, and with open bridges creating long delays for land traffic.

Milwaukee has perhaps achieved a better balance among the diverse uses of the lakefront, with industrial and port development confined to a limited but adequate area at Jones Island, and park north and south of that area. Cleveland has industrial development downtown, with only short stretches of lakefront park. Toronto and Hamilton are fortunate in that they have island- and peninsula-protected enclosed harbour areas within which industrial and port development can take place, with recreational lakefront use outside of the protected area, and on the outer reaches of the lands and peninsulas.

In each city, the pattern and relative extent of each of the diverse uses of the lakefront or riverfront were achieved as the result of an evolution of many years. In some instances the existing investment — public, private, or both — will prevent major changes in the pattern in the forseeable future; in other instances the current concern with urban renewal can be focused in part upon the waterfronts, where extensive redevelopment may be possible. In the United States, many cities are preparing community renewal plans, with federal financial assistance. These plans, in turn, are required to be related to a comprehensive city plan. In Canada, similarly, there is much current activity in the field of urban renewal. Toronto is embarking upon a renewal programme which is analogous in most respects to those of the major American cities.

It would be a great mistake if these plans were to perpetuate the patterns of the past solely or mainly because of traditions, prejudices, or lack of appreciation for the roles of each of the competing waterfront uses. Ports must be on waterfronts; they can be developed up rivers only at great expense to the public, the shipowners, and the industries, and at the cost of loss of the competitive advantages that the port may have, for fast turn-around of ships is a major attribute of the successful port. Likewise, industries which make direct use of water transportation must be located on deep channels which have clear fairways, as free as possible from restrictive bends, depths, and bridges. These should, insofar as possible, have lakefront locations. How they can be provided, and at the same time be compatible with recreational use of the shoreline, is a major challenge for city, metropolitan, regional, national, and international planning within and between the metropolitan areas of the Great Lakes.

11

The Conflict of Salmon Fishing Policies in the North Pacific

J. V. Minghi

Introduction

The North Pacific Salmon Fisheries issue is one of true international proportions, involving Japan, the United States, the Soviet Union, and, to a lesser extent, Canada.

The political geographer is interested in the effects of the competing interests of nations and the differences these interests produce upon the use of natural resources. The salmon are a highly, but not completely mobile natural resource which range across existing political boundaries into areas where unambiguous spatial sovereignty is difficult to maintain. The problem this condition creates is considered in this study both from a legal and a geographical point of view. Conflicts between national salmon fishing policies have been traditionally adjusted by legal means by international treaties, generally according to the wishes of the dominant power. The aim of this paper is to present a survey of the forms, origin and background of the current salmon fishing policies and legal position of the United States and Japan. Also considered is the compatability of existing and proposed legal arrangements with the ecological realities of the salmon cycle and with the economics of salmon fishing in the North Pacific.

Reprinted in edited form from *Pacific Viewpoint*, Vol. 2, no. 1 (1961), pp. 59-84.

Traditionally, marine resources on the high seas can be utilized by all mankind, and become private property only when caught. However, the problem is more than just the conflict over the exploitation of a valuable marine resource of the North Pacific. The peculiar nature of the salmon complicates the problem further. The salmon spawns and hatches in fresh water streams. By beginning and finishing its life cycle within the boundaries of national domains it comes within the full jurisdiction of the coastal state, that is, while it is not on the high seas. Hence, for the coastal state, even the usual basic premise in disputes involving fishing outside territorial water, that the living resources of the high seas are common to all mankind is overshadowed by property claims. This leaves even less common ground than usual among the contestants. In the dispute in question, the United States occupies the position of the coastal state, while Japan which fishes on the high seas, holds to the traditional philosophy of the freedom of the seas. The policy emanating from the United States position is clouded by conflicts among different private interests and government agencies, such as those between the United States Department of the Interior and the State Department, the former giving paramount importance to a policy of conservation, and the latter primarily interested in international relations.

Salmon involved in the dispute in the North Pacific Ocean are spawned and hatched in Asian and American water. The Asian-spawned salmon are mainly from Soviet Siberian streams, while the American-spawned are mainly from Alaskan streams, specifically those flowing into Bristol Bay. Because of their strong homing instinct the salmon, after three to five years on the high seas, return to their parent stream. Salmon in climbing upstream to reach the spawning grounds deteriorate in their physical state. Hence, they are of greater commercial value as they enter fresh water from salt water than at any other time thereafter. The necessary concentration of the salmon as they run towards their parent streams from the open sea renders commercial exploitations easiest at the mouths of these streams.

Commercial exploitation of salmon in Siberia and Alaska began, therefore at river mouths along the coasts. The seasonality of the salmon runs, the remoteness of these areas from markets, the high unit-weight value and the severity of the climate in winter, have given this form of economic activity some peculiar characteristics. The salmon catch, a highly perishable commodity, must be conserved to reach the market in an acceptable condition. This has led to a heavy capital investment in a large canning industry in these remote areas. The salmon run only in the summer months. Since there are few or no off-season employment opportunities, labour in the fishing and canning industries in these isolated areas migrates seasonally. Commercial salmon fishing has continued in this fashion in Bristol Bay under the direction of United States labour and industrial interests and by the Japanese, under a lot-renting system from the Russians, along the Siberian coast. Japan began high-seas fishing for salmon off Siberian waters in the early 1930s. Later in the decade, Japan entered Bristol Bay with experimental and survey vessels with alleged intent to extend large-scale salmon fishing activity to these waters in the future. After protests from the United States Government, Japan announced that she would not fish in Bristol Bay in the future, and withdrew. However, the problem of the conflict between the coastal state and the high-seas maritime nation over the exploitation of salmon had been raised for the first time in the North Pacific.

After the War, measures were taken by the United States to exclude Japan from fisheries where salmon spawned in Bristol Bay streams occur. By the terms of the Treaty of Peace, Japan was committed to enter into negotiations with other countries, and hence joined Canada and the United States as a party to the International North Pacific Fisheries Convention (I.N.P.F.C.) in 1953. In the early 1950s the only Pacific nations with active interests in commercial salmon fishing were Canada, the United States, Japan, and the U.S.S.R. Although the Soviet Union had been actively fishing salmon on an increasing scale since the 1930s, her activity was confined to coastal fishing along the Siberian coast. Added to this was the fact that the Soviet Union shared little common political interest with the other three nations. Hence, it was possible for Canada, the United States and Japan to agree on measures covering most of the North Pacific that would apply to themselves, and would theoretically exclude "newcomers" from catching salmon in convention waters. The area of the North Pacific covered by the terms of the I.N.P.F.C. is 3.2 million square miles, and contains approximately one-third of the world's fish resources.

The I.N.P.F.C. members agreed that, under certain conditions, they would abstain from catching salmon, and also halibut and herring. Hence a "piecemeal" approach to the fishery problem was adopted. The Japanese agreed not to catch salmon of North American origin, and asked if a line might be established in the North Pacific which would facilitate their complying with the agreement.

Thus, on the scientific evidence available at the time, a line at 175 degrees West was established to divide the Asian and American salmon by origin, East of which the Japanese would not fish. This set up a zone contiguous to the American coast within which no parties of the Convention could fish for salmon. It has since become known as the "zone of abstention." At the time, this line was thought to divide satisfactorily American-spawned salmon from Asian-spawned. In international law there is a lack of acceptable procedures and principles for delimiting any contiguous off-shore zone of a coastal state in order to carry out an intended conservation policy. Hence, such a zone as this can only be established by mutual consent between interested parties, and can only be changed under the same terms. The view of the American fishery interests is that the "doctrine of abstention" is an outgrowth of the concept of "historic rights," which in turn is based on the notion that, by virtue of the location of the spawning grounds and the history of sole exploitation, the salmon are an American resource, and hence American property. There is no way for fishermen to recognize the distinction between Asian and American-spawned salmon, and only lately have biologists been able to differentiate. However, the official United States' view, which is that of the State Department, is that the abstention doctrine is valid: (1) when the resource is being fully utilized and there is no waste; (2) when the resource's continued productive state is due to the research and regulations enacted by the countries exploiting the stock; and (3) when all countries presently participating in the fishery are allowed to continue to do so.

Ironically, the present conflict arises as a result of protests by the United States, the architect of the convention's measures, against the activities of Japan in assigned waters. Japan's high-seas fishing catch has been increasing and the runs in Bristol Bay have been falling. The Fish and Wildlife Service of the United States Department of the Interior has adopted a conservation policy which demands that there be a minimum escapement allowed upstream to ensure propagation of the salmon at a sustained yield level. Hence, partly due to Congressional legislation based on inadequate scientific research, catches have fallen more rapidly in Bristol Bay than they would have done, even taking into consideration the diminishing runs of salmon. The explanation of the over-all depleted stocks of salmon has yet to be found. American fishery interests think over-fishing by Japanese fishermen is largely to blame for the depletion in 1957 and 1958, in the belief that the 175 degree West line is, after all, misplaced, and does not satisfactorily divide

Alaska-spawned stocks from Asian-spawned. . . . Consequently, the United States now urges that the abstention line be moved westward. The Japanese argue that the line can only be moved if conclusive scientific evidence can be produced to show that the line does not conform to the convention's intentions.

The convention obligates the signatory powers to carry out scientific research into all aspects concerned with salmon and their movements on the high seas. The results so far show that there exists a broad zone of intermingling of Asian and American-spawned salmon. There is also great variation in the size and movements of stocks of these salmon from one year to another and annually of different species of salmon. Thus, Japan argues that there is no conclusive evidence as yet, and that there will possibly never be a basis for moving the line within the terms of the convention. Obviously a time will come when two lines could be drawn based on biological evidence. One would mark the absolute eastern limit of Asian-spawned salmon, and the other the westernmost limit of American-spawned salmon. If future evidence follows the trends of the findings so far, these two lines would be extremely wide apart, and would contain a number of intermingling salmon. The United States of course, would support the westernmost line, and in fact, has proposed a move westwards of 15 degrees, to 170 degrees East. Japan would use the argument for the eastward line as a counter to the United States proposal, and also as justification for not moving the line from its present position.

From the above reasoning several points arise. The inherent difficulties behind establishing a line running North and South across an ocean to divide salmon by origin can now be seen. The 175 degree West line was meant to be provisional, an administrative procedure to solve an immediate spatial fishery problem. Although this practical solution was meant as a temporary compromise at a certain point in time, inertia set in, as with any provisional line where vested interests are vitally involved on land or on water. The selection of the 175 degree West line in 1952 for the division by origin shows the fallacy of founding legislation on scant scientific evidence, rather than determining if a certain type of legislation would be effective scientifically, and if so, establishing measures accordingly. Lines of absolute limit of one origin or another could eventually be drawn, but any line in between would merely cut through the zone of intermingling. In the case under consideration it seems that in the immediate future no *one* line can be drawn on a scientific basis, whether all parties agree to the principle of equitability by origin or to one of equitability by some quantitative measure involving different species of salmon. Any such line would have to be based on many years of data collection. As with other problems in the natural sciences, many years of intensive research are needed if prediction techniques are to be developed to such a degree that a movable line, or several lines for several species, can be delimited annually. Under presently-known techniques, although there have been considerable improvements, such delimitation would be impossible.

The basic difference of opinion is not one of a scientific nature but one of attitude. Although the United States and Japan are parties to the same convention, Japan does not share the philosophy upon which the convention is based, a philosophy of abstention and equitability by origin. Japan herself however, is in no position to counter American claims with arguments using the same philosophy because the bulk of the Asian-spawned salmon, and by far the greater part of the Japanese catch on the high seas in the post-war period, is of Russian origin. Ever since the 1930s Japan has been progressively constricted in Siberian coastal regions. High-seas fishing temporarily solved this problem, although it has raised others with the United States. Now Russia is evidently also beginning to indulge in high-seas fishing for salmon,[1] further complicating the issue, for although she is fishing largely for salmon of her own origin, she will be competing with Japan, and antagonizing the United States. She is not a member of the I.N.P.F.C. and will presumably fish exclusively under her own regulations. One thing is certain. In the words of Milton E. Brooding, spokesman for the United States National Section at the 1958 I.N.P.F.C. meeting, "Bristol Bay sockeye runs can be exterminated if both of these intensive fisheries—the Japanese high-seas fishery and the United States inshore fishery—are not adequately regulated."[2]

The Japanese Case

Background

Although salmon is not of great relative importance in the total Japanese fishery economy, the great expansion of the export market is largely due to increased exportation of canned salmon to the

---

[1] So far there is evidence only of research fishing. Under Soviet regulations only traps and seines are permitted. Gill nets are outlawed as injurious.
[2] International North Pacific Fisheries Commission, *Proceedings of the Fifth Annual Meeting, Tokyo, Japan, 4 to 10 November, 1958* (Vancouver, I.N.P.F.C., February 1959), p. 53.

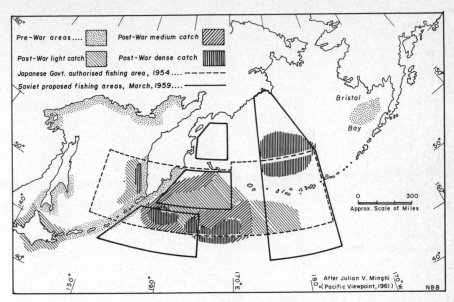

Figure 1. The History of Japanese Salmon Fisheries.

United States, to which 45 per cent of Japan's total value of salmon exports is sent. European demand for Japanese canned salmon has also risen in the last few years.

In the period since 1930 the great feature in salmon fishing has been the increased efficiency of the mother-ship system. Catch per vessel increased tenfold during the period 1930 to 1935. Over the same period the number of catcher-ships increased at the same rate, although through technical advances the number of mother-ships needed to handle this increased productivity has merely doubled. About 90 per cent of Japan's total salmon catch comes under the realm of the mother-ship system. The vessels are equipped with such modern devices as ultra short-wave radio which allows a working radius of 35 miles from the mother-ship, fish detectors, echo-sounders, direction finders, gyro-compasses, radar and even aqua-television. The mother-ship programmes the orderly arrival and discharge of her catchers, to avoid loss of time and confusion. Ever since the resumption of this type of salmon fishing soon after the War, there has been a progressive increase in productivity due to the increase in the efficiency of effort, and to a larger North Pacific population of salmon in the immediate post-war years.

The post-war scene has been characterized by the limitation of Japanese activity in salmon fisheries under various agreements with the U.S.S.R., and under the terms of the I.N.P.F.C. (Figures 1 and 2). The former agreements are flexible in terms of quotas, season and location of fishing, and vary annually. By a Russo-Japanese fisheries agreement for the 1958 salmon season, Japan cut her fleet in the Okhotsk Sea by 50 per cent from the previous year, and reduced her quota from 120,000 metric tons to 110,000. On the other hand, by its very terms, the I.N.P.F.C. has been inflexible and has led to a *status quo* which has been a distinct disadvantage to the United States, the original formulator of the I.N.P.F.C. The Japanese-Soviet Fishery Convention, signed in 1956, gave the Soviet Union a good bargaining position by which to limit Japanese fishing activity still further. The Soviets were in a position to take action on unilateral decisions, whereas, by the terms of the I.N.P.F.C., the United States is not. The Soviets have cut quotas on presumption of depletion through overfishing, and as a result there has been much Japanese irritation over Soviet policy. The Fishery Convention settles no problems on a long-term basis, but resolves itself into a yearly battle in which scientific research is of little or no consideration.

In the present decade, deep-sea fishing has been a basic issue. The 1956 Fisheries Pact between Japan and the U.S.S.R. places restrictions on size of catch in the Northwest Pacific. Questions, however, were settled politically, and not scientifically. Agreements were made on scanty scientific evidence. The Soviets argued for conservation against indiscriminate fishing, and the Japanese maintained that statistical data did not support the thesis that stocks of salmon were diminishing. At a conference in Tokyo in March, 1959, the U.S.S.R. made staggering curtailment proposals for the 1959 salmon fishing season to Japan. After more than a month of discussion, the original Soviet proposal of a quota figure totalling 50,000 tons had expanded, and the Japanese demand for 160,000 tons had contracted to reach an agreed compromise quota of 94,000 tons for the 1959 season.[3]

Although these latest Soviet proposals would place severe limitations on Japanese salmon fishing, they do recognize the right, or necessity, of the Japanese high-seas operation to catch salmon which are mainly of Russian origin. There is, so far, no attempt to prohibit absolutely the catching of Russian-spawned salmon by the Japanese. In this respect the Russians differ in attitude from the Americans. The difference is basically an historic one. The

---

[3] *Pacific Fisherman*, Vol. LVII (1959), p. 1.

Japanese were largely responsible for developing the Siberian fishery, whereas they have no historic rights whatsoever over the North American salmon. Another point raised is the possible conflict between the two treaties, the I.N.P.F.C. and the Russo-Japanese Agreement, over potentially the same waters and resource therein, and involving a member of both treaties, i.e., Japan. This possible conflict of regulations would seem to illustrate as unwise the conclusion of different treaties over waters which essentially form one unit in terms of high-seas fishery regulations. Of course, it can be argued that, although the high seas form a legal unity in the North Pacific, there is a division of stocks based on origin. The intermingling of these stocks during the migration period and the Japanese high-seas fishing activity in the intermingling area, serves to blurr this distinction based on origin-division. As Senator Magnuson of Washington has said, if the purpose of the I.N.P.F.C. is to conserve and perpetuate salmon resources, it "must include all four nations substantially utilizing that resource."[4]

International Law Standing

In general terms the Japanese case rests on the traditional international law concept of the freedom of the seas. Japan is one of the staunchest supporters of the three-mile limit rule. Japan's case is centred on her attitude toward the control of the exploitation of the riches of the sea, and to the doctrines of the contiguous zone, and the coastal state.

Japan maintains that the coastal state is not allowed to claim the exclusive exploitation of natural resources under any other institution than that of the territorial sea. The Japanese distinguish between the problem of marine resources, especially the conservation of biological resources, and the problem of the contiguous zone. The doctrine of the contiguous zone cannot be interpreted to justify a monopoly of fisheries outside territorial limits, since a monopoly can be asserted only as an exercise of the right of sovereignty within an area subject to sovereignty. The maritime states, with ability and improved techniques for fishing on the high seas, will never renounce the rights of exploitation established thereon.

The area between the three-mile limit off the Alaska coast and the 175 degree West line of abstention is certainly in the "contiguous zone" class. The monopolistic connotations of abstention zones declared unilaterally by a foreign state are obvious. The

[4] *Pacific Fisherman*, Vol. LVII (1959), p. 29.

suspicion and fear entertained by Japan over these declarations have been well grounded in the Kamchatka Sea, where, in 1956, a monopoly of high-class salmon fishing was set up by the unilateral action of the Soviet Union. Japan supports the traditional principle that the freedom of the seas cannot be violated by any unilateral declaration or by any new theory. Japan recognizes the need for conservation, but with regulations set up by conventions between interested parties.

One of the notes, discussing the place of the coastal state in a fishery conservation programme, in the Report of the Rome Conference in 1955 states that no conservation measures should be taken by the coastal state on the high seas without international agreement. The reasoning behind this is that conservation measures are based on scientific and technical evidence, and the coastal state has not necessarily got the best, let alone a monopoly of such evidence. Hence, all users should have equal rights to supply information and to formulate measures. Consequently, Japan argues that there is no reason to elevate the coastal state to a superior position. Geographical position alone is not evidence of interest or scientific knowledge about conservation. Mr. Tsuruoka, a member of the Japanese delegation at Geneva in 1958, declared: "As the concept of conservation is primarily scientific, and not political or economic in nature, the coastal state should have no unilateral rights to regulate fisheries by virtue of its geographical position."[5] The argument that the coastal state is in a "special position" based on social and economic reasons is considered untenable. Such an idea could lead to abuse of foreign fishermen, and also to underfishing. The very purpose of a non-coastal state fishing so far afield is explained by the lack of adequate resources available near home to sustain its population. To cut off non-coastal states from these distant resources would deprive a large section of the population of their present standard of living.

According to the Japanese point of view the abstention theory, which forms the basis of the I.N.P.F.C., is held invalid because it lacks a scientific base, and hence has nothing to do with conservation.[6] The main seed of controversy in the dispute hinges on the line of abstention and the "zone of intermingling." The possibility of Asian and American salmon intermingling was realized in 1951,

---

[5] United Nations, "Conference on the Law of the Sea", *High Seas*, A/CONF. 13/31, Vol. V (Geneva, 1958), p. 7.
[6] United Nations, "Conference on the Law of the Sea", *High Seas*, A/CONF. 13/31, Vol. V (Geneva, 1958), p. 41.

and the 175 degree West line was meant to be a temporary measure. To move it, three process stages are provided under the convention: (1) scientific investigation up to a point when conclusive evidence of a discrepancy between the line, and the location and movement of salmon of different origin is available to support a shift; (2) political and diplomatic approval; *and if this fails*, (3) an impartially decided scientific line. The convention is still concerned with stage one. From the American point of view there has been some success because the Japanese have been kept west of the abstention line and away from Japan's alleged just claim of up to the three-mile limit. Japan, who has opposed the abstention principle that she feels the convention forced on her in 1951, is obviously in no mood for further concessions. Japan contends that arguments to move the line westwards are arbitrary, and based on extremely insufficient scientific data, and that to move the line *now* would be to scrap the convention. She also contends that proof is insufficient that there are large proportions of American-spawned salmon among the different species in the intermingling zone.

The freedom of the seas concept is the corner-stone of the Japanese case. In the past Japan has used this concept aggressively, but now she is using it to defend her position against further loss. As a signatory to the convention she has prejudiced her position somewhat. Japan, however, has since taken a very strong position against any further extension of the abstention doctrine and the coastal state concept. She has to be very careful not to set precedents in policy in the convention, which would be detrimental to her position in other fishing disputes with other states.

At present, Japan's population has been increasing by 700,000 annually. To offset the threat of economic chaos the standard of living must be maintained and improved, and the greatest possible resource base must be sought in order that technical and organizational innovations may be fully utilized. In her effort to expand her fisheries, Japan has had to vary her policy to reach compromises in different situations. A programme suggested in 1949 for the future of Japanese fisheries proposed such measures as reorientation and improvements of fishery methods, improvement in collection and computation for production statistics, reappraisal of legislation, improved handling and transportation of fish, exchange of fishery products on the foreign market, and expansion of fishery areas.[7] Since then, under national guidance, all these measures have

---

[7] Ada Espenshade, "A Program for Japanese Fisheries", *Geographical Review*, Vol. XXXIX (January 1949), p. 82.

been carried out, but the expansion of the fishing industry has met with international complications, and Japan has only submitted to limitations on this policy when conclusive scientific evidence has shown that the fishery in question is becoming seriously depleted due to over-fishing. The high-seas salmon fishery operates under such adverse conditions as foul weather (about one-third of the days during the season are impossible for fishing) and conservation measures. There are restrictions on the length of nets, the size of mesh, as well as the distance between nets. Quantity of catch is regulated by quotas, and all fishing is prohibited after 10 August. Even given continuous good weather, the nets are down in water for a maximum of 42 hours a week. The great economic potential, flexibility, a real mobility, and high order of technological efficiency, has given the mother-ship system the greatest possibility of success. With this fact of economic success and that of heavy capitalization in the industry, the other arguments for the Japanese case, those of dependence upon exports on this high-value, low-bulk product, of protein, diet and occupational dependence are reinforced.

The United States Case

Background

Salmon fishing is of only local and regional significance in the United States. It has lost much of its pre-war importance in terms of labour, taxes rendered and installed capital.

The salmon-fishing industry has formed an integral part of the regional economy of the Alaskan coast, and salmon fishing is still the most important fishing activity there in terms of value. Diminishing runs of salmon, domestic conservation legislation and foreign competition have rendered the industry unable to keep pace with the steady growth of domestic and foreign markets. Imports, principally from Japan, are annually more able to compete in the domestic market. Imports of canned salmon for 1958 showed a 25 per cent increase on those of 1957. Japan accounted for 73 per cent of the total canned salmon imports of United States. During the years of increasing catches up to the mid-1930s, the industry was characterized by the domination of a half-dozen large firms which forced the smaller firms out by their ability to lead in the pricing field and by virtue of the economies of scale and vertical integration they enjoyed. Decreasing runs of salmon have led to diseconomies of scale, to the failure to reach threshold requirements, to lower productivity and, consequently, to a finished good at rising cost. Despite this drop in economic importance the industrial and labour interests concerned continue to have a strong political voice. All the companies together have maintained for some 30 years a negotiating body, The Alaska Salmon Industry Inc., while the Alaska Fishermen's Union represents the labour interests of the seasonal workers in the salmon industry. Because of the seasonality of employment, the industry has some extra-regional importance. A large proportion of workers come from the Puget Sound area. There are few opportunities for work in the off-season. The isolation of the industry along the Alaskan coast means that the organisation centre is on Puget Sound. In fact, the capital investment and profit sharing involves many Pacific Northwest interests.

Historical Context of Salmon Fishing.

The development of the industry in Alaska has been basically conditioned by the character and location of its raw material supply. As mentioned above, the peculiar characteristics of the salmon are such that the ideal time and place to catch them is at the river mouths where they run in large schools near the surface before ascending the freshwater streams to spawn and die. Before technical advances made mass-exploitation possible on the high seas, it was most convenient and profitable to begin salmon fishing, as the Japanese had begun in Siberia, in waters close to the shore and at river mouths. It is still sounder economics to fish for salmon at the river mouths, but for obvious political reasons this is no longer possible for the Japanese.

Because of its marginal geographical situation, Bristol Bay did not come under intensive salmon fishing activity until the early years of this century. Due to its physical excellence in terms of factors controlling quality and quantity of salmon runs, it was exploited successfully with increasing returns until the late 1930s. As a result of bitter lessons learned in the past along the entire Pacific Coast, a conservation policy was adopted even in the early days of salmon fishing activity in Bristol Bay. Since early Congressional legislation in 1906 proved not particularly effective, the White Act was passed in 1924. Under the White Act the Bureau of Fisheries was given full power over all fishing in Alaska. The act provided for at least a 50 per cent escapement of all salmon entering the rivers to spawn. It was recognized that the number allowed up the river to spawn, known as the "escapement," was related to the size of the run a few years hence, and that conservation based on a "minimum escapement" policy would render a direct return in the area applied, thus initiating a principle of optimum sustained yield. This would make for a very close spatial relationship between sacrifices made, and benefits reaped.

Up to World War II, the Alaska salmon pack led the world in output. In 1935 Freeman wrote, "so far the Asiatic output has not seriously disturbed our markets."[8] Within the last decade the picture has changed considerably. Salmon runs have been steadily falling since 1935 despite the minimum escapement policy strictly adhered to by the United States Fish and Wildlife Service (F.W.S.). Catches have dropped accordingly. Techniques developed in recent years have been prohibited by law in the interests of conservation. Decisions about areas and times allowed for salmon fishing are often made during the season by the F.W.S. Federal Law forbids United States citizens taking salmon by nets on the high seas. The fish trap which, in economic terms, is the best method of catching salmon, is also forbidden. Quality is a prime requisite for success in the salmon canning industry hence the time between death and canning must be as short as possible. Fish traps are ideal for minimizing this critical period because the supply to the cannery can be stabilized by leaving the salmon alive in the traps, and removing them at such times and in such a number as the cannery might require. The F.W.S. has chosen to legislate in this way to avoid any sudden drastic dislocation in the industry. However, a satisfactory sustained yield has not been realized, and growing inefficiency, despite some organizational changes, has been characteristic of the industry since the War.

In 1957 the situation became critical. Over-fishing by the Japanese was blamed for the drop in the Bristol Bay runs. During the 1958 season the Japanese complied with an American request to fish only a given number of salmon and, if possible, to catch them all west of 170 degrees East. Again this was not an official agreement as the Japanese were much afraid of prejudicing their chances of a satisfactory agreement with the Russians, by openly agreeing to limitation with the United States. After preliminary warnings in December, 1958, the F.W.S. decided in March, 1959, that, to ensure sufficient escapement to maintain the resource, Bristol Bay would be closed to fishing for the 1959 season, although, in late May, 1959, after the Japanese had agreed to reduce fishing intensity for the 1959 season, the Bureau of Commercial Fisheries announced that a limited red salmon catch would be allowed in Bristol Bay. The relationship of escapement to runs has been reasonably good, except for

---

8 Otis W. Freeman, "Salmon Industry of the Pacific Coast", *Economic Geography*, Vol. XI (April 1935), p. 129.

1957, when the Japanese high-seas fishery for the first time operated north of the Aleutians, catching some 20 million salmon, including about 70 per cent of all red salmon taken in the North Pacific that season. The non-materialization of the predicted run is circumstantial evidence that Japanese fishing affected the Bristol Bay run in that particular year. On the assumption that the situation is due entirely to Japanese fishing of Alaska-spawned salmon in water assigned to them under the I.N.P.F.C., both industry and labour have tried by various means to force Japan to agree on a westerly move of the present abstention line. Proposed legislation would also ban imports of Japanese salmon. For the last two years imported Japanese canned salmon had exceeded the total production from Bristol Bay. Further proposals would ban *all* fish imports from Japan. Such proposals have been justified as "conservation measures."[9]

The recent appearance of deep-sea Soviet fishing trawlers in the convention waters has further complicated the issue. Subject to no treaty agreements the Russians feel free to fish salmon outside the territorial limits of Alaska. However, a trawler does not normally fish for salmon, and there is no proof that Russian vessels in the eastern Bering Sea are, or will be fishing salmon. Japanese trawlers have been trawling for bottom fish for several years in the areas where the Russian trawlers have been currently located.

International Law Standing

There are divergent opinions as to exactly what the United States' case is based upon. The views of the fishery interests on this point can hardly be accepted despite the wide support they have been given. The State Department is, after all, the spokesman for the United States in international law. The United States' case is based upon the philosophy and practice of a sound conservation policy, especially in this case where there is a real danger of extinction of the resource. These conservation procedures have been approved and recognized by most nations in both the Rome Conference on Conservation in 1955, and the Law of the Sea Conference at Geneva in 1958. There is also the special interest of the coastal state in a fishery conservation programme. The peculiar nature of the salmon gives the United States presumed grounds for the opportunity of claiming a property right over salmon which are spawned, hatched, have their early development, and return to die in national and territorial waters. Added to these two factors of "special interest" and "property" claims, the United States has also claimed a historic right

---

9 *Seattle Times* (April 3, 1959).

for exclusive exploitation of this resource. The fishermen of the United States and Canada are held to be solely responsible for the maximum development of fisheries, and have enjoyed almost exclusive rights in them.

The first official statement of policy by the United States came in November, 1937, from the then Secretary of State Cordell Hull, after the Japanese high-seas fishing fleet had spent a season researching and catching some salmon commercially in Bristol Bay. In a note to the Japanese Government he argued that both the United States Government and private interests had developed the salmon resource to its present state. A law of Congress protected the salmon and put strict control on fishing activity. All this the Japanese had ignored. In the light of the annual investment of the United States in conservation, the hardship of the industry and steady decrease in total pack, the United States claimed a superior interest in Alaskan salmon, and suggested that it was to be regarded as an American resource. Such doctrines as "prior occupation", "prescription" and "usage" were used to bolster the United States' case. As a matter of policy the United States could not abandon its control in this case without some domestic hostility and public disgrace. The pre-war question was one of conservation and competing national interests, for this affair came at a time when there was growing friction between the United States and Japan on policy in the Pacific area.

Since the War, the United States' case has little changed. In 1943, Tomasevich thought that, in terms of power of protection, fishery conservation should have the same standing as revenue laws or defence of a neutral coastal state against belligerent activities.[10] Even Japan voted for the "coastal state" measures at Geneva in the hope that the extension of exclusive fishing rights would not be pressed by other countries. On the presumption that the production of most fisheries can be maintained at a near-maximum with conservation policies, the United States argues that, with increased activity in fishing, the most important aspect of the international law of fisheries is the promotion of effective conservation. The doctrine of the freedom of the seas has never been absolute, and extraterritorial rights for various functions have always existed. Allen has stated: "There is a definite distinction between the right of

---

[10] Jozo Tomasevich, *International Agreements on Conservation of Marine Resources, with Special Reference to the North Pacific* (Food Research Institute, Stanford University, 1943), p. 35.

sovereignty and the right to exercise protective or preventive jurisdiction over an area outside the national domain."[11]

Two main lines of policy are being pursued at the moment, one
direct and the other indirect. Within the terms of the I.N.P.F.C. the
Japanese are being asked to suspend fishing in the area of intermingling where North American salmon occur in significant proportions. Indirectly the vested interests are attemping to force legislation through Congress that would bring pressure to bear on
Japanese fishing activities through economic sanctions, such as ban-
ning imports from Japan of canned fish. There are also attempts to
use organized labour to take action such as refusing to unload goods
from Japan at the port of entry into the United States.

The Relative Standing of the Two Cases

The reports of the various sub-committees to the Committee on
Biology and Research on the Progress of Research on the Problems
raised by the Protocol of the I.N.P.F.C. contain the best statement
on current expert opinion of all parties to the convention. The Committee's report to the 1958 Meeting of the I.N.P.F.C. in Tokyo provides the latest statement.[12]

The proposed fields of study agreed upon at the first meeting of
the I.N.P.F.C. in 1954 were: (1) the distribution of salmon on the
high seas; (2) the use of various techniques to distinguish origin;
(3) the tagging of salmon to obtain direct evidence of movement;
and (4) oceanographic background study for this salmon distribution and movement data. At the 1957 meeting, the zone of intermingling was delimited as spreading over about 30 degrees of longi-
tude between 170 degrees East and 160 degrees West. In this large
area there is considerable difficulty in observing the distribution of
salmon by their origin. The evidence shows that each stock may
vary from year to year in distribution and size. The present research
programme leaves many gaps, and it is impossible to describe the
high-seas distribution of all the important races quantitatively and
qualitatively. Although the distribution of salmon in 1956 and 1957
prove the year to year variation, they do not contradict some overall general conclusions which can be made.

---

[11] Edward W. Allen, "The American View", *Proceedings of Regional Meet-
ing, American Society of International Law, Marginal Seas and Pacific
Fisheries*, Bulletin no. 12, Part 2 (Seattle, June 1956), p. 22.
[12] International North Pacific Fisheries Commission, *Proceedings of the
Fifth Annual Meeting, Tokyo, Japan, 4 to 10 November, 1958* (Vancouver,
I.N.P.F.C., February 1959).

Tagged red salmon of American origin have been found to predominate over Asian-spawned salmon as far as 175 degrees East and to exist as far as 170 degrees East; yet, Asian parasite characteristics have been found as far east as 170 degrees West. Within the intermingling zone there is a definite north-south apportionment, with American-spawned salmon predominating in the Bering Sea, and Asian south of the Aleutians. However, "the dynamic rather than the static nature of the distribution of red salmon is emphasized." So far any quantitative conclusions on pink salmon are impossible. Marked intra- and inter-seasonal fluctuations exist in number and distribution. No research work on chum salmon had been carried out prior to 1954. After three years of intensive research by tagging and scale analysis, a conclusion that the centre of the intermingling zone falls about 175 degrees West, with a 15 degree spread on either side, can be made. However, measurement of intermingling within the zone in terms of assessed proportions is still quite vague.

Riesenfeld wrote that "in the Law of the Sea national egotism, rash generalisations, insufficient consideration of basic questions have caused more conflicts and uncertainties than in any other aspect of International Law.[13] The present conflict over salmon exploitation in the North Pacific is well illustrated by this statement. Both sides have pursued increasingly incompatible policies. The motives behind these policies have often been influenced by chauvinism and local self-interest, and by political considerations not directly related to the problem in question, rather than by notions of equity.

At the extreme, the fishery interests interpret the United States' case as founded on the premise that she has property rights over the salmon, and relate this to a policy of exclusive exploitation based on origin. Japan, of course, does not recognize this in practice. Hence many arguments are not founded on common ground. By municipal law involving conservation measures, and by such policy as the terms of the I.N.P.F.C., the United States has passed legislation in an attempt to achieve her goal of exclusive rights to exploitation. However, municipal legislation has been flexible, whereas the terms of the I.N.P.F.C. have not. The United States has thus tried to find scientific evidence to substantiate its legislative measures.

More logically, legislation and exploitation should be in the light of scientific evidence because the mass-exploitation has a scientific base. In all fairness, however, it must be pointed out that the pres-

---

13 Stephan A. Riesenfeld, *Protection of Coastal Fisheries under International Law* (Washington, Carnegie Endowment for International Peace, Division of International Peace, Division of International Law, 1942), p. ix.

ent illogicality of the line 175 degrees West, although due to the lack of proper scientific evidence at the time, cannot really be blamed on its creators as it was supposed to be a temporary measure to meet immediate demands. Rash generalizations on both sides have led to serious misconceptions. The Japanese claim that there is no conclusive scientific evidence which related the drop in runs of Bristol Bay salmon to Japanese fishing of salmon on the high seas (Figure 2) and that, moreover, there is no evidence that the Japanese are catching immature salmon or that the small mesh nets used by the Japanese kill or injure young salmon. The Japanese maintain that the need for the stringent conservation measures in Bristol Bay is a result of the coincidence of a cyclical low with an unusual limited escapement (Figure 3) in the two main years, 1954 and 1955, in which the 1959 run was spawned.

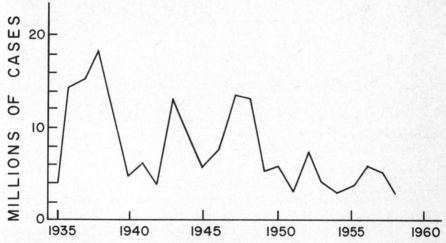

Figure 2. Bristol Bay Red Salmon Packs.

Professor M. Uda, of the Tokyo University of Fisheries, said in the spring of 1959: "It has been prematurely supposed by some that the main cause (of the decline of Alaska-spawned salmon) was overfishing by the Japanese high-seas salmon fisheries. However, the declining trend began before Japanese high-seas fishing. The peaks in the sockeye pack in Bristol Bay were in the decade from 1930 to 1940. The fluctuation in natural environmental conditions such as the falling of water levels and freezing of spawning beds due to climatic change, together with deforestation, water pollution, dam obstructions, effect of natural enemies, predators, etc., and changes in survival, or mortality rates due to changes in ocean climate, may be mainly responsible for such a broad change in sub-Arctic

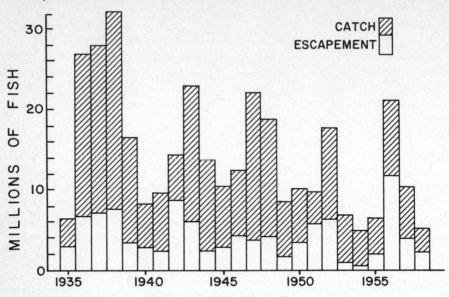

Figure 3. Red Salmon Run in Bristol Bay.

waters."[14] Fisheries experts in the United States are in general agreement with Professor Uda's statement. Dr. William F. Thompson, one-time Director of the University of Washington's Fisheries Research Institute, has stated, ". . . the (United States fishing) industry must not make the mistake of trying to remedy by law something that is a natural occurrence."[15] Obviously a distinction must be made between two trends. There is a definite over-all reduction in salmon runs for which the Japanese cannot be held responsible. However, a yearly fluctuation can also be observed.

The Japanese operate their high-seas salmon fishing industry in a manner similar to the way in which they operate several other industries producing goods deemed essential by the Japanese Government to the country's economy. It is an administered non-competitive industry entered within the hands of several large corporations. The industry, beset by political complications in the international field in which the government participates, receives government support. It is at the same time efficient and inefficient from the economic standpoint. In terms of scale of operation and utilization of available techniques, the Japanese industry is more efficient than the Bristol Bay salmon fishery. However, it is hardly efficient when certain considerations are examined. Such considerations

---

[14] M. Uda, "The Salmon Fisheries", *Fisheries Seminars*, Vol. 3 (Nanaimo, Fisheries Research Board of Canada, March-May 1959), pp. 8-9.
[15] *University of Washington Daily*, April 8, 1954.

would include its short-term policy of a high rate of discount to the future, the increased input necessitated by substituting transport and search costs for the natural concentration found at river mouths, and the failure to allow the salmon to reach full maturity, and hence highest quality which they attain as they begin to run upstream from the open sea. Return per unit effort, if measured by number of salmon per unit of gear fished, is far lower on the high seas where salmon are scattered, than in Bristol Bay where they are schooled. On the high seas twenty-five men and a large boat must fish six to eight miles of net to equal the daily catch of two men in an open skiff using 150 fathoms of net. These questions of technical efficiency and high returns must be considered in the light of short-term exploitation and sacrifice of quality.

The United States' industry, on the other hand, has not been able to use optimum methods of exploitation because conservation legislation has been against this. Fishing techniques have become anachronistic. In 1939, when restrictions were not as severe as now, Deloach stated that " . . . such restrictions . . . serve to reduce the available supply for market purposes as well as to forestall wasteful use of the resource."[16] Up to the early 1950s, regulations were still severe in terms of legislation against more efficient techniques. The tendency has been for the F.W.S. to maintain a technical *status quo* in this manner. There have been various pressures behind such a policy. Ostensibly the desire for the conservation of the resource is fundamental. However, there are other factors, such as the vested interests of the boat owners, and the aspect of the asserted social benefit to the Alaskan native. Some type of benefit/cost analysis would be needed to gauge the validity of the last mentioned factor. There has been heavy investment in the industry to offset the lack of economies brought about by these inefficiencies. However, for the last 20 years, runs of salmon have been diminishing, hence productivity has further dropped. The great feature of salmon fishing is the lack of reliable prediction in terms of quantity, quality and time of species. Obviously, despite the factor of concentration, for the immobile site of the Alaskan industry this unpredictability is going to have a greater effect than for the mobile high-seas operation of the Japanese. This uncertainty means great risk. Up to the early 1920s the small cannery, typical of a risk industry, accounted for the major part of the pack. However, the tendency since then has been towards economies of scale by vertical integration, as the

---

16 Daniel B. DeLoach, *The Salmon Canning Industry* (Corvallis, 1939), p. 39.

smaller canneries began to suffer competition from under-pricing by the bigger companies. As long as the runs did not deteriorate appreciably this was sound economics, and productivity increased. However, with progressive decreases in runs the catch dropped quickly below threshold requirements. The unit cost of the salmon has thus increased, giving the more cheaply produced Japanese article a comparative advantage and strong competitive position in the American market. In fact, despite the low productivity per worker (or per capita unit in gear), caused by the need for search and large area covered by nets, the Japanese can put a lower cost per unit commodity on the American market due to other relative costs of factor inputs in the production process. Primarily lower wages per worker in the Japanese industry enable it to achieve comparable labour costs to the American industry even though the Japanese use more men per salmon catch per unit of time. Secondly the Japanese government subsidizes the industry in technical improvement as compared to government restraint in the United States' policy. These two factors would seem to explain the superior competitive position of the Japanese despite the natural advantage of concentration the Alaskan industry enjoys. Logically, then it would seem that if the United States' policy toward Bristol Bay salmon fishing were changed to one of government subsidies for technical improvement plus restricted entry into the market, the present industry would lower costs of salmon catch, and consequently lower prices of the commodity. This restriction would essentially mean the adoption of a monopoly operation of the industry after the Japanese style. The United States monopoly would never get out of hand as long as Japanese salmon were not restricted from the American market. There is one other important factor which must be considered. Because of the present nature of the resource, its availability rather than the volume of the market might ultimately set the limit.

The pressure for a solution to this international problem is essentially desired from the use or value both parties see in the resource. Therefore a solution to the economics of the salmon business in each country is fundamental in perpetuating the resource.

At the Law of the Sea Conference in Geneva 1958, the United States' case probably gained a little on the Japanese policy in terms of world opinion. The abstention principal found support, conservation was declared the duty of all nations, and the special interests of the coastal state were recognized. The convention must be ratified, and this will be binding only on the states accepting the obligations.

Hence, regional and special organizations must continue to tackle conservation problems.

There is need for a permanent solution to the problem, a solution which must come through diplomacy and international law. However, there are many problems to be overcome before arriving at any agreement. Under the terms of the I.N.P.F.C., if any disagreements should arise in connection with the conclusions of research work, an independent committee is to decide on the recommendations to be made.[17] As Japan has never recognized the United States property claim, there is a question of the "spirit and intent" of the two disputants. Not only are there differences over the interpretation of the protocol of the I.N.P.F.C. but there are also varying opinions regarding the statistical inference of the data collected in salmon research. The accumulated scientific evidence since 1954 shows that disagreements will increase as the data mount. Complications and intricacies, unimagined in 1952, are becoming more evident as the sum of Canadian, American and Japanese data is brought out annually at the I.N.P.F.C. meetings. At the same time, any independent committee would be faced with so many alternatives that an objective solution based solely on scientific data will probably be impossible. Diplomatic compromise would then probably be necessary to settle the issue. Unilateral action can be ruled out as a solution, for it can scarcely be the basis of a fundamental and equitable solution of the fisheries problem. The United States realizes that any policy of extending territorial jurisdiction can be a two-edged sword. Salmon fisheries are not the only important fisheries of the United States. The tuna-fishing industry of California finds the United States in the role of the high-seas state, and there is regional pressure from California against any national policy which would adversely affect the vested interests of the California high-seas tuna fleet.

The Canadians act as independent observers at the I.N.P.F.C. meetings. As they are satisfied that no salmon spawned in Canadian streams cross the 175 degree West line at any time, the Canadians can afford to be neutral. The Canadians state that it is not just a case of picking up the abstention line and moving it a little westwards, as the United States demands. They suggest that several new lines must be drawn to divide the stocks of salmon by species determined by an equal-ration proportion in terms of numbers of each

---

17 United Nations, "Report of the International Technical Conference on the Conservation of the Living Resources of the Sea, Rome", *Objectives of Fishery Conservation*, A/CONF. 10/6 (New York, 1955), p. 47.

species. These lines would have to vary from season to season. If such a solution were to be founded on scientific evidence in the terms that the I.N.P.F.C. demands, then it could only take place when and if sound and conclusive means of predicting salmon movement are developed. So far there is a lack of sufficient evidence for conclusive statements of any fundamental nature. Interpretation of data presently available varies, and allows for no conclusive proof of determinant factors. A mutually satisfactory line based on averages of migration extents seems a long way off.

Japanese and American policies are at opposite poles. Even with some flexibility of either policy, there seems little possibility of a solution coming through the efforts of the contending national and sectional parties. There is a legal deadlock at the international level and disagreement on the interpretation of scientific data. However, diplomacy may yet find a way.

From this study of the conflict over the utilization of the natural resource several features come to light: (1) the limitations and possible dangers of an exclusive fishery pact covering large areas of the high seas; (2) the economic need of Japan to maintain this valuable export at its present level; (3) the basic difference between the economics of the Japanese and American salmon fishing organizations; (4) the basic contrasts in attitudes between Japan on one side, and the two principal "coastal" states, the United States and the Soviet Union, on the other, over the depletion and exploitation of salmon stocks; and (5) the confused state of international law relating to the freedom of the high seas and fishing rights.

Postscript to: "The Conflict of Salmon Fishing Policies in the North Pacific" Julian V. Minghi.

During the decade since this paper first appeared, there have been few basic changes in the nature of the conflict. Until 1966, the Bristol Bay salmon runs continued to decline, and the United States continued, unsuccessfully, to press for a shift in the 175 degrees West meridian eastwards to limit the spatial extent of Japanese high-seas salmon fishing in the North Pacific. The United States in 1965 threatened severe restrictions on the importation of Japanese fishery products, in reaction to continued Japanese fishing and declining salmon runs.

Despite the tremendous improvements in the techniques of biological research, fishery experts have deplored the lack of scientific knowledge upon which the I.N.P.F.C. and other similar treaties are based, and to question the direction which research is taking in its narrow devotion to determining legal lines as part of a static system of ownership of North Pacific salmon.*

By the late 1960's, however, salmon runs at Bristol Bay had increased substantially, and, despite Japanese fishing, the 1969 run was expected to exceed that of any year since Japan started her high-seas salmon fishing activity in the North Pacific.

* W. F. Thompson, "Fishing Treaties and Salmon in the North Pacific", *Science*, Vol. 150, no. 3705 (December 31, 1965), pp. 1786-1789.

12

Water Pollution in Canada by Drainage Basins

J. R. Menzies

Introduction

It has been estimated that of the earth's total water supply about 97 per cent is in the seas, another two per cent is locked in the polar ice caps and only one per cent is fresh water. It is in respect to this one per cent of available fresh water, suitable for use by people, plants and animals, that pollution is of greatest significance. Pollution in salt water which is more limited in its adverse effects, must also be taken into account

The importance of water to the economy and well-being of a nation or any particular area is usually recognized in inverse ratio to its availability, quality and quantity. A firm realization that without it there can be no life, would ensure this national resource a proper place in our present and future plans. Coupled with this is the need for universal recognition of the destructive role which pollution plays.

A publication of the World Health Organization contains the following statement:

"When the forces of sanitary deterioration are considered, such as those that accompany increasing population density and industrialization, it becomes evident that the sanitary control of the environment is slipping backward. In spite of all of a positive nature that WHO and similar agencies have attempted to do, the world

Background Paper, *Resources for Tomorrow Conference, 1961,* Vol. 1, pp. 353-64. Reprinted by permission of the Queen's Printer, Ottawa.

is probably in worse sanitary condition now than it was ten years ago. The forces of deterioration have outstripped the forces of betterment."

It would be unfair to regard this as an accurate statement for all parts of Canada but it accurately portrays conditions in fairly extensive areas where pollution abatement and control are not receiving sufficient support from regulatory authorities and the general public.

Water Use, and Effects of Pollution

Water use may be thought of in several broad categories such as domestic, industrial, agricultural, power, navigation, wild life and recreational. The effects of pollution within these classifications vary widely. For example, pollution resulting from the disposal of human wastes is of major significance to domestic water supplies; of less importance in relation to industrial, agricultural and some forms of recreational use; and of little significance in respect to navigation and power development. Severe pollution from this source can be very destructive to aquatic life. Pollution resulting from industrial wastes is usually significant in relation to domestic use, sometimes in relation to agriculture, to fish and other wild life, and frequently to further industrial use. Waste oil in municipal and industrial wastes and from navigation is often destructive to wild life and damaging to property and recreational activities. Pollution from natural sources affects water use in many ways, some of which are not fully understood. Physical pollution, such as silt from runoff or river bed scouring, is not only detrimental to various water uses but over a period of time decreases the storage capacity of reservoirs.

Broadly speaking, the effects of pollution become a matter of general interest only when they are notoriously bad. The situation arouses public attention when a body of water becomes septic or when fish and wild fowl are destroyed in quantity. Because of modern water treatment methods, water-borne epidemics are infrequent although it is quite possible, even probable, that epidemics of non-fatal character go unrecognized as being water-borne. When tastes or odors develop in a municipal water supply due to pollution, they are usually of local interest.

Two conditions of increasing significance are related to the rapidly expanding use of synthetic detergents. Even with modern sewage treatment methods these detergents are not neutralized or destroyed to the degree that their effects are not recognizable. Because they contain elements such as phosphorus in the form of polyphosphate additives, it is suspected that they may be, in part, responsible for luxuriant growths of algae in the receiving waters. Complaints concerning algae are becoming more frequent. Tastes and odors may result from their decomposition and the cost of water treatment is increased.

Recorded Data

Useful data concerning water have been obtained by the Industrial Minerals Division, Mines Branch, Department of Mines and Technical Surveys. Similarly the Water Resources Branch, Department of Northern Affairs and National Resources has as one of its primary functions the maintenance of the systematic hydrometric program in operation across Canada. Relevant publications of these Departments are listed in Appendix "A".

While these data are necessary to assess our water resources, and include information frequently obtained in pollution studies, they do not provide much information to evaluate conditions relating to pollution. While it is possible to ascertain probable effects of well known types of pollution these effects are influenced by so many conditions peculiar to the receiving body of water that detailed studies are necessary, especially if the effects of pollution have become or may become critical. Such studies are expensive because of the many factors which require determination. This becomes obvious if reference is made to "Objectives for Boundary Waters Quality Control"—Appendix "B". These objectives have been accepted by the Governments of Canada and the United States and are receiving ever-widening use by administrative authorities. They require careful consideration in relation to unusual local conditions and may require modification or elaboration if compliance with them is to achieve the desired results.

The complexity and cost of pollution studies coupled with personnel limitations of most administrative groups are responsible for the comparative scarcity of factual data concerning the effects of water pollution. Boundary waters studies carried out under the auspices of the International Joint Commission have resulted in comprehensive reports of major significance in respect to certain boundary waters. Similarly studies by provincial authorities, and to a lesser degree, by federal agencies, have provided valuable data for some areas. Appendix "C" lists provincial reports on local drainage areas.

Extensive surveys of sanitation problems have been carried out in coastal waters by federal and provincial governments but these have been limited to determining sources of pollution and the bacterial content of the sea water. The studies are essential in respect to the control of shellfish production and to the processing of fresh fish.

Industrial Wastes

Wastes from industries have caused serious water pollution problems and will do so in the future with increasing frequency unless great care is observed in dealing with them.

Chemicals used for industrial purposes are recognized as being responsible for certain pollution problems. Many industries for example use or produce phenolic compounds. When these enter surface sources of water supply they are objectionable even in very small quantities due to tastes which they cause when they react with chlorine. In recent years satisfactory methods of treatment and control have been developed. Numerous industrial plants have taken corrective action but phenols are still a problem in many waters.

Some industries produce toxic wastes. These have been responsible for extensive *fish kills* and may also affect municipal water supplies. Cyanide and chromium wastes are examples. Other industries discharge wastes which contain large quantities of solids. If these settle they can cover and destroy extensive spawning grounds of fish. Pulp and paper production wastes, which are frequently associated with this condition, also make heavy demands on dissolved oxygen.

With new products being developed and new industries starting production throughout the country it is inevitable that disposal of industrial wastes will present problems of increasing complexity.

Municipal Wastes

Many industrial wastes are discharged into municipal sewerage systems and they, together with rapidly increasing volumes of municipal sewage, are creating pollution problems which require corrective action.

The objectionable effects of pollution have been recognized for many decades—and probably centuries when one considers the efforts made by ancient civilizations to secure clean water. The relationship between pollution and water-borne disease was demonstrated first in modern times when an epidemic of cholera was connected with the use of sewage-polluted water from the Broad Street Well in London, England. Similarly numerous other epidemics of cholera and typhoid fever have been traced to polluted water supplies.

Improved methods of water treatment, particularly the use of chlorine have reduced the incidence of water-borne disease so greatly that a false sense of security has developed. Municipal officials are very conscious of the high cost of treatment when the source of supply is seriously polluted and are demanding remedial action, particularly if the pollution originates outside their own community. Some forms of pathogenic bacteria and viruses are resistant to normal treatment methods and it is realized that full knowledge is lacking in regard to certain diseases which may possibly be transmitted by polluted water. It is beyond dispute however, that water can be the vehicle which transmits disease-producing bacteria. Infection develops when the water is consumed voluntarily as a beverage, or unintentionally when swimming. Infections of the eyes, ears, nose and throat are possible when exposure to polluted water occurs while bathing. These are counteracted by prohibiting bathing in polluted areas but this action by the medical health office is unpopular and frequently disregarded.

Gross pollution may have other serious effects. Excessive amounts of domestic sewage in relation to the volume of receiving water, may cause complete depletion of the dissolved oxygen norm-

TABLE I—MUNICIPAL WASTE TREATMENT RELATED TO POPULATION (1960)*

Province	Total Population	Population Served with Sewers	Population Served by	
			Primary Treatment	Secondary Treatment
British Columbia	1,570,000	720,000	24,250	62,350
Alberta	1,220,000	740,000	445,000	295,000
Saskatchewan	906,000	376,000	12,590	260,481
Manitoba	850,040	507,876	408,227	41,352
Ontario	5,500,000	3,775,000	907,574	2,382,650
Quebec	4,628,378	2,380,000	97,500	11,900
New Brunswick	554,616	191,000	2,200	6,000
Nova Scotia	694,717	296,000	1,000	8,000
Prince Edward Island	99,285	30,000	800	8,000
Newfoundland	415,074	133,000	....	4,000
	16,438,610	9,148,876	1,899,141	3,079,733

Sources: 1) Dominion Bureau of Statistics, for data on total population.

2) Public Health Engineering Division, Department of Health and Welfare—sewerage and treatment data based on information received from the provinces and from technical publications.

* Based on 1956 census data, urban communities of over 1,000 population only, and assuming that all the population in each community is served by the sewerage system. The error thus caused by including persons served by individual disposal systems such as septic tanks is offset by small communities with sewage treatment. These data do not include sewage treatment plants constructed and operated by the Federal government. Considering only those plants which serve over 500 persons, about 170,000 persons are served by Federal installations. In addition a very large number of smaller plants serve Federal employees.

ally present in these waters. Those forms of life which depend on the dissolved oxygen are then destroyed. Some instances of this occur from time to time in Canada and demonstrate the serious nature of insufficient treatment or complete lack of it. Fortunately the areas so affected are not numerous but reference can be made to the lower reaches of the Don River, in Toronto, where septic conditions have existed; the lower Thames River, (Ontario) where, during periods of low flow, fish kills have occurred; and the North Saskatchewan River which was devoid of oxygen below Edmonton during periods of ice cover and low flow prior to construction of sewage treatment plants that now serve that city. Partial depletion of dissolved oxygen may also produce adverse effects on aquatic life since some fish require several parts per million to flourish or survive.

Other Chemicals and Insecticides

Water polluted by chemicals used in agriculture and for the control of harmful insects and flora, such as algae, may be unsuitable for certain purposes or of such a quality that the cost of treatment is increased substantially. D.D.T. which is frequently used for insect control, has been associated with fish losses and there is evidence that it may cause bad tastes in municipal water supplies. Radioactive wastes are becoming increasingly important and a sampling program is being planned to evaluate conditions in relation to public water supplies.

Present Status of Waste Treatment

In most industries it is only in recent years that waste treatment has received serious consideration and corrective action taken. Even within individual industries there is little uniformity of action. Local conditions and the zeal, or lack of it, of pollution control agencies are the principal determining factors. It can be said that most industries are willing to take remedial measures when the need for them is demonstrated. These can be very expensive, particularly when they have to be applied to existing plants and it seems unfair to require one plant to treat its wastes while its competitors continue to discharge untreated wastes. Some degree of uniformity in respect to waste treatment would provide less cause for complaint within an industry and between different plants. Nevertheless absolute uniformity of requirements for effluents is impractical because of local factors. Present or possible future use of the receiving waters is of prime importance when assessing the need for and the degree of treatment which is necessary.

Similarly with municipal wastes, it can reasonably be said that all should be treated before discharge. The best possible treatment for all wastes would be an ideal goal but quite unreasonable in many instances. It is this need for consideration of local uses and circumstances that emphasizes the necessity for obtaining exact and reasonably complete knowledge concerning conditions in our rivers and lakes.

It is apparent that major problems of pollution are likely to be found in areas of high industrial development and heavy concentrations of population. These are modified or intensified in relation to the purification potential of the receiving waters.

Inland areas are more likely to have pollution problems than coastal areas. For this reason it is not surprising that the inland provinces have been confronted with the most frequent and serious problems associated with pollution. As a corollary of this it is found that these provinces also show the most progress in pollution abatement. They are Alberta, Saskatchewan, Manitoba and Ontario.

Drainage Basins

The mainland of Canada can be divided into four main drainage basins, namely: Pacific, Arctic, Hudson Bay and Atlantic.[1] The following is a brief description of the pollution problem as it applies to each of these drainage basins.

Pacific Basin (400,730 sq. mi.)

The most important rivers in this basin are the Columbia, Fraser and Yukon with several smaller rivers between the Fraser and Yukon watersheds. Heavy concentrations of population and industries are, with few exceptions on or near the sea. Consequently the rivers in this basin are relatively free of pollution with the exception of the lower reaches of the Fraser. A few inland communities are served by sewage treatment plants but very little has been done to date to treat sewage from coastal communities. Wastes have seriously affected recreation in some areas such as Victoria, and at Greater Vancouver where a primary sewage treatment plant is being constructed. Some wastes are harmful to fish and dangerous to shellfish consumers. Bacterial pollution from domestic sewage is affecting the use of sea water in fish processing plants and some areas have had to be closed to shellfish production to protect the consumer.

1 Map 33, Drainage Basins and River Flow, ATLAS OF CANADA, Geographical Branch, Department of Mines and Technical Surveys, Ottawa, 1957. (In addition there is a small area in southern Alberta and Saskatchewan which lies in the Gulf of Mexico drainage basin.) The map also shows watersheds, area data and rates of flow for the principal rivers.

Pollution in inland streams is always a problem particularly in recreation areas since water may be used for drinking and culinary purposes by persons not fully acquainted with potential health hazards.

Arctic Drainage Basin (1,380,895 sq. mi.)

The most important river in this basin is the Mackenzie. Some domestic and a little industrial waste enters this system. The population on the watershed of this river is very small and the larger centers have been provided with sewage treatment facilities, for example in Inuvik, Yellowknife and Fort Smith. Efforts are being made to control smaller sources of pollution.

Hudson Bay Drainage Basin (1,421,350 sq. mi.)

A large number of rivers are located in this basin, the most important being the Nelson and Moose. The main tributary of the Nelson is the Saskatchewan River which drains a large part of the developed areas in Alberta and Saskatchewan. The low flows in the Saskatchewan River appear to present a real problem so far as future development of those provinces is concerned. Reference has previously been made to conditions in the North Saskatchewan River resulting from the discharge of municipal and industrial wastes. Remedial measures have been employed to correct the most objectionable conditions by treatment of some municipal and industrial wastes but important sources of pollution are still without treatment facilities. Storage facilities now being developed on the upper reaches of the North Saskatchewan River will make it possible to increase minimum flows and thus provide improved conditions. Municipal and industrial wastes are treated at Edmonton. Municipal wastes are treated at North Battleford but not at Battleford or Prince Albert.

Conditions in the South Saskatchewan River have not been as severe as in the North Saskatchewan. Industrial wastes in the Calgary area have been responsible for imparting objectionable tastes to fish. Municipal wastes are treated at Calgary, Lethbridge and Swift Current, located on tributary streams, but not at Medicine Hat and Saskatoon on the main stream.

The Red River drains into Lake Winnipeg and thence to the Nelson River. Most of the wastes entering the Red River in Canada receive some treatment, for example, Greater Winnipeg provides primary treatment. The Assiniboine River, a tributary of the Red River, with its principal tributary the Qu'Appelle River, drains a large area of Manitoba and Saskatchewan. Municipal wastes are treated at Regina, Fort Qu'Appelle, Virden, and Portage la Prairie. Brandon, one of the larger cities on the watershed, has not provided treatment for its sewage.

Another major river in this basin is the Moose. Some communities and industries are located on its tributary streams. Kapuskasing, Cochrane and Timmins, the principal urban communities on this watershed, all have sewage treatment plants. Industrial wastes, principally from paper mills, receive little treatment but this is not too important at present as the flow to the north is largely through wilderness country. Sewage treatment is provided for Federal installations at Moose Factory, near the mouth of Moose River.

Most of the other rivers drain uninhabited or very sparsely settled areas.

Atlantic Drainage Basin (580,097 sq. mi.)

The importance of this basin derives from the fact that the watershed of the St. Lawrence River contains over one-half of the country's population and probably 80 per cent or more of the nation's industry. More than two-thirds of the urban population served by sewage treatment in Canada are residents of Ontario. There is comparatively little sewage and waste treatment elsewhere in the basin although an increasing interest in the problem of water pollution, particularly in New Brunswick, suggests that greater emphasis will be placed on pollution abatement soon. Increasing interest in pollution abatement is also noted in the province of Quebec. Within the scope of this review, however, it is only possible to discuss general areas within the basin.

As on the Pacific Coast, most urban communities in the Maritimes and Newfoundland, are found on or near salt water. Wastes from these communities and from some industries have had detrimental effects on the use of the receiving waters. This has been most obvious in relation to shellfish production in the Maritimes, but fresh fish processing and recreation have also been affected. There are, however, still numerous safe bathing beaches which are easily accessible by automobile.

The Great Lakes have areas of pollution in the vicinity of the towns and cities on their shores, the extent of the polluted area usually being directly related to the size of the community. Similarly, rivers carrying wastes cause substantial areas of pollution where they discharge into the lakes. The rivers connecting the Great Lakes are all polluted to varying degrees. These rivers, Lake St. Clair and small areas of the large lakes near the inlets and outlets of the rivers were studied in detail in 1946-49 by the International Joint Commission. Substantial and continuing improvement has been achieved in these waters in the ensuing years through treatment of municipal and industrial wastes. Further improvements will be required to bring them all into compliance with "Objectives for Boundary Waters Quality Control." The St. Lawrence River has not been studied in detail as yet, but it is known to be heavily polluted in some sections. Many of the streams which empty into the Great Lakes and the St. Lawrence River are comparatively small in volume. Where their watersheds have been largely denuded of forest growth they carry very little water in the summer months.

Pollution in the Ottawa River varies widely since its watershed includes large areas of woodland as well as highly developed sections. Gross pollution extends from Hull and Ottawa to the junction with the St. Lawrence River due to municipal and industrial wastes, the latter originating to a large extent in pulp and paper plants.

Streams in the province of Quebec receive substantial volumes of municipal and industrial wastes in the developed portions of the province while most of those on the north shore of the St. Lawrence are generally unpolluted. The Saguenay River would appear an exception but detailed knowledge of its condition is lacking. The Richelieu River rises in the United States but wastes originating in that country are of minor importance in Canada because Lake Champlain provides natural purification.

Pollution Control Agencies

Because of health aspects most of the authority to deal with water pollution has been assigned to health departments. In recent years, however, other agencies have been established to deal with pollution problems.

British Columbia appointed a Pollution-Control Board to deal with water pollution in the Lower Mainland of the province where it is of greatest concern. The Provincial Department of Health and Welfare is represented on the Board and on its staff and still has the major responsibility for waste control in the province. Other interests, such as the Federal Department of Fisheries, are also involved in pollution control activities.

The Departments of Public Health in Alberta and Saskatchewan administer pollution control in those provinces. Manitoba has a provincial Sanitary Control Commission which functions in collaboration with the Provincial Department of Health and Public

Welfare. The latter may make regulations concerning the prevention of the pollution, defilement, discoloration or fouling of lakes, rivers, streams, pools and waters *in the absence* of any similar edicts under the Pollution of Waters Prevention Act (the legislation providing for the formation and administration of the Provincial Sanitary Control Commission.)

The Ontario Water Resources Commission is responsible for the administration of pollution abatement and control measures related to community and industrial wastes in that province. It has been very active in pressing for remedial measures and improved conditions. The provincial Department of Health deals with private domestic installations.

In 1955 the Province of Quebec introduced legislation relating to control of water pollution. A committee was appointed to study pollution but became inoperative. A limited amount of work was done on river studies but this has not been published. Recent advice suggests that interest is increasing and a new committee has been formed to study water pollution.

New Brunswick has appointed the New Brunswick Water Authority with wide powers to correct and control water pollution. Its activities to date suggest that an aggressive campaign is to be waged against water pollution. This program will be carried out in cooperation with the Department of Health and Social Services which retains an interest in the field due to potential health hazards.

The Health Departments in Nova Scotia, Prince Edward Island and Newfoundland are primarily responsible for pollution control in those provinces. Comparatively little has been done, however, in regard to the treatment of municipal sewage. Industrial wastes such as those from canning plants are treated in waste lagoons in some instances.

On the basis of existing legislation the federal government has very limited control of pollution, particularly in respect to human wastes. The Boundary Waters Treaty of 1909 is of major significance in relation to international problems. When water pollution reaches objectionable proportions the International Joint Commission may be called upon to investigate conditions and recommend remedial action. The correction of transboundary pollution reverts to the States and Provinces in which it originates, and efforts to promote improvements receive the support of the Commission.

Other federal legislation which has a bearing on pollution control includes the Navigable Waters Protection Act. Its purpose is to protect the interests of navigation and it is concerned chiefly with those types of wastes which would tend to obstruct channels and streams.

The Fisheries Act is similar in character and places restrictions on the discharge of materials deleterious to fish life.

The Migratory Birds Convention Act prohibits the deposit or discharge of "oil, oil wastes or deleterious substances—in any water frequented by migratory wild-fowl, or that flows into such water, nor on ice over either of such waters".

The Department of National Health and Welfare Act states that the Minister of National Health and Welfare shall enforce "any rules or regulations made by the International Joint Commission, promulgated pursuant to the treaty—so far as they relate to health". The treaty referred to is the Boundary Waters Treaty of 1909, previously mentioned.

While the Act creating the department does not confer any specific authority in this field beyond that already quoted, a program of cooperation with other departments of the Federal government has been developed. The results have been worthwhile since most large sources of pollution originating on federal property lying outside urban communities have been effectively treated or plans for treatment are well advanced. Most departments of the federal government, and crown corporations, are playing an important role in this general policy of pollution control.

The Criminal Code of Canada, which defines a common nuisance, has not been regarded in the past as a useful means of effecting pollution control because it is difficult to prove the exact cause and locate the source of a common nuisance when several wastes are involved.

The Department of Transport has "General and Special Regulations for the Government of Public Harbours in Canada" which place restrictions on the discharge of various wastes, rubbish and oil. The National Harbours Board Regulations are similar. These regulations are based on the Canada Shipping Act as are the Oil Pollution Prevention Regulations. While this legislation is reasonably effective for the purpose for which it was intended, it has very limited value in the general control of municipal and industrial wastes.

Financing of Treatment Plants

The cost of treating industrial wastes is generally held to be the responsibility of the industry concerned if its wastes are discharged directly to the receiving waters. When the wastes enter a municipal sewerage system the policy regarding their treatment may vary considerably. It is not unusual, however, for a community to require treatment by the industry prior to discharge into the sewer if the waste would be detrimental to the system or would place an undue load on the treatment process.

The cost of treating municipal wastes is, with minor exceptions, a charge borne by the community. The Province of Quebec has agreed to pay up to three per cent interest rates on debts incurred by municipalities of 7,000 population or less in respect to water supply and waste treatment. Alberta at one time loaned money for similar purposes at a rate of two per cent but this practice has been discontinued. The Ontario Water Resources Commission will arrange to finance municipal treatment plants and recover the total cost on an annual basis over an agreed number of years. The New Brunswick Water Resources and Pollution Control Act makes provisions for agreements with municipalities for the control or prevention of the pollution of water, and the agreement may provide for defraying part of the cost of the plan. The National Housing Act provides for federal loans up to two-thirds of the capital costs of sewage plants and trunk interceptor sewers, with a rebate up to one-quarter of such expenditures incurred before April 1963. The prompt response on the part of municipalities encourages the belief that this provision will play an important role in pollution abatement and control.

Present and Future Needs

Because of the very heavy demand for water in many industries, there has been an obvious tendency for industry to locate on the larger rivers and lakes whenever a choice of location is possible. Industry attracts or is attracted by urban communities since large numbers of employees are still necessary in spite of the present trend toward automation. Thus future expansion of present manufacturing plants and new industries will greatly increase the need for unpolluted water. Domestic consumption is also increasing rapidly as a result of labor saving devices in the home. Plans for the future must take these factors into account.

A basic need in such planning would be a more accurate knowledge of present conditions. This will require an increase in water pollution studies by competent authorities, with a related major increase in personnel and equipment. Those departments, commissions, etc. in the federal and provincial governments which are now responsible for pollution control, would seem to be best qualified to undertake such studies.

Similarly means should be sought to reduce wasteful run-off, as for instance by spring freshets. Reference to maximum and minimum flow data for many rivers makes this basic need self-evident. Power development and water conservation projects have been helpful on some watersheds. Associated with this is the need for better control of land use, since many areas best suited to forest growth have been denuded. Reforestation can offer a partial solution since it tends to increase minimum flows.

Possibly the greatest present need is a better knowledge of pollution problems on the part of the taxpayer. So many demands are being made for increased expenditures in urban communities that sewage treatment gets little support in many areas.

In summary, pollution problems of major significance are already evident in Canada and will become more common and more severe as industrial and urban development increases. Hence, a more complete knowledge of present conditions coupled with prompt and effective remedial action, is essential for future national development and expansion.

APPENDIX A

I Industrial Water Reports

Department of Mines and Technical Surveys

Report No. 819
"Industrial Waters of Canada" covering the period 1934 to 1943, (out of print).
Report No. 833
Industrial Water Resources of Canada—Water Survey Report No. 1, *The Aim, Scope and Method of Investigations*, by J. F. J. Thomas, 1953.
Report No. 834
Industrial Water Resources of Canada—Water Survey Report No. 2, *Chemical Quality of Surface and Civic Water Supplies, Ottawa River Drainage Basin*, 1947-1948, by J. F. J. Thomas, 1952.
Report No. 837
Industrial Water Resources of Canada—Water Survey Report No. 3, *Upper St. Lawrence River-Central Great Lakes Drainage Basin*, by J. F. J. Thomas.
Report No. 838
Industrial Water Resources of Canada—Water Survey Report No. 4, *Columbia River Drainage Basin*, by J. F. J. Thomas, 1953.

Report No. 839

Industrial Water Resources of Canada—Water Survey Report No. 5, *Skeena River, Vancouver Island, and Coastal Areas of British Columbia*, by J. F. J. Thomas, 1953.
Report No. 842
Industrial Water Resources of Canada—Water Survey Report No. 6, *Fraser River Drainage Basin*, 1950-1951, by J. F. J. Thomas.
Report No. 849
Industrial Water Resources of Canada—Water Survey Report No. 7, *Saskatchewan River Drainage Basin*, by J. F. J. Thomas.
Report No. 856
Industrial Water Resources of Canada—Water Survey Report No. 8, *Mackenzie River and Yukon River Drainage Basin*, 1952-1953, by J. F. J. Thomas.
Report No. 858
Industrial Water Resources of Canada—Water Survey Report No. 9, *Churchill River and Mississippi River Drainage Basin*, 1952-1954, by J. F. J. Thomas.
Report No. 861
Industrial Water Resources of Canada—Water Survey Report No. 10, *Nelson River Drainage Basin in Canada*, 1953-1956.
Report No. 865
Industrial Water Resources of Canada—Water Survey Report No. 12, *Water Quality at some Canadian Military Establishments*, 1956-1958.
Memorandum Series No. 132
Interim Report on Hardness of Major Canadian Water Supplies, by J. F. J. Thomas.

II   Surface Water Supply of Canada

Hydrometric Survey Data, Department of Northern Affairs and National Resources

Water Resources Paper No. 120:
Atlantic Drainage, including South-eastern Quebec, New Brunswick, Nova Scotia, Prince Edward Island, and Newfoundland.
Climatic Years 1954-55 and 1955-56.
Water Resources Paper No. 115:
St. Lawrence and Southern Hudson Bay Drainage in Ontario and Quebec.
Climatic Years 1953-54 and 1954-55.
Water Resources Paper No. 121:
Arctic and Western Hudson Bay Drainage, (and Mississippi drain-

age in Canada). In British Columbia, Alberta, Saskatchewan, Manitoba, The Northwest Territories and Western Ontario.
Climatic Years 1955-56 and 1956-57.
Water Resources Paper No. 122:
Pacific Drainage: British Columbia and Yukon Territory.
Climatic Years 1954-55 and 1955-56.

APPENDIX B

Revised October 1949
International Joint Commission
Washington, D.C.-Ottawa, Canada

Objectives for Boundary Waters Quality Control

The term "boundary waters" as herein used shall include the waters defined in the references to the International Joint Commission dated April 1, 1946, October 3, 1946, and April 2, 1948, and are as follows:

St. Clair River, Lake St. Clair, the Detroit River, St. Marys River from Lake Superior to Lake Huron, and Niagara River from Lake Erie to Lake Ontario.

These objectives are for the boundary waters in general, and it is anticipated that in certain specific instances, influenced by local conditions, more stringent requirements may be found necessary.

General Objectives

All wastes, including sanitary sewage, storm water, and industrial effluents, shall be in such condition when discharged into any stream that they will not create conditions in the boundary waters which will adversely affect the use of these waters for the following purposes: source of domestic water supply or industrial water supply, navigation, fish and wild life, bathing, recreation, agriculture and other riparian activities.

In general, adverse conditions are caused by:

(A) Excessive bacterial, physical or chemical contamination.

(B) Unnatural deposits in the stream, interfering with navigation, fish and wild life, bathing, recreation or destruction of aesthetic values.

(C) Toxic substances and materials imparting objectionable tastes and odors to waters used for domestic or industrial purposes.

(D) Floating materials, including oils, grease, garbage, sewage solids, or other refuse.

Specific Objectives

In more specific terms, adequate controls of pollution will necessitate the following objectives for:

(A) *Sanitary Sewage, Storm Water, and Wastes from Water Craft*

Sufficient treatment for adequate removal or reduction of solids, bacteria and chemical constituents which may interfere unreasonably with the use of these waters for the purposes afore-mentioned.

Adequate protection for these waters, except in certain specific instances influenced by local conditions, should be provided if the coliform M.P.N. median value does not exceed 2,400 per 100 ml. at any point in the waters following initial dilution.

(B) *Industrial Wastes*

(1) Chemical Wastes—Phenolic Type

Industrial waste effluents from phenolic hydrocarbon and other chemical plants will cause objectionable tastes or odors in drinking industrial water supplies and may taint the flesh of fish. Adequate protection should be provided for these waters if the concentration of phenol or phenolic equivalents does not exceed an average of 2 p.p.b. and a maximum of 5 p.p.b. at any point in these waters following initial dilution. This quality in the receiving waters will probably be attained if plant effluents are limited to 20 p.p.b. of phenol or phenolic equivalents.

Some of the industries producing phenolic wastes are: coke, synthetic resin, oil refining, petroleum cracking, tar, road oil, creosoting, wood distillation, and dye manufacturing plants.

(2) Chemical Wastes, other than Phenolic

Adequate protection should be provided if:

(a) The pH of these waters following initial dilution is not less than 6.7 nor more than 8.5. This quality in the receiving waters will probably be attained if plant effluents are adjusted to a pH value within the range of 5.5 and 10.6.

(b) The iron content of these waters following initial dilution does not exceed 0.3 p.p.m. This quality in the receiving waters will probably be attained if plant effluents are limited to 17 p.p.m. of iron in terms of Fe.

(c) The odor-producing substances in the effluent are reduced to a point that following initial dilution with these waters the mixture does not have a threshold odor number in excess of 8 due to such added material.

(d) Unnatural color and turbidity of the wastes are reduced to a point that these waters will not be offensive in appearance or otherwise unattractive for the afore-mentioned uses.

(e) Oil and floating solids are reduced to a point such that they will not create fire hazards, coat hulls of water craft, injure fish or wild life or their habitat, or will adversely affect public or private recreational development or other legitimate shore line developments or uses. Protection should be provided for these waters if plant effluents or storm water discharges from premises do not contain oils, as determined by extraction, in excess of 15 p.p.m., or a sufficient amount to create more than a faint iridescence. Some of the industries producing chemical wastes other than phenolic are: oil wells and petroleum refineries, gasoline filling stations and bulk stations, styrene copolymer, synthetic pharmaceutical, synthetic fibre, iron and steel, alkali chemical, rubber fabricating, dye manufacturing, and acid manufacturing plants.

(3) Highly Toxic Wastes

Adequate protection should be provided for these waters if substances highly toxic to human, fish, aquatic, or wild life are eliminated or reduced to safe limits.

Some of the industries producing highly toxic wastes are: metal plating and finishing plants discharging cyanides, chromium or other toxic wastes; chemical and pharmaceutical plants and coke ovens. Wastes containing toxic concentrations of free halogens are included in this category.

(4) Deoxygenating Wastes

Adequate protection of these waters should result if sufficient treatment is provided for the substantial removal of solids, bacteria, chemical constituents and other substances capable of reducing the dissolved oxygen content of these waters unreasonably. Some of the industries producing these wastes are: tanneries, glue and gelatin plants, alcohol, including breweries and distilleries, wool scouring, pulp and paper, food processing plants such as meat packing and dairy plants, corn products, beet sugar, fish processing and dehydration plants.

NOTE: The methods of determination of the chemical constituents referred to in the preceding objectives are as given in "Analytical Methods for Boundary Waters Quality Control", as prepared by the Board of Technical Advisers. Bacterial determinations are to include the presumptive and confirmed tests for the coliform group of bacteria as given in "Standard Methods for the Examination of Water and Sewage", latest Edition.

APPENDIX C

Water Pollution Studies and Reports on Local Drainage Areas

Newfoundland

There are no published reports on water pollution studies in the Province of Newfoundland.

New Brunswick

St. John River (1953)—for the International Joint Commission.
St. Croix River (1957)—for the International Joint Commission.
Pollution in the North Shore—for the New Brunswick Water Authority, and East Coast Areas of New Brunswick (MacLaren 1958).
St. Croix River (1959)—for the International Joint Commission.
Pollution of the St. John River—for the New Brunswick Water Authority Estuary (Ballance 1960).*
*This report not published to date.

Quebec

Studies made by Committee of Pollution, Province of Quebec.
Surveys: Riviere du Nord
        St. Francis River
        Matapedia River
        Yamaska River
Report of Pollution of Ottawa River (1954), Lucien Piche, Ph.D.

Ontario

Water Pollution Studies in Ontario
Ontario Water Resources Commission Studies

Aurora Creek
Ausable River
Avon River
Bayfield River
Beaver River
Beaverton River
Big Otter Creek
Black Creek
Black River
Bloomfield River
Blyth River
Bowmanville River
Boyne River
Butler's Creek
Carleton Place Area

Carruthers Creek
Catfish Creek
Cobourg Brook
Conestoga River
Coon Creek
Credit River
Don River
Duffin's Creek
Effingham Creek
Elgin County
Essex County
Etobicoke River
Gage Creek
Ganaraska River
Graham Creek

Grand River
Haldimand County
Harmony Creek—
   see Oshawa &
   Harmony Creeks
Highland Creek
Holland River
Humber River
Kent County
Kettle Creek
Kingston Area
Lakehead Survey
Lambton County
Lucknow River
Lynde—Pringle
   Creek

Lynn River	Otonabee River	Scugog River
Lyons Creek	Oshawa & Harmony	Seine River
Maitland River	Creeks	Shelter Valley Brook
Massey Creek	Ottawa River	Silver Creek
Middlesex County	Otter Creek	Spanish River
Mimico Creek	Oxford County	Stoney Creek
Moira River	Pefferlaw Brook	Sydenham River
Napanee River	Petticoat Creek	Talbot River
New Toronto Creek	Rideau River	Thames River
Niagara River	Rouge River	Thunder Bay District
Nith River	St. Clair River	Toronto Waterfront
Nonquon River	St. Lawrence River	Trent River
Norfolk County	Sarnia & Area	Twelve Mile Creek
Nottawasaga River	Saugeen River	Welland Canal
Onaping River	Schomberg River	Welland County

Other Studies

Burlington Bay (City of Hamilton)

Industrial Wastes Conference Reports.

Manitoba

1. Sanitary Survey of Red River 1952-1955
2.   "   "   " Assiniboine River 1953-56
3.   "   "   " Whitemud River 1954-56
4.   "   "   " Souris River 1955-56
5. Winnipeg River Survey 1957—Lower Winnipeg Lake Survey 1957.
6. Pollution Aspects of Schist Lake and Lake Athapapuskow 1957.
7. Outline of Policy of Provincial Sanitary Control Commission Re Pollution of Bodies of Water 1953.

Alberta

Proposed Objectives for water quality.

Report on Pollution of Stirling Lake, 1952.

Report on Stream Pollution survey of the Bow River and its tributaries.

Report on Pollution of North Saskatchewan River 1950-55.

Report on Air Injection Project, North Saskatchewan River 1955-56.

Report on Pollution of Old Man River and South Saskatchewan River 1953-55.

British Columbia

Water Quality in the Fraser-Thompson River System of British Columbia, B.C. Research Council Report 1952.

Greater Vancouver Water and Sewage District report of Commissioner T. V. Berry 1959.

Sewerage and Drainage of Greater Vancouver Area, British Columbia, September 1953. Gilman, Hyde, Rawn and Oliver.

13

Water Pollution Control and Regional Planning— The Saint John River

R. C. Ballance

Introduction

The Saint John is generally considered to be a New Brunswick river. Actually, more than half of its drainage area is in the State of Maine and the Province of Quebec. Its upper third is entirely within the State of Maine and the next quarter of its length forms the International boundary between Maine and New Brunswick. Only for about the last half of its length is the Saint John truly a New Brunswick river. Even in these lower reaches, several tributaries entering from the west are streams that are principally in the State of Maine. Thus flow control and pollution control in the main stream may only be accomplished by co-operation among two provinces, one state and two countries. Location and watershed area are shown in the map of Figure 1.

The drainage area is slightly less than 20,000 square miles. Estimated population in this drainage area based on 1961 census data

Background Paper, *National Conference on Pollution and our Environment*, B17-1-2, Montreal, 1966. Reprinted in edited form by permission of the Canadian Council of Resource Ministers.

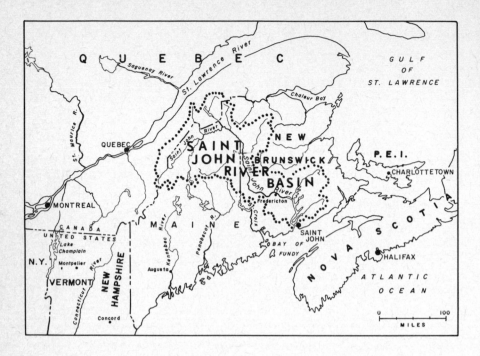

Figure 1. Saint John River Drainage.

is about 250,000. More than half of this total population is rural. Of those living in urban communities, 91,000 live in four general areas. These are Edmundston, N.B.-Madawaska, Me. 18,000, Houlton, Me.-Woodstock, N.B. 15,000, Presque Isle, Me. 17,000 and Fredericton-Oromocto, N.B. 41,000. The remainder of the communities vary in type from peri-rural to peri-urban and range in size from a few hundred to a few thousand.

The watershed has a resource-based economy. The potatoes grown in Carleton and Victoria counties, New Brunswick and in Aroostock County, Maine are well-known for both quality and the size of the crop. Equally well-known are the Maine and New Brunswick forests. Many thousands of acres in the Saint John drainage area are covered with magnificent stands of pine, fir, spruce and hardwood. One cannot help being impressed when flying over this area with the vast panorama of wilderness which is spread out below—a wilderness interlaced only by networks of logging roads and occasionally punctuated by tiny hamlets and villages. Only on the banks of the main river and its larger tributaries can one find the larger settlements.

Present Uses of the Saint John

Navigation

In the past, the Saint John served only as a transportation artery permitting access into the hinterland. Archeological diggings indicate that the aboriginals camped at a number of places along the river banks. The Indians found the summer runs of salmon and bass to be an excellent source of food. Also, after the spring freshet had subsided, they obtained their first supply of green vegetables by picking the delicate fern fronds which emerge from the silt of intervale land.

French explorers in the 1600's and 1700's used the river as a transportation route for trade with the Indians. English loyalists fleeing the American Revolution in 1783 travelled up the Saint John and settled on land granted to them by the monarch. Not only in the summer was the river used as a transportation route. The wife of the military commander in Fredericton wrote on December 14th, 1810: "Now our river is frozen fast, and becomes a post road". In February, 1813, a force of 550 men marched up the Saint John river from Fredericton to Madawaska on their way to Kingston to participate in the War of 1812.

Scheduled riverboat service between Saint John and Woodstock was operated up until 1906. Today navigation is restricted by silting of the channel and low bridges; Fredericton remains accessible, and petroleum products are regularly shipped in from Saint John during periods of open water. Much of the main river and many of the tributaries are used for transporting pulpwood and sawlogs to mills at Saint John.

Recreation and Fishing

There are not many natural beaches on the Saint John River. Those along the Long Reach and Grand Bay within 20 miles of the river's mouth are excellent and are extensively used. Other natural beaches further inland are rarely used and no significant improvements of natural conditions have been undertaken. There is a real and understandable fear of pollution conditions and for this reason natural beach development has been ignored although some excellent opportunities exist.

Boating on the river, especially in the lower 110 river miles, is excellent. There are a number of flourishing boat clubs and marinas at Saint John, Oromocto and Fredericton, as well as several smaller marinas further upstream. In addition there are hundreds of private landings along the shore although the flood flow at

spring freshet makes permanent installations difficult, if not impossible, to maintain. Several areas along the river are suitable for
the landing of float equipped aircraft. These are usually in association with marinas but one such harbour on the Beechwood headpond
is used principally for aircraft.

Sport fishing for Atlantic salmon is very good at several well-
known pools along the river. Hartt's Island pool above Fredericton,
the Hartland pool and the rapid water near the mouth of the
Shiketehawk at Bristol are particularly popular. Many of the tributaries support good populations of salmon and trout although
artificial barriers across the river have made it necessary to install
fish ladders. In some cases migrating fish are transported around
the dams in tank trucks and in this way adequate populations of
adult fish in important tributaries may be maintained. There are
good runs of sea bass (stripers) in early June and angling for these
fish is increasing in popularity.

In the tidal section of the river—from about 10 miles above
Fredericton to the Bay of Fundy—commercial fishing is permitted.
Licensing is restricted to those who can meet stringent requirements. The main yield of the commercial fishery is salmon and
shad, although a few sturgeon and other species are netted.

Power Generation

Two hydro-electric power stations are in operation on the Saint
John River. Grand Falls, with an installed capacity of 60 megawatts, operates under a rated head of 132 feet. The Beechwood
power station has an installed capacity of 115 megawatts and
operates under a rated head of 61.4 feet. A third dam is now under
construction and scheduled for completion in late 1967. It is located
at Mactaquac, 14 miles above Fredericton.

There is virtually no storage above any of these existing dams
and the operation (except during periods of maximum runoff) is
to meet the peak load on the distribution system. Several of the
larger tributaries have been developed for power generation but on
these, too, there is limited storage.

Water Supply and Waste Disposal

Very little use is made of the main river for water supply purposes. Oromocto, N.B. is the only municipal user of surface water
and even here the inlet line draws as much from the Oromocto
River as it does from the Saint John. Two major industrial plants
draw water from the river. They are a paper mill at Madawaska,
Me. and a food freezing plant at East Florenceville, N.B. Tribu-

taries are used more extensively for water supply. A pulp mill at Edmundston, N.B. uses about 65 mgd. from the Madawaska River. Twenty or more potato processing plants operate seasonally and draw their water from tributary streams.

Both municipalities and industries use the river and its tributaries for waste disposal. Of the quarter million population in the drainage area about 137,000 live in cities, towns or villages with sewer systems. Most of these systems discharge untreated sewage— less than 25,000 persons live in municipalities with sewage treatment facilities. Most of the treatment facilities are waste stabilization ponds—there is one activated sludge plant (at Oromocto). Fredericton, the capital city of New Brunswick and the largest urban community in the drainage area, has no sewage treatment facilities.

There are no facilities on the New Brunswick side of the Saint John River for the treatment of industrial waste. In Maine several of the potato and food processors have stabilization ponds. The major industrial polluters are a pulp and paper mill at Edmunston, N.B. and a food processor at East Florenceville, N.B. These two plants discharge wastes that produce more pollution than would be caused by a population of two million people.

The net result of these discharges of untreated waste is to render the river virtually useless for miles of its length. Between Edmunston and Grand Falls, pollution is so bad that nearly every summer there is a complete depletion of dissolved oxygen in the water resulted in a "fish kill". The river bottom is completely blanketed with wood fibre. As anaerobic decomposition takes place in the bottom deposits, methane and hydrogen sulfide are generated and as these gases accumulate they cause sections of the wood fibre mat to float to the surface. These floating mats vary in size from a few inches across to more than an acre in area. On the surface, wave action breaks up the fibre mat, the gases escape and the fibres settle to the bottom only to repeat the same procedure again and again. Thus, material that should be removed from the waste flow at the mill appears 100 miles or more downstream.

Below the food plant at East Florenceville it is not necessary to use sophisticated analytical methods to detect strong evidence of pollution. The eyes and the nose are adequate to see the culls and waste from the plant and to smell the rotting vegetable matter. Evidence of the waste from this industry has been reported as much as 75 miles downstream of the outfall.

Contemplated Development

Hydroelectric Power

The Mactaquac dam, previously referred to, will be completed in the autumn of 1967. Installation of turbines is phased over eight years so that by 1975 there will be six units with a total capacity of 591 megawatts. Operating head will be 110 feet. Currently under discussion is the construction of power dams at the Dickie and Lincoln School sites in the State of Maine. The Dickie dam is planned for an installed capacity of 760 megawatts at rated head of 275 feet and in addition will provide a live storage of 2.9 million acre feet.

At Lincoln School the installed capacity will be 34 megawatts at rated head of 61 feet and 16,000 acre feet of live storage will be provided. The presence of live storage will have beneficial effects on the operation of the downstream generating stations. The capacity of Grand Falls can be increased to 290 megawatts and another station with a 98 megawatt capacity can be economic.

With these installations completed, generating capacity on the river would be increased from the present 175 megawatts to 1888 megawatts. Of this total, the New Brunswick Electric Power Commission would have 1094 megawatts.

Recreation Development

With the completion of the Mactaquac project in 1967, a huge lake will be created. This lake will be nearly 59 miles long and will vary in width from present river width to more than two miles. The banks will be serrated with numerous inlets at the mouths of tributary streams and a total surface of 21,900 acres will result. Such a lake will provide incomparable conditions for both sailing and powerboating. Connection with the section of the river downstream of the dam is to be provided by equipment designed to transport watercraft around the dam.

The present paucity of natural beaches on the river will be partly resolved by the flooding since some sections of the headpond will have bank slopes admirably suited for beaches. Relatively minor and inexpensive improvements can be carried out to create beaches at other sites which have less favourable natural conditions.

To take advantage of the conditions which result from flooding the Province of New Brunswick has embarked upon an imaginative program of Regional Development in the general area affected by the Mactaquac project. Under the direction of the Community Improvement Corporation, a newly formed Crown Corporation, a number of projects aimed at establishing recreation and tourism facilities have been initiated. A major park is under construction just upstream from the damsite. This park, scheduled for construction over a ten-year period, will have its first elements completed by summer 1967. Ultimately it will include a 300 units campsite, a day-use park, a marina, golf course and clubhouse, beach, tennis courts, lodge and chalets. Located at the confluence of the Mactaquac River with the Saint John, the parksite has an area of 1,052 acres and a shoreline of nearly 3 miles. The site is readily accessible from the Trans-Canada Highway and situated as it is on the Saint John can be reached directly by river traffic.

Two other major parks are contemplated in the regional plan. These will provide overnight camping sites and a limited range of recreation facilities. In addition space is allocated for a number of day-use parks along the shores of the future reservoir. Some shore land on the reservoir has been purchased and reserved for private and institutional development. The basic concept that is followed in allocation of shore land use is that the reservoir should be considered as a public recreation resource and this may only be accomplished if land immediately adjacent to the water remains in public ownership. If shore land is sold to private individuals it is only a matter of time until the reservoir is virtually inaccessible to the public.

The new Mactaquac dam will create an artificial barrier which will restrict the normal migration of salmon on their way up river to the spawning grounds. In order to maintain this annual migration the Federal Department of Fisheries has recommended a scheme that is unique in North America but which has proved highly successful in Scandinavian countries.

The proposal is that a hatchery and rearing facilities be built downstream of the dam. About 1000 adult salmon will be captured annually for the propagation and release of a half million young salmon.

The rest of the migrating fish will be trapped in a collecting gallery and transported in specially designed and built tank trucks to points above the Mactaquac dam. Such a combination of techniques is expected to increase the population of anadromous fish in the Saint John River system.

Conflicts in Multipurpose Uses

Maintaining a delicate balance between conflicting uses of water is an extremely difficult task unless virtually complete control of water use is vested in one agency. Most of the serious conflicts are obvious—the most obvious is the conflict between waste assimilation and water supply—the less obvious conflicts may be very minor.

Navigation and Transportation

Commercial navigation produces some side effects which may adversely affect water supply and recreation. Oil spills and waste discharges are the principal adverse effects of navigation. If log driving is classed as "navigation" the complete blockage of the stream during the drive and the bulldozing of logs from the river bank into the stream have serious detrimental effects on all recreational uses. The log driving problems appear to be diminishing as industry converts from river driving to trucking of logs.

Recreation

The use of water for recreation seldom has any effect on other water uses; the main conflicts are among the number of unsympathetic recreational uses. Obviously swimming, boating, water skiing and fishing cannot be carried on at the same place at the same time. Thus areas must be set aside for each of these and the people who participate must be cognizant of the rights of others as well as their own responsibilities.

It must be recognized too that the exhaust discharges of outboard motors can adversely affect water quality. Poorly tuned motors and motors that leak oil and gasoline will cause oil slicks and render the water aesthetically unacceptable for other recreational uses.

Power Generation

The operation of a power dam produces the most serious effects on other water uses. The barrier to migrating fish has been mentioned earlier and the barrier to navigation is obvious. While both of these problems may be circumvented by the installation of engineering works, the capital and operating cost of such works is often not justified by the benefits which may accrue.

While the power dam may, if properly designed and operated, produce storage of water for irrigation and water supply such operation is unlikely to be economic from the viewpoint of power production. Power production requires that the head be maintained as high as possible—irrigation and water supply require that the headpond be drawn down when water withdrawals exceed the runoff.

Any dam—power or otherwise—creates a large stilling basin in the river. Consequently if there are major sources of pollution upstream the headpond provides nearly perfect conditions in which sedimentation can take place. The buildup of sludge in the bottom of the reservoir will inevitably result in biological degradation of water quality. Low dissolved oxygen can result in fish kills if conditions become bad enough, especially since the placid headpond is not as conducive to the reaeration of water as is the flowing stream. These conditions of pollution can render the water unfit for water supply, irrigation and recreation. The importance of strict pollution control upstream of a dam cannot be overemphasized. Pollution control is vital to the maintenance of a healthy headpond and to multi-purpose use of the water resource.

Operation of the power dam can have a serious physical effect on recreational use of the reservoir. Since the Saint John River hydro-electric stations are used to supply peaking power to the system, it is inevitable that there will be intermittent operation. The Mactaquac plant for instance is intended to be operated for peaking during the week but be virtually closed down on Saturday and Sunday. It is expected that the pond will be drawn down about three feet from Monday morning to Friday evening and be built up over the weekend. The resulting rise and fall of the water will inevitably affect the use of beaches and marinas and will be detrimental to the propagation of water fowl. The frequent changing of water level will probably cause erosion problems in certain critical areas of unstable soil.

Water Supply and Waste Disposal

Withdrawals of water for domestic and industrial supply rarely, if ever, adversely affect the other uses of a stream. However, water withdrawals always lead to waste discharges and if the wastes are discharged untreated the value of other uses may be seriously affected. Polluted water affects navigation and power generation only slightly with possible buildup of slimes on the surface of structures and machinery. Recreation and water supply may be ruined completely by pollution and its effects. This terrifying possibility exists in the Saint John River. The status of raw waste discharges from municipalities and industries has already been referred to and although government control has been eminently successful in preventing new discharges of untreated waste, there has been no reduction of the quantity of waste discharged. In fact, industries and municipalities with existing sewer outfalls appear to be able to increase the quantity of their raw waste discharges as long as they do not install new outfall sewers.

If the Saint John River is to supply the existing and future demands for recreation, pollution *must be* eliminated.

Potential for Future Development

A regional development plan sponsored by a Federal-Provincial agreement under A.R.D.A. and administered by the Community Improvement Corporation includes the construction of recreational facilities referred to in the "Contemplated Development" section of this paper. While this regional development plan is quite imaginative and broad in scope, it is restricted to a development period of ten years. Obviously the demand for water based recreation will increase with the increasing affluence and leisure of the population. Beyond the ten years of the development plan the necessity for additional recreational facilities is certain to occur. All aspects of water based recreation must be considered. Beaches must be built; fish hatcheries must increase their output; conservation areas must be set aside for the propagation of water fowl; the scenic beauty of the Saint John Valley must be preserved by sensitive and sympathetic development. Large sections of riverbank must remain in public ownership or else the river will suffer from unsightly ribbon development. Possibly, in the future, it may be economic to practise irrigation of crops although this part of Canada rarely suffers extended drought.

All future beneficial uses of the Saint John River depend on more than just "holding the line" on water pollution. The trend must be reversed and *all* discharges of untreated waste must be eliminated. Are we not intelligent enough to recognize a worsening situation? Do we not have ample evidence that polluted streams are unfit for beneficial uses? Can we not realize that continued use of a stream requires that we *prevent* pollution and not *cure* it after it has happened? Is our technology not sufficiently advanced to provide the techniques of pollution control? Are we unable to perceive that unpolluted rivers are the greatest bequest we can pass on to future generations?

If we cannot, do not or will not appreciate these things then the future of the Saint John River is indeed bleak and someday it will join the ranks of the many rivers that have been wantonly destroyed by a supposedly civilized society.

14

The Great Lakes and Their Problems

M. W. Thompson

The Great Lakes, their Connecting Channels and the St. Lawrence River have been the key to the development of Canada. They opened up the heart of a continent to explorers, fur traders and pioneers. The rich industrial empire of southern Ontario and its accompanying density of population continues to depend on the waters of the Great Lakes. One-third of the population of Canada lives on or near the shores of the Great Lakes.

The hydro-electric plants on the St. Mary, Niagara and St. Lawrence rivers have a total installed capacity of nearly 8 million kilowatts. About 230 million tons of cargo move annually over the Great Lakes route, one of the world's busiest inland waterways. Industry requires clean, safe water for all its operations and municipalities demand water of high quality. Yet, the final disposal of wastes from these same industries and municipalities continues to be an important function of the Great Lakes and their tributaries. Fishing and recreational interests also need water of good quality.

The Great Lakes cover an area of 95,000 square miles and drain an additional land area of 200,000 square miles. Their vast storage capacity makes them one of the best naturally regulated water systems in the world. The maximum recorded flow on the St. Lawrence River is only twice as large as the minimum. By contrast, the maximum recorded flow on the Columbia River at Trail,

Paper presented at the *Conference on Water Resource Management*, Conservation Council of Ontario, Toronto, 1966.

B.C. is 40 times the minimum. Monthly levels of Lake Superior and Lake Huron normally vary over a range of one foot from the seasonal low in winter to the seasonal high in summer; those of Lake Erie about a foot and a quarter; and those on Lake Ontario about a foot and a half. The average outflow from Lake Ontario is 241,000 cfs or, in non-technical language, the average outflow from Lake Ontario in 24 hours is enough to supply all the cities, towns and municipalities in Ontario for one year.

Until recently, most people in Ontario seemed to believe that the Great Lakes contained an inexhaustible supply of fresh, clean water to meet all their needs and in turn had little regard for the downstream riparian interests. How could the largest concentration of fresh water in the world have such problems as pollution and low levels?

Since Lake Superior, Lake Huron, Lake Erie, Lake Ontario and their Connecting Channels are the boundary waters which separate Ontario from six neighbouring American States, problems such as water levels, regulation and pollution are not merely local but are also international problems. The Boundary Waters Treaty of 1909 contains agreed principles and provided for the creation of the International Joint Commission to deal with such water problems along the common frontier, including the Great Lakes.

Canadians are slowly beginning to realize that water is our most valuable asset; and it took the abnormal water levels on the Great Lakes, the deterioration of Lake Erie and an apparent water shortage in the United States to bring this precious resource into its proper perspective.

The first step in solving a problem is the identification of that problem and the causative and related factors. This paper is confined to the identification and a brief explanation of the international water problems in the Great Lakes supplemented by an outline of what is being done about them.

Let us first consider the inter-related problem of levels on the Great Lakes. When high or low water levels occur, and particularly when they persist for several years, they become injurious to one or more interests that depend on the stability of levels and flows. Extreme fluctuations do not affect the various interests in the same way. Navigation is best served by high levels; hydro power by the maintenance of minimum flows especially during periods of high demand for electricity; and shore property interests such as industries, municipalities and tourist resorts are best served by minimizing both high and low levels. The natural balance of any one of the Great Lakes could not be altered without causing some adverse effects to one or more of the interests concerned. The first problem then is to determine what long term range of levels can best serve all interests—local, provincial and international.

Periods of high levels and low levels do not fall in a cyclical pattern. The analysis of 106 years of record establishes that the only pattern is a seasonal variation. What then caused the low water levels of 1964 and the high levels of 1952? The Great Lakes receive their water supply from the rain or snow which falls on the basin. About two-thirds of the normal precipitation is returned to the atmosphere by evaporation and evapo-transpiration. The water supply from runoff to any particular lake varies as much as the precipitation and the return of water to the atmosphere. The immense natural storage of the Great Lakes tends to smooth out these erratic variations. When either high or low water supplies occur for an extended period, corresponding extremes of levels occur and persist for some time after the climatic conditions have changed.

The change in flow from the lakes is small compared to the level variations, let alone the change in storage and supply conditions. For example, there is enough water in one foot on Lake Huron-Michigan to sustain the average flow of the St. Clair River for 2½ months. Yet a one-foot drop or rise in the lake changes the outflow by 7% or enough to sustain the average flow for only 5 days. Thus, the occasional large departures of water levels from normal affect the outflow for several years. It takes 2½ years for only 50% of the full effect of a change in water supply to Lake Huron to be realized in the outflows from Lake Ontario; and 3½ years for 60% of the full effect to be realized. In other words, the lower lakes suffer from abnormal levels long after the upper lakes have returned to average conditions.

This background leads us to the second problem—further regulation. What compression in extreme variations of levels can be accomplished to provide relief to shore property interests and yet attain benefits to power and navigation? What regulatory works are required? Could modifications to lake outflows be provided to prevent adverse effects downstream? In order to achieve desirable stabilization of the levels of Lake Huron the capacity of the St. Clair and Detroit rivers must be increased to carry large water releases, perhaps twice the present capacity. This would necessitate gated control structures and possible locks to compensate for reduced releases during the period of low supplies. Furthermore, if the increased discharge lowered Lake Huron by one foot, it would raise Lake Erie by 4½ feet and if passed down to Lake Ontario, would raise it by 6 feet. The regulation of Lake Huron and Lake Erie would necessitate integrating the regulation of all the lakes as one system to protect all riparian interests.

The other and most critical problem is the forecast of future water supplies. Before one can consider additional diversions into or out of the Great Lakes, he must be able to predict precipitation and losses to the atmosphere not for several months ahead, but for two or three years ahead in order to provide effective relief from the adverse effects of either high or low levels. Such long range forecasts are not available.

Lake Superior and Lake Ontario are regulated in accordance with Orders of Approval and under the direction of the International Joint Commission. The regulation, with the exception of seasonal shifts, follows the natural pattern. Significant changes occur only when high or low supplies are prevalent or expected to continue for some time. Statistical analyses of past records are used to estimate probable future supplies.

Let us now transfer our thinking from the problems in the Great Lakes resulting from natural conditions to those problems caused by the activities of man. I refer to the pollution of these waters.

Pollution is not a new problem on the Great Lakes. Fifty-three years ago the Governments of Canada and the United States requested the International Joint Commission to determine to what extent, by what causes and in what localities these waters were being polluted. The Commission reported in 1918 that the "situation along the common frontier is generally chaotic, everywhere perilous and in some cases disgraceful."

The Commission's 1918 report was not exactly ignored, but neither were its recommendations implemented. Progress in pollution abatement was very slow. With apparently an inexhaustible supply of fresh, clean water, there seemed little reason to spend large sums of money on pollution abatement works which would reduce industrial profits or add to local taxes.

In 1948 the Commission was requested to investigate the pollution problems of the Connecting Channels of the Great Lakes from Sault Ste. Marie to the Niagara River. It found that the bacterial concentration in these waters was in places 3 to 4 times greater than the average in 1913. The Commission's report of 1950 set forth specific water quality objectives intended to restore and maintain the waters of the Connecting Channels in a condition which would not impair the many uses expected of them. It recommended their adoption by the Governments to satisfy the Treaty requirements that "boundary waters and waters flowing across the boundary shall not be polluted on either side to injury of health and property on the other."

Progress in abating pollution in the connecting channels has been good. Most municipalities have either sedimentation and disinfection facilities or have them under construction. A few communities, however, are still in the planning stage. Remedial measures taken by industry has produced remarkable results especially when one considers the scale of industrial expansion which occurred in the same period.

Such progress should not be allowed to conceal the fact that the problem has not yet been solved and further substantial efforts are required by certain industries and municipalities. The IJC objectives are not being met in all reaches of the connecting channels. More efficient treatment is now necessary in those areas where there are large centres of population or heavy concentration of industrial wastes.

For many years the Great Lakes have been receiving the wastes from the rich industrial empire and the municipalities they support. The concentration of pollutants in these waters has been gradually increasing over the last 40 years. The bacteriological, chemical and biological changes induced by municipal and industrial wastes has had a deleterious effect on the water quality. Recent data indicates an accelerated rate of deterioration. The situation, particularly in Lake Erie, is serious. A similar process, though less advanced, is taking place in Lake Ontario. The quality of water in Lake Huron is still good. The water quality of Lake Superior has not been degraded due to its size, depth and sparse population on its shores.

Flowing streams either continually or periodically flush pollutant materials downstream. This is not so in the Great Lakes. These lakes are so deep that the accumulated pollutants in their lower layers remain in them almost indefinitely. The cumulative and almost irreversible effects of pollutant substances necessitates remedial action well in advance of the manifestation of these effects.

This problem is best illustrated by the excessive enrichment of waters by nutrients. The growth of algae like crops on fertilized land, is stimulated by nutrients. Microbiota feed on the algae that die and sink to the bottom of the lake and in the process deplete the dissolved oxygen. The more concentrated the algae growth, the sooner oxygen in the deeper waters is exhausted. The dissolved oxygen in the bottom waters cannot be replaced because they are isolated from the surface layers by thermal stratification. The depletion of dissolved oxygen in the deeper water is followed by a release of nutrients from the bottom deposits which, in due course, promote further growth of algae. Under extreme conditions this high rate of productivity may become self-supporting. The accumulation of nutrients in the lake is so slow and subtle that the onset is seldom noticed. But once the concentration becomes critical the process requires only a few years to become manifest. The rapid change tends to take the general public by surprise. Such is the case in Lake Erie.

The major problem is to recognize that stringent pollution control is necessary. The cost may be high. The immense size of the Great Lakes complicates the problem. This is contrary to popular belief.

This leads us to a second major problem. There is a danger that we may be lulled into a position of believing that there will be no need to extend the pollution abatement works now being constructed to meet the current objectives. It has been estimated that the demand for water for domestic and industrial uses is increasing at the rate of 4% per year. But this small annual increase also means that in 18 years the demand for clean, fresh water will be doubled and so will the quality of pollutants. Will today's pollution cause a water shortage in the future? Pollution problems created by a lack of vision today will be compounded by industrial expansion, population pressure and the growth of water-related recreation.

Pollution cannot be eliminated. Nevertheless, the most effective management of water, our greatest resource, must place emphasis on pollution control. This is our obligation to the succeeding generations. Greater dependence on water that has been used over and over again coupled with an increase in quantity and new types of wastes will necessitate more stringent and additional controls over all effluents discharged into the Great Lakes and their tributaries.

Water pollution takes many forms. Each has its own characteristic properties and each can, in its own way, make water less suitable or even unfit for many purposes. There is a deficiency in the scientific knowledge and understanding of the physical, chemical and biological behaviour of the Great Lakes, particularly in respect to pollutants and their dispersal. How much do we really know about the adverse effects of each waste discharged into the Great Lakes, the cycle of eutrophication, the toxic effects of certain metals and synthetic organic substances, the survival rate of pathogenic micro-organisms, and the most practicable methods of advanced waste treatment? Socrates' statement "all that we know is that we know nothing" is applicable in this instance. The knowledge and understanding gained through research will enhance constructive remedial action and avoid expensive mistakes being made in an effort to control pollution.

The immense size of the Great Lakes has limited research in many aspects of their limnology. A list of the more common species comprising the plankton of Lake Huron would be an original contribution to scientific literature. The equipment and methods developed for investigating streams and small lakes are not applicable to these inland seas. The need for large vessels and special equipment has hampered large scale studies. Until recently, most of the research has been restricted to shallow waters or near shore areas. Consequently, research projects on the Great Lakes generally have been localized, of short duration and lacking coordination. Fortunately, this problem, the lack of research activity, is now being overcome by support from various levels of government in both Canada and the United States.

Extreme water levels and pollution of the Great Lakes have no respect for artificial political boundaries. The consequences are felt by the citizens of both Canada and the United States. These problems, if neglected, can adversely affect the relations between the two countries and their peoples. One of the purposes of the Boundary Waters Treaty of 1909 was to prevent disputes regarding the use of these and other boundary waters. The Treaty provided for the establishment of the International Joint Commission, defined its jurisdiction and authority, and spelled out the principles by which it was to be governed. The Treaty also recorded certain mutual obligations regarding the use of boundary waters and those streams crossing the boundary.

The International Joint Commission is a permanent body with certain quasi-judicial, investigative and administrative powers. It has six members—three from Canada and three from the United States. The Commissioners are not "negotiators" under instruction from their respective governments. The IJC functions as a single body seeking objective solutions to common problems.

On October 7, 1964, the Governments of Canada and the United States requested the International Joint Commission to investigate and report on the problem of the levels of the Great Lakes and the pollution of Lake Erie, Lake Ontario and the International

Section of the St. Lawrence River. These investigations are being conducted by the IJC through technical boards selected by the Commission from qualified experts in both countries. The Commission does not employ a large staff of its own, but it is empowered by the Governments to call upon officials of departments and agencies in both countries. The provincial and state governments concerned also provide experts from their agencies. If it is deemed necessary, the Commission may retain consultants. Thus, the IJC is able to select and deploy the most experienced and competent people in both countries and combine them in these joint investigations.

Like the Commission, its International Boards operate as single units seeking a solution to problems in the joint interest of both countries. There is active cooperation and exchange of current information between agencies of both countries through these international boards. The studies are so large and complex that the programmes of the participating departments and agencies must be integrated to make sure the best possible use is made of the available technical resources in both countries. The Commission's cooperative studies avoid unnecessary duplication.

What is being done to provide solutions to the problems indicated earlier? The Commission's Great Lakes Levels Board is assessing the effects of various levels on shore properties. Regulation plans are being developed, using mathematical models for six combinations of lakes for various ranges of stage on each of the lakes. The effect of further regulation on navigation is being evaluated by studying traffic patterns, composition of future fleets and cost of vessel operation. The dependable capacity and energy output of existing power installations, and the feasibility of further expansion is being determined for each regulation plan developed. Field investigations, designs and cost estimates are being made for the required regulatory works. The private and public interests considered include industrial and municipal works such as water intakes, sewer systems and sub-structures of shore installations; power facilities; commercial fisheries; water related recreation such as beaches, boating and marinas; wild life habitats; and riparian ownership.

The two international pollution boards are acquiring factual information on the source, extent, location, effects and dispersal of pollutants. Intensive studies are being conducted on lake circulation, mixing and diffusion; chemistry, physics and biology of the lakes; the assimilation of pollutants; the development of appropriate parameters; the cycle and effects of eutrophication on aquatic life and water quality; and the effects of fertilizers, pesticides and herbicides on aquatic life. More effective means of treatment of industrial and municipal wastes are being developed. All these studies are being coordinated under the aegis of the International Joint Commission.

The collection and analysis of data and the development of regulation plans, the determination of practical remedial measures and the design of regulatory works is neither spectacular nor suitable as newspaper copy. Articles are read by a much larger audience if they are sensational. Nevertheless, programmes approved by the Commission are being implemented in the most expeditious manner. Nearly all segments of the investigations are proceeding simultaneously.

Over 300 Canadian professional and technical personnel are participating. The Canadian participation will continue to accelerate. Until this year the United States activities in relation to these Great Lakes problems has been more extensive than Canada's.

We cannot afford the luxury of "off the cuff" solutions. With the expenditure of the large sums of money to be involved, we need assurance that all remedial and regulatory works recommended by the IJC will produce the desired results. A methodical and thorough approach is warranted. Granted, extensive research in large scale studies should have started years ago; but original research and thorough investigations on limnology of the Great Lakes has been initiated and will continue to accelerate. This newly acquired knowledge will lead us to the solution of the problems of the Great Lakes.

It will be some time before these investigations are completed. Nature is providing temporary relief from the effect of low water levels. The problem of enrichment of the waters of the Great Lakes, particularly Lake Erie, cannot be left until conclusive evidence is assembled. For this reason the IJC in its interim report last year recommended that the Governments of Canada and the United States, as soon as possible and in association with provincial and state governments, take appropriate action to ensure sufficient purification of municipal and industrial wastes to achieve the maximum removal of phosphates.

When we become anxious about the time it takes to devise solutions to the water problems of the Great Lakes let us ask ourselves: what water levels can best serve all interests; how can we achieve further regulation and yet protect downstream interests; how can we forecast future water supplies; can we diminish the cumulative effects of pollution; avoid the danger of being lulled into complacency; and accept the high cost of more stringent water quality standards? The answers must be practicable, economically feasible and in the best interests of the peoples of Canada and the United States. These are the problems of the Great Lakes.

15

Environmental Control in the Great Lakes—St. Lawrence Region of North America

E. G. Pleva

The Great Lakes, with their great discharge river the St. Lawrence, comprise the most economically significant body of water or water system in North America and perhaps in the entire world. More than 36 million North Americans live in the Great Lakes-St. Lawrence drainage basin: over 25 million in the United States and 11 million in Canada. Many millions more are directly affected by what happens to these lakes and the waters in them or discharging from them. We have estimated that by 1985 the population of the drainage basin will increase to 57 million human beings, of whom about 19 million will reside in Canada. During this period, in other words, an annual increase in population of approximately one million is indicated.

The most important industrial and urban agglomeration in Canada parallels the axis of the lower Great Lakes and the St. Lawrence River. A map of Canada shows that a relatively straight line may be drawn from Quebec City through Montreal, Kingston, Toronto, London, to Windsor, approximately 700 miles long. If one visualizes a belt 50 miles wide (25 miles on each side of the imaginary line) running its entire length, the belt or corridor would be 35,000 square miles in area. Although this comprises less than

Reprinted from *Water Resources of Canada,* ed. C. E. Doleman (University of Toronto Press, 1967), pp. 83-86.

1 per cent of the total area of Canada, this corridor is an extremely important part of the country; for it contains approximately three-fifths of Canada's population, four-fifths of the industrial activity as measured by the value of manufactured goods, and one-third of the commercial agriculture as measured by the value of products sold off the farm. One of Canada's railway champions, Alexander Galt, named this corridor over a century ago. When arguing for a railway to run from the salt water of the St. Lawrence estuary to the heart of the continent in Chicago, he said: "This railway will serve the Grand Trunk of North America."

Obviously Canada has an exceedingly large stake in the maintenance and improvement of the quality of the environment in the Great Lakes-St. Lawrence drainage basin. Yet in this area, the quality of the surface waters, rivers, and lakes, and even that of the groundwater, is decreasing from year to year. There is general agreement that pollution by municipal and industrial wastes is the main cause of this deterioration.

The physical map of North America shows a natural unity of the Great Lakes-St. Lawrence drainage basin: it is one system. However, a political map displays a pattern of fragmentation. This natural unit is shared by the United States and Canada: by the nine states of Minnesota, Wisconsin, Illinois, Indiana, Michigan, Ohio, Pennsylvania, New York, and Vermont; and by the two provinces of Ontario and Quebec. It is generally realized that the local government units of a century ago are inadequate to meet the problems of today's expanding urban areas; but it is not so well known that historically evolved state and provincial boundaries are great obstacles to dealing with large environmental problems. A governor can speak only for his state; a premier can refer only to things being done in his province. There is no unitary system or approach for dealing with the basic problems of this great drainage basin. Ohio cannot speak to Ontario except through the State Department and the Department of External Affairs. This process can take forty years.

Lake Erie, the most critical part of the system, may be regarded as illustrating the complexities involved in trying to reach a unitary basis in the environmental planning of a region fragmented into many political jurisdictions. Every major magazine, newspaper syndicate, and television network seems to have provided a "horror story" on Lake Erie in the past year. The *New York Herald Tribune* invented a new word in its article on Lake Erie—*lacocide*, the death of a lake.

The International Joint Commission, established as a consequence of the 1909 Treaty, has certain obligations and procedural practices. It should be studied as a model for a working framework of some "authority" more closely related to the problems of 1967. The treaty works well and the IJC has a commendable record of activities, but it must be pointed out that the great deterioration of the Great Lakes and St. Lawrence River has taken place since 1909—the period when the IJC was operative. Clearly something has been lacking.

Ontario has excellent water resources legislation in the Water Resources Commission Act. Ohio, likewise, has excellent water legislation. But even if Ontario and Ohio were able to work together, what happens when a substantial portion of the pollution of Lake Erie comes from industrial wastes originating in Michigan? Presumably this is where federal and international cooperation should take over. However, in both Canada and the United States, water is a natural resource that comes basically under the control of the provinces and the states. Here is a very serious dilemma that must be resolved without delay.

Many scientific conferences have been called in the past few years to deal with the problems of the Great Lakes and their alleviation. But the conferences always come up against the hard facts of fragmented political jurisdiction and the absence of any operational mechanism able to produce a unitary approach. No one is so naïve as to believe in some cumbersome centralized political remedy. History has given us our fragments of states and provinces and we must work within this framework.

The recently passed United States Water Quality Act of 1965 (P.L. 89-234), although geared to the cooperative and coordinated efforts of the three levels of government—federal, state, and local—recognizes the comprehensive scope of water resources problems when they transcend boundary lines. Perhaps an arrangement may be worked out by the United States and Canada whereby the five states of Ohio, Michigan, Indiana, Pennsylvania, and New York (operating under the Water Quality Act) could cooperate with Ontario (operating under the Ontario Water Resources Commission Act) to deal positively with the improvement of Lake Erie.

There are some who claim emphatically that more research and more education are needed. These needs are acknowledged, but the most urgent necessity now is to develop the means whereby unitary programmes may be undertaken by fragmented political units. While further research is necessary, we actually lack today the practical means of applying the knowledge we already have.

In the absence of working machinery to deal with regional water resources problems on a regional basis, many proposals involving massive adjustments of the continental water budget are being given great publicity. North America's future may include major water diversion and water transmission projects, but the immediate challenge is to control pollution, the great destroyer of water in the Great Lakes-St. Lawrence basin. This economic region is fortunate in its store of fresh water. But the usage of this water is limited by pollution, and the limitation has now reached critical proportions.

There are several positive consequences to a successful programme in water management and pollution abatement. Water is the most planning-sensitive factor in determining the pattern of new urban growth and the redevelopment of old urban areas. As already indicated, the management of water resources in Ontario is and always has been a provincial responsibility. The Ontario Water Resources Commission Act merely establishes procedures whereby the province exercises its responsibilities. Ontario will double in population in the next quarter-century. All this growth will be in the urban sector. The proper management of water resources, including the supply and distribution as well as the treatment of wastes, will be a major element in developing the kinds of urban patterns that could be a credit to a civilized technology and a humane people.

Conclusions

1. The Great Lakes-St. Lawrence region of North America is one of the world's most important industrial and urban areas.

2. Its water resources are abundant but are being limited in utility by pollution. The seriousness of the condition is increasing.

3. A unitary programme on water management and pollution abatement has been difficult to achieve owing to the political fragmentation of the drainage basin.

4. The most critical area in the system, Lake Erie, may be dealt with on a unitary basis provided that Canada and the United States were to enable Ontario and the five states of New York, Pennsylvania, Ohio, Michigan, and Indiana to work together under the terms of recent existing legislation. The working out of such an agreement would take a high degree of statesmanship. Perhaps the principal decision-makers should convene upon an island in Lake Erie and stay in session until a working agreement is reached.

5. The planning and management of water resources may be the most important factor in achieving a civilized pattern of land

uses in rapidly developing urban areas. Decision-makers must find courage for compromise between potentially competitive uses for water.

6. The people of the region, through research and education, must become more adequately informed in preparation for the decisions that will lead to prudent and rational management of water resources. This knowledge is necessary in order that simple panaceas for water resources problems may be evaluated critically in all their implications, and that projects which are bold in scale and novel in purpose may be appraised intelligently by the tax-payers.

7. Finally, the regional inhabitants must accept and be prepared to underwrite the considerable costs involved in effective water management works.

16

Multiple-Purpose
Development of
Canada's Water Resources

W. R. D. Sewell

Throughout Canadian history water resources have played a vital role in the nation's economic growth. Since the days of the early explorers and fur traders, water resources have influenced settlement patterns and have been a powerful force conditioning industrial and agricultural development. The expansion of the forestry industry and the mineral-processing industries in Quebec and British Columbia has been closely associated with the harnessing of hydro-electric power in those provinces. The water-resources programmes of the Prairie Farm Rehabilitation Administration (P.F.R.A.) have done much to overcome the problems of agricultural readjustment resulting from the drought and economic depression of the 1930s. More recently, the St. Lawrence Seaway scheme has been carried out with overall economic expansion as its major objective. The close association of water-resource development with overall economic growth is further emphasized by the large amount of investment in water-related activities. Recently, capital investment in hydro-power projects in Canada has averaged more than $400 million a year. When expenditures on other water-resource projects are added to this, the total annual capital investment in water projects probably accounts for more than 20% of the total annual capital investment in all activities in Canada.

Reprinted from *Water Power*, April (1962), pp. 146-51.

Cognizant of the importance of water-resource development to their economic wellbeing, Canadians are taking an increasing interest in the manner in which these resources are managed. They have begun to question whether the goals of public policy are broad enough to cope with the emerging problems of water-resource development. They are also asking what roles should be assumed by the federal and provincial authorities in this field. Are the policies and the functions of the various agencies sufficiently coordinated to ensure that the resources will be developed for their most beneficial uses? And are the data, research programmes, personnel, and financial arrangements presently available adequate for efficient management? These, and other related questions, formed the basis of discussions in the Water Sector of the Resources for Tomorrow Conference held in Montreal recently.

Termed by the Chairman of the Steering Committee of the Conference, the Honourable Walter Dinsdale, "a landmark in the economic development of all parts of Canada," the Resources for Tomorrow Conference was organized as a joint venture by the ten provincial governments and the federal government. Its main objectives were to consider the shortcomings of present resource programmes, to discuss the resource problems Canadians face as a nation, and to provide suggestions as to how these problems may be overcome.

To facilitate the discussions, over 80 Background Papers dealing with various aspects of the management of Canada's renewable resources were prepared and distributed to the 700 delegates prior to the Conference. Compiled in two volumes, these Papers provide a wealth of information and constitute a valuable reference guide. A third volume, containing other Background Papers, and a résumé of the discussions at the Conference, is to be published subsequently.

The Conference Sessions were composed of two groups: Resource Sectors dealing with the problems associated with the development of individual renewable resources—water, agricultural lands, forests, fisheries, and wild life; and plenary sessions dealing with problems common to all the resources—such as jurisdiction, administration, research, and so on. In addition, special attention was given to problems relating to recreation and regional development. This article concentrates upon problems associated with the development of water resources in Canada as revealed in the Background Papers and in the discussions at the Conference. Attention is drawn, however, to the interrelationships between water development and the development of other resources. An understanding of these interrelationships is fundamental to the solution of the emerging problems of water management in Canada.

Problems of Water Management in Canada

Most of the problems of water management that have arisen in Canada relate to the increasing competition for the use of the nation's water resources, the division of authority in water matters between several jurisdictions, and the non-coincidence of political and natural boundaries.

As population has increased and as technology has advanced, the number of competing claims for the use of water resources has multiplied. As development proceeds this problem will become more complex and serious disputes are certain to arise. Conflicts over the use of water for different purposes have already appeared, as in the case of fish and power in the Fraser River basin and in the St. John River basin. Other conflicts are brewing over the use of water for irrigation purposes in Alberta, and the development of hydro power elsewhere in the Saskatchewan-Nelson basin. Yet other disputes have arisen over the use of water bodies for the disposal of domestic sewage and industrial effluents. Serious problems of water pollution have occurred, for example, on the Ottawa and St. John Rivers, and threaten to do so in other parts of Canada.

Resolution of these problems is complicated by the fact that jurisdiction over water resources is shared between the federal and the provincial authorities. The British North America Act of 1867 (and its subsequent amendments) grants to the provinces the ownership of resources within their boundaries, but retains for the federal authority certain responsibilities relating to the management of these resources. Specifically, in connection with water, the federal authority has exclusive jurisdiction over the use of water for navigation purposes, and for the fisheries. It also has concurrent jurisdiction over agriculture. Its responsibilities in water matters are further extended by its power to deal with problems concerning international and interprovincial relations. The federal authority also is responsible for the overall economic policy of the nation.

Clearly, such a division of responsibility calls for a maximum of co-operation and co-ordination of policies and activities. Many of the problems that have arisen may be attributed to the lack of co-ordination and co-operation among the various authorities.

Canada possesses some of the largest river systems and lakes in the world. Many of these, such as the St. Lawrence, Saskatchewan-Nelson, the Mackenzie, and the Yukon River systems, extend several hundreds of miles and cross several boundaries, provincial or international. Problems related to the non-coincidence of watersheds with political boundary lines are among the most frustrating of water-management problems in Canada.

Water-resource development, however, does not take place in a vacuum, but within the context of general economic development. Not only is water management intimately interrelated with the management of other resources, but it is also profoundly affected by overall economic policy. In addition, water development is becoming a recognized instrument of economic policy, designed not merely to provide power, or irrigation water, or domestic and industrial water supplies, but to achieve certain broad economic and social objectives. Clearly, therefore, there is a need to integrate not only the various water policies and activities, and other resource-development policies, but also to harmonize overall economic and water-resource development. The need for a more integrated and comprehensive approach to resource management was one of the principal conclusions of the discussions of the Conference.

Adoption of a comprehensive approach to resource management will hinge upon the determination of the roles to be played by the federal and provincial authorities in resource development; adoption of a much broader perspective in planning; the creation of an appropriate institutional framework; and the provision of funds for development.

Federal and Provincial Responsibilities

The division of powers between the federal and provincial authorities, as set out in the B.N.A. Act, has had a number of important effects on the development of water resources in Canada. First, in assigning responsibilities for different water uses to different authorities, it has made more difficult the resolution of conflicts between them. The problem is especially serious because there is no compulsory forum in which disputes between provinces may be resolved. If one province has a dispute with another province over the use of a water resource, the matter could be submitted for Court ruling only if *both* parties agreed to litigation. The resolution of disputes is even more complicated where the federal authority is in dispute with provincial authorities over the use of water resources.

Secondly, it has encouraged the federal authority to concentrate its developmental efforts on those aspects of water use for which it has direct responsibility. Thus projects undertaken by the federal authority have been concerned dominantly with activities related to navigation, fisheries, and agriculture.

Thirdly, there is often confusion as to which authority is responsible for a particular function, and this results in considerable delays in initiating projects. Such delays may be very costly and may allow the problem to get out of hand. Delays in initiating pollution-control projects, for instance, have been attributed to the lack of defined responsibility for dealing with this problem.

The question as to the roles to be played by the federal authorities and the provincial authorities received a great deal of attention at the Conference. The general consensus of opinion in the Water Sector seemed to be that although the provinces own the water resources within their boundaries, and have primary responsibility for their development, there is a very important role to be played by the federal authority. It was suggested that the federal authority should recognize a broad national interest in development which can be applied without infringing upon the proprietary rights of the provinces. The federal role might be to supply leadership through the co-ordination of overall economic and resource-development policies; through co-operation in the investigatory and planning stages of development; and through the provision of finance in the form of grants and low-interest loans.

Planning Water-Resource Development

The second requirement in a comprehensive approach to water management is broadly based long-range planning. Planning in water-resource development to date in Canada has been rather narrow in scope. Usually it has been concerned only with the design of projects to serve rather specific needs, such as the provision of a power supply, irrigation for farms, or water supply for homes and industry. Generally, only the technical and financial aspects of the situation have been considered. The orbit of the planning has rarely extended beyond the local area, and generally has been short-term in perspective, seldom extending beyond 15 years.

As the development of water resources proceeds, however, and as the competition for their use increases, the need to expand planning horizons will grow. More and more it will become necessary to take into account the broad economic and social effects of the projects, and their interrelationships with other projects.

The adoption of a broader horizon in planning, however, will depend upon the provision of more basic data and the extension of programmes of research. It will also require the training and marshalling of the professional skills required in the planning and development of projects, and the development of techniques for the selection of projects.

A. Basic Data

Future planning of water-resource development will require a vast amount of information relating to the physical and economic factors involved. The discussions in the Water Sector revealed that there are some deficiencies in present data programmes, and a number of suggestions were offered regarding ways in which data programmes could be improved to provide the necessary information.

First, there are a number of gaps in the coverage of present programmes. For instance, it has been recommended that for surveying water resources there should be a rain gauge every 200 sq. miles. Only in the most densely populated areas of Canada is this standard approached. One important deficiency is the lack of high-elevation meteorological recording stations; another is the sparsity of snow courses. There are few data available on ground water and on evapotranspiration. Information on the uses of water for various purposes is extremely sparse. Problems in designing certain structures, such as spillways and flood-control works, would be reduced if there were more detailed information on peak flows. Present programmes, therefore, need to be expanded in breadth and in depth to overcome these and other deficiencies in coverage.

Second, greater co-ordination of efforts in planning and operating data-gathering networks would eliminate much duplication, and make possible more extensive coverage. Co-operation in gathering hydrometric and meteorological data, for instance, has yielded very beneficial results. Much, however, remains to be done.

Third, greater use can be made of data that have already been gathered, by advising potential data users as to the extent of coverage to date; by more intensive analysis of data; and by improvements in publication. Specifically, there is a need for lists of data-gathering stations, past and present, and for summaries of data collected to date. This would save the potential data user a great deal of time in his search for information and would materially assist in planning data-collection programmes. More intensive analysis of data is also required. At present far more effort is spent on gathering information than on analysing it. More intensive analysis of data may not only reveal many important new facts, but may also save unnecessary efforts in data collection.

Fourth, scarcity of funds, personnel, and time make it essential to be selective in planning data programmes. In recent years the advantages of statistical sampling techniques have become more and more apparent in data collection. For instance, serious consideration is being given to the development of networks based upon a system of base stations and satellite stations. The former would be permanent, but the latter would be operated for a period and then discontinued. The records from the satellite stations could be correlated with those from the base station.

Finally, the approach to data collection in the future must be more forward-looking than it has been in the past. By and large, the approach to date has been to gather data when requested to do so by the data user. In future, however, data-collecting agencies will have to anticipate to a much larger degree what requirements will be and plan data collection accordingly.

Most of the detailed discussions of problems of data collection and interpretation related to physical data. It was emphasized, however, that in future economic and social considerations would assume ever-increasing importance in planning, and that programmes for collecting, analyzing, and publishing socio-economic data would have to be stepped up accordingly.

B. Research

Throughout the discussions at the Conference there was a call for more research in both the pure and applied fields. Although a great deal of money is spent on research in Canada, much less emphasis is given to this aspect of development than in many other countries. In the United States and the U.K., for instance, more than 2% of the national income is devoted to research; in Canada less than 1% is spent for this purpose. Even more important is the fact that in Canada only a small part of the total research effort is in the field of resource management.

A number of suggestions were offered as to ways in which the necessary programmes of research might be undertaken. These suggestions emphasized the role of government agencies in supplying leadership, but also stressed that industry should place more emphasis on research than it has in the past. Specific proposals for an extension of the research activities included those for an expansion of the National Research Council to include studies of resource-management problems, and for the expansion of co-operative research programmes sponsored jointly by the federal and the provincial governments, and by government and industry.

C. Personnel

Adoption of a more comprehensive approach to resource management will require the marshalling of a wide variety of professional and technical skills to carry out the necessary planning and development. Increasingly, however, it will be necessary for these specialists to familiarize themselves with problems of overall development. The need for cross-fertilization of ideas will become more and more urgent.

How can the types of skills required in future be made available? Four important suggestions were put forward in the Water Sector. First, there should be increased emphasis in university curricula on resource-management problems. A notable step forward in this direction has been made at the University of British Columbia, where a Natural Resources Programme has been launched by the Department of Economics, and involving the Departments of Forestry, Engineering, and Fisheries. Second, government agencies should initiate training programmes similar to those undertaken in other countries. Education would be regarded as a continuing process, welding academic theory with practical experience. Third, much can be gained from exchanges of personnel. In this way, a reservoir of experience would be developed, with benefits to more than one region. Fourth, conferences and seminars should be held to discuss resource-management problems. These should gather together people from a variety of disciplines, rather than from just one. Clearly, each of the disciplines—engineering, social and natural sciences, and so on—has an important contribution to make in planning and development. Only if representatives from these disciplines are brought together can all aspects be considered, and a common understanding be developed.

D. Tools for Evaluation of Projects and Programmes

With the increasing competition for the use of water resources and the growing number of claims on funds for development, the need for tools of analysis to weigh alternatives and select between them is becoming more urgent. To date decisions have been based largely on technical and financial considerations alone. In the future, however, the broad economic and social effects of development will loom larger in decision-making.

Benefit-cost analysis is a technique which makes it possible to take account of these effects in the analysis and evaluation of projects. The technique has been developed and used in various parts of the world, notably in the United States and in Europe. Various United Nations agencies also use it in their analyses of programmes of development, and it has been used in the analysis of some projects in Canada, as for instance the Greater Winnipeg Floodway Scheme, and projects of the Conservation Authorities in Ontario. There is at present, however, no body of generally accepted principles of analysis, and there is wide variation in procedures used to evaluate the various benefits and costs.

Because of the demonstrated usefulness of this tool of analysis, it seemed to the organizers of the Water Sector of the Conference that there would be much merit in discussing the matter in some detail. To assist the discussions, a group of four authors drawn from government, university and industry, prepared a draft Guide to Benefit-Cost Analysis as a part of the research carried out for the Conference. The draft Guide set out the basic principles of the analysis, discussed possible applications of the technique, and recommended a number of procedures for analyzing water-resource projects.

There was general agreement that benefit-cost analysis is a basically useful tool in project evaluation and that it would be very useful to have the Guide published. The Steering Committee of the Conference subsequently agreed to this proposal and the Guide is to be published as a Conference document in the near future.

Agencies for Water Management

A third requirement in the adoption of a more comprehensive approach is the development of an appropriate administrative framework. Over the years a framework of agencies has evolved to carry out the responsibilities and policies of the various authorities in water management. This framework is characterized by a host of agencies at the different levels of administration, much duplication of functions, and a lack of co-ordination within and between the levels. At the federal level, for instance, responsibilities for water management are scattered among nine Departments and their associated Branches and agencies, together with a number of Crown Corporations. In many provinces there are more than a dozen provincial agencies dealing with water matters. The problem is further emphasized by the fact that in some cases the development of a river for a given purpose—say hydro power—may involve a dozen federal agencies, several provincial agencies, and possibly a number of federal-provincial or inter-provincial agencies too!

Efforts have been made to improve co-ordination of policies and functions among the agencies at the various levels of administration. At the federal level, for instance, an Advisory Committee on Water Use Policy was established to improve co-ordination of the policies of the various Departments which have responsibilities in the water field. In addition, from time to time, a number of ad hoc committees have been set up to consider the various engineering, legal, economic, and other aspects of projects in which several agencies have an interest. Even so there are many areas in which co-ordination of policies and activities of federal agencies could be improved. A suggestion for a federal Water Resources Department was given some consideration. Such a Department would be responsible for the various investigatory, planning, and developmental activities of the federal government in the field of water management.

At the provincial level attempts to improve co-ordination have varied in breadth and in depth. In some cases the aim has been to gather together the agencies interested in a particular aspect of water management to decide upon a common policy and to eliminate duplication of functions. Sometimes a new agency has been established to co-ordinate the policies and activities of existing agencies. The New Brunswick Water Authority, for instance, was set up to co-ordinate the activities of the various agencies in New Brunswick that are responsible for pollution control. In Ontario, on the other hand, a new agency, the Ontario Water Resources Commission, has been established to take over some of the functions of existing agencies in controlling pollution.

In addition to efforts at the federal and provincial levels, co-ordination has been improved through the establishment of federal-provincial and interprovincial agencies. These agencies have been largely regulatory or investigatory in nature. Agencies such as the Lake of the Woods Control Board have been set up to regulate water levels and discharges from certain water bodies. Others, such as the Fraser River Board, the Prairie Provinces Water Board, and the St. John River Board, through their joint investigations and studies, have done much to improve mutual understanding of problems and needs in the regions concerned. There have been notably few federal-provincial agencies responsible for the developmental phase of water management.

Despite the progress in improving co-ordination, however, it seems that some substantial modifications in the present administrative framework will be required in the future. The types of agencies that will be required, and the functions they will be called upon to perform, were matters of considerable discussion in the Water Sector. Particular attention was focussed upon agencies required for multiple-purpose development of water resources, and upon the appropriateness of the river basin as a unit for planning and development.

The advantages of the multiple-purpose approach to resource management have been demonstrated in various parts of the world, and perhaps most successfully in the Tennessee Valley of the United

States, where the management of land and water resources is entrusted to a single agency, the Tennessee Valley Authority. While there is no instance of such an all-embracing approach to management in Canada, some important beginnings have been made in devising administrative arrangements necessary for multiple-purpose development and the management of water resources on a river-basin basis. These efforts have been made at local, provincial, and federal levels of administration.

Perhaps the most successful example of an administrative agency for multiple-purpose development at the municipal level of government is that of the Conservation Authorities in Ontario. Thirty such Authorities have been established so far under the Conservation Authorities Act. Municipalities in a watershed may, under the terms of the Act, combine to form an Authority to undertake land and water-conservation projects. Typically they have been motivated by the need for flood control, but usually their interests encompass other phases of land and water management as well, such as control of pollution, reforestation, groundwater investigations, provision of recreation facilities, and so on. The activities of the Authorities are co-ordinated by the provincial Conservation Branch. The Branch also provides guidance and liaison, co-operates in investigations, and administers financial assistance. Their distinctive features are their local sponsorship, their emphasis on the multiple-purpose approach, and their use of the watershed as the basic unit for management. Federal encouragement of this type of development is provided through financial contributions under the Canada Water Conservation Assistance Act.

The Conservation Authority type of structure seems well suited to the development of small watersheds and it is probable that it will be adopted elsewhere in Canada. It has already been adopted in a modified form in Manitoba. Nevertheless, there are a number of problems to be faced. For instance, how large are the projects it can handle? What type of agency would be required where inter-provincial or international waters are involved?

A number of attempts have been made at the provincial level to implement the multiple-purpose concept. The most recent is that of the South Saskatchewan River Development Commission, set up in 1959 to carry out the agreement between the federal government and the government of Saskatchewan relating to the South Saskatchewan project. The seven-member semi-independent Commission is responsible for the co-ordination of the policies and relevant activities of the agencies responsible for various aspects of the project. Upon completion of the project, the Commission will be responsible for the operation and maintenance of the reservoir. A South Saskatchewan River Development Board, composed of federal and provincial officials, was set up to supervise the construction of the project and to provide advice and liaison as required.

The South Saskatchewan River Development Commission contrasts with the Conservation Authorities in Ontario in that the latter are organized on a watershed basis, whereas the Commission is concerned with a specific project in one part of the Saskatchewan-Nelson Basin. Although it constitutes an important step forward in organizing development on a multiple-purpose basis, it is clear that a number of problems remain to be solved. In particular, there are problems of co-ordinating the development of the project with the development of other projects in Saskatchewan, and of harmonizing this scheme with other water-resource developments in the Saskatchewan-Nelson Basin.

An increasing number of efforts are being made at the federal level to develop water resources on a multiple-purpose basis. The most notable examples include the planning and construction that have taken place on the St. Lawrence and Niagara Rivers; financial participation under the Canada Water Conservation Assistance Act and the construction of projects under the P.F.R.A. Act. Further development of this type is envisioned under the A.R.D.A. Act.

The P.F.R.A. was originally set up to carry out programmes designed to overcome problems of agricultural readjustment associated with the droughts and economic depression of the 1930s. Many of its programmes have been based on multiple-purpose development of water resources, providing water for irrigation, stock-watering, domestic water supply, and so on. Over the years, however, the scope of the P.F.R.A.'s activities has expanded and some of its projects embrace other water-development purposes, such as flood control and power.

Despite the progress that has been made by the P.F.R.A., it suffers, as do other federal agencies, from limitations imposed by the B.N.A. Act. Even though it is able to undertake multiple-purpose projects, an agricultural purpose must always be present. Furthermore, it is unable to undertake planning and development on a comprehensive basin-wide basis as many of the projects involved would include aspects that are beyond its jurisdiction.

These examples show that important beginnings have been made, but that a wholehearted adoption of the multiple-purpose and river-basin planning concepts will require much greater co-operation and co-ordination between agencies and between levels of administration. This will be especially important in the case of water resources where:

(a) jurisdiction over water use is divided between the federal and the provincial authorities.

(b) the resources are shared by two or more provinces.

(c) international interests are involved.

Problems such as these at present inhibit development of some of the nation's major river basins, including the Fraser, the Columbia, the Saskatchewan-Nelson, and the St. John. There were a number of suggestions offered in the Water Sector as to the types of agencies required for the development of these basins. Among the suggestions, proposals for the establishment of River Basin Authorities and River Basin Commissions received considerable discussion.

A River Basin Authority is an agency, styled on the TVA model, and vested with broad powers to under take the planning and development of the water and associated resources of a river basin on a comprehensive basis. This type of agency seems to have greatest appeal where the region has not reached a very advanced stage of economic development, where water resources play a dominating role in the development, or where potential conflicts of agencies and of jurisdictions are minimal. It was suggested that it might be the appropriate structure for developing the resources of the less-developed areas in the country, including some parts of northern Canada.

The River Basin Commission has more limited functions. Its role is to co-ordinate the policies and activities of agencies responsible for the different phases of the development of the water resources of the basin, in order to prepare an overall plan. This type of agency has already been adopted for the development of the South Saskatchewan project. A modified form of the Commission was suggested as a means of planning the development of the St. John River Basin, involving the participation of officials from the Canadian and U.S. governments, from the provinces of New Brunswick and Nova Scotia, and from the State of Maine. The main role of the Commission type of agency appears to be that of preparing a plan of development. Other types of agencies, therefore, would be required to put the plan into action.

The discussion of administrative frameworks indicated that there are some deficiencies in the present structure and that some bold changes will have to be made to meet the emerging problems of water management. Although many suggestions were offered, it was clear from the discussions this subject stimulated that it is a problem that merits a great deal more consideration than was possible at the Conference.

Financing Development

Success of a comprehensive approach to management also hinges upon the availability of the necessary funds for development. Several delegates suggested that the construction of a number of projects is held up because the sponsoring agencies are unable to obtain the necessary funds—even though the projects may be economically and socially desirable. Such instances include certain projects in which a number of authorities are involved; and projects in which a number of purposes are involved, especially if non-reimbursible features (such as flood control or recreation) are included.

Many delegates called for a more penetrating look at present financing arrangements, and for the determination of the roles to be played by federal and provincial authorities in this phase of water management. It was noted that the federal authority can exert an important influence in this connection through its control over monetary and fiscal policies, and through its superior borrowing powers. Among the suggestions that received most support were those for the development of co-operative arrangements between the federal and provincial authorities for financing projects of a broad national interest through grants-in-aid, and through the provision of low-cost loans by the federal government.

Summary and Conclusions

Increasing competition for the use of water resources, the complex interrelationships between water development and the development of other resources, and the particularly close association of economic growth and water development in some regions will call for a much broader approach to water management in Canada in the future. Efficient management will require more comprehensive planning encompassing a long-range perspective, and embracing multiple-use concepts of development.

The adoption of a broader approach will necessitate a number of changes in present policies and institutions. First, the roles to be assumed by the federal and provincial authorities must be more clearly defined and goals of policy announced. Second, to carry out the necessary planning, basic data must be collected, analysed, and published; research—in basic and in applied fields—must be undertaken; the appropriate professional and technical skills must be trained and marshalled; and tools of analysis and evaluation devised. Third, modifications must be made in the administrative framework to accommodate changes in perspective in planning and development. Finally, appropriate financial arrangements must be devised. Certain specific suggestions were made as to the ways in which present arrangements need to be modified.

In addition to these specific suggestions related to water resources, a number of other proposals were made concerned with resource management in general. Of these, two are of particular interest: Resources Advisory Councils, and a National Resources Development Fund. There were numerous suggestions as to the form an Advisory Council should take. Some suggested that it should be a body in which all the senior governments were represented and which would have certain research and planning functions. Other suggestions called for the establishment of Inter-Departmental Advisory Councils on Resource Management at both federal and provincial levels of administration. These Councils would co-ordinate policies and programmes at their respective levels and provide liaison with other similar bodies.

A National Resources Development Fund was proposed by several of the delegates, but there were widely diverging opinions as to the form it should take and the functions it should perform. There was fairly general agreement, however, that it should be a fund from which the provinces could draw low-cost loans for projects that were considered to be in the overall national interest. One proposal was that the Fund should be administered in a manner similar to the World Bank.

Perhaps the most notable achievement of the Conference was that it provided a forum for the free interchange of opinions and experience among people from a wide variety of disciplines. The cross-fertilization of ideas that was promoted thereby made it possible not only to identify a number of significant problems and issues in resource management in Canada, but also provided a clear conception of possible solutions.

17

A Water Resource Policy for Canada

T. Lloyd

Those who were brought up on the Bible are familiar with some of the difficulties of living in an arid land where rain seldom comes and the merciless sun beats down on a landscape unprotected by vegetation—where shade is at a premium and water needs to be treasured.

> *I will give unto him that is athirst of the fountain of the water of life, freely.*
> *Stolen waters are sweet.*

Such phrases lose much of their meaning when read in the damp and cloudy climate of western Europe or of eastern Canada where water has traditionally been all too plentiful. Yet to a resident of Utah, Arizona, or the southwestern Canadian Prairies during a drought, they retain all the force of their origin in the deserts of the Near East. And even to a New Yorker, now denied his glass of ice-cold water at lunch, drought can become very personal.

A world map of rainfall demonstrates how very favoured our part of the world has been. For the sake of simplicity we can use three categories of precipitation (which includes not only rain but the water equivalent of snow)—those with less than 20 inches a year, with more than 60 inches a year and those between 20 inches and 60 inches. They may be considered "relatively dry", "wet" and "humid". The map (Figure 1) demonstrates that the eastern part of the United States and Canada and also western Europe are

Reprinted in edited form from *Canadian Geographical Journal*, Vol. LXXII, no. 1 (1966), pp. 2-17.

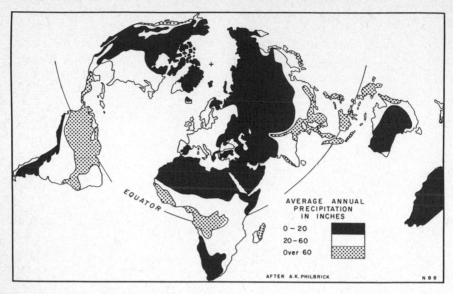

Figure 1. The Arid Crescent.

humid; in fact they form a North Atlantic zone of humidity. With the exception of some mountainous areas, the western part of North America is comparatively dry. These rather crude generalizations need to be refined by taking into account the season when the precipitation comes and also its "reliability", that is the extent to which it can be depended upon from year to year. The *effectiveness* of the precipitation depends to a considerable extent on the temperature, since this influences the amount of moisture which, having fallen, will be evaporated again. Thus four inches a year falling in the Arctic would be far more effective than the same amount in southern Alberta, or still more so than in New Mexico. When these and other factors are superimposed on one another, the composite picture emphasizes even more that western Europe and eastern North America are favoured, as is the Pacific fringe of Canada. The Canadian Prairies and the American southwest and much of the area within the mountain regions are, however, handicapped.

These facts serve as an essential starting point for discussing any major water policies in Canada and in the United States. They do not take into account the transport of water by natural means, for example rivers, which convey the precipitation of one region across country to be useful in another. As the Nile brings water from the tropical rains of central Africa to the arid Mediterranean so does the mountain-fed Colorado River of the United States flow through arid areas of Utah and Arizona; and the Saskatchewan

River, depending largely on the melting snows of the Rocky Mountains, brings water to the drier Prairies. Furthermore, water moves in even greater amounts beneath the ground by way of aquifers—water bearing rocks—and may be tapped at a considerable distance from where it originally falls.

Although precipitation varies from region to region, and may also from year to year, we are dealing in reality with a closed system; the often-cited "hydrological cycle", by which moisture moves between the atmosphere and the earth. Water derived from the oceans, and to a small extent from lakes, is held in the atmosphere until it is precipitated as rain or snow. Part is absorbed into the ground and part runs off as streams and rivers. Without entering the ground it may also be evaporated directly or—and this is important—by transpiration from plants. It has been estimated that there are 33 trillion acre-feet of fresh water somewhere on earth at any one time. Three-quarters of this is in ice and less than a quarter is in groundwater in the aquifers. At any moment a relatively small amount of it is held in the atmosphere, in soil moisture a little below the ground surface, in lakes, or is passing along in rivers. While the amount of moisture at any moment in the rivers and in the atmosphere is small in total, the turnover there is enormous. Of the total precipitation, possibly 30 per cent enters streams and soaks into the ground and so eventually drains off the land towards the sea. It is this stream-water and the underground water, parts of a single complex, which forms the earth's fresh water supply available for human use.

A typically 30-inch average precipitation falling on the United States in a year provides the rivers of that country with about 1.8 million cubic feet per second of flow or in more familiar terms about 5,000 gallons a day per head of the population. Canada with a far smaller population, but much of its river water in remote areas, has apparently a slightly greater total of flow than the United States, namely 2.5 million cubic feet a second. In addition is the water within the ground, a very significant source in some parts of North America but one that has often been extracted at the high price of lowering its level, the "water table", year after year. For example, the water table is now 75 feet below sea level in parts of southern California. Some large Canadian cities have depended on such underground water, Winnipeg being an example. In this case, when a more distant source of fresh water was obtained, the water table beneath that city rose again as the porous clays were recharged.

Such figures as I have cited are of course highly generalized. They do not take account of the contrasts between one part of the United States or Canada and another, or of variations which may be very significant over a period of years. Those who can recall the arid 1930's on the Canadian Prairies and compare the appearance of the landscape then with that of the 1950's will appreciate the significance of such fluctuations, as can of course those who have followed the falling levels of the Great Lakes during recent years in comparison with average levels based on records made during the past hundred years.

In summary, nature has provided a constant cycle of water falling as rain or snow and a system of lakes and rivers and underground routes by which part of it eventually drains off toward the sea. The simple picture is complicated by the presence of vegetation which both serves to delay moisture in the soil longer than it would otherwise remain there, and by contrast to return large amounts of moisture directly to the atmosphere by way of the leaves of the plants themselves. An important additional interruption in the hydrological cycle, of great importance to Canada, is due to the annual lowering of temperature in winter. Large quantities of water are temporarily held as snow or ice on the ground or in water courses, to be released rather abruptly each spring. The natural water cycle is also modified by man. The consequences of this are the main concern of this article. Water is so intimately involved in almost every aspect of life on earth that only a very few aspects can be discussed here.

How Water Is Used

Among users of water we should distinguish two main groups: those who, so to speak, "borrow" it for temporary use and return it to be eventually used by others, and those who take it and use it so that it is no longer available for further use.

In the first category is the housewife who fills the washing-machine with water, in the case of Montreal taken from the St. Lawrence River above the city, and returns it, along with dirt and detergent, to the river below the city. On a larger scale is the utilization of water for raising steam, from which all but about one per cent is returned to be used again. In contrast, the irrigation farmer withdraws water from a stream and spreads it on his cropland (that which is not lost by evaporation en route), so that it is discharged into the atmosphere by transpiration from the crop. This latter is an example of "consumptive use" and is obviously more critical than what I have referred to as "water borrowing".

It is claimed that in the United States about one-quarter of the available 1,300 billion gallons a day is actually "consumed".

In looking more closely into ways in which water is employed, we need to consider only briefly its use in remote areas with a small or scattered population, where human activity can result in only negligible interference with the natural order of things. There come to mind, hunting and recreation in remote areas and the scattered domestic user whose isolated pollution of the local waters could harm few but his own family. So too the small farmer drawing his requirements from a well and returning them when used to mother earth.

In a quite different category are those uses of water which utilize appreciable amounts of water to the detriment of other users. For these, the great majority of cases in North America, regulation of some sort is essential. It is becoming apparent, particularly in the United States, that the complex of local laws and customs evolved over the years cannot hope to ensure the just allocation of water, particularly when it is scarce. To quote Oliver Wendell Holmes: "A river is more than an amenity, it is a treasure. It offers a necessity of life, which must be rationed among those who have power over it." Before considering the implications of this, let us review the main large-scale uses of water:

1. Domestic use in urban areas.
2. Industrial use.
3. Navigation.
4. Power production.
5. Agriculture.
6. Recreation.

Also of importance is water required by fish and wildlife, as is those aspects of water supply involved in flood control. These I shall not discuss in detail.

Domestic Use

A little-noticed miracle of every day life occurs each time we turn a knob on a pipe in our homes, night or day, summer or winter, wet or dry, and a steady flow of clear, pure water streams out. The assumption throughout eastern North America and western Europe that this trick will invariably work, cannot be counted on in much of the rest of the world. We rarely appreciate the cost that the community as a whole pays for this simple yet priceless service. My own first encounter with the elementary economics of water supply came while I lived in Greenland, during World War II. The building—the Canadian Consulate—had the only dependable running water supply in Godthaab, the capital city. Our system demonstrated by simple steps a direct relationship between the turning of a tap or the flushing of a toilet and the digging out of a frozen snowbank of kegs of kerosene. The water originated in a shallow well from which it was extracted by an electric pump, which in turn was operated by batteries, the charging of which was done by an internal combustion engine fueled by kerosene. So much water, so much kerosene. No desert dweller guarded his water supply more carefully than did I, the man who periodically had to seek kerosene in the snowbank.

It is estimated that in the United States about 150 gallons of water need to be provided each day per person. The variety of uses in a typical city range from drinking and cooking, for which water of a high standard of purity is required, through that for bathing, washing clothes, carrying sewage and other wastes, washing cars, watering lawns, for standby use in fire protection, for air-conditioning, a rapidly increasing need, and for use in swimming pools and for even more luxurious purposes. The rapid concentration of population in larger urban areas and the rising standard of living is placing constantly growing demands on water for domestic use. Yet in most cases the cost to the user does not depend directly on the amount used.

Industrial Use

The industrial use of water ranges from that needed to raise steam, to its incorporation in finished products such as bottled drinks. It is also needed in many industrial processes for cooling, for preparation of solutions, removal of impurities and so on, well known examples are the paper industry, oil refining, and meat packing. And finally water is used in enormous quantities for the removal of waste products. This is of course at the root of much of the industrial pollution of lakes and streams. Industrial demands are constantly rising, but fortunately much of the water, estimated at more than 90 per cent, is not really consumed but under favourable circumstances may be re-utilized. Citation of a few figures for particularly industries may indicate the magnitude of the demand for water. The steel industry is outstanding—a typical large mill in the United States employs 250 million gallons a day, enough for a city of about 2 million population. Some paper manufacturing processes employ 100,000 gallons for each ton of paper.

It is in relation to the vast and spreading urban areas that many controversial water supply problems have arisen. Scarcely a large United States city has not at one time or another been concerned that the rising demand for water will outstrip supplies. The recent acute shortage in New York and other parts of the northeastern United States was not unexpected. The city draws on several local and more distant underground and surface supplies, including the Delaware River (use of which was challenged by the State of New Jersey). The low precipitation of recent years has strengthened popular demands that other and more dependable sources must be sought, particularly far upstream in the Hudson River—and there has even been reference to the Great Lakes as a possible source. Detached observers of the New York scene have suggested that the lack of water-meters puts a premium on waste, and that this accounts for an appreciable part of the shortage. This points up the view that so-called shortages may suggest a need for more cautious and conservative use of the available supply, and for avoidance of pollution of existing waters.

In some cities such as Los Angeles, the situation has long been chronic, the inevitable consequence of rapid, unplanned urban growth in a region which should never have been expected to provide sufficient water. It is the only city of more than a million population outside of the humid region of the United States, and has for more than fifty years used distant water supplies. A population approaching 7 million in southern California is now almost entirely dependent on water piped from hundreds of miles away.

Navigation

The use of water for navigation is in many cases not detrimental to other uses, although it may lead indirectly to pollution. Thus the St. Lawrence River above Montreal carries lake and ocean vessels, but also is employed as a domestic water supply and provides for hydro-electric power development. There are possible sources of conflict between different users, and the St. Lawrence Seaway and the Port of Montreal illustrate them. Ships need safe channels of an assured depth, for even a slight lowering of the water level may reduce the cargo capacity of a vessel, and so the revenue earned on each voyage. It has been suggested in recent years that maintenance of a 35-foot channel up the St. Lawrence to the Port of Montreal has been possible only at the expense of interests higher up the waterway—excessive amounts of water having been released from Lake Ontario, thus lowering its level. However, the contrary claim has also been made that the level at Montreal has been allowed to fall below that required, because water has been retained upstream, to the advantage of hydro and other users. In fact it seems that neither claim is correct. It is becoming clear that the many complex and inter-related questions of water depths, dependable flow, safe navigation, currents, and ice movements in the river and at Montreal call for far more research and co-ordinated consideration than has so far been given. Long ago it was said that "The Clyde made Glasgow and then Glasgow remade the Clyde". Montreal is a parallel case. The city's greatness is due in a large part to the St. Lawrence River; this in turn will inevitably be more and more modified to meet the many demands placed upon it. Navigational works such as the Welland Canal and the Soo Locks also make possible regulation of other parts of the Great Lakes, not only for navigation but for many other water uses. Plans have been proposed for comparable controls at the outlets of the other lakes. Any steps to regulate a large natural waterway raise the possibility of providing multi-purpose use, which may include not only navigation but also simultaneously power production, flood control, recreation and so on. Examples of this come to mind from many parts of the world including, of course, the classic case of the Mississippi River, the more recent example of the Volga River in the Soviet Union, and the large-scale undertakings planned for the Mekong River in southeast Asia.

Hydro-Electric Power

Since the turn of the century, Canada has been active in using its rivers for production of power, so much so that most nearby sites are now fully employed. The need to draw on more distant sites calls for far longer transmission lines and higher voltages, and in some cases use of direct current transmission. Despite such new developments it remains necessary on economic grounds as well as for technical reasons to utilize also thermal power stations, also a user of large volumes of water. The time is not far distant when atomic power plants too will be a competing source for large blocks of power; they too will demand water. Some of the very large hydro-electric sites now planned will need to seek distant customers for some of the power. This at once involves possible export to the United States. Cases that come to mind are Churchill Falls in Labrador, falls on the Nelson River in northern Manitoba and sites within the Cordillera of British Columbia. The hazards which may be associated with firm long-term contracts to export power have been widely discussed.

Problems are encountered in assessing a fair share of the costs of water to the various users, for example, hydro power and navigation. Decisions must be made, and not always on clear principle, as to how construction and operating costs are to be allocated.

The use of water for irrigation further complicates the allocation of fair costs. Such situations are made no easier when the interests of several provinces or states, and two countries, also have to be taken into account.

Water for Agriculture

Of all the large-scale uses of water, irrigation has become the most demanding and is perhaps the most controversial. Irrigation of crops in arid or semi-arid areas has of course been practised for thousands of years. What is newer is the involvement of irrigation in production of commercial crops of high value for large industrial users. Combination of the long-influential farming community with large-scale industry makes water users in some parts of the United States and Canada a power to be reckoned with. The demand for irrigation water comes not only from the traditionally sub-humid or arid regions. Increasingly, it is being used to supplement rainfall at critical periods in order to ensure higher yields or better quality. Summer visitors to Vancouver learn with some astonishment that the copious rain provided by nature is no longer adequate; it must be supplemented by the use of giant sprinklers!

Critics of the constantly rising demand for irrigation water charge, among other things that (1) much of the water is wasted, (2) the price paid for the water is far below its real worth and (3) production of some crops in dry areas is, strictly speaking, not profitable, but it is only possible because of direct or indirect subsidy; part of the cost of the water being met by excessive land taxes and too high power rates. It is also emphasized that irrigation water is very largely lost to other users because of evaporation. It has been estimated that in the United States 85 per cent of all water actually *consumed* (rather than "borrowed") goes for irrigation. It is also suggested that in strictly economic terms the use of water for agricultural production is relatively wasteful if it competes with industrial users.

The inter-relationships of power and irrigation are well illustrated from the case of the South Saskatchewan River Project now approaching completion. The plans initiated in 1958 involved construction of two dams to form a lake 140 miles long and store 7.5 million acre-feet of water. Multiple uses for the impounded water, including power production, flood control, domestic and industrial water supply, recreation and irrigation of as much as 500,000 acres of land, then producing grain by dry farming techniques, are planned. The financial success of the irrigation project depends upon a changeover from such grain farming to use of the land to grow different crops by irrigation, crops which would of course be far more valuable. The current controversy, which has arisen because some grain farmers do not wish to be "reconstructed", illustrates the human consequences of such projects, but also endangers the economic basis of the whole scheme. Farther west on the Prairies, particularly in Alberta, there are of course many examples of areas where irrigation has made possible economical use of drier lands. Sugar factories, canneries, freezing plants, seed processing operations have resulted from the production of irrigated crops. The Lethbridge region is a particularly successful example of this.

Recreational Uses

The general rise in living standards in North America accompanied by shorter working hours and vacations with pay, and use of the automobile, have made outdoor recreation a large and prosperous "industry". City dwellers seek in the outdoors some compensation for the restrictions of their daily lives, and streams, lakes and rivers are among the leading attractions. The growing popularity of water sports is leading to intensive use of even remote natural waterways, as well as reservoirs and canals. The steady rise in population in Canada and the United States suggests that this will continue. Thirty years ago the Tennessee Valley Authority took the initiative to include recreation as an important factor in the multi-purpose use of its dams. This proved prophetic. A visit to any reasonably accessible large power project today demonstrates the very great value of this secondary utilization. The lake forming behind the Saskatchewan Dam should transform the rather arid and colourless landscape, and the vast hydro-electric developments taking place in interior British Columbia will have comparable results. This does of course raise again the question of apportioning costs for benefits derived. There still seems to be a tendency to charge a disproportionate share to the users of electricity despite the appreciable services provided for others.

This brief excursion into the changing pattern of water usage and availability raises the obvious question — "Will there be enough water?" To which the only possible reply must be another question. "What are you willing to pay for it?" There seems no doubt that in one way or another sufficient water can be provided for foreseeable needs. The real difficulty is that in most of the United States and in much of Canada it has always been assumed that good water is plentiful and cheap — so cheap in fact that it costs nothing to waste it. Thus in strictly economic terms it is cheap for a householder to let a bathtub tap drip all day and night because this costs him nothing, since the water tax bears no relationship to the amount he uses, while inviting a plumber to replace the washer may be a long and expensive venture.

I suggested that we have become accustomed to good water being *plentiful*. One consequence is that we have rarely taken even elementary precautions to ensure that the water will remain good. Living in broad expanses of a water-strewn land we have customarily dumped the wastes of our homes and industries into convenient lakes and rivers without appreciating until recently the consequences of large-scale pollution. It is now being realized that the costs of correcting such misdemeanours have to be met.

There is no need to refer in detail to the widespread fouling of the waters of settled North America. President Johnson is often quoted as saying that not a single large river in the United States is now free of major pollution. The recently enacted Water Quality Act in that country begins a long-range policy of preventing pollution of rivers and lakes, as well as of correcting it where it exists. Put in the forthright language of our American friends it means that "No one has the right to use America's waterways, which belong to all the people, as a sewer". In Canada we have seen the establishment of the Ontario Water Resources Commission as an initial step in the same direction. More recently the Quebec Water Board demanded "foresight" and "vision", and its director suggested it would take a long time to correct existing pollution. More than a hundred municipalities are constructing sewage treatment plants. There is rising interest too on the Prairies. But this country is wide and the law is often remote. The conference planned for October, 1966, on "Pollution and our Environment", under the auspices of the Canadian Council of Resource Ministers should demonstrate whether we are able to achieve obviously necessary ends by a less direct method than that suggested by passage of the federal act in the United States. If not, we too shall need to call on the authority of the country as a whole to protect the heritage of all of us. River basins do not conform to provincial boundaries and water control problems cross frontiers. In the Missouri-Souris-Red River area of the United States, programmes of pollution control have already been started. Should the Red River eventually pass Emerson, Manitoba, in a sparking new blue guise, it will provide a challenge to Winnipeg to allow it to continue unpolluted toward the sea.

On a far larger scale has come the recent report by The International Joint Commission on pollution of two of the Great Lakes

— Erie and Ontario. Recommendations to both the United States and Canadian governments have indicated ways in which action should now proceed. The problem appears to be that, particularly in the case of Lake Erie, domestic and industrial wastes have been dumped into the water for so long that parts of it are becoming a nutrient solution for the growth of algae. This in turn deprives the water of its dissolved oxygen, making other life impossible. To improve the situation, continuing pollution must cease, so that nature and time can clean up the lake. As a first step, the Government of Canada has arranged to sample the waters of Lake Ontario, Lake Erie and the St. Lawrence, and comparable action is being taken by the United States. It should not be beyond the ingenuity of the authorities to make it expensive for those who pollute the lakes and cheaper to purify their wastes. This has for some years been true of the at-one-time notorious waters of the Ruhr industrial area in Germany, where a graduated tax on effluents is proving effective. In Canada we have been inclined to the use of kindly persuasion in such matters, although the Criminal Code has long provided for action under federal law against anyone committing a "common nuisance" — which may be defined as an act which "endangers lives, safety, health, property or comfort of the public". If greater legal precision is required, advantage might be taken of The Act Respecting Fisheries, Paragraph 33, Section 2, or The Act Respecting the Protection of Navigable Waters, Paragraph 18, both of which were designed to discourage pollution.

To return to the cost of providing sufficient water, which we are accustomed to securing for a few cents per thousand gallons, including treatment needed to ensure purity. Irrigation water in the United States southwest, a region where water is very scarce, costs about one tenth as much. There it is used in enormous quantities, and so casually, that in some regions as much as half is wasted before reaching the cropland. One acre of cotton there may employ four feet of irrigation water, as much as would be used by sixty average United States city families in a year. Much of the demand for irrigation water in the United States southwest is, it seems, due to the very low cost; and this in turn results in wasteful utilization. If there is indeed a shortage of water for irrigation, or any other requirements, it can now be produced, but at several times the present cost, by desalination of brackinsh water or even sea water. The city of Key West, Florida, on a small island, now obtains fresh water through a 135-mile pipeline from the mainland. Within a year it expects to produce more than 2,500,000 gallons a day from the ocean. The use of nuclear power plants to provide the energy for desalination could, at the same time, generate surplus electricity, so that the cost of such water might be brought down to as low as 25 cents per thousand gallons. Use of such water would of course increase appreciably the cost of irrigation. This explains the present demand to use existing water, even though from a great distance.

In summary it seems clear that water can be made available in areas of shortage but at a price. The necessary steps include:—

1. Far greater efficiency in the use of the present supply.
2. Discouragement of waste by realistic pricing.
3. Avoidance of pollution.
4. More effective use of underground water supplies, about which too little is yet known.
5. Distillation of brackish and saline waters.

The search for additional water by cities such as Los Angeles, which began sixty years ago with the Owens Valley scheme, later extended to the Colorado and is now involving sources in northern California, has led to suggestions that the next available water is in the Columbia River. One northwest state governor commented that taking such water would be "pure unvarnished piracy". This is not an unexpected rejoinder when it is recalled that water is at the very basis of the Pacific Northwest economy, which depends on agriculture, forestry, hydro-electric power, the pulp and paper industry, and many auxiliary industries utilizing economical electrical power. But the search for water has not stopped there. In the words of the Governor of California, "Whether we bring it from the Snake, the Columbia or the Volga, we will have to have it". The area of the United States Southwest, from western Texas to the Pacific coast, and including the Great Basin and Colorado Basin, is the focus of rising demands for the introduction of new water into the region, demands which inevitably lead to pressure on Canada, particularly on western Canada. Columbia River water is of course partly Canadian, but the new search extends even farther into British Columbia, the Yukon and Alberta. An example of the scale of such demands is a scheme propounded by an engineering concern in Los Angeles. It proposes nothing less than rearrangement of the river and lake pattern of much of North America. Its immediate objective appears to be as the phrase goes, "to maximize" the amount of engineering construction during the next thirty years, a period when the industry may be less active than it has during the past quarter century. In essence, water from the Canadian Cordillera would be turned south to meet the supposed needs of the United States southwest. Anything which survives after passing Southern California would go on the arid areas of Mexico. An incidental but unavoidable result of the scheme would be to drown out most of the usable level land in interior British Columbia. The water needs of Canada have not been overlooked. The Prairies would be allocated at least as much of the water as Mexico. Other more eye-catching, but less essential aspects of the scheme include canalizing water from the Canadian Rockies via the Great Lakes to Labrador, apparently to facilitate the bulk transport of goods! Another water route would run by way of North Dakota to the Mississippi. A seaway for shipping is also proposed to James Bay, where as is well known, the off-shore waters are so shallow that even a canoe cannot be assured of getting within sight of land at low tide. Clearly we have here an exercise in sophomore civil engineering which has received far greater attention than it ever deserved. It underlines the danger, all too familiar to geographers, of allowing the drawing office to replace acquaintance with the land and the people as they really are. It is sometimes the path of wisdom to prevent the large-scale rearranging of nature, especially when it is based on inadequate knowledge, and hasty and ill-conceived pans.

Entirely apart from this particular proposal, it is apparent that water has now become a subject of major concern within Canada, and that it will influence relations between this country and the United States in the years ahead. Considerable pressure is being exerted from non-official bodies in the United States to accept the concept that all fresh water in North America should be made available wherever it is needed. This "North American" approach has received some support, as for example from the influential Western Canadian-American Assembly, which reported in 1964:

> Canada and the United States are moving in the direction of a new and significant policy for the development of energy resources, particularly water power, on a continental scale . . . The International Joint Commission should undertake long-range continental plans for water resources.

There are of course long-standing arrangements for consultation between Canada and the United States covering boundary waters, through the agency of the International Joint Commission, the continuing body representing and reporting to both countries. Nevertheless it may well be that this machinery alone is no longer adequate. It does not appear, for example, to have worked smoothly in relation to utilization of the Columbia River water. The suggestion has been made that, in a strictly technical sense, Canada has not always been sufficiently skillful to maintain its authority in the partnership. Certainly, water is now infinitely more important to both countries than it was when the Commission was founded, nearly sixty years ago. Examples of major questions concerning boundary waters and related topics which now face this country include those concerned with the Great Lakes, the International Section of the St. Lawrence River, the disposal of water rights on the Columbia River, already referred to, the suggested very large Rampart Dam on the Yukon River in Alaska, the provisions of sufficient water for all of the Prairies as their industrialization gains momentum, as well as the much-touted proposal that purely Canadian water, at present draining toward the north, should be turned southward for the use of United States interests.

While there are in all such cases "technical" questions to be taken into account, for the solution of which expert aid — meteorological, hydrological, engineering and so forth — is needed, there is room for concern that too often the conclusions of the scientists and engineers are liable to be over-ridden by the demands of the politician — who may be sensitive to the pressure of local, short-term interests, rather than to those of the country as a whole.

If only for this reason, geographers and others interested in the wise use of our water resources need to inform themselves of constitutional usages — including the division of powers between the Government of Canada and the provincial authorities. Such matters may require far greater acumen than many of us can hope to command, finding it difficult as we do to understand how the century-old provincial right to control over local works and under-takings — matters of a merely local or private nature in the province, property and civil rights in the province, and similar modest requirements — can have been allowed to over-ride the broad, general federal power to make laws for the peace, order and good government of the country, its trade and commerce, for navigation and shipping, for inland fisheries, and so on. The central government in Canada enjoys constitutionally, I have always understood, some residual advantages not possessed by the federal government in the United States. If this is indeed so, it would seem to be unnecessary to approach discussions on water resources in the rather hesitant way that has sometimes been the case.

In any event the posture of Canada could only be strengthened by prior announcement of clearly defined national policies. There is now a widespread demand for the formulation of such a National Water Policy. It is something which has been commended by leaders of all political parties, and would doubtless secure corresponding support throughout the country. The consensus of informed opinion seems to be that such a policy statement should at the least take into account the following points:

1. Water is of increasing importance to the country's well-being, and is likely to be a critical factor in its future development.

2. The wide geographical extent of many water problems and their inter-relationships require that it be a truly unified and national policy.

3. Such a national policy needs to be arrived at by the Government of Canada — following appropriate consultation with provincial and regional authorities and with public and private bodies actively concerned.

4. The Government of Canada needs to have available more effective expertise concerning all aspects of water. It has been stated that ten separate federal departments and eight additional federal agencies have a continuing, direct concern with water. The reorganization of departmental administration now going on may simplify this somewhat, but there is a continuing risk that the changes will not go as far as strict efficiency would require.

5. Provision for research on water resources within the Government of Canada, in the provinces, and in the universities needs to be greatly extended. This would, incidentally, lead rapidly to the training of far more specialists in water resources than are now available. One example of a broad research topic, which should lead to useful results is: "How do the social and physical consequences of a major water project compare with those intended when the work was planned?"

6. There is urgent need for long-term planning for future water requirements in this country as a whole, without regard to provincial or other local boundaries. We need to be constantly alert to the danger that short-term benefits, or seeming benefits, for one or other local region, may be allowed to endanger the welfare of the country as a whole.

7. After the most thorough and extended investigation of Canadian requirements for the foreseeable future, consideration may be given to possible diversion of waters now entirely within Canada into international river basins or the Great Lakes. Care would have to be taken that any such diversion

did not discourage development of the "Near-North", the region lying at present beyond the main settled area of the country.

In providing this brief list of points to be kept in mind in formulating a national water policy, I cannot claim any originality. All of them have previously received authoritative support. As a scientist I would naturally place greatest emphasis on the urgent need to increase basic and applied research, both in government agencies and outside, and in the training of expert personnel. In the long run the success of this country in its relationships with our large, friendly but often demanding and at present very thirsty neighbour, will depend on the calibre of those who represent us, and on the scientists and technologists who must provide them with factual knowledge and counsel.

Fortunately Canada's participation in the International Hydrological Decade is providing a very necessary fillip to the study of all aspects of water, including its utilization. Steps in the same direction are the recently announced arrangements between the Government and certain provinces for water resource inventories, notably with the three Prairie Provinces concerning the Saskatchewan-Nelson river basin and with Ontario in relation to its northern rivers. This is useful and could well form part of a nation-wide water programme.

Consideration of water resource policy is in many ways a geographical matter, but it is broader than even the all-embracing arms of this mother of the sciences can enclose. It is because of a conviction that in such matters geography is not enough, that I have ventured outside the usual academic pale to comment also on public policy. The subject is so important to the welfare of our people that it should receive the widest possible consideration.

18

Investment Choices in Public Resource Development

I. Burton

I

Evaluating Projects in the Public Sector

The role of government in resource development

It has long been recognized that governments have a major role to play in the management of a nation's resources, especially its renewable resources. This is no less true in Canada where the country's economic progress is closely associated with its store of natural wealth.[1]

All is not well, however, with the part government plays in the use and development of our renewable resources. Responsibilities are poorly defined, and where they are clearly recognized, insufficient funds are made available. No level of government is specifically charged with the overall responsibility for investigation, initiation, and coordination of projects. Nowhere in Canada is there an agency or group of technically qualified and experienced personnel large enough to undertake such tasks. The result is a haphazard, piecemeal process of resource management. Action is taken largely in

---

Reprinted in edited form from *The Prospect of Change*, ed. A. Rotstein (McGraw-Hill, Toronto, 1965), pp. 149-73.

---

[1] Ian Burton and Robert W. Kates, "Canadian Resources and American Requirements", *Canadian Journal of Economics and Political Science*, Vol. 30, no. 2 (May, 1964), pp. 265-269.

response to emergencies or to specific and articulate local demands. The prevailing strategies are to leave it to others (usually some other level of government) or to do nothing. When action is taken, it tends to be uncoordinated and in a politically opportunistic spirit. Efforts to break out of this mould into a program of sound coordinated development are repeatedly frustrated.

The need for direct, systematic and coherent government participation in resource development at the present time is nevertheless clear. Consider, for example, the increasing competition for limited water supplies in some regions, the increase in flood damage potential, and the lack of adequate facilities for outdoor recreation, especially among the lower-income groups in urban areas. Such problems fall more readily to the public sector since the returns upon investment are spread over a long period of time and cannot always be readily aggregated.

Thus we find increasing demands for action which governments at all levels are ill-prepared and ill-equipped to meet, demands both from disinterested professionals and from sectional and regional groups which see some prospect of benefit. Evidence of this can be seen in the submissions to the Royal Commission on the South Saskatchewan River Project.[2] The chairman of the South Alberta Water Conservation Council concluded his brief on the benefits of the proposed project with the opinion that "no matter what the cost, it will eventually pay off."[3] Similarly the President of the Saskatchewan Rivers Development Association assured the commission that, "no Canadian government need feel reluctant to spend tax dollars to improve the lot or secure the welfare of Canadians *anywhere*"[4] [italics added]. The Appendix to the Commission Report includes a number of such statements. Similarly, of the ten resolutions passed at the Annual Meeting of the Western Canada Reclamation Association in June, 1963, nine called for action by federal government departments or agencies.[5] The Association, among other things, requested federal government action in control of pollution of international and interprovincial waters, the establishment of an agency to develop a national water policy, a survey of the resources of the Saskatchewan-Nelson Basin, a general study of river basins and water needs in Western Canada prior

2 Royal Commission on the South Saskatchewan River Project 1952, *Report* (Ottawa, Queen's Printer, 1952).
3 *Ibid.*, p. 278.
4 *Ibid.*, p. 289.
5 Western Canada Reclamation Association, "Resolutions Passed at Kelowna Meeting", *Western Reclamation;* Vol. 3, no. 3 (October, 1963), pp. 4-5.

to the signing of the Columbia River Treaty with the United States and a special study of water use and future needs in the Okanagan Valley.

The prevailing pattern is for these demands to be passed between levels of government without much significant action resulting. From time to time some of the popular demands are met in piecemeal fashion in a number of projected and actual schemes. These include the Columbia and Peace power developments in British Columbia,[6] the Winnipeg flood control scheme,[7] the Toronto recreation plan,[8] and the measures coming under the Prairie Farm Rehabilitation Act, the Maritime Marshlands Reclamation Board, and the Agricultural Rehabilitation and Development Agency. A substantive discussion of some of these measures, in the context of regional development problems is undertaken in Professor Whalen's article. This paper is concerned with the question of selection among the wide range of possible choices for public investment programs in resource development.

The need for choice mechanisms

The contentions, quoted above, that programs should be implemented "no matter what the cost" or "anywhere" cannot be accepted. There are many competing demands for public funds for resource development. Farmers want water for irrigation, city dwellers need recreational opportunities, and flood plain residents, whether rural or urban, want protection from floods. In addition to these sectional demands, there are also regional demands from different parts of the country. Ontario's interest in resource development is quite different from that of the Maritime Provinces or the Prairie Provinces.

A realistic program must therefore involve some selection procedure for picking out better projects and rejecting poorer ones. Phrased in a slightly different way, we may ask of an individual project how its gains or benefits compare with its costs. This figure may then be used to make comparisons between projects.

This paper is addressed to a critical examination, both in theory and practice, of one such selection procedure called benefit-cost

---

6 See John V. Krutilla, *Sequence and Timing in River Basin Development* (Washington, Resources for the Future, Inc., 1960). Also I. M. Robinson, "Peace River Region", *Resources for Tomorrow Background Papers*, Vol. 1, (Ottawa, Queen's Printer, 1961), pp. 505-525.
7 Canada, Department of Resources and Development, *Report on Investigations into Measures for the Reduction of the Flood Hazard in the Greater Winnipeg Area*, Report and Appendices A to H (Ottawa, 1953).
8 Metropolitan Toronto and Region Conservation Authority, *Plan for Flood Control and Water Conservation* (Woodbridge, 1959).

analysis. This method is relatively new in Canada. It may be used to provide more rational and objective criteria for making choices in public resource development. The adoption of this technique of economic analysis as a guide to investment decisions in the public sector offers some attractive possibilities. Ways have been devised to measure in monetary terms the benefits of public investment. Benefits are analogous to the revenues of a private investment project. Important differences, however, are that benefits may be counted "to whomsoever they accrue" and the initial investment may not be recovered for a period of time considerably longer than most private investors are prepared to wait. Indeed, the benefits may not be recovered at all in the sense that the government will never be reimbursed. Usually the benefits are reaped by a large number of people over a long period of time.

The analysis of the benefits and costs of any particular project involves three main elements. The first is the estimation of costs. This is simply the common practice of assessing in advance of an undertaking what each component will cost and summing the individual items to give total cost. Costs of public works usually include such items as the purchase of land and rights of way, materials for construction, the design and execution of the project (labour), interest on money borrowed, and operation and maintenance. At present, many public works are undertaken on the basis of cost estimation alone, without any effort to measure corresponding benefits. A government simply obtains cost estimates and then decides whether or not it can afford to go ahead with the work. Under such circumstances, there is no economic guide to the decision-making process. Projects are selected, designed and approved without reference to any economic criteria.

The second element, therefore, is central to the idea of benefit-cost analysis; it is the notion of measuring benefits. Most discussion of this technique turns around the method of calculating benefits, which are grouped into three main kinds: direct, indirect, and intangible.

Direct benefits are those returns most intimately associated with a project. Some examples are the value of crops produced by an irrigation project, the value of power produced by a hydro development, the value of flood damages prevented, and the value of a lake as a recreational amenity. It is useful also to distinguish between gross benefits and net benefits. In an irrigation project, for example, the total value of crops produced is the gross benefit, but the net benefit is the increase in income from the land after all associated costs such as farm labour, pumping, fertilizer and so on have been taken into consideration. Clearly, in order to realize the maximum net benefit, the costs include not only public expenditure for the dam and irrigation canals, but also private farmers' expenses necessary to take advantage of the irrigation water made available to them. In spite of these complications, direct benefits are relatively easily measured.

More difficult to measure are the many *indirect* benefits. These are additional flows of income created indirectly by the projects; for example, the production of cigarettes from a crop of tobacco grown on an irrigation project, or the manufacture of aluminum with the power from a hydro project. Similarly, the sale of increased amounts of recreational equipment may result in increased production as a result of a reservoir-recreation project. Because indirect benefits extend into many sections of the economy and cannot readily be traced or aggregated, a common device used in benefit-cost analysis is to assume that indirect benefits will be a fixed proportion of direct benefits. Sometimes a figure of 50% is used.

A word of caution is appropriate concerning indirect benefits. They may often be merely transfer payments from one group or place to another, and not involve any real benefit to the economy. If, as a result of irrigation, Canada's tobacco industry was moved from Ontario to the Prairies, this would not necessarily involve any gain for Canada. Clearly, however, it would involve a considerable gain for the Prairie Provinces and a loss for Ontario. In benefit-cost analysis, the viewpoint is important. It should always be made clear whether benefits to the nation or a part of the nation are in question.

The remaining benefits, neither direct nor indirect, may be described as *intangible*. This simply means that they are not susceptible to measurement. The tendency has been for the area of intangible benefits to be continuously narrowed down as new measuring techniques are devised. In a recreation project, for example, it is now quite common to attempt the measurement of recreation benefits in terms of dollars per visitor-day. Values are not yet placed on such "intangibles" as scenic views or human life.

The third element in the analysis consists of a comparison between benefits and costs in the terms of a ratio. A standard rule (given the force of law in the United States) is that projects are considered economically "feasible" if a ratio of greater than unity is obtained — that is, if benefits, exceed costs. Where costs are greater, projects are rejected as not economically "feasible."

It is clear that the growing importance of the public sector of the economy, creates a greater need for such a method as an aid in making investment decisions. In Canada there is an additional reason for the adoption of benefit-cost analysis. The joint operation of two and sometimes three levels of financing and authority in natural resource development — federal, provincial, and municipal — makes the problem of formulating rational decisions in allocating funds more complex still. There is also need for a more rational process of allocating national funds among the competing demands of local, regional and sectional interests.

Legal interpretation of the British North America Act has emphasized provincial control of most resources, although the areas of responsibility of the two senior levels of government are by no means clearly defined.[9] The Provinces tend to guard their rights jealously, but in many cases have insufficient funds and staff to carry out resource development projects on the necessary scale.

Thus most requests for assistance in resource development are directed to the federal government. The government itself does not usually initiate schemes, and its participation is limited to $37\frac{1}{2}\%$ of the cost under the Canada Water Conservation Assistance Act of 1954,[10] with matching provincial funds, and the 25% balance left to local interests. Hence, development tends to occur only where an active sectional group sees an opportunity for profit (as in the South Saskatchewan Dam) or where an emergency exists (such as the Winnipeg floods), or some combination of the two (the Toronto scheme). The function of the province is mainly to pass on the request in appropriate form with its approval.

When the federal government is thus forced to choose among alternative projects in a variety of places, there is a clear need for the objective criteria which benefit-cost analysis purports to offer. Such a guide to decision-making within the existing political framework may provide for more nearly optimal solutions from the standpoint of economic allocation.[11] With this kind of study it becomes theoretically possible to make comparisons among different levels or sizes of one project; to evaluate single projects; to compare several different projects and to set priorities among them. This may be done in terms of the benefit-cost ratio, or in terms of net benefits.

9 Bora Laskin, "Jurisdictional Framework for Water Management", *Resources for Tomorrow Background Papers, op cit.*, pp. 211-225.
10 1-2 Elizabeth II, *An Act to Authorize the Grant of Assistance to a Province for the Conservation of Water Resources*, Chapter 21.
11 O. Eckstein, *Water Resource Development* (Cambridge, Harvard University Press, 1958); John V. Krutilla and O. Eckstein, *Multiple Purpose River Development* (Baltimore, Johns Hopkins Press, for Resources for the Future, Inc., 1958); R. N. McKean, *Efficiency in Government Through Systems Analysis* (New York, John Wiley and Sons, 1958).

Alternatively, such choices can be exercised solely through the political process without benefit-cost analysis, subject to cost estimation, the restraints imposed by budgeting procedures, and financial stringency. There is, however, no reason to believe that the most economically desirable projects will be selected in this manner. The notion that "the wheel that squeaks most should get the grease", is not a sound guide to decision-making, even when financing is a local responsibility.[12] A clear defect of such a method from the political standpoint is that it is difficult to refute the charge of political patronage even when it is not valid.

For these various reasons, the Government of Canada has been including benefit-cost analysis in its requirements for financial participation in some projects. Use of the technique has grown in the past ten years, but in an unsystematic fashion in which the analysis has been performed by a variety of groups and individuals, in as many different ways, under conditions of inadequate financial support.[13]

II

Some Practical and Theoretical Problems
in Benefit-Cost Analysis

It was largely to correct a generally unsatisfactory situation and to attempt to produce a coordinated resource policy that eight hundred resource and planning experts congregated in Montreal in October, 1961, for the Resources for Tomorrow Conference, under Dominion and provincial sponsorship. Eighty background papers were pub-

12 See Ian Burton, "Some Aspects of Flood Damage Reduction in England and Wales", G. F. White (ed.), *Papers on Flood Problems* (Chicago, Department of Geography, University of Chicago, 1961), Department of Geography Research Paper No. 70, pp. 203-221.
13 Examples in Canada include the following: Ausable River Conservation Authority, *Flood Control and Water Conservation Brief: Parkhill Creek Watershed, 1959* (Exeter, 1959). John Davis, "The Economics of Nuclear Power in Canada", Brief presented to the Special Committee on Research, House of Commons (Ottawa, June 1, 1961). Metropolitan Toronto and Region Conservation Authority, *Plan for Flood Control and Water Conservation, op. cit.* Moira River Conservation Authority, *Flood Control and Conservation Measures Brief for the Moira Watershed, 1959* (Connifton, April, 1959). Royal Commission on the South Saskatchewan River Project, *Report on the South Saskatchewan River Project* (Ottawa, Queen's Printer, 1952). Royal Commission (Manitoba) on Flood Cost-Benefit, *Report of the Royal Commission on Flood Cost-Benefit* (Winnipeg, 1958). Upper Thames River Conservation Authority, *Flood Control Brief, 1958* (London, Ontario, 1958). Upper Thames River Conservation Authority, *Supplement "A" to the Brief on Flood Control Measures for the Upper Thames Watershed: Benefit-Cost Analysis,* J. H. Dales (London, Ontario, 1957). Upper Thames River Conservation Authority, *Supplement "B" to the Brief on Flood Control Measures for the Upper Thames Watershed: Benefit-Cost Analysis* (London, Ontario, 1959).

lished and the experts deliberated for six days.[14] This mighty labour brought forth a mouse in the form of the Council of Resource Ministers, which was set up in order to improve communication between resource agencies in provincial and federal governments. Communication may have been improved, but there is as yet little to show for it. The conference itself highlighted many problems and made some attempt to set guide lines for future resource development. No tangible government action has resulted.

One valuable by-product of the conference, however, was the preparation of a *Guide to Benefit-Cost Analysis*.[15] This Guide provides a general outline of the aims and principles of benefit-cost analysis, it examines some of the technical problems involved, and provides a number of examples. On the face of it, the Guide may be thought to offer the possibility of a standard approach to the choice of alternatives in resource management. In fact, the intricacies are such that almost infinite opportunities exist for varying the analysis in small but significant ways. Hence the Guide is not able to perform the function of standardizing procedures. On the contrary, it emphasizes the applicability of benefit-cost analysis to many problems in different ways.

An approach to standardization would require the production of a large and detailed *Manual*. Even were this task to be completed, American experience is not encouraging on the score of achieving uniformity of method. In spite of the continued efforts of the Inter-Agency Committee on Water Resources in the United States,[16] the several agencies continue to practice widely divergent forms of benefit-cost analysis. Even within single agencies, the

---

14 The eighty papers were published as *Resources for Tomorrow Background Papers* (Ottawa, Queen's Printer, 1961) in 2 Vols. A third volume of *Proceedings* was published in 1962.

15 W. R. D. Sewell, John Davis, A. D. Scott and D. W. Ross, *Guide to Benefit-Cost Analysis* (Ottawa, Queen's Printer, 1962).

16 As for example the "Green Book", Inter-Agency Committee on Water Resources Report, *Proposed Practices for Economic Analysis of River Basin Projects* (Washington, Government Printing Office, 1958). Recent American literature on standards and procedures in benefit-cost analysis includes the following: Maynard M. Hufschmidt (Chairman), John Krutilla, Julius Margolis and Stephen A. Marglin, *Standards and Criteria for Formulating and Evaluating Federal Water Resources Developments*, Report of Panel of Consultants to the Bureau of the Budget (Washington, 1961). President's Water Resources Council, *Policies, Standards, and Procedures in the Formulation, Evaluation and Review of Plans for Use and Development of Water and Related Land Resources*, Senate Doc. No. 97, 87th Congress, 2nd Session (1962). See also Edward G. Altouney, *The Role of Uncertainties in the Economic Evaluation of Water-Resources Projects* (Stanford, Project on Engineering-Economic Planning, Stanford Institute in Engineering-Economic Systems, Stanford University, 1963).

Army Corps of Engineers for example, there are variations in methods from district to district although a detailed manual on procedures is widely used and is constantly under review.

In the light of the difficulties in establishing a uniform system of application, there is need for a checking or reviewing system to ensure against the creation of inequalities. For example, one method may consistently lead to higher estimates of benefits than another, and the projects analyzed by this method would be unduly favoured. A check is provided in the United States by competition among federal agencies for Congressional appropriations. The principal construction agencies, the Army Corps of Engineers, the Bureau of Reclamation, and the Soil Conservation Service, keep a close watch on each other's methods. To some extent the Bureau of the Budget also performs an overseeing function.

As the use of benefit-cost analysis increases in Canada, there will be a need for some similar system. Perhaps it will be most naturally provided by competing provinces instead of competing agencies. Benefit-cost studies by competing provinces might then be expected to be made subject to review by an interprovincial organization, or at the federal level by an independent body.

Canada is not alone in this development, and the use of benefit-cost analysis is becoming more widespread in other countries. It has been used extensively in the United States since the formal requirements that benefit should exceed costs was written into the 1936 Federal Flood Control Act.[17] Its use has spread gradually. The new Victoria Line for the London Underground System in England was subjected to a benefit-cost analysis prior to the decision to construct it,[18] and this is symptomatic of the increasing use of benefit-cost analysis in planning new transport developments.[19] Proposals have also been made recently for its use in city and regional planning.[20] It is also being used increasingly in underdeveloped countries—for example in the large-scale river valley developments in India.[21]

---

17 49 U.S. Statutes 1570, Act of June 22, 1936, commonly called the Flood Control Act of 1936.
18 C. D. Foster and M. E. Beesley, "Estimating the Social Benefit of Constructing an Underground Railway in London", *Journal of the Royal Statistical Society*, Series A (General), Vol. 126, Part II, (1963), pp. 46-92.
19 H. D. Mohring and M. Harwitz, *Highway Benefits* (Evanston, Northwestern University Transportation Center, 1962).
20 Nathaniel Lichfield, "Cost-Benefit Analysis in City Planning", *Journal of the American Institute of Planners*, Vol. 26, no. 4 (November, 1960), pp. 273-279.
21 See for example, N. V. Sorani and Nilakanth Rath, *Economics of a Multiple-Purpose River Dam*, Report of an Inquiry into the Economic Benefits of the Hirakud Dam (Poona, Asia Publishing House, for Gokhale Institute of Politics and Economics, 1960).

Benefit-cost analysis is not expensive. It does require more money than governments in Canada have been willing to spend, but in the United States, where considerable experience has been acquired in its use, the total cost has been relatively small. Appropriations for such surveys (including geological, hydrological and engineering studies, as well as administration and miscellaneous items) since 1936 are estimated at $330 million, which is less than 5% of construction costs in the same period. The cost of survey reports in individual cases varies from a few thousand dollars in some instances to several million dollars for a major river basin study.

In principal, the advantages of benefit-cost analysis are substantial, but unless this method is correctly applied and certain pitfalls avoided, experience indicates that it may not help to arrive at better decisions. There is a danger that the whole objective of benefit-cost analysis—to weigh alternatives—may be subverted, and that it may be used merely as a pseudo-scientific veneer to justify decisions made entirely on other grounds. This is not to deny that "political considerations" have a legitimate role to play in decision-making, but simply that benefit-cost analysis has not been designed to act as a prop for ill-conceived ideas. Unless it is executed properly, it can easily come to fulfil just this latter purpose.

A few words of caution, therefore, are in order. Before the analysis is attempted, some fundamental assumptions require explicit consideration and decision. The question of a regional or national viewpoint was raised above. Another instance is the problem of expenditures on labour. At a time of full employment, such expenditures may be reckoned as a cost, while at a time of unemployment they may well be reckoned as a benefit. In some locally depressed areas it may thus be legitimate to claim labour as a benefit, while elsewhere it would be a cost item. It is not my purpose here to offer solutions to these questions, but merely to make them explicit.

In any analysis of benefits and costs, particularly in water resource development, there are many physical variables involved in addition to social and economic factors. Social scientists often tend to assume that the physical variables are much better understood and are much more amenable to prediction than the social and economic ones. This is not always the case. Furthermore, [22] varia-

---

[22] See for example, S. V. Ciriacy-Wantrup, "Benefit-Cost Analysis and Public Resource Development", *Journal of Farm Economics*, Vol. 37 (November, 1955), pp. 676-689. J. Margolis, "Secondary Benefits, External Economies, and the Justification of Public Investment", *Review of Economics and Statistics*, Vol. 39 (August, 1957), pp. 284-291. A. H. Trice and S. E. Wood, "Measurement of Recreation Benefits", *Land Economics*, Vol. 34 (August, 1958), pp. 195-207.

tions in assumptions about physical variables may far outweigh the significance of assumptions about economic variables in terms of their consequences for project planning. For example, a great deal of attention has been given to the question of an appropriate interest rate by economists. Reuber and Wonnacot have concluded in 1961 that 5-6% was a reasonable rate for the opportunity cost of federal funds in Canada.[23] Recent studies in the United States suggest, however, that considerably greater variations in benefit-cost ratios may occur in estimating potential flood damages on the basis of one or two common hydrological assumption as to the frequency of a large flood, than on the basis of two interest rates in common use, namely $2\frac{5}{8}\%$ and 5%.[24]

Nevertheless, the arguments in favour of adopting benefit-cost analysis are many. I rest my case on three minimum claims. First, economic arguments, both sound and unsound, are already a strong weapon in the arsenal of opposing regional and sectional interests that contend in the political arena for and against public projects.[25] Benefit-cost analysis by a government agency, subject to public scrutiny, would therefore help to increase the confidence of the public by restraining the abuse of economic arguments in the political process. We would be less subject to the argument that this project is worthwhile "no matter what the cost."

Second, benefit-cost analysis has undoubtedly had a stimulating effect in expanding scientific understanding of physical and socio-economic variables involved in public resource development and can continue to do so. For example, geographers interested in estimating flood probability and in predicting recreational use of projected reservoirs have had some success in developing geographical analog methods, namely, the transferring of the experience obtained in one place to a similar or analogous situation where particular information is required.[26] A case in point would be the prediction of per capita attendance at the future recreational reservoirs on the fringes

23 G. L. Reuber and R. J. Wonnacot, *The Cost of Capital in Canada* (Washington, Resources for the Future, 1961), p. 112.

24 Robert W. Kates, "The Synthetic Estimation of Flood Damages: A New Approach", unpublished paper presented to the Pennsylvania Conference of Economists (1962). See also G. F. White, *Choice of Adjustment to Floods*, Department of Geography Research Paper No. 95 (Chicago, Department of Geography, University of Chicago, forthcoming).

25 S. V. Ciriacy-Wantrup has made this point in "Benefit-Cost Analysis and Public Resource Development", *op. cit.*

26 See, for example, for recent study of the Meramec Basin, E. L. Ullman, R. R. Boyce, D. J. Volk, *The Meramec Basin, Water and Economic Development*, A report to the Meramec Basin Corporation, 3 Vols. (St. Louis, Meramec Basin Research Project, Washington University, 1962).

of Metropolitan Toronto from the experience of other cities, while making any adjustments that are required. Viewed in this manner, reservoir attendance is primarily a function of population and distance, and it becomes predictable by a simple regression model. Such predictions are fundamental to any assessment of recreation benefits from reservoirs. Problems of this nature have stimulated a greater concern for the development and testing of predictive models.[27]

A third claim for benefit-cost analysis is that it has at least acted as a sieve in eliminating proposals that by no extension of the estimated benefits could be considered economically desirable. While it is true that the sieve has large holes, and that "pork-barrel" projects are justified through benefit-cost analysis in the United States, nevertheless one indication of its effectiveness is seen in the rejection of approximately half of the proposed projects reviewed by the U.S. Army Corps of Engineers. It is true that not all these rejections are made on the grounds of an analysis of benefits and costs, but the analysis does act as a partially effective sieve.

Opposition to benefit-cost analysis has been voiced by some liberal groups who see it as a dangerous weapon which might be used to curtail "desirable" spending in the public sector. While this possibility exists in theory, it has not been realized, and wherever benefit-cost analysis has been introduced, the effect has been to aid in the expansion of programs of public investments in resource development.

Although defensible in principle, benefit-cost analysis is much more open to criticism on the grounds of how it has been applied thus far. The remainder of this paper is devoted to an examination of some of the non-technical or administrative deficiencies of the analysis as it is now being used in Canada.

III

Problems of Selection: Two Cases

First a word about approach is in order. I am going to look at benefit-cost analysis from the geographer's standpoint of examining the possible alternative in human adjustment to the physical environment and to the use of natural resources.[28] To what extent

---

[27] I. Burton, "The Quantitative Revolution and Theoretical Geography", *Canadian Geographer*, Vol. VII, no. 4 (1963), pp. 151-162.

[28] The concept of human adjustment was first clearly proposed and developed in geographic literature by Harlen H. Barrows in his Presidential Address to the Association of American Geographers, "Geography as Human Ecology", *Annals, Association of American Geographers*, Vol. 13 (1923), pp. 1-14.

can benefit-cost analysis be expected to lead to better decisions in resource management and hence to better adjustments to the physical environment? If based on accurate predictions of future events, this technique can be used as a means of increasing the range of choice and of comparing the quality of these alternative adjustments. It should also be noted that there may be subsidiary demands on the public purse as a consequence of implementing measures deriving from benefit-cost analysis. For example, partial flood control may induce accelerated flood plain development leading to demands for a greater degree of protection.

The question of alternatives in adjustment to the physical environment is illustrated by reference to two recent examples. When judged by these experiences, benefit-cost analysis is not now leading to better decisions and is, in fact, in danger of being used to reinforce decisions inferior in their consequences to those which might have been expected in the absence of such analysis.

Both of the cases that I propose to examine involve flood problems, although the issues that arise here have a wider relevance in other areas of resource management and of government spending in the public sector generally.[29] The first is the case of the flood control project in Toronto, and the second, the Moira River Project in Belleville.

The flood control project in Toronto

The Metropolitan Toronto flood control study provides a good example of the way in which benefit-cost analysis may serve to focus attention almost entirely on measures for the control of floods to the neglect of other possible ways of reducing flood losses.[30] This has occurred in spite of the fact that adequate consideration of alternatives is one of the objectives of benefit-cost analysis. The background to this plan also illustrates the inability to take appropriate action until an extreme situation has arisen. This is at least in part a result of existing administrative and jurisdictional arrangements.

There is a wide range of possible adjustments to floods on the technical side.[31] Although this is commonly conceived as a problem of control, other possibilities become apparent if we think in terms

---

29 Professor Drummond, for example, concludes that benefit-cost studies should be made of our growing expenditures in the field of education. Cf. "Some Economic Issues in Educational Expansion", in this volume.
30 *Plan for Flood Control, op. cit.*
31 The classic statement of the range of human adjustments to flood hazards is found in G. F. White, *Human Adjustment to Floods,* Department of Geography Research Paper No. 29 (Chicago, Department of Geography, University of Chicago, 1945), pp. 128-202.

of flood loss reduction. In addition to engineering works such as dams, levees, dykes, floodwalls and channel improvements, losses may also be reduced in the future by flood-proofing of individual buildings, the reorganization and rescheduling of activities, flood warnings, land-use-regulations, building codes, and urban redevelopment. Flood damage insurance is also a possible alternative adjustment which involves a redistribution rather than a reduction of loss.

In 1950 the Don Valley Conservation Authority in Toronto published the following statement:

On the whole the floods of the Don now do only a small amount of damage compared to those before 1880 and there seems little likelihood that the amount will increase. *Flooding is not a very serious problem on the Don and does not call for costly measures of control.*[32] [Italics added.]

Four years later a catastrophic flood associated with the passage of Hurricane Hazel caused considerable property damage in the Toronto area (including an estimated $3.5 million in the Don Valley alone) and resulted in the loss of 81 lives. In 1959 the *Plan for Flood Control and Water Conservation* for the Toronto Metropolitan area was presented to the Government of Canada. The plan stated in part that:

It is the purpose of this plan to point out *the urgent need for flood control* and water conservation measures, to outline a program of proposed measures and to analyze the engineering, economic and social aspects of the proposed program. The Metropolitan Toronto and Region Conservation Authority respectfully requests financial assistance from the Governments of the Dominion of Canada and the Province of Ontario in respect of an integrated flood control and water conservation program for Metropolitan Toronto and Region.[33] [Italics added.]

It is widely acknowledged that Hurricane Hazel changed the view of flood problems in Toronto and Southern Ontario. Although the agencies quoted above are not identical (by 1959 the Don Valley Conservation Authority had been amalgamated along with several other authorities into the Metropolitan Toronto and Region Conservation Authority), nevertheless a major reason for the amalgamation was in order to be able to do more about the flood problem collectively than could have been achieved by the sum of their separate efforts.

The 1959 request was for contributions of $12,795,488 each from Dominion and provincial governments. This request was not entirely or even largely for flood-control measures. As indicated in Table I, only 22% of the benefits were for flood damage reduction and over 40% were to be derived from public recreation.

---

[32] Ontario Department of Planning and Development, Conservation Branch, *Don Valley Conservation Report* (Toronto, 1950), p. 19.
[33] *Plan for Flood Control, op. cit.*, p. 1.

TABLE I. TANGIBLE BENEFITS OF THE METROPOLITAN TORONTO AND REGION PLAN FOR FLOOD CONTROL AND WATER CONSERVATION

Type of Benefit	Value of Benefit	Per Cent
Flood Damage Reduction	$12,447,000	22.4
Recreational Use of Reservoirs	21,203,000	37.6
Indirect benefits	9,335,000	16.5
Others (including water supply, fishing outside reservoirs, pollution abatement, and recreational use of acquired flood-plain lands)	13,240,600	23.5
TOTAL	$56,225,600	100.0

Source: Figures are derived from *Plan for Flood Control and Water Conservation*, Metropolitan Toronto and Region Conservation Authority, Woodbridge, Ontario, 1959. They are expressed in present value, assuming a 100-year life of construction works and an interest rate of 4%.

The recreational benefits were derived in the following manner. Heart Lake recreational area was used as a model. Attendance at this lake in 1958 was estimated at 196,000. The desirable level of attendance (the optimum on grounds of safety, health, and public convenience) was then considered to be 100,000 a year, for a developed area of 50 acres. The value of a visitor-day was put at 75 cents on the basis of an examination of several commercial recreation areas taking into account admission charges and opportunity for concessionary profits. On this basis the equivalent gross annual market value of the Heart Lake services, if operated as a commercial enterprise, would be 100,000 x $0.75 or $75,000. Less depreciation and operation and maintenance costs of $22,534, this amounts to a net sum of $53,466.

The net annual value per acre of these 50 acres of developed recreational land would then be $1,050. The total value per acre (assuming a 100-year life and an interest rate of 4%) is thus about $25,000. This figure is then used as a value on the developed recreational land for the ten proposed recreation lake areas located within and around the boundaries of Metropolitan Toronto. It is argued that the demand for this kind of recreational opportunity is so great, that all ten areas would be utilized to full capacity as soon as they were completed and placed in operation.

The measurement of recreation benefits presents a number of complex conceptual problems,[34] and it is not surprising, therefore,

[34] Some of these are reviewed in A. H. Trice and S. E. Wood, "Measurement of Recreation Benefits", *op. cit.* See also, Lawrence G. Hines, "Measurement of Recreation Benefits: A Reply"; Trice and Wood, "Measurement of Recreation Benefits: A Rejoinder"; and Jack Lessinger, "Measure of Recreation Benefits: A Reply", *Land Economics*, Vol. 34 (November, 1958), pp. 365-370.

that this particular example of Canadian benefit-cost analysis has come under some criticism. A widely accepted principle of the analysis is that an allocated benefit should not exceed the least costly alternative. Eric Baker has claimed that natural lake and waterfront sites were still available at the time of the analysis for $500 an acre.[35] Substituting this figure for the $25,000 an acre actually used, the recreation benefits would have been drastically reduced to the extent of yielding a negative benefit-cost ratio.

Another condemnation of these recreation benefits has been made by the American economist, Ayers Brinser, who states:

The problem here is illustrated in the analysis made of recreation benefits in a Toronto watershed. Having dismissed the benefit-cost ratio as an impediment to responsibility, the planners went on to concoct such a ratio, or a reasonable facsimile. The astronomical (and unsupported) value assigned to recreation was necessary to produce an economic justification for the total investment. Perhaps recreation deserved this weight of value, and perhaps also the only way that value could be stated was as an educated intuition. But to call that intuition a quantified value in a benefit-cost calculation did little more than prove the known fact that the benefit-cost ratio can be reduced to meaninglessness.[36]

In justification of the Toronto plan, it can be stated that a large and expanding urban area like Metropolitan Toronto will require much more public recreation facilities in the future. Over the next 20 to 25 years, the construction of a series of reservoirs around the periphery of the city may well seem to be justified on the basis of recreation alone. The scheme has an air of justice about it and the proponents of the plan may come to be highly praised for their great foresight. But this does not meet Brinser's objection that the benefit figures are inadequately supported.

More sophisticated methods of estimating recreation benefits have been developed, although none of them are completely satisfactory.[37] Because of the nature of the problem, no perfect means can be devised, and this has led some to the conclusion that all attempts to put a dollar value on public recreation should be abandoned. This is especially the view of those who think that all such

[35] See the discussion by Mr. Eric Baker in *Proceedings of the Resources for Tomorrow Conference*, Vol. III (Ottawa, Queen's Printer, 1962), pp. 157-158.
[36] Ayers Brinser, "What the United States Can Learn", a comment on a paper by E. G. Pleva, "Multiple Purpose Land and Water Districts in Ontario", Jarrett (ed.), *Comparisons in Resource Management* (Baltimore, Johns Hopkins Press, for Resources for the Future, Inc., 1961), pp. 189-207. See Brinser's comment on pp. 214-215.
[37] Some of the literature on recreation benefits is found in Paul R. Kipp, *Annotated Bibliography on the Economic Evaluation of Outdoor Recreation and Related Subjects* (Washington, U.S. Department of the Interior, 1960), mimeo.

attempts will underestimate the true value of recreation, thus leading to the disparagement of recreation as compared with other non-recreational developments. The contrary view is that recreation has not been getting its due, and that the attempt to quantify recreational values will help to secure increased attention. Of course, it would be ideal if it could be claimed that the analysis allows objective comparison between such alternatives. Quantification is a move in that direction, but recreational benefits have so far proved to be among those least amenable to satisfactory treatment.

In addition to these criticisms of the way in which benefits were actually measured in the Toronto case, the main objection is that the plan reveals inadequate consideration of possible alternative adjustments. Evacuation of buildings from the flood plain, possibly including urban redevelopment carried out over a ten-year period, might have been much less costly. Such an alternative might also have included flood-proofing and flood insurance for buildings as long as they remained, an improved flood warning system, and prohibition of new construction.

Such alternatives were given only cursory consideration. The benefit-cost analysis for the Toronto plan was carried out by private consultants for the Conservation Authority. The major defects in the analysis are the result of the lack of time and funds. The role of the consultants is also significant. Hired by the Conservation Authority, their task was to present the Authority's case in its most favourable light with a view to obtaining a total grant of over $25.5 million from the two senior governments. Under these circumstances, a consultant does not play the role of an impartial technical expert, attempting to use benefit-cost analysis in order to determine the most favourable course of action. Rather, he performs as a lawyer attempting to put his client's case in its most favourable light.

In consequence, the question of alternatives was only briefly considered. At an early stage in the analysis, it became necessary to select a particular kind of project and proceed to justify it. This still left room for within-project alternatives such as the number of dams, on which streams they should be located, and their size. But the broad range of alternatives which I have described was very rapidly eliminated. In other words, benefit-cost analysis was used virtually *ex post facto* to justify a decision previously taken on other grounds. The other grounds can only be guessed at. Undoubtedly sound engineering considerations entered in. Perhaps also it was realized that a major flood disaster could be used to justify the building of a recreation project for the Metropolitan area.

A more effective use of benefit-cost analysis would have permitted examination of the recreation project without the spur of a major flood. There is clear need for an agency of government at some level to perform and study such problems, and for provision of appropriate financing of such a study by federal assistance if necessary.

If the benefit-cost analysis had been more stringently performed, the result may well have been negative, and Toronto might have been presented with a choice of other alternatives for flood damage reduction, but no recreation project. Likely the citizens of Toronto would have condemned such an outcome and demanded the project. This is not the point. Benefit-cost analysis is a guide to weighing alternatives and making choices, not a means of justifying choices after they have been made.

The Moira River project

A second example is the case of the City of Belleville, Ontario, located on Lake Ontario at the mouth of the Moira River. A brief prepared for the Moira River Conservation Authority and directed to the two senior governments was submitted in 1959.[38] It constituted a request for $165,000 from each government. The relatively small sum of $330,000 is 75% of the total cost of approximately $440,000 of a proposed scheme to provide flood protection (in this case an ice control dam) for the City of Belleville. The city would be required to contribute $107,800 toward the cost or 98% of the balance while other municipalities in the Moira basin would contribute the rest. The benefit-cost analysis included in the brief is confined almost solely to flood-control measures.

The analysis itself was carried out *at the request of the Dominion government,* and it is the most recent of a series of attempts by the City of Belleville to obtain support for such a project.[39] Two previous attempts had been made prior to 1945. These followed the maximum flood on record which occurred in 1936. Both attempts failed and accordingly the city joined with other communities in the Moira basin in the establishment of the Moira River Conservation Authority. It was hoped in this way to present a more powerful united front in trying to obtain senior government assistance for the flood control scheme.

The Authority's first proposal was rejected in 1948 by the

---

38 Moira River Conservation Authority, *Flood Control and Conservation Measures Brief for the Moira River Watershed, op. cit.*
39 The succession of applications is summarized in a mimeographed report to the Mayor and Council of the city of Belleville submitted by the Authority and dated February 13, 1961.

Dominion government on the ground that the stream was not navigable. Negotiations and discussions with both senior governments continued sporadically without much progress for the next ten years. Meanwhile, some work was carried out by the Authority in obtaining designs and cost estimates for the proposed dam.

In 1958, following the change of government in Ottawa, a new approach was made. It was then that the Authority was asked to study the benefits and costs of the project. The damages that would occur in the event of a repetition of the 1936 flood were measured by sending a questionnaire to 233 establishments in the flood plain. Only 79 replies were received and the estimates were based on these answers. In this manner, total direct damages were estimated at $1,202,000. It was estimated that construction of the ice-control dam would permit $1,095,000 of these damages to be prevented and this amount is listed as the benefit from the scheme compared to the cost of approximately $440,000.

The proposal was rejected in December, 1958, by the Dominion government, not on the basis of the benefit-cost analysis, which found a favourable ratio, but on the grounds that projects of less than $2,500,000 were too small for Dominion government participation.

The Authority then decided that there was little point in making further representations to the Dominion government and that the matter should be referred to Belleville for a decision regarding the possibility of proceeding under existing alternative grant systems. The investment put into planning the flood protection scheme included over $3,000 in engineering costs and a substantially larger amount in the form of free services provided by the province. The choice facing the city was to abandon the scheme or to carry it through paying substantially more of the total cost than anticipated. This would have amounted to at least $218,000 on the basis of a 50% provincial grant or $175,000 as a winter works project. The city decided to consult the persons involved, and sent a letter of enquiry with a questionnaire to be completed by all residents and businessmen in the flood-prone area. The response was most discouraging. Of some 800 questionnaires distributed, only 215 were returned and of these only 60 indicated support for the city to go ahead with the scheme. Accordingly, the city drew the conclusion that the people were not sufficiently interested in receiving flood protection and abandoned the project. Interviews [40] conducted in the

---

[40] Conducted by the author with assistance from the following: C. W. Bridge, Michael A. Church, Marta Foty, Heather Gordon, G. J. V. Kokich, Cecil Louis, Douglas Rigby, Janet Westman.

area in September, 1962, reveal that many residents have little or no awareness of the flood hazard. Some did not recall the last severe flood in 1936, and among those that did, there was a widespread impression that such a flood would not occur again. These residents ascribed their optimism to the very existence of the Conservation Authority and to the greater degree of preparation by the city.

This latter reason is valid in part. A flood warning system has been set up for the city in conjunction with the Moira River Conservation Authority and civil defence authorities. Preparations have also been made to meet the flood emergency should it arise, and instructions for city personnel were printed in the City Engineer's *Annual Report* in 1961.[41] Nevertheless, the optimism of residents and businessmen in the flood-prone areas is not justified by the facts. A flood equal to or greater than the 1936 flood could occur at any time in late winter or early spring when ice is being carried downstream and conditions exist for an ice-jam to develop. The Flood Control and Conservation Measures Brief puts the return period of the 1936 flood at 20 years. If this is a correct estimate, floods of much greater magnitude are to be expected over a longer period.

The Moira case study illustrates another deficiency of benefit-cost analysis as now practised in Canada. The choice facing governments at all levels has always been to build the dam as designed or to reject the scheme and be left with no alternative. The brief includes no mention of examination of other alternatives. No doubt others were given cursory consideration, but no careful analysis of the benefits and costs of other alternatives was made and to do so was probably beyond the scope of the investigation. It would have involved extra expense and delay in circumstances in which, as it appears, the Dominion government felt free to reject the scheme on other grounds entirely. It is not clear why a benefit-cost study should have been requested at all by the Dominion government which was aware of the general scale of the project.

Other alternatives which could have been considered for Belleville include flood-proofing, urban renewal or redevelopment, and possibly flood insurance. The redevelopment alternative might in fact be an attractive choice, for it would offer the possibility of opening up the river to public view and providing open space for public gardens and parking in an attractive physical setting. None of these alternatives received adequate consideration. In fairness, it should

---

41 City of Belleville, Public Works Department, *City Engineer's Annual Report for 1961*, pp. 30-40.

be pointed out that no mechanism exists for government participation in such alternatives and that a radical new view of the government's role in flood damage reduction would be required.

No attempts have been made in such a direction. Flood-proofing is regarded as prohibitively expensive, yet it has been shown to be a feasible adjustment in economic terms in some cases.[42] Moreover, if senior governments are prepared to aid the construction of dams, why not provide subsidies for flood-proofing of private buildings where such a method of adjustment seems preferable? Belleville was left with no alternative to its system of emergency preparations which may do little to reduce damage, especially if it is not constantly reviewed.

IV

Toward a Wider Range of Choice

The Toronto and Belleville cases illustrate my contention that the effect of benefit-cost analysis, as it is now being carried out, may be to limit the range of alternatives considered. The prospect of substantial financial help from senior governments seems to mesmerize local authorities and deprive them of a sense of enterprise and a wider view of alternatives. If the money is forthcoming, all is well, even though the best possible project may not have been selected and probably not even considered. If the money is not forthcoming, the search for a solution may simply be abandoned, and the situation allowed to deteriorate until another emergency develops.

Nor is the stance of the senior governments helpful. They mainly stand and wait and their procedures for assistance are such that large-scale engineering projects are favoured while other alternatives are neglected. There are, of course, reasons for this. Perhaps one of them is that in our society it is much easier to build a large engineering project to control the forces of nature than it is to make adjustments in the human society itself. The question of new types of demands on the public purse was raised earlier. Control of nature is at best a partial and temporary solution. For example, floods in excess of those for which flood control works were designed are almost always possible. There is the danger that when great faith is placed in only one such kind of adjustment, frequent and small-scale damages may perhaps be avoided, but we may still be left with

---

[42] J. R. Sheaffer, *Flood Proofing: An Element in a Flood Damage Reduction Program,* Department of Geography Research Paper No. 65 (Chicago, Department of Geography, University of Chicago, 1960).

catastrophic losses at infrequent intervals. We frequently choose short-term and small-scale security at some unknown risk of longer-range and possibly disastrous consequences.

The pattern of decision-making in the public sector, with respect to renewable resource development, as described in this paper, is not adequate. There is need for an agency or agencies to initiate resource development projects and to examine them in terms of benefit-cost analysis. If it is to be useful in arriving at decisions, the analysis needs to be performed according to carefully specified methods, and based on assumptions appropriate to Canadian conditions.

Even if given adequate support, it would still be unreasonable to expect benefit-cost analysis to work perfectly overnight in Canada. Nor will it ever be the sole basis for making decisions. The analysis may be expected to perform the "sieve" function well enough. Beyond this, other criteria would be used, such as extent of danger to life, the extent of other intangible benefits, the ability and willingness of provincial and local groups to provide the necessary co-operation, the existence of budget constraints, the logical sequence of projects in a given river basin, other existing government programs, the special needs of particular areas at particular moments in time, and the need to ensure an equitable geographical distribution of projects within a province or within the nation.

The importance of benefit-cost analysis in guiding decisions on public investment in Canadian resource development is likely to increase whether federal participation in these projects grows, or whether provincial jurisdiction is accompanied by greater financial ability to meet its responsibilities. Since benefit-cost analysis is to be used, it would be well to ensure that it is used to permit adequate consideration of alternatives. In that way it may become as useful a guide to investment choices in reality as it is in theory.

19

The Nodal Water Region of North America

A. K. Philbrick

By way of introduction this is a paper in applied cultural geography emphasizing the importance of innovative perception. Human culture is a complex cyclical phenomenon operating at three distinct levels simultaneously. These are the levels of human values or tradition, ways of doing things, and works expressed in patterns of the human organization of area, like a palimpsest in successive stages upon the face of the earth.

The cyclical nature of the culture process may be formalized by writing the three words, *values, ways, works* under one another in a list with directional arrows pointing downward on the right and upward on the left.

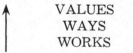

VALUES
WAYS
WORKS

The downward arrow on the right signifies that already-formulated widely-held cultural values are implemented by established routines of conduct which produce familiar and dependably predictable results. The upward arrow on the left signifies that innovative perception in the fulfillment of felt need requires new procedures which continuously pose increments of change in the creating of new human values.

Old traditions are well established and conservative. They are difficult to change or dislodge because they have the strength of

Reprinted from *Canadian Geographer*, Vol. VIII, no. 4 (1964), pp. 182-87.

long-established commitment. Fragments of emergent tradition are weak and may easily be pushed aside because they normally have few adherents.

Where water is concerned there are two very strong traditional views. First, all water that is to be of any use to satisfy the needs of land animals and vegetation must be derived either directly or indirectly from precipitation through the hydrologic cycle. Secondly, because the hold which living matter has over its water content is purely temporary, practically no water is ever withdrawn permanently from the cycle; so there cannot be said to be any real shortage of water, only problems of distribution and of human stupidity in water use, which proper attention to correct conservation practices can set right.

But these traditional views are not necessarily the last word on the subject. In innumerable situations over the face of the earth practical problems of a pressing nature over a long period of time have led men to yearn for other ways of doing something about a water supply than to accept complete dependence upon the natural hydrologic cycle.

Let us suppose, for the sake of the record, that the American Atomic Energy Commission is correct in reporting on its experiment *work** (the final word of the three describing the culture cycle) and that fresh water may, in the future, be produced by desalinization of sea water for eight cents per thousand gallons in a plant delivering a billion gallons per day using breeder reactors, and for possibly as low as five cents per thousand gallons with electricity for one-half cent per kilowatt hour into the bargain. Ask yourself, what is the impact of such conjecture upon the possible *ways* (the second of the three words in the cultural cycle) of supplying water at the right time in the right places to accommodate human need? And ask yourself, also, what is the impact of such implications with respect to ways of getting fresh water upon our *traditional ideas* concerning water supply (the first concept of the culture cycle)?

Is there a difference in the kinds of policy and programme appropriate for developing run-off water of the natural hydrologic cycle from those appropriate in quest of fresh water from the sea? The answer is so emphatically yes that we should re-examine how we really do expect to obtain the fresh water for our ever increasing multi-purpose uses.

---

* *Science News Letter*, LXXXIV, no. 6 (August 10, 1963), p. 82.

In the case of capture, storage, and use of controlled run-offs from precipitation in the natural hydrologic cycle, *river basins* are inherently logical planning units. In projecting use of desalinized sea water, on the other hand, an entirely different kind of functional and planning unit becomes necessary. We are no longer required to think only in terms of given natural drainage units. What I shall call the *nodal water region* now becomes an effective operational unit. A nodal water region is one of human organization, unifying water resources of any type in some optimum way for the delivery of maximum amounts of water of the most appropriate quality to the greatest number of users with maximum effectiveness at minimum cost.

When one considers the possible locations of sea-water desalinization plants in terms of resource versus market orientations one is struck by the apparent but deceptive simplicity of the problem. There are, after all, so many millions of square miles of ocean and so very many tens of thousands of linear miles of sea coast, to say nothing of the numerous large underground sources of saline waters from which to choose! When we imagine desalinization plants all along our coasts to supply water deficit areas, then we begin to ask where are we going to store water processed in this manner? How are we going to deliver it to users? How are we going to minimize costs of production by concentrating a relatively few large producers for maximum efficiency in the most wisely selected places? In response to such thoughts we begin to feel the need for co-ordinated nodal systems of strategically located desalinization and pumping plants. We begin to cast our eyes about the world for the most suitably distributed circumstances for natural storage and delivery which are also adjacent to large populations in need of additional supplies of water.

If past experience is any criterion we shall both scatter and concentrate desalinization projects, just as we have experienced similar results in the controversy between advocates of the big dams on the major rivers and the advocates of far up-stream control. Man-made hydrologic cycles serving large locally market-oriented needs may, indeed, justify localized individual desalinization works; yet, it remains true that the public interest will be best served generally by the policy of the broadest possible effort to secure optimum co-ordination among diverse water resource and market-oriented interests within the context of a new water resource tradition—the nodal water region based upon development of a man-made hydrologic cycle.

Such a policy statement is background for discussion of the specific illustration of a nodal water region which is the geographical focus of this paper—a co-ordinated international programme of engineering facilities and political statesmanship which will assure the status of the Great Lakes of North America in perpetuity as the mid-continent fresh water reservoir for both Canada and the United States. Indeed, there are four separate statements of policy needed to complete that background, including the above.

(1) *The nodal water region rather than the river basin* is the most appropriate unit for planning and operation under co-ordinated policy and engineering developments.

(2) From prior tradition, *let there be continued and ever strengthened conservation, purification, and multiple re-use of existing water supplies.* Such measures can delay and reduce the need for supplemental man-made hydrologic cycles, extend the time period over which development of desalinization works can take place, and thus facilitate their construction by allowing them to be in response to a more gradually increasing need than otherwise would be the case.

(3) *Water used in excess of annual precipitation will be replaced* within a reasonable time. Surface and ground water are to be regarded as a "water bank" against which our people have been borrowing since the beginning of European settlement. Prospects of man-made hydrologic cycles at strategic locations raise possibilities for the deliberate re-investment in this water bank through recharging of aquifers.

(4) *Users must pay* for water so that the capital as well as current operating costs may be met. Such policy will encourage thrift. Private works for purification and re-use of water taken into closed systems from public sources will be cheaper over the long range for many to construct and maintain than the continuing purchase of large amounts of new water.

Research and development on an international scale can implement such policies. Plans and programmes must take into account continuing advances in engineering technology which can reduce costs of desalinization and power production, the selection of optimum locations for facilities and distribution channels, and the direct as well as indirect effects of such policies and developments upon local, regional, and national economies in the equitable distribution of benefits among the political entities involved.

The Great Lakes Nodal Water Region of North America will be used to illustrate these ideas. The states of the United States bordering the Great Lakes and the province of Ontario, Canada, combined, withdraw from ground and surface sources approximately 80 billion gallons per day (66 billion English gallons, 303 million kiloliters) — one fourth of the total water withdrawn by the two countries. It is estimated that at any given time no more than one-fourth of this amount is unavailable for re-use and that existing quantities of water are withdrawn for use and re-use at least four times. Given adequate control, we could thus double the available water supply by desalinization and introduction into the Great Lakes of 20 billion U.S. gallons (16.5 billion English gallons, 75 million kiloliters) of fresh water per day processed from the world ocean. On an annual basis this is 7,300 billion U.S. gallons.

In round numbers there are 20,000 billion U.S. gallons in the top one foot of the Great Lakes' surface water (91 billion kiloliters). One year's additional supply of water for the Great Lakes region could therefore be stored in less than five inches (12.7 cm.) of rise in the level of lakes. This vast 95,200-square-mile (246,558-square-kilometer) alignment of the Great Lakes, shown in Figure 1, containing 9,511 cubic miles of fresh water (39,641 cu. km.), already in unregulated use, is not only the world's largest fresh water supply, but it is also the world's largest natural storage reservoir, available free for use without the building of a single dam, large or small.

The responsibility for the quality control and re-supply of these waters so that they may be used in excess of their natural supply is a grave trust. The long-range prosperity of North America is at stake in the wise development and multiple-purpose use of these waters.

Diversion of rivers draining into Hudson Bay is one source for additional water for the lakes. Precedent for use of this source already exists in diversion of water from the Albany River. The amount of water which can be diverted, however, is less than the potential requirement; and there are limits beyond which supply from this source will adversely affect the ecological balance of the region. In principle it is a poor policy which requires us perpetually to rob Peter to pay Paul.

An unlimited supply of seawater for desalinization is accessible from Hudson Bay, 350 miles (563 km.) northeast of the highest of the Great Lakes, Lake Superior, 602 feet (183.5 m.) above mean sea level. When engineering pilot plants now in operation and others being developed demonstrate that desalinization, power, and pumping phases for a co-ordinated continental desalinization and

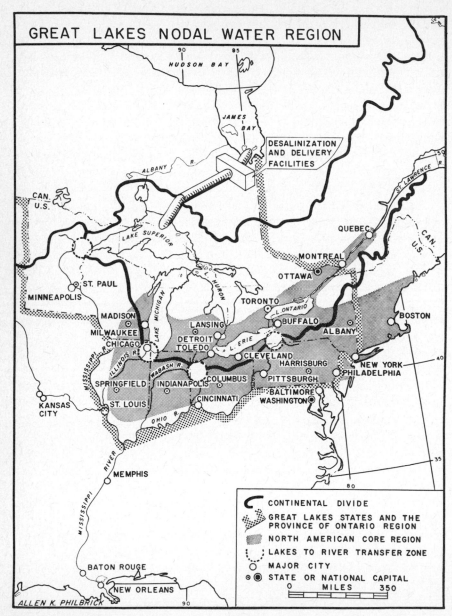

Figure 1. Great Lakes Nodal Water Region.

water delivery system are economically competitive, a programme for such a large-scale man-operated hydrologic cycle should be ready for construction and operation.

The choice of James Bay and Lake Superior as the salt water source and reservoir of initial storage, respectively, for such a system is geographically logical from many viewpoints. Each point in the following summary should be considered in relation to the map in Figure 1; and it should be understood that their combined significance is multiple rather than additive.

(1) *Storage.* From Lake Superior water can flow eastward by gravity throughout the system.

(2) *Salt.* Salt from demineralized seawater may be returned to the sea, stored as sludge for final evaporation in the processing of by-product minerals and chemicals, or used as a basis for storing fissionable wastes.

(3) *Access.* Including the St. Lawrence River to the Lambert Locks at Montreal, water users have access to supply from 10,000 miles (16,093 km.) of fresh water coast, divided approximately evenly between the United States and Canada. The region thus served is the industrial heart and the greatest nodal regional market for water on the continent.

(4) *Access.* Because of the circumstances of glacial origins in the formation of the Great Lakes-St. Lawrence drainage system, there are many widely distributed points of near contact between the lakes and the outstretched headwaters of the Mississippi's dendritic drainage pattern. By short siphon-pumping transfers at many points, fresh water could be made available to downstream communities in controlled amounts all along the major Mississippi tributaries.

(5) *Power.* Power derived from the head of water stored at various points down-river could, within a co-ordinated international system, at least reduce costs of original pumping of desalinized water into Lake Superior.

(6) *Evaporation control.* Winter storage of desalinized water production during late summer and fall would minimize evaporation loss, because much of the lake area is roofed by ice during the winter.

(7) *Seasonality.* Conversely, heavy withdrawal during early spring would correspond with the season of greatest natural re-supply from run-off. Varying degrees of seasonal and regional co-ordination of production, delivery, storage, and consumption are possible within an international nodal system serving half a continent.

(8) *Silting.* Silting, which plagues builders of reservoirs within river basins because of upstream erosion, would not represent a

major inherent difficulty in using the Great Lakes as a continental reservoir supplied in this manner. The savings through avoidance of eventual reservoir reconstructions costs would be very large.

(9) *Balance*. Uncontrolled use of surface and ground waters under present and probable future demands promises increasingly to upset the balance of nature. Implementation of a more positive policy of water production by man-made and operated hydrologic cycles will create the opportunities for people to restore and to stabilize such balance as investment in the natural "water bank" for any dry day in the future.

(10) *Cost*. A policy of scarcity ensures disagreement over rights and privileges of water use. Controlled-production water policy provides the basis for enlightened international agreement and a wise division of responsibility within a co-ordinated system. Under such a system, the only limitation on water withdrawal would be the willingness to pay a reasonable cost of guaranteed water replacement. As already indicated, responsible estimates of future costs of as little as five cents per thousand gallons and cheap electricity into the bargain have been made by the Atomic Energy Commission. Even if one doubles this figure to ten cents and redoubles it to pay power and financing costs of mass water production, it is reasonable to predict on a long-range pay-as-you-go basis the doubling of the region's annual water supply for twenty cents per thousand gallons.

To treat water as a mineral to be mined, beneficiated, and delivered through use of existing lakes and rivers, by the construction of a minimum of concentrated engineering facilities, to provide an absolute increase in fresh water available for industrial, agricultural, domestic, municipal, and all other purposes *is* a revolutionary idea. Its full impact can be appreciated only when the manner in which its multiple advantages reinforce one another is understood. This can best be appreciated by viewing the spatial association of the variables as outlined above in this article in applied cultural geography emphasizing the role of innovative perception.

From the sea around us water seems as universal as the world ocean. But the mathematics of optimum location and the significance of geographical position of supply and demand gives to *human perception* the opportunity to plan and execute a programme of water development which will give an entirely new and more positive direction to future water policy in North America and the world.

20

Alberta and The Prairie Provinces Water Board

S. Raby

The surface water supplies of the Saskatchewan-Nelson River
Basin are playing an increasingly critical rôle in the expansion of
the Prairie economy. As investment in the development of these
resources should be designed to achieve maximum social satisfactions, comprehensive, integrated policies are taken to be a necessary prerequisite for the successful management of these waters.
Unfortunately, many deficiencies and shortcomings persist in their
present administration which severely restrict implementation of a
satisfactory programme. Assuming that this framework cannot be
made to cope successfully with such objectives, it is desirable to
find institutional alternatives which would serve as vehicles to
plan and implement efficient development in the best possible way
within a meaningful unit.[1] As a preliminary step, there is an urgent
need for a survey of the existing physical, economic, and social
conditions in order to allow the established Prairie Provinces Water
Board to carry out its stated objectives, and to help determine an
areal framework of authority which would be both effective and
reasonably tolerable to the interests involved.

Reprinted from *Canadian Geographer*, Vol. VIII, no. 2 (1964), pp. 85-91.

[1] Though emphasis is here laid upon federal-interprovincial relations, such
comment is pertinent to water resource allocation in general. See, for
example, M. M. Gaffney, *Comparison of Market Pricing and Other Means of
Allocating Water Resources*, Paper presented to the Southeastern Water
Law Conference (unpublished ms.) (Athens, November 9, 1961).

Integrated River Basin Development

Defined as "the orderly marshalling of water resources of river basins for multiple purposes to promote human welfare,"[2] integrated river basin development has become a major tool in the task of making optimum use of the world's water resources. The need for it stems from the complex relationship between the availability of water and its possible uses in the various parts of a drainage basin. Maximization of net benefits demands at least the broad outlines of a basin plan, for "integrated river basin development with the aim stated involves the coordinated and harmonious development of the various works in relation to all the reasonable possibilities of the river basin."[3]

Both comprehensive and allied multiple-purpose development are essential concepts in this integrated approach.[4] Even if the former is thought premature but conceded as desirable on a long-term basis, several problems immediately arise. These include such questions as the protection of reservoir and dam sites, improved basic data coverage (an essential factor in the realization of scale economies), experiments and innovations in development procedure, and the allocation of management and research functions. It is conceivable that, on the basis of experience in the United States, the federal interest might be restricted to basin-wide stream regulation, leadership in research, pilot plant experimentation, and other technical activities. In the adoption of comprehensive policies, several major difficulties have to be faced, namely, the variety of purposes to be considered, the modification of deeply embedded policies and institutions, and the rapidity of social and technological change.

In the light of these observations, the Saskatchewan-Nelson River Basin should be examined to find out what benefits would accrue from treating it as a suitable planning unit, and also the processes by which such planning might be accomplished. Here, the successes achieved by the United States in the application of integrated multiple-purpose design and management deserve apprecia-

---

[2] United Nations Organization, *Integrated River Basin Development* (New York, Department of Economic and Social Affairs, 1958), p. 1.
[3] *Ibid.*
[4] Askerman defines comprehensive development as the application of integrated multiple-purpose design, planning, and management which include joint consideration of ground and surface waters, conservational and other measures for "engineering" of demand, and the treatment and management of waters having substandard quality. (United States Senate Select Committee on National Water Resources, *The Impact of New Techniques on Integrated Multiple-Purpose Water Development* (Washington, Committee Print no. 31, 1960), p. 2.

tion. With the swing away from single water services, development efforts become increasingly focused upon river basins, and what has been termed the "river basin problem" has arisen.[5] This refers to conflicts that occur when attempts are made to organize multiple-purpose resource development on the basis of valley regions. However, as Craine has emphasized, "the solution is not to be found in the independence of the river basin but rather in setting up channels of inter-action between river basin development and other related aspects of human affairs."[6]

Although the whole Saskatchewan-Nelson Basin might be difficult to comprehend and to deal with effectively through a single organization, if it is not so managed then how can the individual planning units be co-ordinated; how can significant spill-over effects be internalized and net benefits maximized for a given investment? In a paper to the annual general meeting of the Engineering Institute of Canada fifteen years ago, Manitoba's Deputy Minister of Mines and Resources commented that the co-ordinated development of the water and related resources of the Saskatchewan River system represents "one of the most important and one of the most complex problems in the field of resources development with which Canada is faced today."[7]

The Present Institutional Framework

The existing basis for water resource management in the basin derives from two fundamental and inter-connected developments: the interpretation by the courts of the British North America Act and the proliferation of agencies and policies directly involved in this particular field. Under the act, responsibility for administration and control of resources devolved upon the respective provinces, with the exception of several facets placed under federal or joint interest. The Dominion acquired exclusive jurisdiction to legislate for the peace, order, and good government of Canada, and for the regulation of trade and commerce, navigation and shipping, seacoast and inland fisheries, and inter-provincial and international transportation systems. Further, it may theoretically gain exclusive jurisdiction over local works by declaring them to be for the general interest of Canada or two or more provinces. Of especial importance

---

5 L. E. Craine, "Lead-off Speech, River Valley Regions Workshop A: The Scope for Multiple Resource Development Within River Basin Regions", *Proceedings of Resources for Tomorrow Conference (Montreal, 1961)* (Ottawa, Queen's Printer, 1962), p. 324.
6 *Ibid.*
7 D. M. Stephens, "The Saskatchewan River and Manitoba's Water Problem", *Eng. Journal,* Vol. XXXI, no. 9 (September 1948), p. 471.

is federal spending power which enables a measure of indirect regulation through conditional grants. Although the Dominion and the several provinces have concurrent powers relative to agriculture, the primacy of the provinces regarding water resources derives from their being given jurisdiction over property and civil rights, matters of a local and private nature, and local works and undertakings.[8] As Laskin has shown, even where federal power appears exclusive, complementary provincial powers and interests exist.[9]

There is serious confusion on the question of allocation of interprovincial waters, and it is difficult to see how far United States' precedents are applicable, especially because there is, in practice, no equivalent to the Supreme Court. Provisions exist for such a development, but pending action under the Exchequer Court Act there is no way for a province to bring another province or the federal government to court. This body of law undoubtedly comprises a perplexing obstacle which must be accommodated in the provision of an administrative scheme capable of encouraging a comprehensive, regional approach to water resource planning and development.

The administrative framework for water resource management is characterized by a wide array of institutions and policies on private, provincial, and federal levels, many with interests in planning and development. Each of these interest groups has its own particular economic and social objectives, must subserve particular legal restraints, and must respect its individual economic limitations. Co-ordination within either the federal or the provincial network appears weak, and there is a lack of clearly defined responsibilities among the various levels of government. There is also a lack of lucid resource development policies. As is shown below in discussion of the South Saskatchewan Project and the Prairie Provinces Water Board, a major obstacle is the tendency of the provinces to assert their sovereign "rights" over the administration and development of natural resources present within their boundaries to the deterrence of necessary overriding controls or effective national leadership. (Here it is assumed that such controls and leadership merit respect in lacking partiality and seeking honourable ends.)

Discussion of the need for a re-appraisal of water resource development in the Saskatchewan-Nelson River Basin can be framed

---

[8] See T. M. Patterson, "Administrative Framework for Water Management", *Resources for Tomorrow, Conference Background Papers*, Vol. 1 (Ottawa, Queen's Printer, 1961), pp. 227-248.
[9] B. Laskin, "Jurisdictional Framework for Water Management", *ibid.*, pp. 211-225.

within two major considerations, one concerned with past experience, the other with potential requirements for suitable management criteria. Out of the fractious debates regarding the South Saskatchewan Project and subsequent postures adopted by the respective governments emerges some pertinent comment upon the status of the Prairie Provinces Water Board and the attitudes of those governments to integrated development of the whole basin.

The Prairie Provinces Water Board

The Prairie Provinces Water Board was set up by an agreement signed in July 1948 between the governments of Canada, Manitoba, Saskatchewan, and Alberta. An inter-provincial Western Water Board had been formed 2½ years prior to this agreement without Federal participation, its main purpose being to make a comprehensive overall study of the basin in co-operation with Dominion government departments. The Canadian Minister of Resources and Development then stated that the Dominion government would step out of the irrigation picture, and according to opposition members the situation provided an excuse for his backing down upon extensive western commitments. Consequently, the provinces sought the formation of a new board.

Of particular interest are the Prairie Provinces Water Board's functions and duties as defined in the agreement. Under the former, the board was

> to recommend the best use to be made of interprovincial waters in relation to associated resources in Manitoba, Saskatchewan and Alberta and to recommend the allocation of water as between each such province of streams flowing from one province into another province.

The Board's duties were

> (a) to collate and analyze the data now available relating to the water and associated resources of interprovincial streams with respect to their utilization for irrigation, drainage, storage, power, industrial, municipal, navigation and other purposes; (b) to determine what other data are required from time to time in order to reach decisions on questions referred to it and to make recommendations to the appropriate governmental organizations concerned for the carrying out of (studies) . . . which the Board considers necessary to supply information required for the proper performance of its duties; (c) upon the request of any one of the three provinces or the Dominion to recommend the allocation of the waters of any interprovincial stream among the respective provinces; (d) to report on any questions relating to specific projects for the utilization or control of common river or lake systems at the request of one or

more of the Ministers or authorities charged with the administration of such river or lake systems.[10]

Although the Board has performed a useful function in providing a forum for discussion, in preparing several valuable reports, and in allocating common waters, it possesses only advisory powers. Its recommendations with respect to any matters referred to under subsections (c) and (d) quoted above become effective only when adopted by orders in council passed by Canada and by each of the affected provinces.

Alberta and the South Saskatchewan Project

Considerable perplexity faced the board at a meeting that was held in September 1951 to discuss a second application by the government of Saskatchewan for an allocation of almost one million acre-feet of water annually for use in the South Saskatchewan Project, a multiple-purpose scheme lying wholly within Saskatchewan. The representative from Alberta created procedural difficulties by submitting that an alternative joint Alberta-Saskatchewan project making use of Red Deer and diverted North Saskatchewan River waters should be studied by the board before he would vote for a permanent allocation. He argued that as a board member he was carrying out the function of the board in determining the best use of the water.[11] An interesting altercation followed. The chairman stated that the matter of invesigating this alternate project was one of government policy and that the extent of further investigations would have to be determined because there was no official request from the Alberta government to have the combined project investigated to its ultimate conclusion.

Instead of pressing for an over-all basin survey under its own auspices, the board at that time agreed to a further two-year "reservation" and awaited the then forthcoming report of the Royal Commission on the South Saskatchewan to provide evidence to guide its eventual decision. It is curious that, although this suggestion was made to the board by Alberta's representative, that province's submission to the commission in the following year maintained that such investigations should be initiated by the Prairie Provinces Water Board itself.

The commission's terms of reference were to investigate and report upon two issues. First, it was asked to ascertain whether the economic and social returns to the Canadian people on the invest-

---

10 Quoted in Royal Commission on the South Saskatchewan Project, *Report* (Ottawa, Queen's Printer, 1952), pp. 422-423.
11 *Ibid.*, pp. 420-421.

ment in the proposed South Saskatchewan River Project would be commensurate with its cost, and, secondly, it was to decide whether the project represented the most profitable and desirable use which could be made of the physical resources involved.[12] Unfortunately, although these were reasonably comprehensive assignments, they were not wholly relevant to the board's problem, and, further, the commission itself investigated them only in a rather limited fashion. In finding that the present economic returns on the investment in the project were incommensurate with its cost, the commission recommended "that without delay a comprehensive, long-range program be developed that would result, over the years, in the most beneficial use being made in the interests of the people of Canada of the waters of the Saskatchewan River from the headwaters to the sea [sic]."[13]

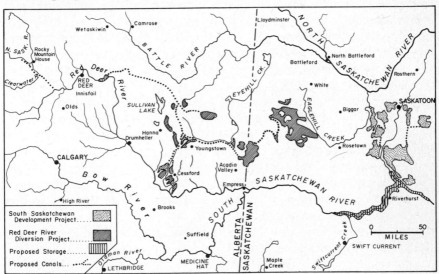

Figure 1. Location of the South Saskatchewan Development and Red River Diversion Projects (1952 plans).

Alberta's viewpoint was that the two projects involved should be considered on their merits and not from any provincial standpoint. This attitude was shared, to some extent, by the commission which, in making a negative answer to the second question above, recommended that further study be given to the merits of the William Pearce Scheme (North Saskatchewan River Diversion Project). This alternative had the advantage of leaving unappropriated

12 *Ibid.*, p. xi.
13 *Ibid.*, p. 7.

South Saskatchewan water available for future use in Alberta in that only Red Deer and diverted North Saskatchewan system supplies would be used in the irrigation of 500,000 acres in the Youngstown and Cessford areas of Alberta and of some 200,000 acres in the Kindersley-Kerrobert-Rosetown districts of Saskatchewan.

The Provincial Case

In the same year as the board was set up, Burfield of Alberta's Water Resources Branch made note that diversion of water is necessarily subservient to the division of federal aid, and that allocation of funds tends to be by provinces rather than by projects.[14] Alberta's participation in the water board, though tardy, was based upon at least some appreciation of the need to treat the basin as a whole to the best use of available water supplies "in so far as possible by regions in the drainage basin rather than by provinces."[15] However, alarm was soon expressed at the apparent trend in board policy to respect the claims of individual provinces ahead of other considerations. These fears were only reinforced by the reversal of the commission's proposals on the South Saskatchewan Project by the Diefenbaker government in July 1958 when, it was contended, no sufficient justification had been set out for deciding financial allocations between that and the William Pearce Scheme.[16]

It should be noted that disapproval of the commission's findings soon after their publication had been strongly expressed by the then Liberal federal government and also by members of the Prairie Farm Rehabilitation Administration. Ironically, Alberta's support for its own suggested project had been stigmatized as "provincial in outlook" in the Saskatchewan submission to the Royal Commission. The same document pleads that "Saskatchewan has been largely by-passed in federal resource development programmes since the early days of its settlement despite its wealth of undeveloped resources and actual known projects awaiting development. . . . It would not only be unjust to Saskatchewan but detrimental to the nation if part of the waters of this great river were not utilized in the Province of Saskatchewan."[17] Were, in fact, the interests of

---

[14] F. R. Burfield, "Discussion of Prairie Water Problems", *Eng. Journal*, Vol. XXXI, no. 12 (December 1948), p. 648.

[15] Letter from B. Russell, Alberta Director of Water Resources, to L. B. Thomson, P.F.R.A., Director of Rehabilitation (February 14, 1950).

[16] A brief outline of the agreement made between the Saskatchewan and Canadian governments and of subsequent developments is included in South Saskatchewan River Development Commission, *South Saskatchewan River Development Project, Progress Report for 1961* (Regina, 1962).

[17] Government of Saskatchewan, *Submissions of the Province of Saskatchewan to the Royal Commission on the South Saskatchewan Project* (Regina, 1952), pp. 32, 95.

maximum social welfare as they appeared at that time being sacrificed to the doctrine of equitable apportionment? Here, Saskatchewan's case partially rests upon the dubious premise that to stabilize all parts of the nation is the same as the most profitable and desirable use of the physical resources involved. Attention is drawn to a persuasive document produced by the Saskatchewan government in reply to the commission's findings, which were said to conflict with "the seemingly overwhelming economic, social and political evidence in favour of the (South Saskatchewan River) project" and to be built upon "an argument replete with gross exaggerations on the cost side and with gross understatements on the benefit side and confounded with a multitude of 'blind alleys' of alternative resource uses, none of which have any basis in fact."[18]

Had the Prairie Provinces Water Board by that time been in a position to present a scheme for the best use of investment in developing the water resources of the basin and thus dispel any feelings of partiality, the subsequent decisive rupture might have been avoided. The board was unfortunately not in agreement even regarding whether or not it should consider the economic factors involved in a given project, and these projects were discussed with but little reference to the general requirements for water and other resource development in the prairies as a whole, or to the interests of Canada.

The 1958 decision by the federal government was undoubtedly a critical factor in strengthening the attitude taken by the Alberta government to the work and objectives of the board. Alberta's intransigence has since become a major stumbling block in attempts to motivate a detailed river basin study of the type outlined by Durrant in 1960.[19] Effective discharge of the board's duties assuming their reasonable interpretation, which were assented to by all four governments concerned, would appear impossible given the current lack of basic information dealing with the economic and social significance of water resource development in relation to human activities and needs. If provincialism is to function as a veto even to this preparatory work by such an impotent body, then the possibility of transferring power to a basin authority seems not a little remote.

---

[18] Government of Saskatchewan, *Saskatchewan Replies to the Royal Commission on the South Saskatchewan River Development Project* (Regina, 1953), pp. 2, 7.

[19] E. F. Durrant, *Preliminary Report on an Integrated Basin Plan for the Saskatchewan River Basin and the Nelson River* (Regina, Prairie Provinces Water Board, 1960).

The Present Dilemma

Alberta is not dependent upon the other two prairie provinces for its water supplies and has been inclined to adopt a somewhat patronizing attitude towards involvement in basin-wide activities. For example, this strategic advantage has been used to assert the primacy of irrigational water-use by hostility towards firm allocations of water for power purposes downstream, even though such developments might acquire a legal basis in primacy of use of supplies. Of interest is Alberta's view that the best or most economical and beneficial uses of the water supplies of the Saskatchewan River drainage basin (so far as irrigation and water power development are concerned) occur in the basin's foothills reaches, and, as that province's submission points out, "this foothill region happens to be in the province of Alberta."[20]

This ardent provincialism found expression in two statements by the head of the Engineering Division of Alberta's Water Resources Branch. Speaking at a Western Canada Reclamation Association Conference in the fall of 1962, he said that

> Alberta . . . , although interested in an integrated basin plan, would certainly oppose any suggestion of any sort of inter-basin or interprovincial authority on the administration of the Nelson-Saskatchewan Basin. We feel that the development of the water resources, or any resources for that matter, should be retained by the provinces. . . . It seems that the policy of the [Alberta] government at the moment is not to become too involved or tied down too much to an integrated basin plan. Perhaps it is due to a feeling of reluctance . . . to commit themselves to abiding by the findings of the study in the event that they might not just agree wholeheartedly with what has been proposed.[21]

In its submission to the 1952 Royal Commission, Alberta had argued that it would be difficult to administer the water resources of the basin properly without a single administrative authority in charge.[22]

Unless a basin authority is able to enforce its decisions, these will be left to the whim of political forces in Ottawa, the ultimate authority in that only they have access to the necessary financial resources. The provinces' distrust of such forces is understandable in the light of past experience. Hence there has arisen the current

---

[20] Royal Commission on the South Saskatchewan Project, p. 405.
[21] *Western Canada Reclamation* (Redcliff, Western Canada Reclamation Association, November 1962), pp. 4, 6.
[22] Royal Commission on the South Saskatchewan Project, p. 405.

dilemma in which discussion of means to improve federal-interprovincial arrangements may be only of academic interest.

Cass-Beggs of the Saskatchewan Power Corporation has set out a provincial solution, and argues for separate provincial development, provided that it is possible to develop an adequate authority for allocation of water for consumptive use and provided such applications can be made at an early date and can be adequately policed and maintained into the future.[23] It is contended that provision of suitable finances on some equitable basis to the three provinces, together with a limited degree of interprovincial action are all that is needed for satisfactory water development in the basin. Past experience of water resource management by the provinces and the observations made above leave one a little disconcerted with this solution .

Prospect

The *volte face* by the government of Alberta away from its initial guarded enthusiasm for integrated development may derive in part from resentment that federal funds were not made available to the dominantly Albertan William Pearce Scheme rather than to the South Saskatchewan Project, but it does show that the Prairie Provinces Water Board is in no position to carry out its stated objectives, limited as they are, and, further, that a commission administration, let alone a regional basin authority, would have to overcome serious obstacles before being granted legality within the existing permissive legislation. First, the major interested parties must set about to discover the extent to which they have common interests that could be advanced by comprehensive planned development of the water resources within the basin.

---

[23] D. Cass-Beggs, "Panel Speech, Water Workshop A: Organizing for Multi-Purpose Development in River Basins", *Proceedings of Resources for Tomorrow Conference (Montreal, 1961)* (Ottawa, Queen's Printer, 1962), pp. 135-137.

21

Multiple Purpose Land and Water Districts in Ontario

E. G. Pleva

In many characteristics of soils, climate, and population, Southern Ontario, the area with which we are primarily concerned here, has much in common with neighboring sections of the United States. Most of our problems, no less than our accomplishments and opportunities, will be familiar to readers south of the U.S.-Canadian border.

Southern Ontario has flood hazards and local difficulties with water supply, soil erosion, needs for farm drainage and for reforestation; rapid growth of its cities accentuates demands for outdoor recreation and creates difficulties of land use on the rural-urban fringe. Nearly all of the land is in private ownership, much of it in farms. Relationships between government and the individual are central to a diversity of programs of financial or technical assistance to landowners.

There is little that is unique, then, in Southern Ontario's problems of land and water development or in the physical techniques of dealing with them. Much more distinctive, I believe, is the multiple purpose land and water resources district as a device for carrying out a coherent set of programs that draw upon the ex-

Reprinted from *Comparisons in Resource Management, Six Notable Programs in Other Countries and Their Possible U.S. Application*, Resources for the Future Inc. (Johns Hopkins Press, Baltimore, 1961), pp. 190-207.

perience and skills of several departments of the provincial government. For those reasons I shall devote most of this essay to an account of the structure and functions — the formalities, if you will — of Ontario's multiple purpose local Conservation Authorities and an examination of the Conservation Authorities Act under which they were established and are operating. It will be useful, however, to begin with a glance at Southern Ontario as a whole, as the geographical background of these activities, and to close with a brief sketch of other legislation that bears on present and prospective land and water programs under the Conservation Authorities Act.

Ontario, the central province of Canada, lies near the economic heart of North America. Its southern border adjoins a populous and highly industrialized area of the United States.

Ontario, with a total area of 412,562 square miles (80 per cent of which is land), is Canada's second largest province. It is half again as large as Texas and nearly five times the size of Great Britain. It accounts for one-half of the country's industrial output and one-third of her population — about 6 million out of a total of 18 million people. Ontario is heavily urbanized and predominately English-speaking, although there are important pockets of French-speaking population in the northern and eastern sections. More than any other part of Canada, southern Ontario resembles the major northern and midwestern areas of the United States.

The province is made up of two dissimilar areas of unequal size — northern and southern Ontario; the natural division between the two sections occurs where the French River, Lake Nipissing, and the Mattawa River cut across a relatively narrow extent of land between Georgian Bay and the Ottawa River.

Northern Ontario has 93 per cent of the province's total area and 12 per cent of its population. It is in general a land of potential and actual mineral, forest, and recreational wealth. A rigorous climate, rocky terrain, and scarcity of agricultural soil combine to preclude agriculture throughout most of the area. The great bulk of the land is still in public ownership, consisting for the most part of Crown lands administered by the provincial government.

The southern section, with about 29,000 square miles and more than 5 million people, contains only 7 per cent of the area of Ontario but 88 per cent of the total population. It is in the main an area of level to undulating sand and clay plains and rolling hills, and it has a climate suitable for agriculture. Nearly all of the land is privately owned. At present about 80 per cent of the people of southern

Ontario live in cities or towns of more than 5,000. The remainder is divided about equally between farm and rural nonfarm families. And the towns and cities still are growing fast. In another decade the problem of fringe development may well have spread over nearly all of the area. It is almost entirely in southern Ontario that work under the Conservation Authorities Act is being carried out.

The operation of multiple-purpose land and water resources districts in Ontario is related to the Conservation Authorities Act, passed by the Ontario Legislature in the early part of 1946.

The Conservation Authorities Act permits the local municipalities within a drainage basin to organize as an Authority for purposes of flood control, reforestation, land-use programs, fish and wildlife management, farm ponds construction, wet lands programs, and any other scheme related to the conservation of natural resources within a drainage basin. In Ontario, a municipality is, by definition, a city, town, rural township, or county. The municipality, in effect, is the unit of local government. Under this system we have found that rural interests, on whose lands many of the programs are actually carried out, are quite adequately represented.

The first step toward setting up a Conservation Authority must be taken by the municipalities wholly or partially within a watershed. Although the initiative for organizing the Authority must come from the local municipalities, the Act sets out clearly the provincial responsibility at the organizational and subsequent stages.

The process of organization is relatively simple. Two local municipalities within a given watershed must first by resolution petition the Minister of Commerce and Development to call a meeting to determine whether an Authority should be established. The Minister then sets the time and place of the organizational meeting, to which representatives from all the municipalities are invited. The representation is on a population base, as follows: municipalities below 10,000, one representative; over 10,000 but not over 50,000, two; over 50,000 but not over 100,000, three; over 100,000 but not over 250,000, four; over 250,000, five. Two-thirds of the representatives must be present to make the meeting legal.

At the organization meeting, the legislation is explained and the merits and limitations of the proposed Authority are discussed. Finally the vote is taken and if two-thirds of those present are in favor, a resolution is sent to the Minister asking that an Authority be established. The Authority is made legal by an Order-in-Council and under the Conservation Authorities Act becomes a body corporate with representatives from all the municipalities within the

watershed or drainage basin. The membership includes those municipalities which voted against its establishment as well as those
municipalities which may have abstained from voting or were
absent at the organization meeting. In brief, membership by the
municipalities in the watershed is total and complete.

The establishing of an Authority is, then, a simple legal matter.
Since the Act was first passed in 1946 not one request for establishing an Authority has been refused.

At the beginning of 1961 there were thirty Authorities in Ontario. (Figure 1.) Together, they covered an area of 19,671 square
miles. Total membership of 695 included 434 different municipalities. The number of members from a given municipality is based on
the same population formula as for representation at the organization meeting. In one district—the Grand River—there also is a
Commission, which antedates the Authorities Act and continues to
carry out responsibility for flood control.

The Authorities vary greatly in size from one with an area of
86 square miles and 8 members to one with an area of 2,614 square
miles and 78 members.

The powers of an Authority as set forth in Section 15 of the Act
are as follows:

> To study and investigate the watershed itself or by its engi-
> neers or other employees or representatives, and to determine a
> scheme whereby the natural resources of the watershed may be
> conserved, restored and developed and the waters controlled in
> order to prevent floods and pollution or any of such matters; sub-
> ject to the Lakes and Rivers Improvement Act, to erect works
> and structures and create reservoirs by the construction of dams
> or otherwise; to purchase or acquire and without the consent of
> the owner enter upon, take and expropriate any land which it
> may require and sell or otherwise deal with such land or other
> property; to purchase or acquire any personal property which it
> may require and sell or otherwise deal therewith; to enter into
> such agreements for the purchase of materials, employment of
> labor and such other purposes as may be necessary for the due
> carrying out of any scheme; to enter into agreements with
> owners of private lands to facilitate the due carrying out of any
> scheme or conservation project; to determine the proportion of the
> total benefit afforded to all the participating municipalities which
> is afforded to each of them; to use lands which are owned or con-
> trolled by the authority for such purposes, not inconsistent with
> its objects, as it deems proper; to acquire lands, with the approval

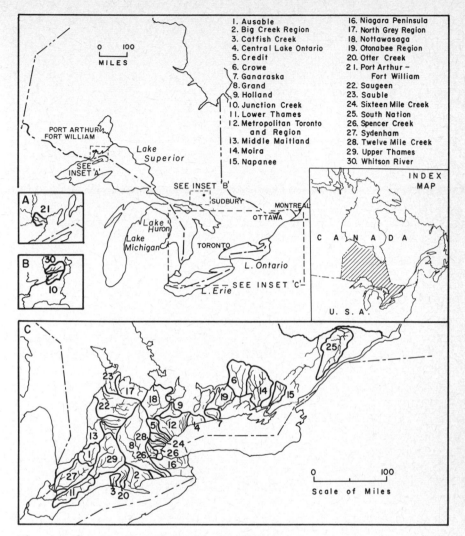

1. Ausable
2. Big Creek Region
3. Catfish Creek
4. Central Lake Ontario
5. Credit
6. Crowe
7. Ganaraska
8. Grand
9. Holland
10. Junction Creek
11. Lower Thames
12. Metropolitan Toronto and Region
13. Middle Maitland
14. Moira
15. Napanee
16. Niagara Peninsula
17. North Grey Region
18. Nottawasaga
19. Otonabee Region
20. Otter Creek
21. Port Arthur – Fort William
22. Saugeen
23. Sauble
24. Sixteen Mile Creek
25. South Nation
26. Spencer Creek
27. Sydenham
28. Twelve Mile Creek
29. Upper Thames
30. Whitson River

Figure 1. Conservation Authorities in Ontario.

of the Minister, and to use lands acquired in connection with a scheme, for recreation purposes, and to erect, or permit to be erected, buildings, booths and facilities for such purposes and to make charges for admission thereto and the use thereof; to collaborate with departments and agencies of government, municipal councils and local boards, and other organizations; to plant and produce trees on public lands with the consent of the Minister of Lands and Forests, and on private lands with the consent of the owner, for any purpose; to cause research to be done;

generally to do all such acts as are necessary for the due carrying out of any scheme.

Surveys and Reports. The early Authorities set up in Ontario were brought into existence because of the recurring threat of flooding. However, all Authorities are aware of the necessity of comprehensive and integrated measures in a regional conservation program. The Authorities themselves were not staffed or equipped to carry out the necessary studies in land use, reforestation, woodlot management, pollution control, water supply, fish and wildlife, and recreation. The Ontario Department of Commerce and Development, through the Conservation Branch, carries out at no expense to the Authority the necessary preliminary surveys and investigations. The technical staff of the Conservation Branch then appraises the conservation needs of each drainage basin or watershed. Finally a detailed report is submitted to each Authority outlining the Conservation measures that should be followed.

The report is in the form of a working plan and is intended primarily for Authority members. The full report tends to be a rather bulky document since it contains fairly detailed information on the watershed. A typical report for one of the larger watersheds runs to 600 pages, 100 maps and charts, 150 pictures, and 75 specific and detailed recommendations. In addition to the full report, a summary report in printed form is issued for general distribution throughout the watershed and is especially valuable for the schoolteachers. Every schoolroom has a copy of the local survey on its reference shelf.

The full report is based on survey work and is written up under six general headings: History, Land Use, Forestry, Water, Wildlife, and Recreation. The scope of the studies varies with the conditions and needs of the area investigated. The findings reported to the Authority have direct application to the problems the Authority must face and solve.

History: A background of history is necessary to give the proper perspective to immediate problems. The residents of the watershed must have as localized a picture of past conditions as possible. The historical approach often promotes an interest in conservation among people who would otherwise be indifferent.

Land Use: The relations between soil, forestry, agriculture, and water are carefully studied. All available information dealing with this relationship within the watershed is drawn together. Soil surveys by the Soils Department of the Ontario Agricultural College and physiography studies by the Ontario Research Foundation provide the basis for detailed field work and aerial photograph inter-pretation.

Forestry: The condition and extent of the original forest, the history of the wood-using industries, the conservation measures in progress, the inventory of existing forestry resources, and the recommendations for future conservation measures make up the forestry section.

Water: A careful examination is made of all hydrometric and meteorological records for the watershed. Much attention is given to flood records. A careful hydrology survey indicates the number, size, and location of reservoirs needed to control floods and to regu-late summer flow. The survey includes a mapping and examination of all lakes, ponds and old mill dams.

Wildlife: General inventories are made of all species of wildlife, both game and non-game. Special emphasis is given to vanishing or threatened species. Streams are classified for fish management.

Recreation: The present and projected future populations of the area are studied and the facilities needed now and in the future are estimated and described.

A survey of a given watershed may take several years to make. The field work is done largely during the summer months when students from the universities carry out the investigations under the direction of the provincial scientists and technicians. A typical sur-vey may give professional training and summer employment to thirty students.

The Authority, when presented with the report, must assume responsibility for undertaking the schemes recommended. The Authority usually initiates action on those projects it considers most urgent; in some cases, however, the Authority may take many years before starting on any part of the program. The legislation through-out is permissive, and even after an Authority has been set up, the carrying out of the program depends on the favourable action of the Authority.

Operation and Financing. If one or more schemes have been ap-proved by an Authority, it becomes the Authority's responsibility to make approaches to the government departments or other bodies from which it requires assistance, whether financial, technical, or otherwise. A land-use program would involve the assistance of the Department of Agriculture; a forestry or wildlife program, the Department of Lands and Forests; a flood-control project, the serv-ices of an engineer accredited by the Department of Commerce and Development and the Department of Public Works, who does the engineering and designing up the point of calling for tenders and carrying the work through to completion of the structures. The Authorities, that is, are not staffed for specialized conservation work. Neither is the Conservation Branch of the Ontario Department of Commerce and Development which works most closely with them. But the technical assistance of the operating departments is available to the Authorities, and they use it.

The financing provisions of the Conservation Authorities Act recognize three classes of expenditure. The first is related to capital expenses such as dams, reservoirs, reforestation land, and conservation areas such as parks and floodways. The Authority's share of payment for capital expenses is borne by the member municipalities which benefit from the scheme, on the basis of a fixed percentage of estimated benefits. A second class of cost is related to the maintenance on capital projects and is paid entirely by the Authority in the same way. A third class relates to administration costs and includes all the things an Authority might be expected to do that do not fall into the categories of capital or maintenance costs. The Authority meets its share of these costs by charging the municipalities proportional shares based on the assessment of lands within the drainage basin. Administration costs include salaries, office rent and equipment, tree-planting and other portable conservation machinery, exhibits, audio-visual materials, continuing investigations of farm ponds, reforestation lands, and other small conservation projects, printed material and traveling expenses.

Grants are made by the Ontario government for the first and third classes: capital expenses and administration costs. Grants have not been made so far for maintenance of capital projects. Grants are a matter of policy and may change from year to year. At the present time the grants from the Ontario government for each of the following is 50 per cent: a flood control scheme costing less than $5 million, a large-scale reforestation land purchase, a conservation area in which a park is located, the acquisition of flood-plain lands, and all items included under administration costs.

A flood-control scheme which costs more than $5 million is eligible for a $37\frac{1}{2}$ per cent contribution of the Government of Canada under The Canada Water Conservation Assistance Act. The Province of Ontario contributes an additional $37\frac{1}{2}$ per cent of the cost, leaving the Authority with a 25 per cent responsibility.

Receipts coming to the Authority from nontax or non-governmental sources, such as camping fees or boat rentals, are used for the development and expansion of the general progress of the

Authority. Receipts coming from the municipalities are raised by taxation and show clearly in the mill-rate levy on every land-owner's tax bill. Each municipality collects and turns over to the Authority the amount of money represented in its levy. Grants of the senior levels of government are paid to the Authority and do not go through the treasuries of the member municipalities.

Even so brief a review as this of the cost-sharing provisions of the Act suggests four points worth noting. First, the local muni-cipalities through the Authority must initiate the programs and are responsible for a significant share of the financing. Second, the Government of Canada is under no legal obligation to assist the province in conservation work because the terms of the British North America Act of 1867 specifically place the control of natural resources under the jurisdiction of the provinces. In practice this has meant that the benefiting area must feel convinced that the project is worthwhile enough to warrant a considerable outlay of local money, and also that the case for assistance must be presented and defended adequately to warrant the expenditure of money at the higher levels of government, particularly from the Government of Canada.

Third, although the Act has plenty of teeth in it, to be used if necessary, we have thus far in practice been able to keep things from coming to the point of coercion. For instance, the law clearly provides for expropriation of land, if necessary, in carrying out an approved program. Neither the officials nor the private citizens like the word "expropriate." A few years ago, when 5,000 acres had to be acquired for the Conestogo Dam, the Authority negotiated sales with the landowners with such success that the indemnity price of only four or five out of ninety-four parcels had to go to arbitration.

Fourth, for work that benefits private land as well as contributes to an area program—like tree-planting, farm drainage, and the building of farm ponds—the farmer himself must contribute, usually through hiring labor or supplying it himself, or through buying trees that the government offers at a nominal price.

All important decisions are made by the full Authority. Many of the large Authorities have executive committees that carry out the routine work. An important feature of the Conservation Autho-rities Act is the provision for the appointment of advisory boards or committees for any subject considered necessary to the effective work of the Authority. Membership on an advisory board is not limited to members of the Authority, and consequently the people with special or technical skills in the area are put to work. Subjects dealt with by such boards or committees include: flood control, conservation, education, public relations, farm ponds and little dams, reforestation, land use, water pollution, parks and recreation, and historical sites and properties. Final decisions must always be made by the accredited members of the Authority but often it is the work of the various boards and committees that brings the meaning of conservation and land use to every person living in the drainage basin.

The Upper Thames Authority. The Upper Thames River Conservation Authority is an example of what can happen in a drainage basin under the legislation. The Authority was organized by Order-in-Council on September 18, 1947, and is one of the oldest Authorities in Ontario. (Figure 2.)

The Authority was organized primarily to develop a program of flood control on the Thames River. There has been a steady evolutionary development of the conservation idea in the watershed so that flood control today is just one aspect of an integrated river valley development program. After the provincial officers completed the survey shortly after the organization of the Authority, a series of meetings and conferences led to the first major project, the construction of Fanshawe Dam upstream from the city of London on the north branch of the Thames River. Fanshawe Dam was built with contributions from three levels of government: Canada $37\frac{1}{2}$ per cent, Ontario $37\frac{1}{2}$ per cent, and the local municipalities through the Authority 25 per cent. Fanshawe Dam, together with Fanshawe Park, have become a kind of prototype for similar projects elsewhere in Ontario. The permanent lake extends back from the dam over four miles and has a width averaging one-quarter of a mile with a total area of 650 acres. The ten miles of shoreline and 1,600 acres of fringe land owned by the Authority are available to the public for recreation. Motor boats of all types, including outboard motors, are prohibited on the lake; as a consequence the sailing of small boats, the organization of rowing clubs, and fishing have become important on Fanshawe Lake.

Most of the park acreage at Fanshawe Lake is in reforestation, nature preserve, and various development stages under the resources programs of the Authority. It is impossible to predict what future generations will need in their space requirements for outdoor recreation. The obligation of the Authority is to acquire sufficient superlative land, to establish a program of natural reconstruction, and if necessary to put the area in a kind of mothballing to await the needs of future populations. The Authority is acquiring land without trying to justify an intensive use for each square inch.

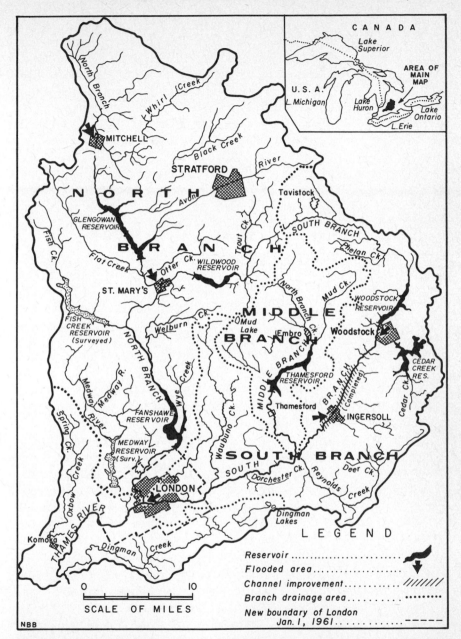

Figure 2. Upper Thames River Watershed.

The Upper Thames River Conservation Authority has undertaken many other projects besides the Fanshawe Dam as part of its blueprint of development. A number of small dams have been built, several channel improvement projects have been completed, millions of trees have been planted on public and private lands, hundreds of farm ponds have been planned, built, or subsidized on private lands, and scores of well-devised conservation education programs have been carried out. These programs included projects in pollution abatement, fish and wildlife management, land-use improvement, farm planning, soil conservation, windbreak planting, woodlot improvement, recreational land use, tours, contests, and demonstrations participated in by school children.

Representatives of the federal and provincial governments met at Fanshawe in January, 1961, to sign the agreement providing Federal aid for the construction of nearly $10 million worth of projects to complete the river valley program begun fifteen years before. The completion of the program in ten years will put the Upper Thames drainage basin under complete water management, the first drainage basin in Canada to be developed on a conservation basis. Five dams and three channel improvement schemes are included in the project. By 1970 the remedial works will control floods and increase summer flow throughout the 1,325-square-mile drainage basin.

The experience of the Upper Thames River Conservation Authority may be summarized as follows:

1. The Conservation Authorities Act is an effective body of legislation to enable the people in a drainage basin to work together for a regional conservation program.

2. It is necessary to prepare as complete a survey and plan as your financial resources permit.

3. It is imperative that the report with its recommendations be placed in the hands of the people who are most concerned specifically with the future, namely the elected and appointed officials, the teachers in the elementary and secondary schools, and the residents of the area. All means of public information and education should be used to inform the public and to earn its support.

4. The timetable of projects must be realistic. It is impossible to get public acceptance for a complete program immediately. The first project should aim at a partial solution of the major regional problem and at the same time give promise of beneficial side effects. For example, the right first project for the Upper Thames Valley was Fanshawe Dam which lessened the flood hazard at London and at the same time offered the extra dividend of an excellent recreational site for residents of the area and their visitors.

5. Research and practice will modify the long-range plan as the program is developed. The Conservation Authorities Act, when given meaning through action by an Authority operating in a watershed, is an extremely important legal device to enable the citizens to work out democratically and carry through to completion a comprehensive development program based on sound conservation theory and practice.

The Conservation Authorities Act is, as we have seen, a self-contained piece of legislation under which a wide variety of land and water programs is being carried out. In addition, however, it is related, in some instances quite closely, to three other broad lines of public action that involve planning for the future. In conclusion, let us at least mention these further elements in Ontario's long-range management of natural resources.

1. The Planning Act, first passed in 1946 and since then extensively amended, enables a municipality to establish a planning board to direct the development of the community towards socially desired goals. The Minister of Municipal Affairs may designate several municipalities or parts of municipalities as a joint planning area. This Act has proved to be effective and over two hundred planning areas in Ontario have been established under it. Chief among the several responsibilities of a planning board are to prepare the official plan for its area and to forward the proposed plan to the council of each municipality involved. When adopted, the official plan indicates the desired pattern of development, and municipal zoning by-laws must be in accord with it.

2. The Water Resources Commission Act, passed in 1957, established the Ontario Water Resources Commission to deal with the problems related to water supply and sewage disposal. The Commission has broad powers in pollution abatement. The government recognized water resources as a regional problem that must be solved on a regional, not a local basis. The legislation permits the province to enter into agreements with local municipalities or combinations of municipalities for purposes of water supply and sewage facilities. The Commission arranges the financing of the projects, builds the facilities, operates the installations, and recovers the costs from the local authorities over an extended period of time. In 1961 the Federal government enacted legislation whereby contributions may be made to the provinces for projects related to sewage disposal and pollution control. The Commission estimates that over $2.5 billion worth of projects will have been completed in the province by 1975.

3. Under the Highway Needs Program the Ontario government has prepared a twenty-year plan for highway construction. The plan, developed by the Minister of Highways and his department, has two related parts: the first deals with the provincial highway grid of major thoroughfares and the second deals with local roads and the roads and streets within the municipalities. In effect, the official plan of the province indicates the general framework of development. It will not give specific siting for a highway but will indicate clearly that a limited access dual highway shall be built between two traffic-generating areas. The local planning groups, however, are given considerable information of the evolving road pattern.

By way of example, let us glance briefly at how London, Ontario, is using the three types of program. (Because the city is located within the Upper Thames River Conservation Authority it is not necessary to make further note here of how the Conservation Authorities Act is applied in the area.) London is a central city with a population of 162,000. The area of the city was increased from 11 square miles to 67 square miles on January 1, 1961. The Ontario Municipal Board, after an extended series of hearings on the city's application to annex portions of surrounding townships, ruled that the urban area is better administered and planned as a unitary municipality including sufficient land to give complete control over the urban fringe. The official plan, drawn under the authority of the Planning Act, recognizes agriculture as a legitimate land use and makes indirect provision for its protection against the premature blighting of urbanism. For instance, to control fringe development, the minimum size of lot is 25 acres in the development zone immediately around the built-up part of the city. In the agricultural zone farther away from the city the minimum size of lot is 5 acres. The official plan also states that urban development shall take place only when municipal water supply, sanitary sewers, and complete sewage disposal are available. And then, urban development may proceed only by a registered plan of subdivision.

The city of London now has three sewage disposal plants with four in process of construction. The new plants are being built by the Ontario Water Resources Commission and will be paid for by the municipality in 35 years. At least two more disposal plants in London are in the planning stage.

Up to the present time the basal gravels have given London an excellent water supply from deep wells in and immediately around the city, but increased per capita use and an increased population indicate that alternative sources of supply must be developed. Plans being worked out by the city and Water Resources Commission call for a 50-mile pipeline from Lake Huron to supply the London area with water of unusual quality in abundance. (It is a commentary of our times that the designation "unusual quality" means simply *good* water.)

The London area has an official plan of major thoroughfares which reflects the provincial planning as applied to a locality.

Thus a given urban district such as London is able to plan its future through the use of legislation devised to enable the citizens through their elected councils to steer the elements of growth and change towards socially desired goals.

There is no conflict in the application of the four kinds of legislation to the problems of a specific area or region. The Planning Act and the Conservation Authorities Act enable local municipalities to organize for the solution of problems that are related to day-to-day orderly development in fixed locations. The use of the legislation depends primarily on the initiative of the local municipalities and is adaptive in nature. The municipalities already firmly established in local government join together in joint planning and operational devices for the purposes of regional or area urban development and conservation projects and programs.

The Water Resources Commission Act and the Highway Needs are related to circulation: in the one case the supply of water and its subsequent treatment after use, and in the other the movement of goods and people. Provincial initiative is necessary in dealing with the dynamic problems of this kind.

Thus any area or region may use all the legislation without conflict. For example, a given urban center will join with its surrounding municipalities under the Planning Act to control urban growth; it will join with all the other municipalities within its drainage basin under the Conservation Authorities Act to promote the conservation of regional resources; it will enter into agreements with the province for the financing, construction, and operation of water supply systems and sewage disposal plants; it will relate its program of street and road construction and maintenance to the official plan of roads through the grants structure.

Planning is essentially a dynamic process in which a democratic people may decide the kind of a future it wishes to have. But planning requires legal sanction in order to be effective. Ontario has enacted some effective planning-sensitive legislation and the people of the province are learning to use it.

22

Pipedream or Practical Possibility?

W. R. D. Sewell

A dam three times as high as Grand Coulee; a reservoir 500 miles long storing more than 500 million acre feet of water (enough to supply the needs of 20 cities the size of New York for a whole year); and a seaway stretching across Canada from the Great Lakes to the Pacific Coast: each of these sounds like an item straight out of science fiction. Far from being fantasy, however, they are key elements in a massive scheme which has been proposed for diverting huge quantities of water from northern North America to southern Canada, the United States, and Mexico. First proposed in 1964 by a firm of engineering consultants, J. M. Parsons and Co. of Los Angeles, the proposed scheme has come to be known as Nawapa, a short title for North American Water and Power Alliance, an international organization that would run the project if it were built.

The scheme has been described by some as "bold, imaginative, and farsighted," and has garnered support in several quarters in the United States. Many Americans, especially in the arid West, see it as a potential solution to the water crisis anticipated in the United States by the end of the century. Senator Frank E. Moss of Utah, perhaps the most enthusiastic supporter of the proposal, points out that U.S. water withdrawals presently amount to about 300 billion gallons per day, or about 27 per cent of the available streamflow. By

Reprinted from *Bulletin of the Atomic Scientists,* Vol. 23 (1967), pp. 9-13.

the year 2000, he says, they will have risen to 900 billion gallons per day, or about 80 per cent of the available streamflow. Even more critical is the fact that some regions are already experiencing water shortages, notably the Upper Rio Grande, Colorado, the Great Basin, and Southern California. If these shortages continue, claims Senator Moss, the development of such regions will be stifled and the economic growth of the nation impaired. The Nawapa scheme, he suggests, represents an attractive way out of this dilemma.

There are some, however, who feel that the scheme is no more than an engineering pipedream, an interesting idea but of little practical value. Others suggest that even if it were technically possible, it would be economically unfeasible. Yet others point out that a scheme of this magnitude could have numerous unanticipated side effects, some of which could prove to be disastrous.

While there appears to be growing support for the proposal in some parts of the United States, it has aroused relatively little enthusiasm in Canada. In fact, some Canadians are openly hostile to the whole idea, viewing it as an attempt to plunder Canadian resources. While Canadians have been prepared to export many of their natural resources to the United States—even non-renewable ones such as oil and gas—and even though they have co-operated in many resource development projects of interest to the two countries, the export or joint development of water resources is regarded as something quite different. Water is regarded as a special, "priceless" asset. "Nothing else could possibly be worth as much to us as our resource of water, and no government in its right mind would give this advantage away," said one Canadian government official recently.

Premiers of several of the provinces that would be involved have stated firmly that they are not interested either in export of water or in joint development. The Canadian federal government is opposed to the scheme as well, and has rejected proposals from various U.S. sources for joint investigations.

An impasse has thus been reached. A number of groups in the United States are busily engaged in promoting Nawapa and in gathering support for it. They seem to have found a fairly sympathetic ear in Washington, D.C., and several federal agencies are now engaged in studies relating to various aspects of the proposal. But while some Canadians recognize the possibility that there may be profits to be made from the sale of Canadian water to the United States, political opinion in Canada is firmly opposed to water exports.

The situation seems likely to arouse increasing emotion on both sides of the border. Americans in some parts of the United States experiencing water shortages will no doubt charge that the Canadian embargo on the export of water is "an unfriendly act." It is conceivable that some of them will call for pressure to be applied on the Canadian government to change its policy, backed up perhaps by sanctions of various kinds. Suggestions that Canadians have an obligation to share their water resource with the United States, however, are bound to arouse feelings of animosity in Canada. Unfortunately, the outcome of this interplay of national emotions may be a solution which is much less advantageous than the solution which could be arrived at by rational analysis. On the one hand, a continental water system is not the only way in which the United States could deal with its water problems. In Canada, on the other hand, an adamant policy of non-export of water does not seem particularly rational when the available resources are so vast. Arguments that keeping the water in Canada will encourage industry to move there rather than locate in the United States do not make much sense either. The cost of water is such a small item in the total costs of most industries that water availability is seldom the critical factor in the decision to locate.

It seems opportune to pose four major questions relating to the Nawapa scheme: (1) Is it technically possible to transfer efficiently such huge quantities of water? (2) Does it represent the cheapest way of providing the benefits claimed for it? (3) Would it have any adverse side effects? (4) Are there any legal, jurisdictional, or political obstacles to be overcome?

Basic Elements

The basic notion underlying Nawapa is the capture of part of the flow of certain major northern rivers in huge reservoirs for diversion southward to other parts of the North American continent. This would be accomplished by the construction of a series of high dams in the headwaters of certain major rivers in Alaska, the Yukon Territory, and British Columbia to divert their flows into a chain of reservoirs including the Tanana, the Yukon, the Peace, and the Rocky Mountain Trench.

The largest reservoir would be the Rocky Mountain Trench, which would have a capacity of 518,200,000 acre feet, or 16 times the capacity of Lake Mead, North America's largest manmade lake. Water from the upper reaches of the Columbia, Kootenay, and Fraser Rivers would be diverted into the Rocky Mountain Trench reservoir. It would then be discharged southward to serve the various subsystems of the proposed scheme.

From the southern tip of the Rocky Mountain Trench Reservoir the water would flow into Montana and then into central Idaho where it would be pumped over the mountains by six huge pumping stations. A canal 630 feet wide and 35 feet deep would carry the water into Utah, Nevada, and back into Utah. From this point the water flow would be split into two branches: one, the Colorado Basin Aqueduct, would carry the water southwest into Nevada, California, and finally Mexico; the other, the Southwest Aqueduct, would carry the water into Arizona and New Mexico before branching off into Mexico and looping up into Colorado as the Colorado Aqueduct.

Another branch of the scheme would start from the Peace River Reservoir in British Columbia. This would be the Alberta-Great Lakes Canal, a 73-foot wide, 30-foot deep waterway which would link the Prairie Provinces with the St. Lawrence Seaway. It might even be extended to the Pacific Coast with a terminus at Vancouver, B.C., thus creating the fabled Northwest Passage which the early European explorers sought in vain.

Other subsystems have also been proposed including a Hudson Bay Seaway, connecting the northern tip of Lake Manitoba with Hudson Bay; a North Dakota Barge Canal, connecting the Saskatchewan River in Canada with the Mississippi River at Minneapolis; a James Bay Seaway, connecting James Bay with Lake Huron; and Knob Lake Barge Canal, which would link the mineral rich Quebec northlands with the Great Lakes. The major interest however, is in the southern diversions and the Alberta-Great Lakes Canal.

The scheme is massive in every respect. It would involve the construction of at least 50 different diversion and control works, including dams, canals, tunnels, and reservoirs. Some of these structures would be several times the size of anything so far constructed for water use anywhere in the world. The Copper River Dam, for example, would be over 1,700 feet high, nearly twice the height of the largest dam ever constructed, the 988-foot-high Inguri Dam under construction in the Soviet Union. Fifteen of the reservoirs would be larger than Lake Mead. In addition, the operation of such a vast system would pose a major challenge to data collection and analysis. The Parsons Company envisions a computer center with a complex network of microwave systems, land lines, and relay stations covering two-thirds of North America. This system would relay the instructions from the center's computers to deliver the water as required.

The plans of course are only in a formative stage. There are few data on certain critical aspects, and more detailed studies need to be done. Doubts have been raised, however, about the technical feasibility of transferring such large quantities of water over such a long distance.

Costs and Benefits

The proponents of the Nawapa scheme claim that its benefits would far exceed its $100 billion cost. They point out that it will be continental in scope, providing water for seven provinces in Canada, thirty-three states in the United States, and three northern states in Mexico. It would furnish at least 120 million acre feet of water. Of this, 78 million acre feet would be delivered to the United States, 22 to Canada, and 20 to Mexico. This, they claim, would make it possible to irrigate an additional 40 million acres of land in the United States. In Mexico it would make possible a threefold expansion of irrigated acreage, or eight times as much new irrigated land as the High Aswan project will provide in Egypt. It would provide sufficient water to irrigate an additional seven million acres in Canada, too.

Nawapa would also generate over 70 million kilowatts of electric power, of which 38 million would be generated in the United States, 30 million in Canada, and two million in Mexico. Revenues from power sales, it is estimated by the Parsons Company, would exceed $4 billion annually. The project would also provide water for industrial and domestic purposes, and would help to deal with the problem of regulating the level of the Great Lakes, a problem of increasing concern to the shipping industry and to industrialists and recreationists in recent years. Another benefit would be the provision of additional water to flush wastes from polluted lakes and streams in various parts of the country.

Over 80 per cent of the water would come from Canadian streams. Proponents of the Nawapa scheme, however, point out that Canada would benefit considerably from its development, since it should make available over 22 million acre feet of water for agricultural, industrial, and municipal use in Canada, and furnish over 30 million kilowatts of power in that country, more than the total Canadian output in 1965. According to the report, the plan would increase electric power output at Niagara Falls by over 50 per cent. Canada would also benefit from raising the level of the

Great Lakes during natural low water years. It was also estimated that national income in Canada would increase by at least $9 billion per annum as a direct result of the plan.

Unanswered Questions

Despite the huge benefits that are claimed, there remain serious doubts as to whether it represents the most economic solution to the problems it is intended to solve. The principal problem is thought to be that of an anticipated water shortage in the United States by the end of the century. An objective examination of the situation suggests, however, that not only is it unclear that there is in fact an impending water shortage, but it is also doubtful whether long distance transfers of water are the cheapest way of dealing with such alleged shortages.

A Shortage in the United States?

In North America we seem to have a predilection for technological solutions to problems, especially if the solution involves the construction of an impressive structure. This has been particularly evident in the approach to urban water supply. Typically, communities have tended to go further and further afield for new supplies. Los Angeles already brings in water from hundreds of miles away and is now looking for new sources, also far away from the city. New York and many other cities are casting their nets wider and wider as their populations continue to expand. The long-distance aqueduct and the large-scale reservoir are becoming symbols of modern urban development.

Concentration on an "extensive" approach to urban water supply, however, has tended to deflect attention from possibilities of making better use of existing supplies. Water use in almost every city in the United States could be substantially reduced if efforts were made to minimize the amount of water used in various industrial processes; if recycling were more widely adopted; if realistic pricing policies were instituted; and if leaks in city water systems were repaired. Studies have shown that there are wide variations in the amount of water consumed by different plants involved in the same industrial process. A kilowatt hour of electricity generated by steam turbines takes as little as 1.3 gallons of water at some power stations and as much as 170 gallons at others. In some steel plants more than 25,000 gallons of water are required in the production of a ton of finished steel, while at other plants only 1,400 gallons are needed for the same purpose. Requirements in the production of a pound of artificial rubber range from 13 gallons to 300 gallons. There are no doubt opportunities here for major reductions in water requirements.

The re-use of water also offers important possibilities for the reduction of water demands. Some factories have installed elaborate equipment which enables the same water to be used over and over again. Some communities, such as Manhattan, use nondrinkable water for other purposes, such as street cleaning. Compared with the possibilities, however, re-use of water is minimal. One reason is that industrial, domestic, and other users have been given little incentive to install recycling equipment, or to use nondrinkable water for purposes not involving human consumption. Water prices often do not reflect costs of supplying the water. If these prices were raised, say the economists, much more efficient use of the nation's water resources would follow.

Increased water prices would also provide an incentive to cut down water losses due to leaks in water systems. It has been estimated that such losses amount to about 100 million gallons per day in the New York area. This is almost equivalent to one-third of the total daily consumption in London. A recent study of urban communities in the United States with populations over 10,000 shows that losses of between 2 and 54 per cent of total production were sustained in water systems in those communities. Assuming an average loss of 14 per cent, total losses in such communities in the United States may amount to over three billion gallons per day.

Not only is there major waste of water in the United States, but a considerable proportion of the water used in the country is used in sub-optimal occupations; that is, it is used for purposes in which it earns lower returns than it could in alternative uses. In the West, particularly, water is used for agriculture purposes although it could earn much higher returns if used for industrial or municipal purposes. How does this happen? As Professor Crutchfield points out, law and historical precedent often prevent water moving into its most economic uses.

In view of the apparent waste of water, and the use of water in sub-optimal occupations, it is difficult to justify arguments that there is an impending water shortage in the United States. Greater emphasis on "intensive" rather than "extensive" solutions would result in large reductions of water demands. If better use were made of existing supplies massive augmentations to such supplies would be unnecessary.

The Cheapest Alternative?

Even if it could be shown that there was a need for the huge quantities of water which Nawapa is anticipated to provide, it is unclear that this is the most economic means of providing it. What are the alternatives? Several possibilities suggest themselves, including desalinization, weather modification, increased use of ground water supplies, and depollution. Professors Crutchfield and Tinney point out that although desalinization and weather modification are still in the research and development stage, there are encouraging signs on the horizon that technical difficulties will be overcome, and that water can be supplied by these means in some regions at costs lower than those involved in large-scale water diversion. Other possibilities of augmenting supplies are also being investigated. One is the possibility of collecting water from streams flowing into the Pacific Ocean along the Central Pacific coast in reservoirs and then transferring it by undersea aqueducts to other parts of the country. Promoters of this scheme (the National Engineering Science Company [the Nesco Scheme]) claim that undersea transfer would be much cheaper than overland transfer and that it would be economically feasible. Other research is being devoted to means of reducing water losses from evapo-transpiration. Various types of films are being tested, as are floating concrete blocks painted white to reflect heat.

Another means of augmenting present water supplies would be increased use of ground water. At present ground water wells supply only one-sixth of the water used in the United States, even though there may be more than 3,000 times more water in underground aquifers than in surface streams. Costs of trapping these aquifers may be considerably less than bringing in water from elsewhere.

The apparent shortage of water in some regions of the United States results partly from the rapid increase in population and the growing per capita consumption of water as the standard of living rises, and partly from the increasing use of water bodies for waste disposal. A consequence has been that almost every major stream or lake in the country has become polluted with industrial or municipal wastes. Many of them have become open sewers, carrying water no longer fit for human consumption. Depollution of some of these water bodies could provide major additions to the nation's water supplies.

Weather modification, desalinization, undersea transfers of water, evaporation control, increased use of groundwater, and depollution are but a few of the possible alternatives to large-scale long distance transfers of water. In some instances they may well provide water at much lower costs than the latter.

Possible Side Effects

The development of any scheme generally implies a decision to forego other alternative uses of a given resource. Thus the construction of a hydro-electric power dam may involve the creation of a reservoir which will inundate a potential mining area, valuable agricultural land, or spawning grounds for anadromous fish. The decision whether to proceed with development of such a dam will generally be made only after a conscious weighing of the various sacrifices to be made. As the scale and complexity of water development schemes increase, however, it becomes much more difficult to predict what the effects might be and what alternative uses may be precluded.

Some adverse effects of Nawapa can already be anticipated. Part of Whitehorse, the administrative capital of the Yukon Territory, would be submerged by one of the proposed reservoirs, and several communities in interior British Columbia would be inundated. The Rocky Mountain Trench Reservoir would interrupt east-west rail and road communications across British Columbia, as well as submerge potentially valuable mineral deposits in the Trench. Other similar sacrificed alternative uses of resources would be involved elsewhere along the route of the Nawapa project.

Beside these anticipated effects, there would be others whose precise impact is difficult to estimate at present. Dr. Raymond Nace of the U.S. Geological Survey suggested recently, for example, that there might be serious effects on the physical geology of the areas in which the major reservoirs would be located. He pointed out that the Rocky Mountain Trench reservoir would place a massive load on an area whose geology is relatively unknown. How would the area react to this new load stress? He also noted that the scheme would place large volumes of unfrozen water over permafrost areas. Would this result in major landslides? Moreover, large quantities of cold water would be delivered to more southerly latitudes where available heat would warm the water, and increase evapo-transpiration. What effects would this have on the micro-climates and meso-climates in the regions of export and import of water?

These questions are but a few of the possible ones that might be raised about potential side effects. Some of these could be extremely serious, if not disastrous. Major efforts should be made now to determine possible consequences.

Institutional Obstacles

Even if it could be assumed that the Nawapa scheme were technically and economically feasible, and even if there were no serious doubts about adverse side effects, there would be several institutional obstacles to overcome. In the first place it would require a major change in political opinion in Canada, and in some parts of the United States, such as the Pacific Northwest, to make inter-basin transfers of water possible. Once this obstacle had been overcome it would be necessary to obtain agreement among the various jurisdictions involved as to the precise terms upon which they were prepared to participate. This would be a monumental task, since it would involve three national governments, possibly seven provincial governments in Canada, maybe thirty-three or more states in the United States, and three states in Mexico. Each would have to be convinced that the arrangement was in its own best interest and that it had obtained a satisfactory bargain.

The difficulties involved in reaching a mutually acceptable agreement in joint development of water resources are illustrated by the negotiation of the Columbia River Treaty. The United States government and the Canadian government came to terms in 1961 but objections from British Columbia delayed ratification for three more years. Canadian officials said bargaining with B.C. was even tougher than with the U.S. government. It is conceivable that bargaining on a scale required for Nawapa could take several decades.

The Broader Context

The Nawapa scheme is exciting and imaginative. It illustrates the twentieth century emphasis on the application of technology on a massive scale to solve human problems. This emphasis is not peculiar to North America. Proposals for diversion schemes of continental magnitude have been put forward in the Soviet Union several times in the past two decades. An intricate system of diversions is almost completed in the western part of that country, involving interconnections for various rivers draining into the Caspian Sea and rivers draining into the Arctic Ocean and Baltic Sea for reason of navigation and transport.

The desire to interconnect river systems parallels the growing interest in the possibilities of interconnecting electric power systems. Intricate power pooling systems have developed in Europe, the Soviet Union, and North America. Successes in this regard have perhaps encouraged interest in the possible advantages of inter-basin transfers of water.

Like the integration of electric power systems, however, the integration of water systems is not inherently good. It may be advantageous under certain circumstances but not others. The problem now at hand, therefore, is the determination of the circumstances under which water transfers are more advantageous than other solutions to water problems. In some cases an "extensive approach" or the diversion of water from other regions will prove to be the best solution. In many others, however, more intensive use of existing supplies will be much more economic. As John Heywood, the sixteenth century English poet put it, "Much water goeth by the mill that the miller knoweth not of."

23

Toward a North American Water Policy

F. E. Moss

It is a singular honour to be invited to address the Royal Society of Canada, the senior learned society of your country and one of the world's leading associations of scientists and men of letters. I do not know whether some of my colleagues in the United States Senate have preceded me on this platform, or whether my appearance here today sets some sort of precedent. But I am sure that such an appearance is rare, and I shall treat it with respect.

I am by custom and courtesy in a position to bring you greetings from the American people. I do so with warmth. We Canadians and Americans have inherited jointly the loveliest and most richly endowed of all continents. We share the job of preserving its beauty and the responsibility of developing its natural resources for the greatest benefit, not only of this generation, but of unborn millions who will follow us.

At the beginning, let me make my position clear. I do not speak as the representative of the Executive Branch of the United States government. I speak as a member of the United States Senate — as the Senator from the water-conscious state of Utah. I will try to set forth what I believe *should be* the policies of my government. Many in my country share these views.

Speech made to the Royal Society of Canada, 1966. Reprinted from *Water Resources of Canada,* ed. C. E. Doleman (University of Toronto Press, 1967), pp. 3-15. By permission.

I always feel very much at home in your country. A recent U.S. Department of the Interior publication describes Utah as a panorama of peaked mountains, lush valleys, and wind-swept plains, where the taming of the wilderness made "the history of Utah an epic of hardship, determination, and triumph." I am sure those same words could have been written about many parts of Canada. Timber, trapping, minerals, farming, and incredible beauty have been as much a part of our Utah lives as of yours. One of the first white men to see the Great Salt Lake, nature's identifying monument in my state, was a Canadian trapper named Etienne Provost. The first white settler in Utah came from St. Louis, whence he had come from Quebec. His name was Antoine Robidou — I am told there are still Robidous in Quebec. Again, just as the railroads helped to knit Canada, Utah is proud to be the place where the last spike was driven in the bands of steel which first linked our western and eastern coasts of America.

What is more to the point in today's discussion, however, is the nature and intensity of our common interest in the preservation of our natural resources. Our lives and our future depend upon the care we take of them, particularly the care we take of our water. In Utah we have an almost sacred respect for water, which shares the indispensability of its life-giving role only with the air we breathe. Its value is determined everywhere by nature's pattern of distribution. In my state there is no more precious thing.

I am sure that Canada, which has a very large portion of the earth's freshwater supplies, does not value water less. The problem of assuring an adequate supply of water for Canada's future differs from the problem in the United States more in degree than in substance. The pollution and levels of the Great Lakes, for example, are bringing as many grey hairs to you as to us, and the flow in the St. Lawrence is as vital to the Port of Montreal as the flow of the Hudson is to New York. Time may be crowding you less, but the challenge of preserving your water resource is clear and near. The challenge looms larger and closer for us. We are already feeling the sharp pinch of necessity. Our demands are quantitatively greater than yours, and the pattern of population growth and industrial development in the United States is putting tremendous pressure on us.

Two factors must be weighed in considering the speed and manner of growth of economic development in the United States and Canada, and the intensity of the exploitation of natural resources in the two countries. First, there is considerable disparity between our two countries in total population and in gross national product. This is unavoidably a source of strain between Canadians and Americans. Such disparity tests the skills of professional diplomats as much as it calls for good manners and broad understanding on the part of all of us. We beg your understanding of our problems and expect you to ask the same of us. Secondly, there is a melancholy lesson for Canada in the economic and natural resource history of the United States. This is a lesson in the importance of taking care of water resources. We in the United States are learning it late and under stress. You have the opportunity to learn it in time to apply it purposefully and according to plan.

The thrust of my message today is a plea to you as members of the influential Royal Society of Canada to support the long-range studies, the surveys, the appraisals, and the planning, which will provide without unnecessary delay a sound basis for effective management of your vast water resources. In order that there be no misunderstanding in this area, let me state my position clearly. After you in Canada have measured your water and projected your own ultimate requirements, it is my hope that you will find that you have water for export, over and above your own foreseeable needs. I assure you that you will find a profitable market for it south of the border in both the United States and Mexico.

Preliminary studies indicate that it is technically feasible and economically sound to collect, store, and redistribute *unused* runoff water from the northern reaches of the continent. Unlike oil and uranium, water can be marketed on a sustained yield basis. If the producing areas are properly managed, they will continue without depletion to produce a profitable "crop" for export. But first you must answer the basic question as to whether it is clearly to your advantage to export water. This question cannot be answered definitively until Canada's water-harvesting capabilities are fully and accurately measured.

Let me clarify a few points of possible misunderstanding. Borrowing from the techniques of the practice of law in both our countries, I want to remove from argument, by stipulation, two very important assumptions which underlie my discussion today. These assumptions should constitute the permanent foundation for continuing relations between our two countries.

The first stipulated assumption is that we Americans and Canadians are mutually desirous of living together in peace on this continent for a very long time to come, preserving the sovereign values of *both* our nations and our societies, and developing our respective talents constructively for the greatest good of the greatest number. The second stipulation is that we two peoples, in addition to all of our intangible blessings, have been endowed and entrusted with a very valuable piece of real estate, a section of the earth which is conducive to life and worthy of our care and affection, and that we are equally interested in preserving it and enhancing it as a region for human habitation.

Now, these are not assumptions to be stipulated in isolation. They are not points to be agreed upon in passing, and separated from the real world of politics, economics, and diplomacy. If you agree to such a dual stipulation, then the course ahead should be carefully plotted in both countries and clearly coordinated for the mutual benefit of both. In other words, if we want to continue to live in constructive peace on this richly endowed continent of North America, and to grow "in wisdom and stature," then we must co-operate in taking care of it.

I would not dare to come here and utter such seeming platitudes were it not for my confidence in the traditional good manners of Canadians. If this audience were to indulge in the habits of old-fashioned American politics, you might drown my voice in loud guffaws and say "Look who's talking! Why don't you clean your own house first?" Indeed, I must plead guilty to this basic charge made against the United States: that we have not taken proper care of our own waters. How then can we qualify to address our neighbours on the subject? I answer on two grounds. First, we have tardily learned our lesson and are doing something about our wasted waters. Secondly, we can help Canada to avoid the onerous costs of trying to recover lost ground after too many years of neglect. Our experience should be valuable to you.

A Canadian businessman recently observed to an American associate, in a friendly but meaningful sally: "You Americans have muddied your own water, now you want to muddy ours." He added (I hope more in jest than justice) that to part of the U.S. press, Idaho water was "American" but British Columbia water was "continental." My response is that really we are not the reprobates we are sometimes made to appear. In my own discussions I have been careful to talk about continental *planning* and not continental *water*. I trust most of my countrymen intended to do the same.

A certain amount of Canadian scepticism is a normal reaction to the widespread discussion in the United States on continental water planning, and particularly to the great attention that has been given to the North American Water and Power Alliance—the NAWAPA concept. Let me point out first of all that the concept relates to a continent-wide water *system,* and not to continental *water.* Then allow me to put into proper perspective the actual status of NAWAPA in the United States.

The concept was developed by the Ralph M. Parsons Company of Los Angeles. Its central idea came from one of the outstanding water-planning engineers of the West. Over the years it has been broadened to include parts of many regional plans which have been discussed on both sides of the border, and expanded into an integrated system. The resulting proposal or concept is based entirely on maps and analysis of published topographical, climatographical, and hydrological data. In many areas there have been no on-site investigations.

The Parsons Company has put the concept or plan in the public domain. While no funds other than his own have been invested in it, Ralph M. Parsons, the head of the company, makes no proprietary claims. The project has been entirely an in-house research and development effort in a field of special competence of the firm. The concept is, I understand, still being revised and refined. When it was brought to my attention, it seemed to me to warrant the attention of the Senate Committees on water resources. At my request, a Special Subcommittee on Western Water Development was appointed and directed to look into the matter. I was named Chairman. The Subcommittee made a rough comparison of this NAWAPA plan with an inventory of all the water projects anticipated by our U.S. federal agencies over the next twenty years.[1] The Committee's general conclusion was that for about 25 per cent greater total cost, the NAWAPA concept could deliver nearly twice as much water as could be provided by the large number of American projects envisioned by the four U.S. federal agencies having water resource development responsibilities.

Our review admittedly was hasty. The degree of refinement of the NAWAPA concept at that time did not warrant more detailed study. I believe that now it does. The United States still has a lot of homework to do. I hope Canada will feel that she does too. Before discussing this homework, let me review for you the essentials of the NAWAPA concept.

In one sentence, it is a continent-wide plan for collection, redistribution, and efficient utilization of waters now running off to the

---

[1] *Western Water Development,* compiled by the Special Subcommittee on Western Water Development of the Committee on Public Works, United States Senate (Washington, U.S. Government Printing Office, 1964).

Figure 1. Conceptual Plan—North American Water and Power Alliance.

seas totally unused or only partially used. It would collect about 15 to 18 per cent of the excess runoff from the high-precipitation, medium-elevation areas of Alaska and of western and northern Canada. It is important to keep in mind that the concept deals with *surplus* water. By proper diversion and storage, optimal flows can be maintained downstream and flood peaks levelled. This collected, surplus water would be diverted southward and eastward through a continent-serving system of tunnels, canals, and improved natural channels, linking chains of reservoirs. Such controlled distribution of the waters from the North, pooled with waters from the interconnected producing areas of both countries, would benefit one territory and seven provinces of Canada, thirty-five states of the United States, and three states of Mexico.

NAWAPA would create a vast power generation system across Canada, pivoted in the West on your great Peace River Project. It would supply new industrial and agricultural water and would provide low-cost water transportation to the Prairie Provinces. It would stabilize flows in both the Columbia and the St. Lawrence rivers—with protection for the Port of Montreal—and permit stabilization of the levels of the Great Lakes with living new water from both the Northwest and from the James Bay watershed.

In the United States, NAWAPA would permit increased flow in the upper Missouri and upper Mississippi rivers during low-flow periods. It would provide ample supplies of clean water for all the arid states of the West, including supplies for restoration of groundwater where it has been depleted. NAWAPA would also provide new high-quality water for Mexico in amounts many times greater than those the Egyptians will garner from the Aswan high dam.

Although Canada and the United States share the benefits of all the water in the Great Lakes, in case additional Canadian water were to become available from the North, the question of actual water export via the Lakes is worthy of investigation. Undoubtedly, the system of stabilized optimal levels in the Lakes would aid gradual restoration of their biological health.

The proposal to transfer James Bay water to the Great Lakes is not exclusive to NAWAPA. The idea has been proposed in only slightly different form by Thomas W. Kierans of Sudbury, Ontario, whose Grand canal scheme embodies the possibility of converting most of James Bay into a great freshwater reservoir. Mr. Kierans' expanded plan now covers almost as much territory as does NAWAPA; but NAWAPA would add water from the Northwest as well as from the James Bay watershed. There is no point at this time in attempting to make a choice between the Kierans and NAWAPA proposals for diversion of water into the Great Lakes. There is certainly sufficient promise in both proposals, however, to warrant the detailed survey and appraisal work which is necessary. Once these studies are completed. Canada may then want either to develop one of these plans or a combination of the two, to design a third plan, or to reject the whole idea.

One undeniable value of the NAWAPA idea is that it stimulates resource study. The least that should be said for continental water planning is that it justifies investigation of all the water resources which might be incorporated in the system. Rational discussion of the specifics of any and all of the plans must await more precise technical data. Assuming that Canada actually produces the surplus water which today's sketchy climatological and hydrological data indicate she does—and I belive detailed engineering studies will confirm and expand the amount—NAWAPA would substantially benefit *both* countries, and bring direct profitable return to Canada.

Thus the bulk of that homework mentioned earlier involves the actual field engineering determination of whether the initial assumptions are true. A determination of real precision—one in which the public can have confidence—must be made and it must demonstrate clearly that Canada does, in fact, have sufficient water-harvesting capacity to consider export to her neighbours to the south. It would make little sense for us to debate further at this time any of the details of the continental planning concept, or even the question of whether it is a good idea for either country. But it makes a lot of sense to go after the facts on which to base definitive judgments. It also makes sense to examine the condition of the continent we share, to survey and appraise its total life-support capability in terms of water supply. Then we should plan the best way to preserve and, if possible, expand this resource. Finally, we must plan its most advantageous use for both our countries and for Mexico.

Let me now stipulate a third point: the people of the United States cannot expect the people of Canada to consider entering any arrangement such as this unless it is demonstrably and unquestionably in Canada's long-term best interest—and is so found by Canadians. We Americans have no right to suggest or to expect any water transfer scheme which might provide water in the United States for the next thirty or forty years, but which would leave Canada too little to meet her own future requirements.

I want to emphasize this point because the engineers, administrators, and parliamentarians who are scrutinizing the NAWAPA concept as a conceivable long-range answer to water supply problems in the United States are *not* conspiring to steal Canada's water. We are not devising a scheme to trick Canada. We are not even trying to arrive at a minimum price at which we might cajole and persuade you into selling us some of your water. As a matter of fact, we are working with dedication to *avoid* the prospect of dependence on imported water. The United States is now embarking on every possible venture to stretch our own water, creatively and ingeniously, and to find out whether we might have enough to see us through. We realize that only through an intensive effort can we find out just how much we can do on our own. After that we will know whether we must seek to import water and if so, how, where, and at what cost?

Our labours have a strange duality. The things we must do to get ready to import water, in case it *is* offered, are, to a very large extent, the things we must do if the water is *not* offered. In my opinion, however, transportation of unused water from an area where usability is meagre or impossible is all but inevitable. Population, economics, and common sense demand it.

Historically, there have been three great surges of federal interest and activity in water resource protection and development in the United States. One was under Theodore Roosevelt, when Gifford Pinchot led the movement for protection of forests. The second was under Franklin Roosevelt, when conservation received a mighty boost from depression-stimulated economic recovery programmes. Neither of these efforts, however, compares in scope or pace with the third surge now taking place under President Johnson. I think it is safe to say that in the past three years the Congress has passed more constructive water legislation than in any other time of our national history. I shall mention only the most important programmes.

The Congress has enacted the *Water Resources Planning Act,* a landmark measure which places water resource planning on a river basin basis. It recognizes the fundamental fact that water does not stop at state or county or municipal boundaries, and that any planning which does not take this into consideration will be piecemeal planning—with piecemeal effect. (As an aside, may I add that water does not recognize international boundaries in its interaction with either terrain or gravity.) The Congress has launched a *Water Research Programme,* which will invest nearly $100 million a year for ten years on basic water research. This is over and above the programme to bring desalting of water into economic balance, both in North America and elsewhere in the world. The Congress has established a *Water Pollution Control Administration,* which will conduct and oversee a broad public and industrial pollution control programme. We have greatly increased the federal funds available to communities for the construction of waste treatment plants and other pollution control facilities.

At this session we have legislation before us which will coordinate attacks on water pollution *within each river basin.* To make the programme more effective, we have just transferred the Water Pollution Control Administration from the Department of Health, Education and Welfare to the Interior Department, where other river basin planning is centred. We are also considering in the Senate at this time a bill which would establish a *National Water Commission,* to be composed of distinguished citizens outside the government, who will consider all aspects of our complex and inter-related water problems and will recommend long-range policy solutions. This emphasis on long-range planning makes our discussions of the same subject here today even more timely. Again, there is pending in Congress—with hearings scheduled for some time this fall—a bill which I have introduced to reorganize our federal water resource management, and to place all agencies concerned with it in one department to be called the *Department of Natural Resources*. At the present time, a score of agencies in five departments have some kind of statutory responsibility for water.

In February, 1966, the Committee on Water Resources Research of the Federal Council for Science and Technology published a recommended programme for ten years of water research. It would cover techniques of planning, organization, and water law. The programme recognizes the need for better methods of weighing costs and benefits of water resource development. In addition, it would expand research in waste treatment, in water-consuming industrial processes, in agricultural practices, in conservation of watersheds for improved yield, in desalting, weather modification, and many other fields. Altogether, it may be said simply that there is a welling up of interest in and activities concerned with water throughout the federal government, and throughout the country. Water is truly front and centre in the United States at this time in our history.

Sometimes I think we make the water problem appear more complex than it really is. There are four general categories of effort, and we must invest in all of them. The first is *conservation*, or taking care of water-producing areas. This means attention to trees and grass on the watersheds, as well as adequate flow control through systems of retention pools and reservoirs to prevent floods and soil erosion.

The second category is proper *water handling*. This includes pollution abatement, cleaning up the water courses, treatment of water for recycle, improvement in water-consuming processes. We must be able to define legitimate water requirements in order to bridle growing demand. Such disciplinary measures as metering come in this category.

The third category is the search for *new sources* of usable water. One way is the desalting of the seas and inland brackish water. Another is rain-making, or weather modification. I recently heard a most descriptive term applied to the latter: "Stimulated Atmospheric Transport."

The fourth is *water resource development,* which covers the collection and storage of surplus water, interbasin transfers, and recharging of aquifers. In this category we find the multiple-use projects for domestic and industrial water supply, irrigation, recreation, transportation, power, and wildlife support.

While redistribution systems, such as the NAWAPA concept, fall essentially in the fourth category, they play an important role in the others. Continental planning makes no sense unless we practise conservation, pollution control, and efficient utilization of water. Economic exploitation of desalting and rain-making both depend upon efficient distribution.

It will cost billions of dollars to restore and to extend the water resources of the United States over the next two or three decades. Were this a meeting of the Chamber of Commerce, I would say to you that the business to be done in the water improvement field during the last third of this century will be greater than the economic explosion of railroad building over two-thirds of the nineteenth century. For example, the NAWAPA concept has a price tag, obviously very loosely attached, of $100 billion for a 25- to 30-year construction programme. Of course this sounds like a lot of money, but it is not unprecedented. The U.S. Interstate Highway programme is a 15-year programme to cost between $45 and $50 billion.

Parsons' engineers estimate that about 48 per cent of the NAWAPA investment would be in Canada, slightly less in the United States, and about 5 per cent in Mexico. The total revenues from NAWAPA activities and services, from the sale of water and electric power, and from other charges for use of facilities, are estimated at about $4 billion a year. Annual operating expenses are estimated at less than $1 billion, leaving $3 billion for capital financing. This makes the scheme quite practical for amortization within the usual time for water projects in my country.

Most of the water revenues would come from the United States. While more than half of the power available would be generated in Canada, the United States would, in the normal course of events, provide a market for large amounts of this Canadian-generated power. More of the navigation benefits would accrue to Canada. Recreation benefits would be about evenly divided. The benefits of such a continent-spanning water collection, saving, and distribution system are very real. They would be felt throughout the continent.

The level and purity of water in the Great Lakes would be restored and sustained, and the Lakes could be used as a distribution manifold, as is proposed specifically in the expanded Kierans' Plan. The flow of water in the Columbia and the St. Lawrence would be stabilized for both power generation and navigation. We could write *finis* to destructive floods on these and other rivers. The collection and redistribution system established in the Prairie Provinces would end floods there, provide a water supply, and mesh into a nation-wide system of water transportation. The new lakes and recreation areas would make the northlands even more attractive. Canada's recreation lure is already beckoning countless thousands of Americans. Their numbers would increase and, with almost limitless stretches of new waterways, the boating boom would become continent-wide.

British Columbia would have the greatest NAWAPA investment, in storage, power, and navigation facilities. The town of Prince George would be the centre of a complex of waterworks unrivalled anywhere in the world. British Columbia would be the site also of what might be the single most controversial feature of the initial NAWAPA concept. This is the proposal to make a huge lake out of the natural defile known as the Rocky Mountain Trench, along the west side of the Canadian Rockies. Studies must be made, of course, to determine the ecological impact of such a man-made, inland, freshwater sea. If this project were judged to be too costly in terms of real estate and wilderness impact, other routes for the transfer of water could doubtless be found, but the value of such a great, useful, spectacular new lake should also be considered.

First-hand studies, including bio-environmental studies, hydrological and geological surveys, and field engineering work may reveal flaws in the NAWAPA proposal. The United States may find it more beneficial to build a great collection and storage complex in Alaska, and then ask Canada for right-of-way to transfer some of this water to the contiguous states. It has been proposed that we might do this by a plastic pipeline which could be submerged in the Pacific Ocean. Both America and Canada must determine what we should do—and determine it fairly soon.

To help make such a determination, I introduced a resolution last summer to provide for the use of the mechanism of the International Joint Commission to investigate the NAWAPA proposal. I chose this Commission because it is an existing and qualified agency through which both countries can work. I am now beginning to have some reservations, however, about using the IJC, not because of principle but because of timing and the scope of the job. The task is broader than the Commission's charter, and there are several years of American and Canadian homework to be done merely to develop instructions for an international agency. Besides, IJC studies of pollution and on control of water levels of the Great Lakes must be speeded up because of the pressing importance of corrective action in that region. The lessons to be learned in working out joint programmes for the improvement of this shared water resource should point the way to broader programmes involving the transfer and export of more distant waters.

I predict that you will see a big change in the overall water outlook in the United States in the next ten years. I *hope* that our domestic water programmes will be so successful that America will not need to seek any of Canada's bountiful supplies. But, even so, we would be happy to join with Canada in a continent-wide conservation and development water study. Canada's investment in water resource development would extend, without limit in decades or acre-feet, the producing lifetime of your water harvest areas, and would evolve a better distribution system. Such a programme would head off more expensive Canadian investment later on. Common sense and prudence dictate that both countries keep an eye on a possible continental system as each of us designs national water resource projects. Let us make sure that while we are making up our minds about the value of a continental approach we do nothing to make it unworkable.

One final thought—the total amount of moisture in the earth's life-support envelope is fixed and constant: the number of people to use it is not. Their numbers expand; their water uses change and increase; their modes of travel, their industries, and their residences shift. Should the United States and Canada approach the solution of the problem of water supply versus water demand separately or together?

24

A Monstrous Concept—
A Diabolical Thesis

A. G. L. McNaughton

I should like to thank the Royal Society of Canada for giving me this opportunity to set forth my views on the uses of Canada's water. I should also like to thank the Society for providing a forum for discussion of the important questions of the exploitation of Canada's water and whether it should be diverted to the United States, and the related questions of the development of the resources of this country and perhaps even its survival and growth as a nation.

Canada has been endowed by Divine Providence with abundant resources which confer immense advantages upon this country. It is our responsibility to use these resources with discretion, and to treasure the more basic of them for the generations of Canadian citizens who will come after us is a paramount responsibility. Of our many resources, two are fundamental: land and water. In Canada, they are closely related, and we alienate or squander either only at our peril.

For this reason, vital and important questions are raised affecting this country's future by propositions such as that currently being touted under the somewhat pretentious name of the North

Speech made to the Royal Society of Canada, 1966. Reprinted from *Water Resources of Canada,* ed. C. E. Doleman (University of Toronto Press, 1967), pp. 16-24. By permission.

American Water and Power Alliance, or NAWAPA for short. Of course this proposal is not concerned with an alliance at all: it is nothing more than an attempt by the Ralph M. Parsons Company, of Los Angeles, California, a private engineering firm, to drum up business for themselves.

A great deal of publicity has been created for these proposals in the United States and much attention has been directed to them in Canada. I feel obliged to say, therefore, that they are quite unacceptable, and to set forth the position which should be taken by Canada and the provinces. Despite some temporizing pronouncements which have been issued by distracted politicians, I believe that this position represents the view being taken by our best-informed technical and administrative officers and by responsible members of our engineering profession, who are best qualified to judge the merits and demerits of any physical arrangement of this kind.

There are similar, and indeed possibly associated schemes, being put forward in Canada by such people as Thomas Kierans of Sudbury, whose Grand canal scheme would divert rivers flowing into James Bay, and more recently by Professor Edward Kuiper[1] of the University of Manitoba, who would reverse the flow of a large part of the Nelson and Churchill rivers flowing into Hudson Bay. The origin of the waters affected in these schemes lies for the most part in several provincial jurisdictions, except for the Red River, a small part of which may represent a re-export of some waters originating in North Dakota and Minnesota. With this one exception, these rivers are all *national* rivers of Canada—that is, they flow entirely within Canada, from source to mouth, and therefore the benefits which accrue from them belong *wholly* to Canada. Over national waters, the jurisdiction of the nation in which they are situated is supreme. Canada would be foolish indeed to recognize or permit any international character to be ascribed to these national waters, and they would assume just such a character if they were to be subjected to any international study.

Within Canada, the rights to ownership of interprovincial rivers, as between upstream aand downstream provinces, is by no means clear. One might suppose that claims could be based on any of the various doctrines which may have superseded that of riparian rights. In any event, the physical jurisdiction rests largely with the particular upstream states concerned, and they have made their views quite explicit. British Columbia, Alberta, and Saskatchewan

1 E. Kuiper, "Canadian Water Export", *Engineering Journal,* Vol. 49 (1966), pp. 13-18.

have made the clearest declarations against the sale of Canadian waters; and Quebec is too well informed and too intimately concerned over water for the public welfare to be drawn into export, especially for compensation in the form of a silly project like a canal to Knob Lake, which forms part of the Parsons scheme. An example of the position taken by provincial governments is that of Premier W. A. C. Bennett, who said that British Columbia "will sell the U.S. hydro-electric power but *not* water. Even to talk about selling it is ridiculous. You do not sell your heritage."

It should be noted that no government or government agency on this continent has commissioned any technical study of the NAWAPA scheme. Indeed, there has been very little formal government discussion on even the possibility of such studies. I have not overlooked the discussion of NAWAPA by a United States Senate subcommittee. Nor have I overlooked the fact that the United States government has not seen fit to act on a Congressional resolution to refer the NAWAPA scheme to the International Joint Commission for study.

It should be noted also that the Canadian government, in referring the problem of Great Lakes levels to the IJC, expressly forbade studies of plans such as the Kierans Grand canal scheme, involving purely national Canadian waters. At the same time, it must be noted that a joint Canada-Ontario stock-taking of northern Ontario waters is proceeding. To this must be added the fact that Quebec, where some of these rivers for diversion are located, has declined to answer an invitation to join in these federal-provincial studies.

One independent scientist who has spoken out is Trevor Lloyd, Professor of Geography at McGill University. In a paper delivered in February, 1966, Dr. Lloyd had this to say about NAWAPA: "Clearly, we have here an exercise in sophomore civil engineering which has received far greater attention than it ever deserved. It underlines the danger, all too familiar to geographers, of allowing the drawing office to replace acquaintance with the land and the people as they really are."[2]

Canada is a vast land, whose many resources are so great that we have yet to take the measure of them. We have a great deal of fresh water, but the available amount, it seems to me, tends to be frequently overstated. We have suffered in the past from permitting such overstatements to remain uncorrected, and they are being

---

[2] T. Lloyd, "A Water Resource Policy for Canada", *Canadian Geographic Journal*, Vol. 73 (1966), pp. 2-17.

made with growing intensity in the propaganda with which we are being deluged.

Canada is a land of hundreds of thousands of lakes. These lakes are full of clear water, which has accumulated there as the glaciers receded thousands of years ago. The large surface of these lakes has a profound effect in modifying our climate from the harsh extremes of the continental effect which would prevail without their presence. But this is water in inventory; if removed it will not be replaced. Moreover, its removal could reduce the amount of rainfall and therefore reduce the supply of running water. Only the running water can be regarded as available for use, for it is only this water which is replenished by rain and snowmelt. Only this water can be regarded as perpetual and, even then, only if it is properly managed. It may come as a surprise to some, but this second kind of water, the kind we can use, is by no means as abundant as is generally supposed. In fact, our total streamflow in Canada is not limitless, as is so often imagined, but is of a similar order of magnitude to that of the United States.

The United States also has vast supplies of water in inventory, but a great proportion of theirs is underground, which means that it is situated beneath space that can be used for living. In Canada, we have much less habitable and arable land, which means that in the future we may have to conserve this for ourselves, and in turn that we have to consider carefully before we put any more of it under water.

The NAWAPA scheme seems to be based on the premise that there are large quantities of surplus water in Canada. Any large-scale withdrawal of our water from the North raises questions which need careful analysis before any major discussions can be permitted, even in Canada.

The first of these that I would mention has recently been called to attention by H. A. Neu of the National Research Council. His advice is that a Canadian committee be formed on water, weather, and vegetation, to carry out certain studies before any system of water diversion is brought under consideration at all. Even the slightest changes may have far-reaching effects; the danger lies in the fact that if water flows were altered, the related climatic changes could affect vegetation and biological life. With decreases in local streamflow, the climate of a region could assume a more continental character—hotter during the warm months, and colder during the winter and fall. Because of temperature changes, plants might not be able to survive the heat of summer or the cold of winter. Conceivably, such changes in climate also might alter the water supply, because of a change in the regime of precipitation.

Then there is the question of permafrost, which occurs in Canada in large lenticular masses embedded in the soil at considerable depths. If these are subject to inflow of heat by flooding of the surface, the permafrost will melt and constitute a dangerous foundation upon which to impound the vast areas of storage water which have been indicated.

The NAWAPA propagandists love to talk of great quantities of water spilling unused into the Arctic Ocean. But the major sources for the scheme are hundreds of miles from the Arctic Ocean. They are in fact the rivers of the Canadian Cordillera, which provide a great series of prime power sites; rivers which form the basis of one of the world's great concentrations of the forest products industry: rivers which provide some of the finest salmon runs in the world. There are detailed plans on Canadian drawing-boards, and there are projects now under construction to harness these flows. The associated mineral and forest resources are already staked out, and the required human and financial resources are being attracted to the region. The NAWAPA promoters would move all of this out of Canada—the people, the industry, the water. It can only be described as madness to believe that Canada has surplus water in an area that is so obviously earmarked for major resource development, and where so much activity to that end is already taking place.

Of course, NAWAPA has nothing to do with the maximum development of these rivers or resources in Canada. Its purpose is to flood the valleys in Canada, and to drain off the water in regulated flow for beneficial use in the United States. But the valleys themselves are of vital importance to British Columbia, because they contain the level land which is so vitally needed for roads and railways, for industries, for people, and for agriculture. Whitehorse and Prince George would be submerged, and their land with them, as would countless miles of railway and highway. These irreplaceable assets would be destroyed in the name of trans-mountain navigation.

The grandiose concept starts with the collection of the waters of the Yukon and the Peace in the Rocky Mountain Trench, that great intramontane valley which stretches through our western Cordillera at an altitude of half a mile above sea level. It reaches from Montana to northern British Columbia, and they would put it all under water .

This scheme ignores all the plans which have been made in Canada for the use of the waters and the lands of the Rocky Mountain Trench. For example, it ignores Canadian plans to capture the waters of the Yukon River by backing them into the Atlin Lakes and thence through a head of something over two thousand feet for power in Taku Inlet. It ignores the fact that the Peace River is being harnessed for power at this very moment; it ignores the development plans which now exist for the Fraser and Thompson rivers. It seems to ignore developments which are under construction on the Columbia River, from which the United States will receive some 50 million acre-feet of Canadian water in the form of regulated flow, at a cost to the United States which is less than the cost to Canada of constructing the dams. Surely this is enough pillage in the appropriation of our waters, without further extension into the national domain.

If, in the course of development of British Columbia waters, there is water left over, the Rocky Mountain Trench is the natural reservoir for it, and the Canadian West—not the United States Northwest, or Southwest, or Midwest—is the logical beneficiary.

The natural reservoir sites of the Rocky Mountain Trench were not discovered by Parsons' engineers. The Peace River waters now being dammed up by British Columbia will be held in the Trench by structures outside it. The Trench will provide a reservoir for water of Canadian origin from the Kootenay branch of the Columbia River, to be impounded by the United States at heavy cost to Canada in terms of sacrificed opportunities, as well as in benefits which should, in equity, be payable for Canadian waters used for consumption in the United States.

Parsons' engineers did not originate the idea of pumping water over the Rocky Mountains from reservoirs in the Trench. The capture of Columbia and Kootenay river waters in the Trench, and their diversion over the Rockies, is the logical first step in development of additional water supplies for the Canadian Prairies.

Studies made or under way by the provinces of Alberta and Saskatchewan have already laid the groundwork for extensive utilization of the Saskatchewan River system. Saskatchewan studies even cover the underground water courses of this system. Tentative agreement has been reached for a joint federal-provincial inventory of the water resources of the entire Saskatchewan and Nelson river systems. This covers a network stretching from Hudson Bay and the Lake of the Woods to the Rocky Mountains. Joint Canada-Manitoba studies for extensive power development of the Nelson River, including diversion from the Churchill River, were completed early in 1966. Work on Nelson River power sites is already under way.

The Canadian Prairie region can look forward to maximum development of its agricultural potential being made possible by water for irrigation. It can also anticipate major developments in mineral, fossil, and forest resources. The logical consequence of such development will be a major petrochemical industry, metal-producing industries, pulp and paper industries—and these all call for large supplies of water from the annual flow available.

The northward course of our Prairie empire is already being staked out by prospectors and timber cruisers. It has already reached the great tributaries of the Mackenzie River system — the Peace and the Athabasca rivers. Massive lead-zinc deposits are being mined at Pine Point on Great Slave Lake, one of the huge natural balancing reservoirs of the Mackenzie system. The federal government is financing a feasibility study for a smelter at Pine Point. Mineral resources have already been staked out in the region of another great Mackenzie reservoir, Great Bear Lake.

Considering the vast potential for development of the Canadian Prairies, it seems unlikely that the waters of the Canadian Cordillera would ever reach the Great Lakes as NAWAPA proposes. What does seem possible is the re-routing of waters flowing into Hudson Bay to the Prairie region. NAWAPA, however, offers to bring western water to the Great Lakes—an offer which had rather more appeal in 1964 when the levels were low than is the case today, now that they have recovered. Here I am dealing with a matter in which I have had a close personal interest and responsibility, as Chairman of the Canadian Section of the IJC in the flood year of 1952 and later. The proponents seem to be quite unfamiliar with the experience during the high-water of 1952, and with the very careful studies made then and subsequently.

These studies showed the sensitivity of the basin to the cumulative effects of even a short succession of years of supply only slightly above normal. The limiting factors are the great industrial and municipal developments which have taken place along the shores of the Great Lakes, and more particularly along the connecting channels, whose capacities have been formed by the rivers through long ages to accommodate natural flows. Any cumulative increase in net supply is accompanied by large sustained increases in levels, and the damage, even for very small changes in levels, is disproportionately severe. This was noted in the surveys conducted by the IJC in 1952-53, and is reflected in the damage claims made at that time—for which, even after the lapse of more than a decade, Canada is about to be sued by interests in the United States.

The costs of channel enlargements to correct this situation in high supply years would be very large, and such enlargements would accentuate the difficulties in low supply years. Moreover, the investigations showed that the time required for changes in supply to pass through the system is very long, and the relationship is very complex. Consequently, for controlled changes in the inflow to the system to stabilize levels and flows, would require an ability to predict natural supply for a period further into the future than is foreseeable. Without this ablity to predict, artificial changes in supply would aggravate periodic crises and in particular increase the danger of flooding, which already causes the greatest anxiety.

In my address to the Canadian Club in Montreal in October, 1965, I referred to some of the serious legal and political implications of the NAWAPA scheme. I observed at that time that this is a monstrous concept, not only in terms of physical magnitude, but also in another and more sinister sense, in that the promoters would displace Canadian sovereignty over the national waters of Canada, and substitute therefor a diabolic thesis that *all* waters of North America become a shared resource, of which most will be drawn off for the benefit of the midwest and southwest regions of the United States, where existing desert areas will be made to bloom at the expense of development in Canada.

Evidently the NAWAPA proposal contemplates that the complete jurisdiction and control will rest with a corporation which, although it might be nominally international, would in reality be dominated by Americans, who would thereby acquire a formidable vested interest in the national waters of Canada. With this mammoth inroad into Canada's lawful rights and interests, the corporation would inevitably, in the nature of things, have to assume quasi-sovereign power to administer large areas of Canada at the expense of Canadian sovereignty.

I was very interested to hear an American, William S. Foster, editor of *The American City*, speak of the implications of water export on a CBC television programme on the politics of water, on April 11, 1966. Mr. Foster said:

There's a great deal of risk. Offhand, at first glance, you would say that the risk is great for the southwest because the water belongs to Canada, and presumably at Canada's wish it could simply turn off the valve and the water would not be there any more. But there is a more subtle threat than that. I wonder just what would happen to the sovereignty of Canada if a nation like the United States and a nation like Mexico would suddenly say that "you no longer have the right to deny us the water even though you need it in your own industrial and agricultural development." I've often thought about that and wondered what the really long-range risks are to Canada, and I think they're considerable.

The situation in the U.S. Southwest is that any additional water which becomes available is forthwith applied to irrigation; and so if cheap Canadian water is supplied, as it is now under the Columbia River Treaty, and would be under the NAWAPA plan, it will be immediately appropriated by the irrigators. Large increases in population and investment may be anticipated, and there does not appear to be any *cheap* replacement should the Canadian water be recalled.

You will appreciate the serious probability of conflict in such a situation when I mention that the Canadian Minister of External Affairs has given assurances to the External Affairs Committee of Parliament that under the Columbia River Treaty, the Protocol, and the Sales Agreement, Canada can make use of waters of Canadian origin for consumptive purposes at any time and in conjunction with power generation in transit. When Canada does exercise this reservation, which I regard as inevitable, will the United States acquiesce in this interpretation of provisions in the Protocol agreed to by the United States Executive, but not included in the ratification by the Senate?

I believe that such a situation is much too hazardous to be left to a giant corporation dominated by United States interests. Canada faced a similar situation 25 years ago when it exported electric power to the United States on yearly permit. When under dire necessity of war we wanted it back we met a curt refusal. I do not think Canada should ever again expose herself to such an outcome, particularly over water, which is an even more sensitive matter.

To me it is obvious that if we make a bargain to divert water to the United States, we cannot ever discontinue or we shall face force to compel compliance. There is nothing in our experience to date which indicates any change in the vigour with which our American friends pursue objectives which they deem in their national interests, however much this may hurt a neighbour who has unwittingly made a careless bargain in other circumstances. Instance after instance can be cited in support of this observation, from the case of the Similkameen River after World War I to the most recent example, when the Columbia River Treaty was hailed in the Senate of the United States as having achieved one major American objective, which was to prevent Canada making best use of her waters of Canadian origin in the Basin[3].

The imperative lesson is that we must be very careful in our discussions of vital problems related to water with the United States, and very, very careful over the bargains which we may make to ensure that the rights we think we have are admitted and confirmed beforehand.

One of the ironic things about all of this fuss regarding the export of Canada's water to the United States is that the United States has abundant supplies of water for all of its needs. What is scarce in the United States is *clean* water. This could be provided at less cost by proper administration and pollution control than by importation from Canada. In fact, I am inclined to believe that in the long run perhaps one of the most unfriendly acts that Canada could do to the United States would be to offer our water at bargain prices. Because if we did, the attack on pollution might then be postponed until the problem was no longer soluble, or the cost would be astronomical. This cost is large enough today, and it rises with every passing year at an accelerating rate.

In the foregoing, I have sought to indicate some of the perils which face Canada with respect to the commitment of our water resources at this time. We have everything to lose by hasty and ill-considered action, and we have everything to gain by waiting until the essential information is available upon which we can make our own assessment of the subject of sharing resources, and our own plans as to the course of action we shall adopt.

---

[3] Senate Hearings, May 8, 1961, Udall.

25

Water Yield Improvement Research in Canada: Needs and Future Trends

W. W. Jeffrey

Introduction

This paper deals in part with future trends. This is a difficult and somewhat thankless task, where the best result to be anticipated is the most general of approximations.

It is probably desirable however that, in a time of technological and management change, one tries to some extent to look into the future in relation to new and pertinent topics within the work area of a professional field. Water yield improvement in forest land management is one such relatively new topic in the forestry profession.

Water Yield Improvement: Terms of Reference

Water is usually considered in terms of three characteristics: (1) yield (quantity), (2) regime (timing), and (3) quality. Water yield improvement deals with quantity and timing of flow. However, considerations of water quality can never be ignored, and inevitably one consistently is obliged to return to consideration of the water quality characteristic. In addition, it is in relation to water quality that foresters most frequently find themselves, in the present state of Canadian forest management, in controversy with workers in other disciplines or with the public at large.

Paper presented to the Annual Meeting of the Canadian Institute of Forestry, Banff, Alberta, 1966.

The improvement of water yield has a number of facets. For the improvement of flow regime, it is possible to carry out artificial recharge of deep surficial deposits during the peak flow period (water spreading), or to manipulate deliberately the depth and pattern of snow accumulation in the alpine zone above timberline. These practices do not generally appear to result in any significant increase in the total amount of water produced, but rather in a change in the time of delivery of water at points of use. Since they deal with rather specialized conditions and objectives, they are not considered further.

Research has been carried out using chemical anti-transpirants sprayed directly on tree foliage. On individual trees under experimental conditions these have shown interesting results. On an area trial basis their initial promise has not yet been fulfilled. Other studies have dealt with the development of genetic strains of grass, specifically Bermuda grass (*Cynodon dactylon* (L.) Pers.), having lowered transpiration rates. This, again, is in a wholly experimental setting also.

It is in the realm of forest manipulation that much of the research into water yield improvement has been carried out. Tests undertaken in calibrated experimental watersheds in a number of areas have shown that the removal of tree cover has resulted in a statistically significant increase in total water yield. Forest removal has been either total, as in some of the Coweeta experiments, or partial, as at Fraser, Colorado and Workman Creek, Arizona.

In the U.S.A., these tests began in the Wagon Wheel Gap experiment in Colorado, the results of which were published in 1926, continued at Coweeta, North Carolina, and have been extended into various other parts of the continental United States in the post-war years. Probably the most celebrated of these studies is that carried out on the Fool Creek watershed at Fraser, Colorado, where results have been coming out subsequent to the mid-1950's.

Yield increases have ranged from a high of 16 inches from complete cutting in one of the Coweeta experiments, to low increases in the Workman Creek (Arizona) watersheds, where a relatively small volumetric increase was found to result from treatment of a small proportional area of high transpiration site.

The studies carried out in the United States have concerned themselves primarily with total water yield and have dealt with flow timing to a lesser extent. In some areas, however, flow timing is a primary waterflow characteristic, since the possibility of artificial storage in which to impound increased flows may be slight, or lacking entirely. Research has been carried out into shading of the snowpack in forest cuttings, in an attempt to retard snow-melt for flow regime improvement.

In all of these tests, considerations of water quality have not been ignored. Sedimentation resulting from logging and road system construction has typically been measured, it being generally agreed that more water will only be valuable if it is of a quality fit for use when it reaches its points of use.

There are relatively few figures dealing with the total potential for water yield improvement. One U.S. source (U.S. Senate, 1960) has made estimates according to forest types in the United States. Increases in some western U.S. forest types, which are present in Canada, ranged from 16 to 22 per cent of present yield, or 3.0 to 4.5 inches water yield increase. These figures refer to treated area and not to whole watersheds.

In this brief summary, no mention has been made of phreato-phyte or other riparian vegetation removal to improve water yield. Considerable research has been done on this topic also.

Another type of water yield improvement could be considered. This is flood avoidance or flood control. This, however, is a separate topic in itself and will not be discussed.

Why Should Foresters be Concerned?

The preceding paragraphs of this presentation have trafficked largely in the standard statements dealing with water yield improve-ment. It is now meet to consider the basic question of why foresters should at all concern themselves with water production from forested lands. Too frequently this question is overlooked under the bland, and oftentimes erroneous, assumption that the answer is obvi-ous to everyone, and that there is general agreement that this is a legitimate forestry concern. There frequently appears, however, a more-or-less widespread feeling among foresters that their primary concern is with wood production, to the virtual, or total, exclusion of other resources. This opinion tends somewhat to be fostered by the organizational make-up of many of our government serv-ices, where different organizations (often in poor, or practically negligible, contact and liaison) are responsible for different land products, and whose leaders must predominantly, quite often, be engaged in furthering their own politico-organizational interests and the interests of their own particular product.

In Europe, it is true that in some countries the forestry service has been for many years the service of "waters and forests", so that there exists there a tradition of long-standing recognition of the interrelationships of wood and water resources. However, this argument, if pressed, is certain to evoke the reasonable response that no one is particularly influenced by the developmental history of resource-management thinking in Europe. Therefore the contention that in other parts of the world there has been a well recognized bond between forests and water is likely to create few ripples in Canada.

The products of wildland are varied: wood, water, fur, game, fish, grazing, recreation and minerals. In the past, the forestry profession has been primarily identified with wood products. This in large degree has been a function of our university training, in which we have learned either exclusively timber management, or primarily timber management with lip service given to other resource needs. Under such circumstances, it is unfair to fault the individual forester when he tends to reflect this orientation in his professional practice. The fact that, in certain sectors of the community, fault may nowadays be found with the forester who, in this way, faithfully parrots the lessons and attitudes he learned at his instructor's knee, is a measure of changing social conditions.

Land management in Canada may soon be entering an era of vastly increased attention to resources other than wood products. The motive force seems likely to be public opinion, manifesting itself as public pressure upon all levels of government. This evolution of opinion has its origin in development of living standards, availability of leisure time, use of leisure time, easy travel, and rapid, universal communication. Vast changes have occurred from the depression days of the 1930's, when the public preoccupation was economic; today's interests are more social and aesthetic, and to a considerable degree deal with maintenance of the environment. One need only consider recent developments in pollution—consciousness to assess the direction and spread of this trend.

Public awareness is now beginning to focus upon the interrelationship of forests and water. This is not always an informed awareness; this defect does not, however, particularly in the absence of demonstrable regional fact, in any way reduce its political potency.

Current examples of popular generalized opinions in the public mind are:

1—"Logging dries up the streams"
2—"Logging kills the springs"
3—"Logging increases the freshet"
4—"Logging reduces late season flow"

5—"Logging silts the creeks"

6—"Logging ruins the fishing"

Such public generalizations do little to ease the foresters' burden.

Many land management (or so-called conservation) pressure groups, now gaining in strength, and (more significantly) in organization, are concentrated in large metropolitan areas. This is a general phenomenon; city people often have a vicarious concern over resource management, along with a vicarious enjoyment of what they consider to be unspoiled nature. (This is particularly evident in wilderness preservation groups in the United States.) These persons also have minimal contact with the wood-harvesting and wood-using industries.

Nevertheless, lack of personal contact notwithstanding, to many of these groups the image of the logger is that of a collective "hairy beast", a giant, remorseless, insensible agent of total destruction, a generalization which seems unfair to a productive industry. In this image the professional forester is not entirely unconnected. He often occupies a similar equivocal stature in the eyes of water resource specialists, agriculturists, engineers, recreation specialists, fish and game biologists and soil scientists, as being, perhaps not in the "hairy beast" category, but certainly as being primarily wood-oriented with little patience and concern for other land values.

Unpalatable as this may be, it is often not without a certain plausibility. However, we can live, if not proudly at least tolerably with a poor image, and so, of course, can the logging and wood-using industries.

Unfortunately, the images above, where they exist, tend (to put it mildly) to alienate public support, and to help generate public pressures. In turn, this is likely to be an important factor in public policy. In the future, such influences upon public policy cannot logically be expected to diminish.

If we ignore public pressure, and the often-legitimate concern it expresses, we may be setting the stage eventually for increased and harmful regulatory control of timber harvest. The day may come, in some areas, when the legitimate and proper harvesting of wood products may be severely inhibited by unnecessarily restrictive legislation.

While there can be little doubt that logging standards and land management practices are economically capable of considerable improvement, it would not necessarily be a forward step in land management were an "over-reaction" to current laxity in practice to inhibit Canadian industrial development.

Assuming that, in one degree or another, such an "over-reaction" is possible, it remains to examine what alternatives are available to us to counteract it should it show signs of developing. Basic to this examination, is the fact that data on forest-water interactions in Canada are everywhere sparse, and in many areas so sparse as to be for practical purposes non-existent. Furthermore, in the current state of hydrologic knowledge, severe limitations exist in the extrapolation of results developed elsewhere into Canadian conditions, without further testing of their regional validity within Canada.

The solution may be to accept without reservations the interdependence of water resources and timber management practices. This inevitably means that we must obtain, through research and trial, the factual material needed to form a base for what in effect may be considerably modified land management policies. Moreover, we have to do this at some time sufficiently in advance of the danger period and not as a "crash program" in response to a need which has already become crucial and immediate.

By the development and proper substantiation of pertinent and adequate facts, and their skilful public presentation, a useful alleviation of public concern can be established. A by-product would be modification of the image we have in some sectors, and its replacement by the concept of the forester as a genuine resource manager. Should adverse public opinion and public pressure continue to develop, such an approach, based fundamentally upon adequate and continuing research in forest hydrology, will allow us to take a positive attitude in developing a base for watershed and water yield improvement. The alternative seems to be perpetually under suspicion and permanently on the defensive.

The fact that a similar argument may be made for recreation, fishery, game and other resources is obvious. While it will not be explored, it seems eloquently provocative of thought about the development of the forestry profession, and it is not inconceivable that it may come to signify that if we do not ourselves develop more than we have in the past, into *bona fide* resource managers, many of us may find in time that we are working for men, trained in other professions, who have.

It would be unrealistic, lightly to dismiss the problems which such a step would present. These must be recognized and placed in perspective. Inevitably, acceptance of responsibilities in wildland hydrology as an integral part of forest management means that cutting may have to be foregone in some areas, and that in others it may have to be postponed pending the development of adequate management practices through research. It is likely, however, that areas in which cutting must perpetually be prohibited would be relatively small in area. It probably means considerable management reorientation and intensification. It certainly means a large program of forest hydrology research.

A special problem is posed in company limits. Where a management objective is to improve waterflows, the question arises as to how much responsibility a company has to provide for improvement of the general good. Where the public holds strong opinions, it does not necessarily follow that these are accepted by shareholders. In fact, it may occur that individuals may hold two divergent sets of opinions, one as a member of the public at large, the other as a corporate investor. This of course applies to other resource uses in addition to water, and seems likely to develop into a difficult problem in many parts of Canada in the future.

Present Status of Water Yield Improvement Research in Canada

The most comprehensive Canadian program of water yield improvement research is that presently underway in the Saskatchewan River headwaters in Alberta (Jeffrey, 1965a). In this program, in effect since the early 1960's three fully instrumental experimental watersheds are being put into operation. Two at least of these have a primary function of water yield improvement research, dealing with subalpine (*Picea-Abies*) and lodgepole pine forests. The third is concerned with montane trembling aspen forests. The possibilities of water yield improvement in this basin appear somewhat lesser in scope.

More significant, perhaps, than the total number of research basins involved, are the facts that the program has been developed so that an inter-disciplinary research team may carry out a sustained program of investigation, and that the basins are not operating *in vacuo,* but are only one integral part of a program of research going on at all levels of detail.

Compared to the East Slopes program, no other present program of research can be considered equally comprehensive or sustained. Some work is being done in the Montmorency Research Forest at Laval University in Quebec, where a research basin has been set up, and some studies have been carried out, or are underway, at the University of Toronto.

In British Columbia, an experimental watershed has been put into operation in the Okanagan area. This watershed deals primarily with flow timing effects resulting from logging. It is the beginning stage of a larger research program of forest manipulation effects upon all water characteristics in the Okanagan area, to be instituted by the University of British Columbia, in co-operation with such agencies as prove interested in the research program. In conjunction, analysis by UBC graduate students seeks to establish the utility of already existing data pertinent to forest cutting-waterflow interactions.

It is, of course, true that some work which is to one degree or another pertinent is being carried out in cognate fields. A recent resumé of this work is available (Jeffrey, 1965b).

In summary, water yield improvement research in Canada, a few years ago non-existent, is presently meagre and scattered.

Research Approaches in Water Yield Improvement: Possible Future Trends

In most expositions of water yield improvement research, it has been customary for attention to be concentrated upon research basin studies. Certainly, such studies have produced most of the generally quoted yield increase figures. This resulted for a time in widespread over-emphasis upon experimental basins, or in a lack of understanding of the place occupied by the research basin in the overall scheme of water yield improvement research.

The experimental watershed research, which has attracted attention in the United States and elsewhere, has been properly of a demonstration nature. As such, it has settled a number of controversial questions and provided data which no other research tool could produce. These studies, carried out as they were, had a proper place in the initial phase of water yield improvement research.

As a result of these studies there, however, developed an unfortunate tendency to regard the unsupplemented experimental basin as an adequate and sufficient tool for water yield—forest manipulation research. This opinion was far from correct. Any research basin, no matter how carefully chosen, is a complex system. Simply to carry out a gross treatment in such a situation and to observe the results, does not lead to vastly improved understanding of the system, nor does it tend to cast any brilliant illumination upon the hydrologic processes and mechanisms at work within the system. How they may have been affected by treatment, and how they interact one upon the other under treatment conditions, are not greatly elucidated.

Nowadays, some dissatisfaction and disillusionment has resulted from these past limitations of calibrated basin-treatment experiment research. This type of gross demonstratory experiment has been described as a sequence as "calibrate, cut and publish". While no thoughtful person today will advocate repetition of calibrated watershed experimentation, exactly as it has been done in the past, to be exaggeratedly critical of it is to show a lack of understanding of the stage of development within which such studies were carried out. Moreover, this reaction against, and disappointment with, the experimental watershed has created a danger of dispensing altogether with calibrated watershed experimentation.

Such a development would be unfortunate, since certain necessary data can only be obtained through basin treatment experimentation. These data are usually required at a rather late stage in research development. Since a long period is needed to instrument, survey and calibrate a set of experimental watersheds, by instituting a program of research basin instrumentation at the inception of a program of research a good calibration may be available at the time when research has progressed to the point that a treatment experiment is justified. In other words, while the results of basin treatment by cover manipulation usually belong to a late stage of research, initial basin instrumentation cannot be delayed until this stage.

Properly utilized, the research basin in water yield improvement research should function as an overall "integrator" of the results of many more limited and detailed studies, dealing with specific hydrologic processes and mechanisms. A refined hypothesis can thus be tested in the basin treatment experiment, and a base is made available for the rational design of this terminal experimental treatment.

It is in the implementation of these limited and detailed studies of hydrologic processes and mechanisms that emphasis will be placed in the future. Such studies will seek to elucidate the various terrestrial components of the hydrologic cycle, and to make comparisons between forest types, forest conditions and forest sites.

Much work needs to be concentrated upon evapo-transpiration estimates to solve the basic questions of how much water on a per acre basis is evaporated under given conditions in a given unit of time, and how such losses compare between forest situations and between vegetation types. Considerations of forest type, composition, density, structure, and site will have to be examined in such research.

Such research is needed to provide a basis for intelligent experimentation in gauged and calibrated research basins. In study of this type, dealing with hydrologic processes in a vegetated landscape, the benefits of research are not confined to forest hydrology. Consideration of a partial list of research topics (viz. water movement in the forest ecosystem, stomatal reaction, heat loads, energy partitioning, rooting, depth, water uptake, water availability) demonstrates the utility of such study to knowledge of forest autecology.

A prime research need is that of identification of high transpiration sites, areas where due to specific conditions (e.g. sub-irrigation by groundwater) transpiration loss is higher than in other parts of the landscape. These situations, once identified, are logical locations for the concentration of research and of specialized forest-watershed management practices. In this identification process we may expect to see higher utilization of remote-sensing techniques, and the development and refinement of ground methods to check the validity of remote-sensing data.

In the field of snow-forest relations a great deal of companion study research is required. Such topics as snow interception by forest canopy, over-winter water losses from forest snowpack, snow-melt and soil moisture recharge, soil frost, and snowmelt retardation for flow regime improvement, may be cited, along with the basic question of forest-snowmelt-flood interactions in appropriate areas.

While companion studies are underway to provide a basis for experimental watershed research, certain research avenues may be expected to be followed in the study of small basin hydrology. One of the largest watershed management problems is that of extrapolation of results from experimental watersheds. Methods of hydrograph synthesis from hydrologic data will receive study, as a means of attempting to predict flows and flow patterns in ungauged areas. Such hydrologic "model-building" may be expected to receive a major share of research attention. Hand-in-hand with this development will be research into basin instrumentation requirements. A first step towards this is the recent development of a Canadian set of current guidelines for such studies (Can. Nat. Comm., I.H.D., 1966).

Where flow regime problems are a major regional consideration it may be expected that short-term research basin studies will be implemented to provide data. One example of this research trend is the University of British Columbia research basin in the Okanagan which is being designed to test the influence of forest cutting upon hydrograph shape and the timing of flow delivery.

In other areas, it is likely that research will be concentrated upon forest-groundwater inter-relationships, whether of shallow water tables close to the soil surface (paludification) or the effect of logging on larger areas of groundwater recharge.

However, it would be misleading to leave this topic without consideration of some of the broader needs of research. The first topic, and an obvious one, is that of research into the economics of a products-mix from wildland areas, and of assigning costs and values to waterflows originating in forested areas. Another need is the necessity to integrate research with that required in the management of other resources, particularly the fishery resource, whether of recreational sport fishery or of anadromous fish of direct commercial value.

Finally, we may safely say that as time goes on more attention will come to be paid to "time trends", the durability and decay rates of water yield increases resulting from forest manipulation.

Where is Research Needed?

To evaluate forest hydrology research needs in Canada would require a major effort, preferably by a qualified team. It would be presumptuous to attempt this evaluation here. However, certain generalizations may be made with some degree of confidence.

Research seems needed in three main avenues:

(1) study in those regions suffering from water problems in which vegetation is a pertinent factor.

(2) investigation to establish which portions of research done elsewhere may safely be used as a base for more advanced studies in Canada.

(3) estimation of the past and current hydrologic effects of existing cover disturbance.

Only the first of these potential research avenues lends itself at all readily to further discussion. Areas where water yield improvement research may readily be undertaken could be identified by some or all of the following standards.

1. areas where water is *presently* short and at a premium for municipal, industrial or agricultural use, or for pollutant dilution.

2. areas where water is *potentially* in short supply due to probable increase in population, industrial development or irrigation requirements.

3. areas from which water might be diverted through engineering works into other drainage basins, thereby creating a deficit within the basin from which the water is being taken.

4. areas with present or potential hydro-power developments

which would be capable of handling more water if it were available.

5. areas having a significant recreational load and where increased waterflow might be the basis for an expanded sport fishery.

It would be incorrect to apply these criteria solely on a broad regional basis. It is likely that even in relatively humid regions, as management guidelines, these have application of direct pertinence to small basins supplying water for municipal or domestic use, for irrigation or for other agricultural use. In such situations, water yield increases through forest watershed management might be a more economical solution to water shortage than diversion from other basins or by large pumping lifts from large bodies of water at lower elevations. Furthermore, anticipated population increases and the rural-to-urban shift in population are likely to expand considerably the areas to which these criteria currently apply, within a relatively short period in the future. Lastly, it is to be noted that these criteria deal only with water yield improvement and not with watershed protection or watershed rehabilitation.

Obvious large areas to which the criteria apply are the Saskatchewan River headwaters of Alberta and much of the dry interior of British Columbia. The Okanagan, the East Kootenay and the Kamloops-Ashcroft-Merritt regions may be identified in the latter instance. However, these are only the results of broad, regional evaluations. On a smaller scale of evaluation, the pertinence of water yield improvement might appear considerably more widespread geographically.

It is likely, furthermore, that in some areas increased water yields resulting from conventional timber harvest are already apportioned and licensed, and that in the absence of special management, water will be in short supply once full vegetative recovery takes place.

Conclusion

In summarizing this presentation, only the major points will be recapitulated.

(1) Predicting future requirements is a difficult and frequently thankless task.

(2) We are dealing with only one portion of forest hydrology subject matter, and should not forget the even more important topic of water quality.

(3) Water yield improvement concerns itself with both yield (quantity) and timing of flow delivery.

(4) For our purposes we are concerned primarily with yield improvement through forest manipulation.

(5) Yield increase potentialities in water deficit areas seem fairly high.

(6) Public awareness in forest-water interactions is growing.

(7) Because of the likelihood of this awareness generating increased public pressures, it is in the interests of the forestry profession to accept responsibility for water production and water quality maintenance from forest lands, and to institute an adequate research program to provide a sound basis for reasonable management.

(8) Consideration of water production, as is also true of other wildland resources, pose a difficult problem in the management of company limits.

(9) There is not much water yield improvement research underway in Canada at the present time.

(10) Future research approaches are likely to involve a combination of research methods, of which the calibrated watershed technique will be only one, albeit an important component.

(11) More attention is likely to be paid to flow timing.

(12) Some areas where research is needed can be recognized on a broad, regional basis.

(13) It is likely that the application of a few logical criteria would result in recognition of localized situations in many other parts of the country.

(14) It is necessary to plan for future population shifts and increases in sufficient time for research results to be available when needed.

26

The Contribution of Social Science Research to Water Resource Management in Canada

W. R. D. Sewell

Section I

Introduction

One of the most significant features of the past decade has been the increasing public debate about the management and use of Canada's water resources. Water resource development has often aroused public discussion in Canada, particularly because such development has had important economic, social, and political consequences. What is new is the intensity and the continuousness of the debate. Water problems have now become major issues in political campaigns. They have been the basis of bitter disputes between the provinces and the Federal Government, and between Canada and the United States. In recent years they have claimed an increasing proportion of the time of the House of Commons and the various provincial legislatures as well as a growing amount of attention in the various media of mass communication.

Reprinted in edited form from *Water Resources Research in Canada,* Special Study No. 5, Science Secretariat (1968), pp. 117-40. By permission of the Queen's Printer, Ottawa.

There are several reasons for the recent awakening of public concern about water problems in Canada. One of them is the increasing number and complexity of conflicts in water use.[1] As population has grown, as industry has expanded, and as urbanization has proceeded, competition for the use of particular water supplies has intensified and has sometimes resulted in severe conflicts of interest between water users. A second reason is rooted in the increasing demand for a higher quality environment. Canadians are no longer satisfied with merely increasing their income; they also wish to improve the environment in which they live, work, and recreate. Suddenly an awareness of the effects of urbanization and industrialization has developed. Problems of air and water pollution are now among the most popular topics of public discussion in many parts of the country.[2] At the same time increasing affluence has led to an increase in leisure time and this in turn has given rise to growing demands for outdoor recreation.[3] More and more pressure is being placed on governments to deal with pollution problems and to increase opportunities for outdoor recreation.

A third source of public debate relates to the roles that the various levels of government can most appropriately play in developing the nation's water resources. The BNA Act gives the provinces title to the resources within their territory, and apart from the use of such resources for certain purposes (namely navigation, fisheries, and agricultural purposes), and except for those cases in which inter-provincial or international problems arise, it leaves the provinces free to develop them in whatsoever way they wish.[4] It has become increasingly clear in recent years, however, that many

1 For discussions of these problems, see Canadian Council of Resource Ministers, *The Administration of Water Resources in Canada* (Montreal, 1965), and K. Kristjanson and W. R. D. Sewell, "Water Management Problems and Issues in Canada", *Resources for Tomorrow Conference Background Papers* (Ottawa, Queen's Printer, 1961), Vol. 1, pp. 205-210.

2 See Canadian Council of Resource Ministers, *National Conference on Pollution and Our Environment, Background Papers and Proceedings* (Montreal, 1966).

3 For a discussion of increasing demands for recreation in Canada, see Lloyd Brooks, "Demand for Recreation Space in Canada", Ralph R. Krueger, F. O. Sargent, A. de Vos and Norman Pearson (eds.), *Regional and Resource Planning in Canada* (Holt, Rinehart and Winston, 1963), pp. 200-211. For a discussion of increasing demands in a region, see J. Howard Richards, "Gross Aspects of Planning and Outdoor Recreation with Particular Reference to Saskatchewan", *Canadian Geographer*, Vol. XI, no. 2 (1967), pp. 117-123.

4 See Bora Laskin, "Jurisdictional Framework for Water Management", *Resources for Tomorrow Conference Background Papers* (Ottawa, Queen's Printer, 1961), Vol. 1, pp. 211-226.

water problems by their nature and magnitude are of greater than provincial concern, particularly in those cases where water resources are shared by more than one province, or where provincial financial resources or technical expertise are not adequate to ensure efficient development.

Proposals relating to the diversion of water from Canada to the United States have also been the subject of public discussion. Among the various proposals, the NAWAPA scheme[5] and the Grand Canal scheme[6] have received particular attention. Although it is widely claimed that Canada possesses vast water resources, opinion is divided as to whether, and under what circumstances, the export of water to the United States should be sanctioned.[7] The arguments against export rest mainly on claims that "Canada may need the water in the future" and that "export today may mean higher cost water for Canadians tomorrow." Unfortunately it is not possible to appraise the validity of these claims as data relating to water use in Canada and as to probable costs of developing new sources of supply are presently lacking.

A fifth source of debate about water management in Canada stems from the increasing demands on the public purse to supply goods and services derived from water resource development, particularly those which are not ordinarily supplied through the market mechanism, such as recreation facilities, de-pollution of lakes and streams, and flood hazard reduction. Questions have been raised as to what criteria should be applied in determining how much the public sector should invest in this regard, and in selecting between competing alternative claims on Federal and provincial budgets.[8]

Debates about the foregoing matters have brought into serious question the adequacy of present policies, laws, and administrative arrangements to deal with the emerging problems of water man-

---

5 The NAWAPA scheme is described in U.S. Senate, Committee on Public Works, Special Subcommittee on Western Water Development, *Western Water Development* (Washington, U.S. Government Printing Office, 1966).
6 The Grand Canal scheme is described in Thomas W. Kierans, "The Grand Canal Concept and the Great Lakes", Canada, House of Commons Standing Committee on Mines, Forests and Waters, *Minutes of Proceedings and Evidence*, No. 9 (Ottawa, Queen's Printer, March 11, 1965).
7 For a summary of the various viewpoints, see W. R. Derrick Sewell, "A Continental Water System: Pipe Dream or Practical Possibility", *Bulletin of the Atomic Scientists* (September, 1967), pp. 8-13. See also Blair Fraser, "Water Crisis Coming", *Macleans* (March 5, 1966), p. 7 and pp. 30-33; T. Lloyd, "A Water Resource Policy for Canada", *Canadian Geographical Journal*, Vol. 73, no. 1 (July 1963), pp. 2-17; and E. Kuiper, "Canadian Water Export", *The Engineering Journal* (July 1966), pp. 3-8.
8 See P. H. Pearse, "Public Management and Mismanagement of Natural Resources in Canada", *Queen's Quarterly* (Spring 1966), pp. 86-99.

agement in Canada. It is evident, for example, that some past policies have failed to attain their objectives. Flood losses continue to mount despite expenditures on flood protection.[9] Pollution continues to increase despite the enactment of laws and regulations to control it.[10] It is also clear that the objectives of water management are broadening. No longer is it only a matter of finding the best technical and financial means of solving a given water problem. Increasingly it involves the consideration of effects on other water uses, relative costs of alternative solutions, aesthetic values and so on. At the same time the need to accommodate the goals and objectives of several levels of administration in water planning is becoming increasingly apparent. Means must be found, therefore, to co-ordinate policies and functions of the agencies concerned.[11] In the future, economic, social, and political considerations are likely to play a more and more important role in water management decisions. As a consequence, greater emphasis will need to be placed on social science research to provide the necessary information and guidelines for choice-making.

At present, expenditures on social science research in the water management field in Canada are extremely small. From the survey undertaken by the Study Group, and from supplementary data, it appears that such expenditures amount to less than $280,000 a year,[12] about 3.3 per cent of all research expenditures on water problems in Canada. This sum is minute when compared with investment in water development in Canada, some $750 million a year, or expenditures on physical science aspects of water management, estimated by the Study Group to be about $8,110,300 a year.[13] Many of the problems that are now on the horizon can be traced in part to the lack of attention to the human dimensions of water management. It is clear that there must be a vastly increased research

[9] See W. R. D. Sewell, *Water Management and Floods in the Fraser River Basin* (Chicago, University of Chicago Department of Geography, Research Series No. 100, 1965).

[10] Canadian Council of Resource Ministers, *op. cit.*

[11] See T. M. Patterson, "Administrative Framework for Water Management", *Resources for Tomorrow Background Papers* (Ottawa, Queen's Printer, 1961), Vol. 1, pp. 227-279.

[12] These data relate to expenditures reported under categories 601, 602, 603, 604, 605, 606, 607, 608, and 700 specified in the Questionnaire circulated by the Science Secretariat. They related both to "in house" research undertaken by government agencies, research carried out under contract to such agencies, and research supported by grants in aid to universities.

[13] These data relate to the remaining categories not covered by economic, social, and institutional research. Detailed breakdowns of these expenditures appear above in the Science Secretariat's Special Study No. 5, *Water Resources Research in Canada.*

effort in this connection. How much more money is needed? What are the questions that are most urgently in need of answer? How can the present obstacles to an expansion of the research effort be overcome? What modifications are needed in existing institutional frameworks to ensure that the results of research efforts will find their way into water resources planning and development?

Section II

MAJOR WATER RESOURCES PROBLEMS IN CANADA: POSSIBLE CLASSIFICATIONS

What are the major water management problems in Canada? Several attempts have been made to answer this question in resources conferences,[14] hearings of the Standing Committee on Mines, Forests and Waters,[15] and various studies undertaken under the auspices of the Canadian Council of Resource Ministers.[16] The reports which have resulted provide a useful though incomplete source of information. An attempt was made by the Secretariat of the Canadian Council of Resource Ministers to update this data for the purposes of the present study. There may still be gaps in the updated listing, but it is believed that it does provide a reasonable starting point for the purposes of this paper.

To facilitate a review of needed social science research the various water problems must somehow be classified. Several classifications are possible and five have been selected for discussion here, namely: emerging issues, geographical incidence, disciplinary or professional interests, phases in the planning and development process, and decision-making elements.

1. Emerging Issues

Water resources problems may be classified according to the extent to which they arouse public concern. There is a broad spectrum of problems ranging from those which arouse little or no concern to those which give rise to intense public debate.

At one end of the spectrum are problems which arise in the day-to-day operations of a water management project, such as a

---

[14] See, for example, *Resources for Tomorrow Conference Background Papers, op. cit.;* Canadian Council of Resource Ministers, *op. cit.;* and B.C. Natural Resources Conference, *Transactions of the 14th Conference* (Victoria, 1962).

[15] Canada, House of Commons Standing Committee on Mines, Forests, and Waters, *Hearings* (Ottawa, 1960 and 1965).

[16] Canadian Council of Resource Ministers, *The Administration of Water Resources in Canada* (Montreal, 1966).

local water supply reservoir. Such problems are usually fairly simple, and responsibility for dealing with them is allocated to the operating agency. There is seldom any need to consult public opinion as to the appropriate course of action. Generally such problems can be solved within the framework of existing policies and agency organization.

At the other end of the spectrum are problems which arouse considerable public debate, particularly where the decision might lead to an irrevocable course of action or preclude the development of other uses or alternatives. Typically such problems excite a questioning of past policies and the adequacy of the existing institutional framework to deal with the problem under discussion. Usually there is great pressure for an immediate decision. Problems of this type might be termed issues. They can be local, regional, provincial or national in scope. An illustration of a national issue in the water management field is the growing pressure for a definition of the responsibilities of the various levels of government. What functions should the Federal Government perform? In what circumstances should it actively participate in development?

In between these two extremes are the other water problems, not yet sufficiently critical to arouse concern. Decisions can still be made within the existing framework of policies, laws, and administrative organization, or with only minor modifications to it. Flood problems fall into this category. So also does the matter of agricultural rehabilitation and development. Some of the problems now in this category may eventually become Issues. Problems which appear to be on the threshold of becoming issues include water pollution, criteria for the allocation of public funds to water resources development, and the manner in which mounting flood losses should be dealt with.

2. Geographical Incidence

A second type of classification is one based on the geographical incidence of the problem. One might classify problems, for example, on a local, provincial, national or international basis. Another classification would be along "regional" lines, using various criteria for defining a region (such as urbanization, political boundaries, or watersheds). Classifications on a geographical basis have been one of the most frequently used in discussions of Canadian water problems.

For present purposes a classification based upon local, provincial, inter-provincial, national, and international categories has been adopted.

For the most part local problems, such as drainage, are of relatively minor importance and can generally be dealt with effectively by either municipal or provincial agencies. There are other problems, however, that are much wider in their incidence, and these sometimes cover a major area of a province and in certain instances two or more provinces. Major floods occur in several provinces and cover vast areas, notably in British Columbia, Manitoba and Ontario. Water scarcity has become a major concern not only in the Prairie Provinces but in certain parts of southern Ontario. Pollution is widespread in several provinces. Problems of this type might be termed "regional". To some extent they can be handled effectively by existing provincial machinery, but it is becoming increasingly clear that innovations in institutional frameworks of laws, policies and administrative arrangements will be needed as these problems grow in magnitude and geographical incidence. New Federal-provincial and inter-provincial agencies and programs will be required for this purpose.

Still other problems can be considered to have national importance. Those which involve the United States are national by definition, such as matters relating to the use and development of international lakes and rivers. Other problems are national in the sense that they are Canada-wide and consequently involve all or most of the provinces. Pollution is becoming a national problem of this type. There are certain problems, however, which, though widespread in incidence, are not clearly national problems. Floods and droughts are cases in point. The effects of these problems are felt far beyond the areas where they occur but there is no indication as to the extent to which losses sustained affect the national economy. Thus far no studies have been undertaken which would help to assess the overall impact of such losses.

3. Disciplinary Interests

A third classification might be based on the assumed interests of various disciplines. Thus matters relating to the evaluation of economic impacts of development, or the financing of such development could be classified as economic problems. Similarly problems relating to the social disruption caused by reservoir construction, or the determination of the rate of adoption of the services which a new project would provide might be classified as sociological problems. Problems of defining jurisdictional boundaries and interpreting the law would be termed legal problems, while matters concerning the inter-action between levels of government or reorganization of administrative structures would be placed in a category of "political considerations," or "institutional problems".

Classifications organized along disciplinary lines generally contain only two or three categories. Engineers, for example, frequently speak of "engineering problems" and "other problems". Economists on the other hand often classify problems as "physical" (or technical), economic, and other (usually implying social, biological, etc.). However, many of the problems are of interest to various disciplines. For example, the operation of river development systems is a matter of interest to engineers, economists, ecologists and geographers and doubtless other disciplines too. Similarly the factors underlying water demands are economic, sociological and psychological in nature. The solution of many of the problems that are now on the horizon will require inter-disciplinary research efforts.

4. Phases in the Planning and Development Process

Water problems can also be classified according to their relationship to a particular phase of the development process. Categories that might be included under this classification are research, data collection, planning, financing, implementation, and management. Sometimes research and data collection are included as parts of the planning phase although they may not all be undertaken by the same agency. Similarly financing and management (which is taken to mean the operation of the project once it has been developed), might be included with implementation.

One of the principal problems that relate to the research phase is the present lack of research funds for studies of economic, social, and institutional aspects of water management. The amount of money devoted to research in the natural resources field as a whole in Canada is small, but the amount devoted to social science aspects is minute. Of the research that is undertaken in the water resources field, most attention seems to be paid to the physical dimensions, particularly the hydrological and biological aspects. The present emphasis is in part a reflection of the manner in which funds are made available for research, such as through the National Research Council which has a physical science orientation. Other Federal government agencies when they have been involved in social science research have generally funded it on a very small scale for a limited period of time, and generally with a mission-orientation. Moreover, much of the social science research has been undertaken by the agencies themselves.

The pertinent question is, therefore, what changes in the present research funding process are required to facilitate more social science research in the water management field? Other problems relating to the research phase include those of determining priorities between competing claims for funds, the lack of personnel skilled and available to undertake the needed research, and the lack of communication between those carrying out the studies and those who might be able to use the results.

There is a general lack of data required for studies of economic, social, and institutional aspects of water management. Often the data collected relate to areal units that are too large to be useful for the studies in question, or it is not collected frequently enough to reflect human impacts on water management. Land use surveys, for example, provide a useful indication of land use patterns as of a particular moment of time. The following year they may alter radically due to other changes, for example, cropping patterns. There are other problems stemming from the lack of uniformity in data collecting procedures, such as in information relating to municipal water supply or industrial water supply. Data collection agencies are not entirely to blame for such deficiencies. Social scientists are sometimes prone to state merely that data are lacking rather than specifying precisely what data they need, in what form, and how often the information should be collected. Nevertheless, it is clear that if social scientists are to provide the advice that is needed on the human dimensions of water problems, data collection and analysis programs must be considerably expanded. Other problems relating to data collection include those of determining the economic gains from additional information, development of more sophisticated techniques of data storage and retrieval, and increasing the usefulness of data by expanding data-analysis programs.

There are numerous problems associated with the planning of water resource development. One of the most important is that of ensuring that economic, social, and institutional studies are undertaken in phase with other investigations rather than as an afterthought once the latter have been completed. Another is that of linking water resources planning to planning for the purposes, such as for regional economic development. There are also problems of co-ordinating planning within and between levels of government. The problem today in North America is not so much the lack of co-ordination between planning agencies, each of which has its own particular view of what is required. Another source of concern is the fact that so many plans end up on the planner's shelf instead of in the legislator's portfolio for action.

In the field of financing there are problems of determining the manner in which various levels of government ought to participate in water resource development. Should the Federal Government provide funds for development as well as for other phases of water management? If so, on what terms should it do so? Another difficulty is that demands are being made for the investment of federal funds in developments that have hitherto been assumed to be the responsibility of other levels of government.

Problems of implementation and management raise numerous questions about the legal and organizational frameworks. It is evident that there are weaknesses in some of the present laws relating to water management, particularly where they encourage suboptimal uses of water resources or where they facilitate only one course of action to be taken. Confusion as to what are the responsibilities of various levels of government and particular agencies in water management present additional difficulties. Other problems relate to the lack of co-ordination within and between levels of government in the water management field.

5. Decision-Making Elements

Another approach is to classify problems according to elements that may enter into decisions about water management. Gilbert White has suggested that six main types of considerations can enter such decisions.[17] He designates these as:

    (a) the range of choice
    (b) the estimate of the resource
    (c) available technology
    (d) economic considerations
    (e) spatial linkages
    (f) social guides

(a) *The Range of Choice*

The range of choice relates to the possibilities for using a given water resource for different purposes on the one hand, and to the alternative ways in which these purposes might be accomplished on the other. For example, a given water resource might be used for such purposes as irrigation, hydro-electric power generation, muni-

---

[17] This framework of analysis is described in Gilbert F. White, "Contributions of Geographical Analysis to River Basin Development", *Geographical Journal*, Vol. CXXIX (1963), pp. 412-446. Its application to flood problems is described in Gilbert F. White, *Choice of Adjustment to Floods* (Chicago, University of Chicago, Department of Geography Research Series No. 93, 1964).

cipal and industrial water supply, navigation, recreation, flood control or for the support of fish runs. Each of these purposes could be accomplished in a variety of ways. Flood problems, for example, can be dealt with by building protective works, flood proofing structures, taking emergency measures, enacting flood plain zoning ordinances, providing compensation for flood victims, or establishing flood insurance schemes. Typically, however, only a narrow range of possible uses and alternative strategies for development is considered in water management in Canada.[18]

(b) Estimate of the Resource

A critical consideration in decisions relating to water resource development is an estimate of the quantity and quality of the water resource and associated land resources, such as soil and minerals. Information on resource availability is important not only to the engineer who designs the structures, but also to the economist who estimates the value of the goods and services that might be derived from development, and the sociologist who examines the possible consequences of various kinds and magnitudes of development.

(c) Technology of Water Management

Any assessment of the possible use and development of water resources requires assumptions as to the technology that is likely to be applied in the collection, storage, transport, use, and disposal of water. Can it be assumed, for example, that the most advanced techniques of hydraulic and mechanical design will be employed by those who are involved in drawing up plans for structures to control water resources, or that farmers or industrialists will employ the most efficient techniques available for the utilization of the water that will be provided?

(d) Economic Efficiency

Economic considerations often play an important role in many decisions relating to water resource development. This role seems certain to grow in the future, particularly as the competition for scarce capital funds intensifies, and as water development is used increasingly as an instrument for promoting economic change. It will become increasingly necessary to determine the economic efficiency of proposals for water resource development, and to trace the economic consequences of various alternatives.

---

[18] This appears to have been the case particularly in connection with floods. See W. R. D. Sewell, *Water Management and Floods in the Fraser River Basin, op. cit.*

Considerable progress has been made in recent years in developing techniques for the evaluation of water development projects. The concepts of benefit-cost analysis are being refined and procedures for identifying and measuring the various gains and costs are being improved.[19] Increasing use is being made of systems analysis in the evaluation of proposals for water development.[20]

Despite this progress, however, techniques of economic analysis used in the appraisal of proposals for water development in Canada are still fairly crude. *A Guide to Benefit-Cost Analysis*[21] was published as a part of the proceedings of the Resources for Tomorrow Conference. Its major objective was to provide a set of principles that could be used as a basis for the development of techniques of economic evaluation used by government agencies and others in the appraisal of resource development projects. It has been only partially successful in achieving this objective. Some provincial government agencies undertake benefit-cost analyses and so do a few agencies of the Federal Government. Many of those who undertake such analyses, however, do not adhere to the principles set out in the Guide, and in several cases the techniques have been grossly misused.[22] A major problem, therefore, is that of increasing the level of sophistication of methods of evaluation used by government agencies and ensuring that such methods are correctly employed.

(e) *Spatial Linkages*

Another factor that may influence water management decisions is the effects that a given water use may have on other water uses, or the effects that a given water development project may have on activities beyond the project area. The effects of alterations in streamflow patterns resulting from the construction of a dam, for example, may be expressed in significant changes in biological systems and social systems as well as in changes in outputs of goods

---

[19] See A. R. Prest and R. Turvey, "Cost-Benefit Analysis: A Survey", *The Economic Journal,* Vol. 75 (December 1965), pp. 683-675; and A. Wildawsky, "The Political Economy of Efficiency: Cost-Benefit Analysis, Systems Analysis and Program Budgeting", *Public Administration Review* (December 1966), pp. 292-310.

[20] See, for example, A. Maass et al, *The Design of Water Resource Systems* (Cambridge, Harvard University Press, 1962); and M. Hufschmidt and M. Fiering, *Simulation Techniques for Design of Water Resource Systems* (Cambridge, Harvard University Press, 1966).

[21] W. R. D. Sewell et al, *Guide to Benefit-Cost Analysis* (Ottawa, Queen's Printer, 1961).

[22] See Ian Burton, "Investment Choices in Public Resource Development", Abraham Rotstein (ed.), *The Prospect of Change* (Toronto, McGraw-Hill, 1965).

and services. Analyzing the impact of a given change in a hydrologic system on the other interlocking systems is a highly complex task. Important advances have been made in recent years, however, particularly through the use of high speed computers and the development of systems analysis techniques. Nevertheless, much work remains to be done before the precise effects of a given change in the hydrologic system can be predicted, even within one system.

(f) Social Guides

Decision-making in water management is profoundly affected by the encouragement or constraint which society imparts through its customs, attitudes, laws, and organizations.[23] Collectively, these may be referred to as social guides. Knowledge of their influence is essential if water resources planning is to be effective in attaining its objectives. The record is replete with examples of water development schemes, which, although engineered to a high degree of proficiency, have failed because of lack of attention to the potential reaction of those who would be affected by the scheme or attention to the capacity of the existing institutions to implement it effectively. Thus flood control schemes may fail to reduce flood losses unless measures are also taken to restrict further occupance of the flood plain; the provision of electric-power may not result in predicted industrial expansion unless accompanied by appropriate pricing policies, tax policies, and the development of an infrastructure; and a plan for water development may merely gather dust on the planner's shelf it it is formulated without reference to the social, legal, and administrative factors on which it will depend for its implementation. Social guides, therefore, can be one of the most important elements determining the outcomes of decisions in water management.

6. Combining the Classifications

Each of the approaches noted above has advantages and disadvantages, depending upon the purposes for which the classification is to be used. Used in combination, however, they serve to point up the most urgent questions that relate to a particular resource management problem, and the types of social science research that would be helpful in the search for a solution.

---

[23] For a discussion, see Harold E. Thomas, "Cultural Control of Water Development", *CIBA Journal* (Autumn 1964), pp. 25-32; and Gilbert F. White, "Formation and Role of Public Attitudes", Henry Jarrett (ed.), *Environment Quality in a Growing Economy* Baltimore, Johns Hopkins Press, 1966), pp. 105-127.

Section III

NEEDED SOCIAL SCIENCE RESEARCH RELATING TO WATER MANAGEMENT

It is evident from a review of the emerging problems of water management in Canada that knowledge is lacking in many important areas. It is also clear that a major expansion of the present research effort is required. Not all the needed studies can be done at once and so priorities must be assigned. Bearing these considerations in mind, five major types of research appear to be especially urgently required:

1. determination of the magnitude of the resource;
2. determination of the potential uses of water resources and the alternative solutions to water problems;
3. identification and measurement of the economic impacts of water development;
4. determination of impacts of various social guides on water management and development of improved frameworks of laws, policies, and administrative arrangements;
5. determination of the value of additional information and of expanded research efforts.

Detailed discussions of the types of research that might be undertaken in the fields of economics, geography, planning and political science appear in the reports of the individual members of the study group.[24] The following discussion notes the accomplishments to date in the various categories of research, and the gaps that need to be filled.

1. Estimating the Magnitude of the Resource

As noted earlier, knowledge of the nature and extent of the resource is a prerequisite to sound planning. Various types of study

---

[24] One of the reports is concerned with problems relating to the weighing of economic considerations in water management decisions. See Richard W. Judy, *Economic Problems in Water Resources Management*. Another is focussed on the difficulties involved in attaining desirable social goals within the legal and institutional framework that conditions water management in Canada. See Lionel Ouellet, *Programme for Basic Legal and Institutional Research in Canada*. A third is focussed on past and potential contributions of geographical research to water management in Canada. See W. R. D. Sewell, *The Role of Geographical Research in Water Management in Canada*. All of the individual reports discuss the general problem of getting the research done. The fourth report, however, concentrates specifically on this matter, and outlines various strategies that might be pursued towards this end. See Michel Chevalier, *Planning the Development and Use of Social Science Research for the Problem of Canadian Water Resources Management*.

are needed in this connection. Many of them are physical in nature and might best be undertaken by physical scientists and engineers. Several reports prepared for the Study Group have specified the areas of research on the physical dimensions of water management that are most urgently needed. These reports and a number of other studies[25] have drawn attention to the lack of data on the spatial and temporal distribution of water resources in Canada, and to gaps in the understanding of factors which influence the hydrologic cycle.[26] They note the need for research on streamflow characteristics; the inter-relationships between precipitation, temperature, evapotranspiration, soil moisture, groundwater recharge and other factors; the behaviour of sediment loads; and on the incidence of floods and droughts. Studies are also needed on means of increasing water resource availability, such as reduction of evapotranspiration,[27] and weather modification.[28] Research is also required for the assessment of potentials of other related resources, such as soils and minerals.

The problems of estimating resource availability have traditionally been principally the concern of the physical scientists, the natural scientist and the engineer. Social scientists, however, can make useful contributions to the needed research. Geographers in particular have long interested themselves in studies relating to resource estimates. In the water resources field they have undertaken particularly valuable work relating to water balances, hydrographic mapping, the identification of areas subject to floods and droughts, and factors affecting streamflows.[29] The effort of Canadian geographers in this connection has not been large but a number of useful contributions have been made, particularly during the past decade.[30] Several of them are now engaged in investigations of streamflow characteristics, factors affecting the hydrologic cycle,

---

25 Various studies prepared for the Resources for Tomorrow Conference draw attention to this problem. See especially, D. Cass-Beggs, "Water as a Basic Resource", and R. H. Clark, A. K. Watt and J. P. Bruce, "Basic Data Requirements for Water Management", in *Resources for Tomorrow Conference Background Papers, op. cit.,* Vol. 1, pp. 173-189 and 191-201, respectively.
26 For a discussion, see R. H. Clark and J. P. Bruce, *Introduction to Hydrometeorology* (Toronto, Pergamon Press, 1966).
27 See A. E. Ackerman and G. O. G. Löf, *Technology in American Water Development* (Baltimore, Johns Hopkins Press, 1958).
28 See National Academy of Sciences-National Research Council, *Weather and Climate Modification* (Washington, 1966); and National Science Foundation, Special Commission on Weather Modification, *Weather and Climate Modification* (Washington, 1966).
29 See W. R. D. Sewell, *The Role of Geographical Research in Water Resource Development in Canada, op. cit.*
30 *Ibid.*

sedimentation and subsurface drainage. With increased availability of funds other geographers would participate in these and other investigations relating to water resource estimates.

Geographers have also undertaken studies in connection with the inventory of other related resources such as agricultural land, forests, and mineral resources. Many of them are now engaged in the Canada Land Inventory. Gradually the methods used in collecting the data for such surveys have been improved. At the same time data storage and retrieval systems have been modernized through computerization, making information much more readily available. There remain a number of weaknesses in present land use surveys, however, and research is needed to overcome these deficiencies. The emphasis in such surveys continues to be on the mapping of what physically exists on a given plot of land. Only infrequently is information collected as to the economic, social, and institutional factors that are responsible for land use patterns. Obviously it is only with information on these latter considerations that predictions as to future land use are possible. Studies need to be undertaken to determine how land use surveys can be made to reveal not only physical possibilities, but also the changes that seem likely to take place, given various economic, social, and institutional considerations.

2. Determination of Water Uses and of Alternative Solutions to Water Problems

Of all the types of research that are needed in connection with the human dimensions of water management in Canada, perhaps the most urgent is that relating to the determination of water uses, and the identification of alternative solutions to water problems. Several studies have drawn attention to the lack of data on water use in Canada,[31] and the implications of this for water resources management.[32] It acts as a major inhibition, for example, to policy-making in connection with such matters as inter-basin diversion and water export. In addition, the narrow range of alternatives commonly considered in water resources decision-making is a major source of potential inefficiency in resource allocation.

Several types of research need to be undertaken to make possible precise estimates of future water needs. These include economic base studies which would provide information relating to

---

[31] See R. H. Clark, A. K. Watt and J. P. Bruce, *op. cit.;* and D. Cass-Beggs, *op. cit.*
[32] See T. Lloyd, *op. cit.* and E. Kuiper, *op. cit.*

population growth and expansion of various economic activities; water service-demand studies, including inventories of present use by households, industries, agriculture, recreation, and other non-consumptive activities; analytical studies to assess the influence of water availability on industrial location, agricultural development, and urban growth, to determine the influence of price increases on water consumption, and to evaluate the effects of the introduction of new technologies on water consumption; and studies to derive multi-variate demand functions based on data provided by the other investigations.

It is essential that these studies be undertaken *before* any attempt is made to undertake an evaluation of the benefits and costs of a water resource development project, and that water use inventories be kept up to date. A series of water use studies should be undertaken in each of the provinces of Canada and an attempt then made to consolidate these into an overall review of water use in the nation as a whole.

Research on water use in Canada to date has been very meagre. Apart from some exploratory work on recreational water use,[33] Canadian social scientists have shown little interest in this matter. Government agencies have not examined it very much either. Some valuable work has been done in the United States and elsewhere in the past few years, however, in developing conceptual frameworks and techniques of measurement,[34] and these might be applied with some modification in Canada. Studies of these problems might be undertaken by universities, consulting firms and government agencies.

Research designed to expand the range of choice has also been fairly limited. There is as a consequence little innovation in the alternatives considered for dealing with water problems. Concentration on construction alternatives remains a dominant characteristic in water management in Canada. Even within that limited range, there have been only modest attempts to innovate, as is illustrated in the cases of adjustment to floods or to pollution. Studies need to be undertaken to identify what are the theoretical possibilities for solving various water problems, and to determine what are the fac-

---

[33] See, for example, P. H. Pearse, "A New Approach to the Evaluation of Non-Priced Recreational Resources", Paper presented to the 1967 Annual Meeting of the Canadian Political Science Association (June 1967); and Canada, Department of Fisheries, *Economic Aspects of Sport Fishing* (Ottawa, Queen's Printer, May 1965).

[34] For reviews of progress in this connection, see Allen V. Kneese and Stephen S. Smith, *Water Research* (Baltimore, Johns Hopkins Press, 1967).

tors which inhibit such factors being taken into account. This is an area of research that has been little explored to date, but could result in a major payoff in terms of improved efficiency in water management.

3. Identification and Measurement of Impacts of Water Development

Another major category of research that needs to be pursued relates to the identification and measurement of impacts of water development. Water management is generally undertaken with some economic or social goal in mind, even though such a goal may be rather vague and not well articulated in policy statements. It is important, nevertheless, to determine whether a proposed scheme is likely to attain the implied objective. In addition, because water development involves the alteration of natural flows of a stream, it inevitably results in differential effects on various water users and on the biological systems within the river basin. Some of these effects may be beneficial to certain users but adverse to others. Careful appraisal of relative gains and losses therefore is required.

A considerable amount of the social science research effort relating to water management in recent years has been devoted to the development of theoretical frameworks and techniques of measurement for assessing the impacts of water management. Most of this work, particularly in the field of economics,[35] has been undertaken in the United States, but several Canadian economists have made useful contributions both to the development of theory and of techniques of measurement.[36] Research on sociological impacts and on political consequences of water resource development in Canada, however, has been very meagre.

There remain important conceptual problems relating to impact measurement, not the least of which is that of specifying the social welfare objective that is to be pursued.[37] Ideally, in welfare economics the objective is to pursue those courses of action which result in increasing income without making anyone worse off. Water resources development projects and measures, however, generally cause shifts in the distribution of income among members of society. Such redistributions may benefit one geographical area while harming another; or they may reward one class of citizens at the expense

---

[35] *Ibid.*, see also Turvey and Prest, *op. cit.;* Maass et al, *op. cit.;* and Hufschmidt and Fiering, *op. cit.*

[36] For a review of these contributions, see R. W. Judy, *op. cit.*

[37] See, for example, Otto A. Davies and Andrew B. Whinston, "Externalities, Welfare, and the Theory of Games", *Journal of Political Economy*, Vol. 70 (1962), pp. 241-262.

of another. Consequently, the social welfare function (or objective) must be specified in terms of a desired income redistribution. Research is needed into the theory and practice of specifying such income redistribution constraints.[38] Other conceptual problems requiring study relate to the treatment of time, uncertainty, opportunity costs, externalities, indivisiblities, and intangibles.[39]

Besides the conceptual problems, there are difficulties attached to the actual identification, measurement, and evaluation of impacts. As noted earlier, a good deal of attention has been focussed on these matters in recent years and considerable progress has been made. There still remain, however, problems of identifying and measuring the value of goods and services that do not normally enter the market mechanism, such as recreation, pollution abatement, and flood loss reduction. Research designed to determine what consumers would be willing to pay rather than do without such goods and services is now being pursued by a number of Canadian economists. This research should be encouraged aand expanded. There are also problems of tracing the broad impacts of various alternative developments through the economic, social, and biological systems. Much progress has been made in this connection in recent years through the application of computer technology, and the building of mathematical models.[40] Most of the applications thus far have been in connection with economic impacts, but increasing use of these techniques is now being made by biologists and others concerned with effects of resource development. The design and use of digital simulation models is a very young art. The technique holds great promise for water resources management because it creates the analogue of the laboratory in which alternative system designs can be tested and evaluated. Research in this field should be enthusiastically supported, especially at the universities.

Another type of research connected with impact measurement that is urgently required relates to the valuation of the actual performance of water development projects. Generally evaluations are undertaken only *ex ante,* that is, prior to the decision whether or not to proceed with implementation of a proposed program. Studies are needed to determine whether in fact the perceived objectives have been attained. In this way planners would have a means of

---

38 See, for example, A. Myrick Freeman III, "Six Federal Reclamation Projects and the Distribution of Income", *Water Resources Research,* Vol. 3, no. 2 (1967).
39 See R. W. Judy, *op. cit.*
40 See, for example, Maass et al, *op. cit.;* and Hufschmidt and Fiering, *op. cit.*

determining how good their estimates were, and in those cases where the goal was not attained, they would be motivated to search for the reasons why. Care would need to be exercised in undertaking such studies. Hindsight appraisal is, of course, much easier than prediction. Nevertheless, an objective appraisal, taking into account the various factors that appear to have influenced the outcome, would be invaluable for future decision-making. Hindsight studies should be undertaken of particular projects, such as the South Saskatchewan project or the Mactaquac project in New Brunswick, or of particular policies, such as those embodied in the PFRA Act, ARDA,[41] or the Canada Water Conservation Assistance Act.

4. The Role of Social Guides in Water Development

A fourth category of social science research that should be accorded high priority relates to the influence of various social guides in water management. As noted earlier, social guides comprise a wide variety of influences that encourage or discourage development taking place in particular ways. They include informal influences such as social mores, customs, and attitudes, and formal influences such as laws, policies and administrative arrangements. Knowledge of the effects of such factors is essential to sound water resources planning. Thus far, however, very little study has been given to such matters by Canadian lawyers, political scientists, sociologists, or psychologists.[42]

Among the types of research that are most urgently required in connection with social guides, five appear to be particularly important, namely: (a) a review of the effectiveness of the present legal and administrative framework in dealing with the emerging problems of water management; (b) the examination of the criteria that need to be applied in water between competing users and in selecting among competing projects; (c) the determination of the potential effectiveness of incentives to private action in dealing with water problems; (d) studies of the role of perceptions and attitudes in decision-making; and (e) the determination of the appropriate areal units for water management.

Water resource development in Canada is profoundly affected by the jurisdictional division of powers imposed by the BNA Act, vari-

---

[41] A pioneering study of this type was undertaken recently under the auspices of the Economic Council of Canada. See Helen Buckley and Eva Tihany, *Canadian Policies for Rural Adjustment: a Study of the Economic Impact of ARDA, PFRA, and MMRA* (Ottawa, Queen's Printer, 1967).

[42] For a discussion see W. R. D. Sewell and Ian Burton, "Recent Innovations in Resource Development Policy in Canada", *Canadian Geographer* (December 1967).

ous laws that have been enacted for allocating water among competing users, the structure of administrative organizations that have been established to guide the management of water resources, and by government policies. Laws and administrative structures give expression to the views and circumstances of the time in which they were established. To be effective in dealing with water problems, however, they must be sufficiently flexible to accommodate new social and political ideas, new technologies, and problems that were not on the horizon when the laws were enacted or the administrative structures were established. Rapidly changing ideas, the emergence of new technologies and the intensification of competition for the use of certain water resources in Canada, have placed increasing demands on the legal and administrative framework.[43] Some changes have already been made and others are now underway. In general, modifications have been made on an *ad hoc* basis to accommodate particular problems as they have arisen. There is no way at present of determining how effective such modifications have been or, even more important, whether some other modification might have yielded better results.

One of the most valuable types of research that could be undertaken in the field of water management in Canada would be a thorough review of legal and administrative frameworks, examining present systems against an 'ideal' system of laws and agencies designed to achieve specified goals. Such a study might be undertaken in four parts or phases, which are methodological rather than chronological; in other words, they could be undertaken simultaneously, although at a given point of the research the conclusions of the preceding phases must be known before the planned research program could be continued. The four phases would consist of the development of a model of 'ideal' legal and administrative frameworks, based upon legal principles and principles of administrative organizations designed to attain specified goals; the inventorying of present systems of water law and water management agencies, a comparison of the present system with the ideal system; and the consideration of institutional changes that might be made to improve water management, given various political and other constraints.

A *second,* and related type of research, is concerned with criteria for choice. As the number and complexity of the claims for the use

43 See Morris Miller, "The Developmental Framework for Resource Policy and its Jurisdictional-Administrative Implications", *Canadian Public Administration Journal* (Toronto, June 1962), pp. 133-155.

of given water resources continue to grow, the problem of selection among them will become increasingly more difficult. Traditional criteria of law and historical precedent will prove to be inadequate and will need to be supplemented by others, such as economic efficiency and social desirability. Similarly, as claims on the public purse continue to expand, and especially as the demand for collective goods continues to grow, more sophisticated economic criteria will need to be applied. In addition, as inter-jurisdictional projects grow in number and in size, the need for means of reconciling the goals of the various jurisdictions will become more urgent. Studies are needed to assess the influence of criteria that have been used in the past in water management in Canada. To what extent, for example, is the present pattern of water use a reflection of legal doctrines rather than economic consideration? Does the present system ensure that water resources will move into their economically most profitable and socially most desirable uses? What influence has the misapplication of techniques of economic analysis had on the development of water resources?

Studies are also needed to assess the outcomes of the application of various criteria to particular resource allocation cases or resource development projects. What would be the effect, for example, of applying economic criteria to all the water allocations that now exist? Would there be major changes in the relative allocations to various types of water use? What would be the effects of relaxing the requirements in the present Canada Fisheries Act relating to the protection of anadromous fish runs? Would such a relaxation be economically sensible and socially desirable? Is the insistence upon uniform standards for water quality, based on drinking water criteria or criteria for protection of particular fish species, likely to produce the kind of environment that society desires for working and recreating or are additional criteria required for this purpose? Many water management decisions in the past have been based on the use of single criteria. In the future, competing social goals will call for the application of several criteria. Research should be undertaken, therefore, to trace the outcomes of the application of various criteria and combinations of them.

A *third* type of needed research concerned with social guides relates to the provision of incentives to private action. Social goals can be pursued in the development of water resources in several ways, such as by the enactment of regulations, the provision of goods and services through the use of tax funds, or the provision of incentives to encourage private initiative. Each of these courses of action has advantages and disadvantages in resource allocation depending on the circumstances. Generally, it is believed, the most satisfactory allocations of water between users and the provision of the social or most desirable level of goods and services will occur when there is the greatest freedom of individual choice, and especially when this can be expressed through the mechanism of the market.[44] Some water-derived goods and services, however, are not generally provided through the operation of the market, notably collective goods, such as recreation facilities, de-pollution and flood control. Since the provision of such goods is thought to be socially desirable, the government often undertakes the responsibility for providing them. The problem arises, however, as to how much to provide.

One possible guideline for the provision of such water-related public goods and services as recreation facilities, flood protection, or de-pollution is the price people would be willing to pay for such services rather than go without them. Research is needed on this matter. Studies also need to be carried out to assess the effectiveness of other incentives to private action. In the case of adjustment of floods, for example, studies might be undertaken to determine the overall effects of an edict making it mandatory for flood-plain dwellers to purchase flood insurance, or the effects of building codes which only permit the construction of buildings that can withstand floods up to a certain specified level (such as the largest flood on record).

A *fourth* area of needed research relates to the role of perceptions and attitudes in decision-making. The way in which decision-makers perceive water problems and potential solutions to them conditions, to an important extent, the choices which they make. As noted earlier, problems are often perceived imperfectly and the range of solutions considered is typically narrow. Attitudes as to what the people want, and as to who should initiate action to deal with a given problem, also appear to play an important role in actual decisions.[45] Some pioneering work[46] has been done in determining the role of perception

---

44 For a discussion of this view, see J. Hirschleifer et al, *Water Supply: Economics, Technology and Policy* (Chicago, University of Chicago Press, 1958), pp. 74-86.
45 For a discussion see Gilbert F. White, "Formation and Role of Public Attitudes", *op. cit.*
46 See, for example, Robert W. Kates, *Hazard and Choice Perception in Flood Plain Management* (Chicago, University of Chicago Department of Geography Research Papers, No. 78, 1962); Gilbert F. White, *Choice of Adjustment to Floods, op. cit.;* and Ian Burton and R. W. Kates, "The Flood Plain and the Seashore: a Comparative Analysis of Hazard Zone Occupance", *Geographical Review,* Vol. LIV (1964), pp. 366-385.

in decision-making relating to floods and droughts,[47] and in connection with the use of recreational areas.[48] Studies relating to the role of attitudes have also been carried out in connection with pollution[49] and weather modification.[50] Such investigations, however, have been few in number and much remains to be learned about the factors which condition perception and attitudes, and the extent to which the latter vary from one set of geographical circumstances to another. The relative importance of perception and attitudes in decisions about different water problems is still unknown. Do attitudes towards responsibility for initiating action play a greater role, for example, in the case of pollution than they do in the case of domestic water supply? Greater understanding of perceptions and attitudes would make possible improvements in policy-making and implementation for it would permit the prediction of likely reactions to various alternative courses of action. Research in this connection, therefore, is likely to have a very high payoff, not only in terms of increasing understanding of human behaviour, but also in terms of improving decision-making.

Among the various types of studies that are needed in this connection, the following seem to be of particular urgency in what ways do people perceive particular water problems (such as floods, droughts, or pollution) and what do they see as potential solutions (in the case of floods, do they see flood plain regulation, flood proofing, and flood insurance as well as flood-control works, evacuation, and compensation?); do the perceptions of the layman differ significantly from those of the specialist; how do attitudes about the nature of the problem and questions about who should initiate action, and what should be done, affect actual decisions; are there major differences in attitudes between the various groups that participate in the decision-making process (individuals, pressure groups, industrialists, administrators, and politicians); in what ways

[47] Thomas F. Saarinen, *Perception of the Drought Hazard on the Great Plains* (Chicago, University of Chicago Department of Geography Research Papers, No. 106, 1966).

[48] Robert C. Lucas, "Wilderness Perception and Use: the Example of the Boundary Water Canoe Area", *Natural Resources Journal* (1964), pp. 394-411.

[49] See, for example, D. R. Lycan and W. R. Derrick Sewell, "Pollution as an Element of the Urban Environment of Victoria", *The B.C. Geographer* (Fall, 1967).

[50] T. F. Saarinen, "Attitudes Towards Weather Modification: A Study of Great Plains Farmers", and W. R. Derrick Sewell and J. C. Day, "Perceptions of Possibilities of Weather Modification and Attitudes Toward Government Involvement", both in *Human Dimensions of Weather Modification*, W. R. Derrick Sewell (ed.), pp. 323-328 and pp. 329-344, respectively.

can attitudes be changed; and, most importantly, how do perceptions and attitudes vary from one place to another?

The determination of appropriate areal units for water management constitutes a *fifth* area of needed research. The river basin has often been suggested as the ideal unit,[51] and it has become increasingly popular in many parts of the world as the areal basis for planning.[52] Water management in the United Kingdom is now organized entirely on a river basin basis. It has been adopted so far to only a limited extent, however, in Canada.[53] Various explanations have been offered for this, including the problems of divided jurisdiction, the effects of historical precedent, and the large size of many of Canada's river basins.[54] There has also been debate as to whether other areal units, such as urban-based regions might not be more appropriate as units for planning and development.[55]

Research needs to be undertaken on the various administrative forms that might be applied to the management of water resources, to determine which are the most appropriate for the various phases of such management. Should data collection, for example, be organized on a river basin basis? Should the river basin be used as a basis for outlining technical possibilities for development and then combined with other units, such as broader economic regions (which may encompass only part of the river basin or which may cover several river basins) for purposes of development? What factors inhibit the adoption of a river basin approach to water management in Canada? How can these be overcome? One of the most

51 See United Nations, Department of Economic and Social Affairs, *Integrated River Basin Development* (New York, 1958). For a discussion of the underlying concepts of the river basin approach, see Gilbert F. White, "A Perspective of River Basin Development", *Law and Contemporary Problems*, Vol. XXII (Spring 1957), pp. 157-187.

52 See Tennessee Valley Authority, *T.V.A.: Symbol of Valley Resource Development* (Knoxville, Tennessee Valley Authority, June 1961).

53 See T. M. Patterson, *op. cit.* For discussions of actual applications see J. W. MacNeill, "Law and the Agencies", Transactions of the *Fourteenth B.C. Natural Resources Conference* (1962), pp. 133-142; and E. G. Pleva, "Multiple Purpose Land and Water Districts in Ontario", *Comparisons in Resource Management*, H. Jarrett (ed.) (Baltimore, Johns Hopkins Press, 1961).

54 See J. W. MacNeill, "Water Resource Administration in Canada", in *Proceedings of the Resources for Tomorrow Conference* (Ottawa, Queen's Printer, 1961), pp. 331-336.

55 See W. R. Derrick Sewell, "Multiple Purpose Development of Canada's Water Resources", *Water Power* (April 1962), pp. 146-151; and J. W. MacNeill, *loc. cit.*

fruitful avenues of research in this connection would be an intensive study of a particular river basin, exploring the possibilities and difficulties of managing it on that basis.

5. The Value of Additional Information and Research

Viewed in terms of the seriousness of emerging problems, the inefficiencies that have occurred in water management, or what is spent in other advanced countries, investment in water resources research in Canada is extremely small. It is clear that a major expansion of this investment is required if optimum use is to be made of these resources. The need for much greater investment in social science research is especially urgent. The question arises, however, as to *how much* more money should be spent in this connection. Decisions must also be made as to the types of research that deserve priority, and as to which research agencies (government departments, universities, or private individuals or firms) should be supported. Such decisions are difficult to make, particularly because it is not easy to specify what the return on the investment will be. There is no simple relationship between research and payoff.

Nevertheless, criteria must be developed so that objective decisions can be made about the appropriate scale of investment in research and about the types of research that should be supported. A good deal of attention has been given to this matter in recent years[56] but there remain weaknesses in methodologies that are used for the economic evaluation of research. One of the most important is the assumption that there is a direct relationship between the investment in research and the economic payoff.[57] Another is that there is seldom an attempt to weigh the payoff from a specified type of research with alternative types of research on which the money might be spent.[58]

Studies are needed to improve methodologies for evaluating the economic benefits of research. With the findings it would be possible

---

[56] See, for instance, U.S. Committee on Science and Astronautics, *Basic Research and National Goals* (Washington, U.S. Government Printing Office, 1965); Alvin Weinberg, "Criteria for Scientific Choice", *Physics Today,* Vol. 17 (March 1964), pp. 42-48; and F. M. Scherer, "Government Research and Development Programs", *Measuring Benefits of Government Investments,* R. Dorfman (ed.) (Washington 1965), pp. 12-70.

[57] See Robert W. Kates and W. R. Derrick Sewell, "The Evaluation of Weather Modification Research", *Human Dimensions of Weather Modification, op. cit.,* pp. 347-362.

[58] See James A. Crutchfield, R. W. Kates and W. R. Derrick Sewell, "Benefit-Cost Analysis and the National Oceanography Program", *Natural Resources Journal,* Vol. 7, no. 3 (July 1967), pp. 361-375.

to determine the appropriate magnitude of the research effort and the studies to which the investment might be profitably allocated.

Section IV

TOWARDS AN EXPANSION OF RESEARCH ON THE HUMAN DIMENSIONS OF WATER MANAGEMENT

The purpose of the foregoing section was to outline the types of social science research that are most urgently required in the water resources field in Canada. The list is highly selective, but judged on terms of the past record, in terms of the present availability of funds and personnel, or in terms of various institutional impediments to the expansion of research, it is a very formidable one. It is evident that changes must be made in policies relating to research funding, that liaison between those who do the research and those who use its results must be improved, and that better methods of disseminating information about research must be found.

Research Funding Policies

As noted earlier, investment in social science research in the water resources field in Canada has been very small. Less than $280,000 a year is presently allocated for this purpose, even when a very liberal definition of research is used.[59] Most of this money is provided by the Federal Government, principally through the action agencies (such as the Departments of Agriculture; Energy, Mines and Resources; and ARDA), the Canada Council, and the National Research Council. Provincial government agencies have supported social science research in this field to only a very minor extent.

---

[59] The small amount of money allocated to social science research in the water resources field is symptomatic of the inadequacy of support for social science research in general and in Canada. At present less than $2 million is allocated to such research each year in this country. This represents less than 1 per cent of the total expenditures on scientific activity in Canada. For a discussion of the implications of this lack of support, see S. D. Clark, "The Support of Social Science Research in Canada", *The Canadian Journal of Economics and Political Science* (May 1958), pp. 141-150.

Index